INDEX MAP

# The Great Alaska Earthquake of 1964

## BIOLOGY

National Research Council.

COMMITTEE ON THE ALASKA EARTHQUAKE
OF THE
DIVISION OF EARTH SCIENCES
NATIONAL RESEARCH COUNCIL

NATIONAL ACADEMY OF SCIENCES
WASHINGTON, D.C.
1971

Geology

Seismology and Geodesy

Hydrology

Biology

Oceanography and Coastal Engineering

Engineering

Human Ecology

Summary and Recommendations

*Available from*
Printing and Publishing Office
National Academy of Sciences
2101 Constitution Avenue
Washington, D.C. 20418

ISBN 0-309-01604-5

Library of Congress Catalog Card Number 68-60037

Printed in the United States of America

FRONTISPIECE    The nearly 34 feet of uplift at MacLeod Harbor, Montague Island, in Prince William Sound destroyed the entire littoral zone (the tidal range) and 24 feet of subtidal ocean bottom. The biological zonation of intertidal animals and plants is shown by dark and light colored bands. Photograph by G Dallas Hanna.

# COMMITTEE ON THE ALASKA EARTHQUAKE

---

### G DALLAS HANNA

#### 1887–1970

With sincere regret, we report the passing on November 20, 1970, of Dr. G Dallas Hanna, Curator of Geology at the California Academy of Sciences. Born on April 24, 1887, Dr. Hanna was a geologist, a paleontologist, a naturalist, and an inventor, as well as an author and a member of the Panel on Biology that prepared this volume. Word of his death came while the volume was in press; we wish he had lived to see it completed.

KONRAD B. KRAUSKOPF
GEORGE Y. HARRY, JR.

# Foreword

Soon after the Alaska earthquake of March 27, 1964, President Lyndon B. Johnson wrote to Donald F. Hornig, his Special Assistant for Science and Technology:

It is important we learn as many lessons as possible from the disastrous Alaskan earthquake. A scientific understanding of the events that occurred may make it possible to anticipate future earthquakes, there and elsewhere, so as to cope with them more adequately.

I, therefore, request that your office undertake to assemble a comprehensive scientific and technical account of the Alaskan earthquake and its effects. . . .

In defining the scientific and technical questions involved and the related informational requirements for collection and assessment, I hope that you will be able to enlist the aid of the National Academy of Sciences. . . .

In discussions that followed, the Academy was requested by Dr. Hornig to establish the Committee on the Alaska Earthquake, to be charged with three principal tasks—to evaluate efforts being made to gather scientific and engineering information about the earthquake and its effects, to encourage the filling of gaps in the record, and to compile and publish a comprehensive report on the earthquake.

Under the chairmanship of Konrad B. Krauskopf of Stanford University, a twelve-man committee was formed of specialists from related scientific and technical disciplines. Their first meeting was held on June 15, 1964.

The resulting documents, prepared by the Committee and its seven specialized panels, constitute perhaps the most comprehensive and detailed account of an earthquake yet compiled. The Committee has attempted to compile from the available information and analysis a useful resource for present and future scholars in this field. As a result of the present study, much that is new and useful has been learned about earthquakes as well as about natural disasters in general.

In addition to the membership of the central committee, the work of several hundred scientists and engineers is represented in the Committee's report. Many of these are staff members of government agencies that have gathered facts and data about the earthquake and its effects; others are from universities and nongovernmental scientific organizations with an interest in earthquake-related research. Their help and cooperation in making this report possible is deeply appreciated.

PHILIP HANDLER
*President*
National Academy of Sciences

# Preface

South central Alaska (Figure 1), including Prince William Sound and the Aleutian area, is one of the world's most active seismic regions. On March 27, 1964, at about 5:36 p.m. local time (0336, or 3:36 a.m. GMT, March 28), an earthquake of unusual severity struck the Prince William Sound area. Seismologists record earthquake occurrences in Greenwich mean time (GMT). The U.S. Coast and Geodetic Survey, therefore, uses 03h 36m 14.0 ± 0.2s GMT, March 28, 1964, as the time of the earthquake. The coordinates of the epicenter of the main shock have been calculated as lat. $61.04° ± 0.05°N$ and long. $147.73° ± 0.07°W$, and the focus was within a few tens of kilometers of the surface. Not only was this earthquake of large magnitude (between 8.3 and 8.6 on the Richter scale, on which the greatest known earthquake is 8.9), but its duration (3 to 4 minutes) and the area of its damage zone ($50,000$ mi²) were extraordinary. Probably twice as much energy was released by the Alaska earthquake as by the one that rocked San Francisco in 1906.

The shock was felt over $500,000$ mi². A tsunami (a train of long waves impulsively generated, in this case by movement of the sea floor) or "tidal wave" swept from the Gulf of Alaska across the length of the Pacific and lapped against Antarctica. Water levels in wells as far away as South Africa jumped abruptly, and shock-induced waves were generated in the Gulf of Mexico. An atmospheric pressure wave caused by the earthquake was recorded at La Jolla, California, more than 2,000 mi away. Seismic surface waves, with periods of many seconds, moved the ground surface of most of the North American continent by as much as 2 in.

The magnitude of the earthquake can be calculated only from teleseismic records, and its duration can be estimated only from eyewitness accounts, because no seismic instruments capable of recording strong ground motion were in Alaska at the time. The range of uncertainty in the magnitude calculations (8.3-8.6) is far greater in terms of energy release than the figures suggest; from the most generally accepted relation of magnitude to energy release, it can be calculated that magnitude 8.6 represents approximately twice the energy release of magnitude 8.3.

Measured crustal deformation was more extensive than the deformation related to any known previous earthquake. Areas of uplift and subsidence were separated by a line of zero land-level change trending both southwestward and eastward from the vicinity of the epicenter, about 80 mi east-southeast of Anchorage; this line parallels the major tectonic features of the region. Areas north and northwest of the zero line subsided as much as 7.5 ft; areas south and southeast rose, over wide areas, as much as 6 ft. Locally the uplift was much greater: 38 ft on Montague Island and more than 50 ft on the sea floor southwest of the island. The zone of uplift was along the continental margin of the Aleutian Trench. Not only was the earth's crust displaced vertically, but horizontal movements of tens of feet took place, in which the landmass moved southeastward relative to the ocean floor. The area of crustal deformation was more than $100,000$ mi².

The mechanism of the earthquake remains to some extent uncertain. Fault-plane solutions for the main shock and the principal aftershocks, of which there were 10 of magnitudes greater than 6.0 within 24 hr after the initial shock, are consistent either with thrusting of the continent over the ocean floor along a plane dipping 5°-15° north or northwest, or with downward slip of the continent along a near-vertical plane; in either case the strike of the fault is northeast in the vicinity of Kodiak Island to east in Prince William Sound, parallel to the dominant tectonic trend. Although the fault-plane solutions do not permit an unambiguous decision between the two possible planes, several other lines of evidence strongly favor the low-angle thrust alternative.

The strong ground motion induced many snowslides, rockfalls, and landslides, both subaerial and submarine. The submarine landslides created local sea waves or tsunamis, which, together with the major tsunami generated by the crustal deformation, smashed port and harbor facilities,

ix

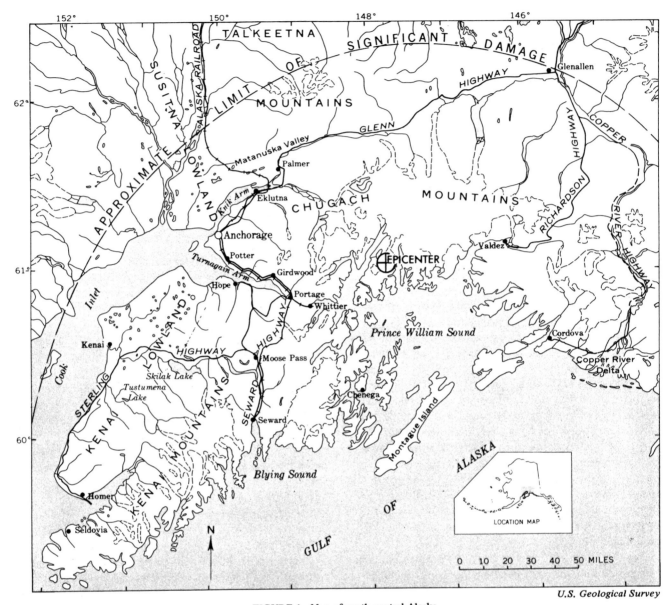

FIGURE 1 Map of south central Alaska.

U.S. Geological Survey

covered sessile organisms and salmon-spawning beds with silt, disturbed and killed salmon fry, leveled forests, and caused saltwater invasion of many coastal freshwater lakes.

The tectonic elevation and depression caused extensive damage to the biota of coastal forests, migratory-bird nesting grounds, salmon-spawning waters and gravels, as well as shellfish habitats, and initiated long-term changes in littoral and stream morphology. Clams, barnacles, algae, and many other marine and littoral organisms perished in areas of uplift. Spawning beds, trees, and other vegetation were destroyed in areas of depression.

Except for the major tsunami, which caused extensive damage in British Columbia and took 16 lives in Oregon and California, violence to man and his structures was restricted to the area of tectonic land-level change. Tsunamis, major and local, took the most lives. Landslides caused the most damage.

The number of lives lost in Alaska, 115, was very small for an earthquake of this magnitude. Factors that contributed to the light loss of life were the sparse population, the fortuitous timing of the earthquake, a low tide, the absence of fire in residential and business areas, the generally clement weather, and the fact that the earthquake occurred during the off-season for fishing. The earthquake came on the evening of a holiday, when the schools were empty and most offices deserted, but when most people were still wearing their warm clothing. The low tide and the absence of fishermen and cannery workers mitigated the destruction and loss of life from tsunamis.

Public and private property loss was over $300 million. Hundreds of homes were destroyed. A multistory apartment building (fortunately not occupied), a department store, and other buildings in Anchorage collapsed. Oil storage tanks at Valdez, Seward, and Whittier ruptured and burned. Many other structures were destroyed or damaged. Most of downtown Kodiak was inundated by the major tsunami.

Damage to surface transportation facilities was extensive. The Alaska Railroad lost its port facility at Whittier, its docks at Seward, and numerous bridges on the Kenai Peninsula. Many highway bridges, especially on the Seward and Copper River highways, were damaged. Many port and harbor facilities, especially at Seward, Valdez, Kodiak, Whittier, Cordova, and Homer, were destroyed.

The earthquake crippled Alaska's economy because nearly half the people of the state live within the damage area and because the land- and sea-transport facilities on which the economy depends were knocked out.

Relief came quickly. The extensive military establishment proved a great source of strength in implementing emergency measures designed to reduce the loss of life, to ease immediate suffering, and to restore needed services promptly. Financial assistance for relief purposes was provided immediately by the Office of Emergency Planning under provisions of the Federal Disaster Act.

Recovery was rapid. Of major importance in the reconstruction effort was a congressional program to provide additional federal aid not possible under existing authority. This program was recommended by the Federal Reconstruction and Development Planning Commission for Alaska, a unique body appointed by President Lyndon B. Johnson on April 2, 1964. The additional aid included transitional grants to maintain essential public services; an increase in the federal share of highway reconstruction costs; a decrease in the local share of urban renewal projects; debt adjustments on existing federal loans; federal purchase of state bonds; and grants for a state mortgage-forgiveness program. An estimated $330 million of government and private funds financed Alaska's recovery from the earthquake.

The Alaska earthquake is the best documented and most thoroughly studied earthquake in history. Attempts have been made to draw lessons from both the physical event and the human experience. Strong-motion seismographs and accelerographs were installed in Alaska shortly after the earthquake, providing a basis for study of the stronger aftershocks. The tsunami warning system for the North Pacific was greatly improved within a few months, mainly by establishment of three new seismograph stations in south central Alaska as the basic elements in the system. Risk maps for Anchorage, Homer, Seward, and Valdez, based upon exten-

sive geological studies, were prepared by the Scientific and Engineering Task Force of the Reconstruction Commission and were used discriminatingly as a basis for federal aid to reconstruction and as guides to future builders. The entire town of Valdez was relocated. Communities and state and professional organizations in seismic areas outside Alaska reexamined codes and programs related to earthquake hazard in light of the Alaska experience. Finally, the Alaska earthquake turned the nation's attention again, and sharply, to the problems of improving the elements of a national natural-disaster policy: zoning and construction codes; prediction and warning systems; rescue and relief organizations; disaster-data collection and analysis; and disaster insurance and reconstruction aids.

Thus the earthquake had many facets. It was a natural scientific experiment on a grand scale, providing data on a variety of long-standing problems regarding the mechanism and effects of earthquakes. It served as a test of man-made structures under extreme conditions, and as a guide to improvements in the location and design of such structures to make them better able to withstand seismic shocks. It was an object lesson in human response to disaster, pointing the way to increased effectiveness of warning systems, of emergency measures during disasters, and of relief and recovery operations.

The charge to the Committee on the Alaska Earthquake was made to ensure that as much technical and scientific information as possible would be wrung from the earthquake experience and that the results would be assembled into a comprehensive report. At its first meeting the Committee decided that its initial task of evaluating and encouraging efforts to gather scientific and technical information could best be carried out by panels representing the major disciplines involved in the data-gathering: engineering, geography (human ecology), geology, hydrology, oceanography, and seismology. Biology, at first included within oceanography, was later made the basis of a separate panel.

As information for a comprehensive report accumulated, it became clear that the report itself could most appropriately follow the panel structure. Accordingly, this report appears in eight volumes, seven put together by the separate panels and a summary volume prepared by the full Committee.

In the early meetings of the Committee, and especially as it became apparent that many of the physical-science and some of the engineering aspects of the earthquake would be treated comprehensively in government publications and individual studies, there was considerable discussion of the appropriate content of the Committee's final report.

The Committee finally decided that the advantages of having available, under one cover and in one place in a library, a truly comprehensive report on the earthquake would justify the expense of duplicating some material already published. In addition, the Committee agreed, a complete report would provide a better basis for the inclusion of cross-disciplinary papers, for pointing out lessons learned from the Alaska experience, and for making recommendations designed to reduce the loss of life and property in subsequent major earthquakes.

As a model for its work, the Committee could look back to the classic report on the 1906 San Francisco earthquake, published by the Carnegie Institution in 1908. To emulate the comprehensiveness of this magnificent report seemed possible, but not the unity and coherence that it gained from the encyclopedic knowledge of its editor and principal author, A. C. Lawson. The breadth and depth of scientific interest in earthquakes have increased so greatly since 1906 that no one man can hope to master, as Lawson did, a great part of existing technical knowledge on all aspects of earthquakes. A report today must necessarily have many authors and must reflect in its length and diversity the extraordinary development of disciplines and instruments over the past half century.

Despite the Committee's attempt to make the report broadly comprehensive, there are unfortunate and obvious gaps in the record, mainly in those subject-matter fields not included in the work of government agencies. Such gaps are identified in the appropriate volumes of the report.

Apart from these gaps, the report covers a wide variety of subjects in engineering, natural science, and social science. Ranging from seismology to human ecology, it sets forth what is known about the structure of the earth's crust in south central Alaska, especially in relation to possible earthquake mechanisms and to tsunami generation; describes the effects of the earthquake on geologic processes, rocks, and soils; outlines the seismic history of Alaska and gives the seismic parameters of the earthquake; presents the results of energy-release, strain-release, and focal-mechanism studies of the main shock and aftershocks; describes the effects of the earthquake on groundwater and surface-water bodies and on glaciers and snowfields; discusses the generation, propagation, and effects of earthquake-induced tsunamis; describes immediate as well as long-term effects on plants and animals of abrupt land elevation and depression and of slides and tsunamis; sets forth in detail, with analyses, the response of man-made structures to the earthquake; chronicles in narrative form both the physical and human events of the earthquake; describes the impact of the earthquake on individuals, communities, and organizations; and puts forward recommendations that range from geologic mapping for hazard zoning, through methods of assuring site-suited earthquake-resistant construction, to means of improving the human response to disaster.

This volume on biology is one of the eight parts into which the report is divided. Its papers describe the effects of the earthquake on the plants and animals of south central Alaska and the shallow waters along the coast. The shock itself caused little disturbance to most organisms, but the widespread changes in land level produced ecological dislocations whose effects will persist for many decades. Few earthquakes in history have altered life environments so profoundly and over so large an area.

The most obvious immediate biological consequence of the earthquake was the killing of land plants in areas flooded by salt water and of marine life in intertidal areas that became dry land. The devastation produced new habitats that were rapidly invaded by organisms that could cope with the changed conditions. Seldom have biologists had such an opportunity to study in detail the sequences of plants and animals that establish themselves on newly created expanses of land and shallow sea floor.

Of paramount economic interest to Alaskans was the effect of the earthquake on the salmon-fishing industry. The spawning grounds of salmon in the shallow coastal streams were vulnerable to drastic change or destruction as a result of the shift in sea level. Some of the spawning grounds were submerged in salt water, some were buried under sand and gravel, and some were partly eroded. There was reason to fear that egg-sac fry in the gravel had been immediately destroyed and that there would be heavy losses of eggs in succeeding years from meandering and erosion of salmon streams. Problems of shellfish mortality and the continued viability of shellfish in habitats altered by uplift and subsidence were also of considerable, though lesser, economic importance. Biological studies devoted to such problems naturally make up a large part of this volume.

Biological studies limited to a few years after the earthquake are necessarily incomplete; the adaptation of plants and animals to completely new conditions is a very slow process. An important function of this volume is to establish a firm basis for more definitive investigations in the future. In an area as remote as coastal Alaska, future biological work will be handicapped by scarcity of information on the normal preearthquake flora and fauna. To supplement the meager existing background data, several papers give new details of the normal plant and animal assemblages, as well as treating the changes produced by the earthquake.

The Committee experienced great difficulty in finding adequate financial support for biological research other than that related to commercial fisheries. Several promising studies had to be abandoned or curtailed, and the volume is accordingly not as complete as we had wished. It should nevertheless have value as a pioneer effort, probably the first intensive and coordinated study of the biological consequences of a major seismic event.

KONRAD B. KRAUSKOPF
Stanford University

# Acknowledgments

The Committee on the Alaska Earthquake and the Panel on Biology are particularly indebted to the National Science Foundation, the U.S. Coast and Geodetic Survey, the U.S. Geological Survey, the Office of Emergency Preparedness, the Army Research Office, the Atomic Energy Commission, the Advanced Research Projects Agency, and the Office of Naval Research for support of the Committee under Contract NSF C-310, TO 89; to the Department of Housing and Urban Development for similar support under Contract H-1229; to the Department of the Interior for special support; and to the National Science Foundation for publication support under Contract NSF C-310, TO 208.

The Committee and Panel greatly appreciate the time and effort provided by Donald W. Hood, Donald B. Lawrence, and John W. Marr for their comments and suggestions as reviewers for the Division of Earth Sciences.

The Panel thanks the various government and private organizations that made available the time of the authors whose works make up the volume. Special recognition is due the Bureau of Commercial Fisheries, the National Oceanic and Atmospheric Administration, the California Academy of Sciences, the Alaska Department of Fish and Game, Michigan State University, and the University of Montana for making it possible for some of their personnel to serve as Panel members, authors, and reviewers. Similarly, the Panel expresses its appreciation to Stanford University, the California Institute of Technology, Texas A&M University, the University of Hawaii, the U.S. Geological Survey, The Geological Society of America, The Ohio State University, the University of Colorado, the U.S. Bureau of Commercial Fisheries, the University of Southern California, Clark University, the University of California at Berkeley, the U.S. Coast and Geodetic Survey, the Environmental Science Services Administration, and the National Oceanic and Atmospheric Administration for making available their personnel for service on the parent Committee; and also to the Office of Science and Technology, the National Science Foundation, the Department of Defense, the Army Research Office, the Advanced Research Projects Agency, the U.S. Coast and Geodetic Survey, the Environmental Science Services Administration, the National Oceanic and Atmospheric Administration, the U.S. Geological Survey, the Office of Emergency Preparedness, the Atomic Energy Commission, the Office of Naval Research, the Department of the Interior, and the Department of Housing and Urban Development for the time and assistance provided by their liaison representatives to the Committee.

The Panel is grateful to the University of Idaho, the U.S. Geological Survey, and Emory University for making the services of editors and indexers available; to the California Academy of Sciences, the Bureau of Commercial Fisheries, the U.S. Geological Survey, the U.S. Coast and Geodetic Survey, the U.S. Army Corps of Engineers, and the Alaska Department of Fish and Game for assistance with maps and illustrations; to the U.S. Army and the U.S. Air Force for transportation to the affected areas; and to the University of Alaska, the Auke Bay Biological Laboratory, the Pacific Power and Light Company, the State of Oregon, the University of Washington, the University of Arizona, the Z. J. Loussac Public Library, and the California Academy of Sciences for furnishing meeting places for the Panel.

Since 1964, reorganizations within federal agencies and departments have involved several of the Committee's supporting agencies. On July 13, 1965, the U.S. Coast and Geodetic Survey and other component agencies were combined to form the Environmental Science Services Administration, under the Department of Commerce. On October 3, 1970, the Environmental Science Services Administration, together with several other organizations, became the National Oceanic and Atmospheric Administration (NOAA), also under the Department of Commerce. Elements of the Department of the Interior's Bureau of Marine Fisheries became the National Marine Fisheries Service of NOAA. Although the Bureau of Commercial Fisheries, the Coast and Geodetic Survey, and the Environmental Science Services Administration no longer exist as organizations, their names are used for historical accuracy, as is that of the Office of Emergency Planning, which was renamed the Office of Emergency Preparedness on October 21, 1968.

# Contents

xv

# General Introduction, Summary, and Conclusions

The Alaska earthquake of March 27, 1964, caused great destruction not only of the works of man but of the natural environment. Intertidal areas that had been covered with the salt water of incoming tides for many centuries were suddenly raised far above the reach of the highest tides, and the exposed complex communities of marine plants and animals were almost immediately obliterated. In areas of subsidence, terrestrial zones abruptly became intertidal zones. Walls of water that surged into estuaries scoured out beds of clams and other organisms or deposited layers of mud and debris that suffocated the life below. Tsunamis washed into low-lying lakes, changing fresh water to brackish water. Estuarine areas that had been ideal nesting grounds for ducks and geese were uplifted enough to make them unsuitable for waterfowl production or were submerged beneath the sea. Ocean agitation and underwater mud slides probably caused extensive damage to life in deeper waters, although such changes have been difficult to evaluate.

Scientists realized immediately that as much information as possible on the great Alaska earthquake and its effects should be assembled and published in one series. To accomplish this purpose, the Committee on the Alaska Earthquake was established under the direction of the National Academy of Sciences-National Research Council. At the first meeting of the Committee (June 15, 1964), no representative of the biological sciences was present, and as a result there was little discussion of biological implications of the earthquake. A Panel on Oceanography was established, however, and the suggestion was made that this Panel might include marine biology in its work. At the Committee's second meeting (August 29-30, 1964), in Anchorage, an oceanography work group consisting of Doak C. Cox (Chairman), Eduard Berg, and George Y. Harry, Jr., was organized. After discussing the need for information on the effects of the earthquake on plant and animal life, the work group recommended that a separate panel on biology be established.

The first meeting of the Panel on Oceanography was held December 21-22, 1964, under the chairmanship of Doak C. Cox. Of the six members of the Panel, three (G Dallas Hanna, California Academy of Sciences; George Y. Harry, Jr., U.S. Bureau of Commercial Fisheries; and Gerald W. Prescott, Michigan State University) represented the biological sciences. At this meeting, the Committee chairman, Konrad B. Krauskopf, stated that the charge of the Committee and its panels was to review the work being done on the earthquake, to detect any gaps that might exist in action or planning, and to recommend ways of filling those gaps. The Committee was also to compile a comprehensive report on the earthquake and its effects. All biological aspects of the earthquake would be handled, for the time being, by the Panel on Oceanography.

The Panel biologists agreed that the vast earthquake-caused changes in many littoral areas, especially those changes having no direct economic consequences, were not being adequately studied. They proposed that such a study be made in Prince William Sound in 1965. This study was subsequently sponsored by the California Academy of Sciences, financed jointly by the Atomic Energy Commission and the National Science Foundation, and carried out under the direction of Dr. G Dallas Hanna. The results are reported in this volume in papers by Hanna, Eyerdam, Haven, and Johansen.

During the summer of 1965, the Panel on Biology was organized to include the three biologists of the Panel on Oceanography and Wallace H. Noerenberg, Alaska Department of Fish and Game. At the first meeting of this panel on January 12-13, 1966, in Portland, Oregon, problems discussed included the financing of research projects, especially those not mission-oriented. The panel recognized the need for additional research in the outer coastal areas, in areas of

1

submerged lakes and streams, and in the Kodiak Island area,
especially the intertidal section that had been investigated
by James Nybakken in 1963 (Nybakken, this volume). Attempts to find funds for such studies were unsuccessful.

To acquaint scientists at the University of Alaska with
the work of the Committee and its Panel on Biology, two
meetings were held on the campus at College, one in August
1966 and one in January 1967. At these meetings the University of Alaska was urged to request funds from various
federal and private granting agencies to carry out immediate
and long-range research on the biological effects of the
earthquake. The University expressed considerable interest
and submitted proposals to several grant-funding agencies,
but without success.

The Alaska earthquake caused sudden and widespread
changes in the environment and in its living creatures. Such
dramatic ecological changes occur only rarely, and their
study was important in understanding the effects of this
particular earthquake. Research on the biological effects of
the earthquake could contribute even more to an understanding of the principles of ecological relationships under
circumstances that would be impossible to simulate in any
controlled experiment. This volume represents the results
of the studies stimulated by the Panel.

The papers in this volume reflect the fact that most of
the funding for biological studies came from mission-oriented
state and federal agencies and also that research was concentrated on Prince William Sound, where the destruction
of economically important species was greatest. Eight of the
thirteen research papers relating to the effects of the earthquake are by state or federal employees. Four papers resulted from the 1965 investigation sponsored by the California Academy of Sciences, and the remaining investigation
was supported by a National Science Foundation grant to a
University of Alaska scientist. Eleven of the papers deal primarily with earthquake effects in Prince William Sound, one
discusses intrusion of salt water into lakes of Kodiak Island,
and one summarizes the overall damages to fish and shellfish resources of Alaska.

Damage to fish and shellfish was greatest in Prince
William Sound, where state and federal agencies fortunately
had already accumulated a great deal of knowledge about
this resource. The Alaska Department of Fish and Game and
the U.S. Bureau of Commercial Fisheries had a considerable
amount of information about the size of salmon runs in
Prince William Sound and the survival of eggs and alevins
(yolk-sac fry) in the gravel. In 1960 the Bureau of Commercial Fisheries had established a field station at Olsen Bay in
Prince William Sound to make a general study of salmon
biology in an important intertidal spawning stream. Within
a few days of the earthquake, state and federal biologists
began an assessment of possible damage to salmon runs.

## SUMMARY

### IMMEDIATE EFFECTS OF THE EARTHQUAKE

The earthquake caused spectacular changes in the appearance of many beaches, especially in Prince William Sound
where uplift in some areas exceeded 30 ft. Many miles of
new beach, sometimes several hundred yards in width, were
thrust up from the sea, creating habitats for terrestrial organisms where no marine plants and animals could survive.
The earthquake triggered landslides and avalanches that
stripped forests and soil to bedrock in some places. Beneath
the sea also, avalanches must have destroyed much life.
Temporary dewatering of streams and lakes because of landslides and land tilting probably caused some loss of living
organisms; for example, the lower part of Ship Creek near
Anchorage was dry for 18 hours immediately after the
earthquake.

Tsunamis that followed the earthquake surged into bays
and inlets and swept away many square miles of soft sediment that was redeposited, often in deep water but sometimes in shallow areas, smothering underlying life. At the
time of the earthquake, most young salmon had hatched
but were still in the gravel; many of them were killed by
mechanical shock or by lack of oxygen caused by siltation.
Many coastal lakes were inundated by tsunamis that swept
salt water into their basins and in some instances washed
away their outlets. In contrast, salmon runs were benefited
in a few areas of Prince William Sound when land subsidence
eliminated impassable falls and velocity barriers and opened
up many miles of new habitat suitable for salmon spawning.

In Prince William Sound, thousands of large red rockfish
(*Sebastes*) and cod (*Gadus macrocephalus*) were reported
dead on the surface of many miles of water near Chenega
Island and in Valdez Arm (Hanna, this volume; Rae E.
Baxter, personal communication). These fish had probably
been forced to the surface by violent water turbulence and
were unable to return to deep water because their air bladders had expanded. Large numbers of dead flatfish were also
seen floating in Knight Island Passage on March 29, 1964
(W. H. Noerenberg, personal communication). Some of the
smaller fishes living among the rocks and algae of the littoral
zone were destroyed in locations where ocean waters no
longer reached them.

The damage to the clam resource was extensive, especially
in Prince William Sound, where 11–40 percent of each species of economic importance were destroyed (Baxter, this
volume). The mussel, *Mytilus edulis*, probably the most
plentiful mollusk in Prince William Sound, sustained a loss
of about 90 percent. Razor clams, *Siliqua patula*, also suffered heavy mortalities in areas of uplift.

At Olsen Bay in Prince William Sound, high mortality of

littleneck clams (*Prothothaca staminea*) in the new +5- to +6-ft zone indicated that clams of this species living in the uppermost foot of the preearthquake range of the species were not able to survive (Hubbard, this volume). The habitat range of the hardshell clam (*Saxidomus giganteus*) was sufficiently uplifted to annihilate the species over the entire preearthquake range of Olsen Bay.

Barnacles are a conspicuous element of the invertebrate fauna of Prince William Sound and form a broad distinct band on the rocks. The upper limit of this band is generally well defined. After the earthquake this upper limit of barnacles served as a benchmark for determining the extent of elevation or subsidence. Thus, in spite of sophisticated modern instrumentation, it was the lowly barnacle that was used to a great extent to determine changes in elevation caused by the earthquake (Plafker, *Science*, v. 148 [June 25, 1965], 1675–1685).

The earthquake affected marine invertebrates primarily by vertical displacement of animals into different habitats. The results of displacement ranged from immediate and complete mortality of invertebrates lifted above the reach of tides to more subtle effects caused by disruption of permanent burrows, shifting of silt by earthquake-generated waves, and alteration of substrate stability along the shoreline. Even more subtle were changes in the microclimate, such as exposure of sedentary organisms to longer drying periods, to longer periods of high temperatures during summer months, and to freezing in winter.

In the coastal areas of Alaska, elevation changes affected extensive expanses of marshland previously suitable for waterfowl. Uplift of the Copper River Delta area caused a drastic change in the principal nesting ground of the dusky Canada goose (Crow, this volume). This goose restricts its nesting to one kind of vegetation found in the delta area, and biologists fear that rapid change in nesting habitat of this bird will affect its abundance. A change in waterfowl habitat in the Chickaloon Flats waterfowl area in Turnagain Arm was caused by a subsidence of approximately 4 ft that permitted high tides to cover much of the marsh with layers of mud and to inundate freshwater areas with salt water. Temporary loss of waterfowl habitat resulted (David Spencer, personal communication).

Alaska's major industry is based on fish and shellfish in the ocean, estuaries, and rivers. The immediate damage to the vessels that harvest this living resource and to the canneries that process it was extensive. On Kodiak Island and surrounding smaller islands, five canneries processing king crab, clams, and salmon were completely destroyed, with a loss of over $2 million (Noerenberg, this volume). Losses at seven other canneries, which were rendered completely or partly inoperative because of flooding caused by land subsidence, were about $1.5 million. In the Port of Kodiak, 13 vessels were lost and 19 went aground or were swamped, representing a financial loss of about $1 million. If other damaged or lost vessels are included, the value of vessels and facilities lost in the Kodiak area totaled about $6 million, in addition to the loss of about $200,000 in stored fishery products.

In the Cook Inlet–Kenai Peninsula area, tsunamis destroyed all fish-processing facilities and vessels at Seward, and land subsidence caused extensive damage to canneries at Homer and Seldovia. The Kenai Peninsula is an important recreational area because of its proximity to Anchorage, Alaska's most densely populated region. The Seward Highway, which connects the Kenai Peninsula with Anchorage, was temporarily closed because of land subsidence, and even during the period of repair in 1964, the road was open for only short periods each day. This restriction resulted in a severe reduction of sport fishing in the peninsula.

In Prince William Sound, the Port of Valdez was severely affected. All its fish-processing plants, waterfront docks, and warehouses were demolished, and 15 seine-fishing vessels were destroyed. Land uplift in the Prince William Sound area caused a number of transportation problems for the fishing industry. The Crystal Falls Fish Company salmon cannery, located at Mountain Slough, became inaccessible to fishermen, and the owners declared it a complete loss. In other parts of Prince William Sound, dredging of waterways, harbors, and dockside areas was necessary to carry on routine fishing operations.

## LONG-RANGE EFFECTS OF THE ALASKA EARTHQUAKE

Because of the great economic importance of the salmon fishery in the Prince William Sound area, state and federal agencies are making extensive studies of the long-range changes in salmon production caused by the earthquake. In Prince William Sound, most salmon spawn in the lower reaches of streams, in intertidal areas that were greatly changed by uplift or subsidence. Of the 223 salmon-producing streams in the Sound, 138 were uplifted 3–31.5 ft, 43 subsided as much as 6 ft, and 42 remained essentially at the same level (−1 to +2 ft). Serious long-range effects on the abundance of salmon have resulted.

The size of the salmon runs was affected primarily by a change in the quality of the spawning gravels in the intertidal areas of streams. Much scouring of streambeds and horizontal movement of channels occurred in regions of uplift. Rapid changes in stream channels were observed in 1964 and 1965 in newly uplifted streams. Salmon eggs deposited in this changing stream environment were subjected to adverse conditions and suffered heavy mortalities. Adverse effects included dislodgment of eggs and alevins by scouring of streambeds, desiccation and suffocation by horizontal meandering of streams, smothering of eggs and alevins from filling of some parts of streambeds, and generally unfavorable conditions for survival in the silt and sediments of newly created intertidal zones.

In areas of subsidence, especially where falls or cascades in streams prohibit upstream movement of spawning salmon, the area of productive spawning was reduced. Formerly productive intertidal zones of streams in subsided areas are now covered with tidewaters much of the time and are rarely used by spawning salmon.

State and federal biologists in the Prince William Sound area have estimated the decrease of salmon fry caused by the earthquake. For the entire period 1964–1967, about 700,000 pink salmon from a spawning population of about 4.2 million were observed on newly created spawning beds in poor-quality unstable environment. A substantial number of pink salmon therefore spawned in areas where few eggs and alevins would survive. By 1967, the newly created intertidal salmon-spawning areas had not improved a great deal in terms of salmon-fry production.

An intensive study at Olsen Creek, Prince William Sound, after the 1965 spawning season, showed that egg losses from scouring or filling of the stream channel amounted to about 7.3 million pink salmon eggs and 1.1 million chum salmon eggs (Thorsteinson and others, this volume). This loss represents a significant portion of the eggs deposited by the females that spawned in the postearthquake intertidal area.

Roys (this volume) estimated the economic loss in Prince William Sound caused by the decline in numbers of salmon after the earthquake. For the 3-year period 1966–1968, the fishermen of Prince William Sound lost about $3.5 million in income, or about $6,000 per fisherman. The approximate gross value lost to the canning industry during this same period was $9.6 million, and the retail loss was about $14 million.

Returning runs of pink and chum salmon in Prince William Sound will probably remain lower than preearthquake runs until major stream regrading is completed and spawning beds regain their former stability. The Alaska Department of Fish and Game and the U.S. Forest Service are trying to speed up stabilization of streams by an extensive rehabilitation program. Upstream zones in subsided areas have been cleared of logjams and other barriers, and intertidal zones in uplifted areas have been regraded into single channels excavated to levels of low-flow water tables. After 3 years, the rehabilitation program appeared to be showing signs of success.

In early 1969 the Alaska Department of Fish and Game requested the Secretary of the Interior to declare the Prince William Sound salmon industry a fishery disaster within the meaning of Section 4B of Public Law 88–309 and requested funds for an engineering study to develop methods of restoration of salmon runs by stabilizing streambeds and restocking streams. The Department of Fish and Game based the request on the loss of salmon-spawning areas, which had resulted in a massive decline of salmon runs throughout Prince William Sound. As an example, they cited the runs to streams of Montague Island: Before the earthquake, approximately 700,000 salmon spawned there each year, but in 1969 only about 20,000 were expected.

An important question in the management of salmon stocks in Prince William Sound is whether the fish that spawn in intertidal areas are discrete populations. The behavior of salmon in areas of uplift after the earthquake sheds some light on this question. In 1964, 61 percent of the pink salmon deposited eggs in the intertidal zone of Olsen Creek, which had been uplifted about 4 ft by the earthquake; 15 percent spawned in that portion of the old intertidal zone, now a freshwater zone, that had been used by about 60 percent of the intertidal spawners in 1962. In 1964 and 1965, most of the pink and chum salmon that spawned in Olsen Creek below the preearthquake high-tide level used the new intertidal zone. This information supports the hypothesis that intertidal spawners belong to discrete populations and select their spawning location according to tidal elevation, although they may also be influenced by the quality of the spawning beds. Observations after the earthquake at Wild, O'Brien, and Swanson creeks in Prince William Sound demonstrated that pink salmon in these streams consistently selected spawning areas on the basis of present tide levels, although some of the areas had never before been used.

Recent information received from Roys indicates that salmon runs on Montague Island are still in poor condition (1970) and the area remains closed to commercial fishing. Furthermore, the even-year run of pink salmon in Prince William Sound is still producing below-average runs, but the rehabilitation program initiated in 1966 has improved runs to 30 specific streams. Little rehabilitation work is being done on Montague Island because aid to recovery would be immensely expensive. Newly created spawning areas of unimproved uplifted streams have shown signs of improved production, but streambed movements are a continuing cause of above-average mortality of eggs and fry.

The intrusion of tsunamis into low-lying coastal lakes of Kodiak and Afognak islands resulted in another long-range effect on fish. Broad Point No. 40 Lake, near the town of Kodiak, received a large quantity of saline water from the tsunamis (Marriott and Spetz, this volume). This seawater inhibited growth of freshwater plankton, and within the first year after the earthquake the lake became virtually sterile. The hypolimnion soon became severely depleted in oxygen and now does not support fish or plankton. A few species of fish survive in the epilimnion; otherwise, the lake has become unsuitable as a fish habitat and is likely to remain so for many years.

Other low-lying lakes in subsided areas now periodically receive salt water at high tides. Lake Rose Tead, a shallow lake of about 234 acres near Kodiak, now receives intrusions of seawater from tides greater than 9 ft. Subsequent mixing with fresh water produces an environment unsuitable for either marine or freshwater plankton, yet growth and survival of coho salmon fingerlings in the lake seem to have improved after the earthquake. This improvement is probably caused by marine food transported into the lake. The magnitude of coho salmon spawning runs into Lake Rose Tead increased dramatically from 1966 to 1968. Sockeye salmon returns also increased in 1968. In the spring of 1969, sport fishermen caught large numbers of 8- to 10-in. coho salmon smolts, indicating that the stimulation of freshwater growth was continuing.

The optimum habitat of most of the economically important species of clams in the Prince William Sound area before the earthquake was at a tide level of between −3.5 and +1.5 ft (Baxter, this volume). In uplifted areas, most species of clams survived to about the postearthquake 6-ft tide level, except in the Olsen Bay area, where littleneck clams showed evidence of high mortality in the postearthquake +5.0- to +6.0-ft zone (Hubbard, this volume). As in the other areas, survival of adults was good at elevations of +4.0 to +5.0 ft. The limiting factor for establishment of mature clams at upper tidal levels seems to be the inability of young clams to survive in this habitat. It is likely that clams in areas uplifted higher than mean low water will gradually disappear because the adults will not be replaced. Much of the new potential clam habitat in the uplifted zone of Prince William Sound consists of preearthquake subtidal silty material unsuitable for clams.

Most of the areas of subsidence in Prince William Sound could immediately support larval clams because they were composed of sand, gravel, and broken shells and contained a minimum of highly organic silt. The zone below the present lowest low tide probably will not remain suitable for young clams if the expected siltation occurs.

In 1965, dense hatches of small postearthquake mussels were common. Most had settled on underlying algae rather than on solid rock, and the beds were generally somewhat lower in the intertidal zone than were the preearthquake adult beds (Haven, this volume). Although mortality of adult mussels had been very high, it was evident that replacement would be rapid because of the heavy set in 1965. By 1968, beds of mussels were again attached mainly to rocks or barnacles rather than to algae.

One of the curious effects of the earthquake was a reversal in dominance of the two common species of barna-

cles found in Prince William Sound (Haven, this volume). *Balanus glandula* was the dominant preearthquake species whose tests were found on uplifted rocks, whereas tests of *B. balanoides* were scarce or absent. The immediate postearthquake settlement was mainly by *B. balanoides*. One possible explanation of the reversal in dominance of the two common barnacles could be based on the supposition that at the time of the earthquake, *B. balanoides* may have just released its larvae into the water, but larvae of *B. glandula* may not yet have been released. Larvae of *B. balanoides* would then have been free to colonize the newly uplifted rocks. By the summer of 1968, *B. glandula* had once again become dominant and had replaced *B. balanoides* in much of the preearthquake upper midlittoral zone.

In the summer of 1965 the California Academy of Sciences gave considerable attention to the effect of the earthquake on the algae of Prince William Sound. By the time of the 1965 study, much of the midtidal zone of moderately uplifted areas was well populated with a mixture of algal survivors and new postearthquake algal growth (Johansen, this volume). *Fucus* that had colonized after the earthquake was common at most stations in 1965, with the notable exceptions of MacLeod Harbor and Hanning Bay, areas of extensive uplift on Montague Island where *Porphyra* was dominant. It seems probable that no fucoid reproductive bodies were available in these areas because the earthquake had lifted all the plants above the reach of salt water.

An interesting biological question that developed after the earthquake was the nature of ecological succession in the new intertidal zone. Plastic settling surfaces, placed in the littoral and upper sublittoral zones near Cordova in 1965, indicated that diatoms and filamentous green algae probably were the first algal colonizers of barren surfaces that were depressed or uplifted into these zones by the earthquake (Johansen, this volume). The settling surfaces were found to be remarkably devoid of animals. Other workers have previously reported that algae precede animals in occupying new or denuded intertidal surfaces.

Observations on postearthquake rocky shores in 1965 indicated that the next stages of community development were sometimes relatively rapid and direct, involving colonization by the same species that were dominant before the earthquake. Evidence of more protracted succession was also found, however, including the dominance of an algal film rather than the lichen *Verrucaria* in the uppermost zones and the previously mentioned differences in midlittoral barnacle species and in attachment of mussels and the dominance of *Porphyra* rather than *Fucus* in the areas of greatest uplift.

Observations in August 1968 (Haven, this volume) generally confirmed the rapid successional nature of several aspects of the postearthquake communities as interpreted from the 1965 data and indicated that with few exceptions (notably the *Verrucaria* zone), these communities had essentially returned to their preearthquake condition.

Biologists of the U.S. Bureau of Sport Fisheries and Wildlife have made periodic observations on changes in the Chickaloon Flats waterfowl area in Turnagain Arm since the inundation and vegetation kill caused by the earthquake (Robert A. Richey, personal correspondence). The 1965 spring waterfowl migration was substantially less than in previous years. Examination of the flats revealed that most of the area was covered with a heavy layer of silt 10–20 in. deep. Erosion from high-tide runoff formed numerous sloughs filled with muddy silt.

In early October 1965, beach arrowgrass, *Triglochin maritima*, was invading the silt layer of Chickaloon Flats and once again was attracting waterfowl. Ducks began to use the area on September 1 and continued to do so until October 18. During the last week of that period, an estimated 10,000 Canada geese and 5,000 ducks were using the area. In 1966, a spring increase of waterfowl was attributed principally to partial recovery of the habitat from the effects of the earthquake. The 1967 spring migration appeared normal; several thousand birds used the flats during this period and returned to them in the fall. In 1968 and 1969, vegetation once again covered most of the affected area and waterfowl use conformed to past seasonal records.

The great Alaska earthquake provided an opportunity to gather information on relationships between bog and forest communities over a much shorter time than was previously possible. A simplified working hypothesis is that the loss rate of surface and immediate-subsurface water increased in areas of uplift (compared to rates before the earthquake) and decreased in areas of subsidence (Neiland, this volume). In the summers of 1965 and 1966, permanent transects were established across a bog-forest transition in areas of known vertical displacement, and various natural characteristics were recorded. Transects were established in the Prince William Sound area and on northeastern Kodiak Island. An early conclusion regarding the effects of rapid and temporary saltwater invasion of bogs is that any effect on vegetation is transient. In 1965, areas invaded by sea waves on Kodiak Island and Montague Island did not differ noticeably from their preearthquake condition. All transects will be sampled at intervals in the future to detect shifts in the relative position of the two major vegetation types.

The Copper River Delta, composed of National Forest uplands and state tidelands, lies generally between the Eyak River and the rugged mountains just east of Cordova. Approximately 330,000 acres of the best waterfowl habitat lying between the Copper River Highway and the Gulf of Alaska have been established as a cooperative game-management area by the U.S. Forest Service and the state. The Forest Service, realizing that extensive habitat changes in this area of uplift might influence future management practices, photographed a series of aerial transects to record the status of the waterfowl habitat after the earthquake. In the spring of 1966, 12 parallel transects, approximately 3 mi apart, were flown across the area. The transects began on the Copper River Highway and terminated at the beach. The objective was to provide a base from which possible future changes in composition of the vegetation on the delta could be measured. It was originally intended to repeat these transects in 5 years. It is now apparent, however, that 10-year intervals will show more significant changes.

Much of the information that could have been obtained by intensive studies of intertidal plant and animal communities affected by the earthquake was not accumulated because of the rapid changes that took place in the environment. The basic information on plants and animals of the intertidal zone collected by the 1965 California Academy of Sciences expedition to Prince William Sound is, however, available for future comparative studies. Future studies of the long-range effects of the earthquake on plant and animal communities undoubtedly will be concentrated on the Prince William Sound salmon runs because of the economic loss sustained by the salmon industry there. Some of the authors of this volume have expressed an interest in continuing their research, and a few have been able to make additional studies of earthquake effects. The publication of this volume and contacts made by the Panel on Biology may stimulate additional research.

## CONCLUSIONS

The most serious biological problem emphasized by the great Alaska earthquake is the lack of fundamental information on plant and animal communities in Alaska. Several mission-oriented state and federal agencies are collecting limited information on Alaska's natural living resources, but these studies are usually not well coordinated, and no agency is primarily concerned with understanding the general biology and ecology of land and water areas. It is not feasible to collect base data for all the biological environments where a disaster might occur, but it is possible to make ecological studies of representative types of aquatic and terrestrial natural environments. Such studies are needed to understand our changing environment and to provide the basis for research after a natural disaster. No single federal or state agency is capable of carrying out major research on representative plant and animal communities, but a good beginning would be to make one of the federal agencies responsible for coordinating such studies.

Collection of information on biological changes after an earthquake is obviously necessary, but this requires contingency planning and advance arrangements for funding to avoid the loss of ephemeral data and to ensure that studies of the long-range effect of the earthquake on the environment will be undertaken. A separate fund for this purpose should be established, perhaps in the National Science Foundation.

The earthquake caused the immediate death of many plants and animals, mainly by elevating or depressing intertidal areas, by generating tsunamis, and by causing slides on land and beneath the ocean.

Long-term effects of the earthquake on plants and animals resulted from meandering and scouring of streambeds in elevated areas, changes in habitat caused by uplift or subsidence, and periodic tidal flooding of depressed lowland lakes.

Alaska sustained a heavy economic loss from earthquake-caused damage to the fish and shellfish resource and to the facilities and vessels used by the fishing industry.

Coordinated studies of the biological effects of the earthquake should continue to document ecological conditions that will change constantly for decades until the preearthquake level of stability is reached. An agency of the State of Alaska, such as the University of Alaska, or a federal agency, such as the Fish and Wildlife Service, should be designated as a center for registering information on biological research relating to Alaska earthquakes.

GEORGE Y. HARRY, JR.
National Marine Fisheries Service,
National Oceanic and
    Atmospheric Administration

G DALLAS HANNA
CALIFORNIA ACADEMY OF SCIENCES

Reprinted with minor changes from
*Pacific Discovery*,
"Biological Effects of an Earthquake"

# Observations Made in 1964 on the Immediate Biological Effects of the Earthquake in Prince William Sound

ABSTRACT: A seldom-mentioned aspect of earthquake damage is the effect on animal and plant life. In the uplifted newly exposed former littoral zone along the shores and on the numerous islands of Prince William Sound there was total destruction of the animal and plant life in 1964. Some uplifted sand and silt areas in the Sound had contained economically valuable clam populations.

Earthquake-triggered landslides, avalanches, and tsunamis destroyed much land vegetation. In the depressed areas, seawater now extends into the formerly green forest.

How much time will be required to establish a new littoral life zone over the vast area affected by the earthquake? The effect of previous earthquakes on the flora and fauna of the shaken area has been little studied, and there is no precedent on which to make a prediction.

An aspect of earthquake damage that is seldom mentioned is the effect on the fauna and flora of the shaken area. Observations of such effects resulting from the Alaska earthquake are reported in this paper. These observations were made during May and June 1964, when I had the good fortune to accompany a party of U.S. Geological Survey investigators, led by George Plafker, to the Prince William Sound area.

The primary objective was to determine the amount of elevation or depression among the many islands and inlets of Prince William Sound, for the epicenter of the earthquake was known to have been in that general area. The Sound itself covers roughly 20,000 mi$^2$, but destructive effects extended over a much greater region. Valdez and Cordova are the principal towns on the Sound, and Whittier is an important railroad terminal. There are numerous deep fiords and many large and small islands along this part of the Alaskan coast. Heavily forested lowlands, steep high mountains, and dozens of glaciers make this one of the most scenic areas of the state. The marine life is very rich and of considerable economic importance.

The first step necessarily was the establishment of a datum plane from which to make measurements; that is, a reasonably accurate determination was needed of where sea level had been in relation to the land before the earthquake. Tide gages were few and widely separated, and the bench marks on which they were located had become displaced along with the rest of the land. The Survey geologists decided to use a biological datum plane based on the zonation of marine animals and plants. The senior scientist and former Director of the California Academy of Sciences, Dr. Robert C. Miller, had made a special study of such zonation; his publication on the subject, as coauthor with George B. Rigg (Rigg and Miller, 1949), was invaluable.

FIGURE 1 A close view of a cliff on Latouche Island showing the dark *Verrucaria* zone at the top and the barnacle zone immediately below. The junction of these two zones is a reliable datum plane from which to compute elevation of the land.

## OBSERVATIONS

Mean high tide is sharply delineated by the line between the lichen *Verrucaria* above and the barnacles and the alga *Fucus* below (Figure 1). Measuring from this plane (Figure 2), the geologists found that the area had been elevated a maximum of about 35 ft at the south end of Montague Island (Figure 3) and had been depressed 6½ ft at the heads of some western inlets (Figure 4). It is now known that the coastline for many hundreds of miles was elevated.

The newly exposed littoral areas, covering many hundreds of square miles and once densely populated by a varied fauna and flora, became completely desolated. At the time of our investigation, a new littoral zone had not yet formed where the uplift was more than 10 ft, the normal tidal range in the Sound. Most of the soft-bodied creatures had decomposed or had become food for birds. The many species of marine plants, so conspicuous along most coastlines, were gone. The *Fucus* had turned black in desiccation; the calcareous red algae were bleached white, and so were the many species of green algae. The great fields of big brown

FIGURE 2 Measuring the distance from the waterline to the top of the barnacle zone in College Fiord. This distance, together with the time and stage of the tide, is used to compute the elevation or depression of the land. Many hundreds of such measurements were made.

FIGURE 3   Former sea bottom on Montague Island, now far above the present highest tides. Encrusting animals and algae—red, green, and brown when alive—were all bleached snow white at the time of the investigations 2 months after the earthquake.

kelp, *Laminaria* or *Nereocystis* (once under water), were gone, but the individual stalks and holdfasts remained, black and bent over, a menace to the unwary observer on foot.

In many places there were great accumulations of dried starfish, and at one locality, the dried necks of clams formed a solid mass covering about a square yard. We could only speculate on the manner by which these organisms congregated. In some places a shovel could have been used to collect almost pure concentrations of small shells. Bleached remains of Bryozoa (Figure 5) and calcareous algae were so

white that the rocky beaches rivaled the adjacent snow-covered mountains in brightness.

There is no known eyewitness to the actual rise of the land to its greatest elevation, so whether the uplift was abrupt or gradual is uncertain. In Cordova, where the uplift was about 7 ft, it seemed to one observer, William O'Brien (oral communication, 1964), that the rise accompanied the highly destructive wave action. It would be expected that free-swimming fishes would have readily escaped; this was not true for a species of red rockfish, which floated to the

FIGURE 4   This glacial moraine, the former nesting ground of many birds, is obviously in a depressed zone—otherwise the fragment of ice could not have reached this area.

FIGURE 5  Bryozoa. Many square miles of former sea bottom were covered with species of this and other groups of encrusting animals and plants.

surface in Valdez Narrows and near Chenega Island in sufficient numbers to cover the water. The destruction of these fish may have been caused by submarine slumping known to have taken place near both of these localities.

Some large sand and silt areas in Prince William Sound in the past have contained a huge and highly valuable population of clams. Where these areas were uplifted, the clams were destroyed. What the economic result will be has not yet been determined, but in this area, most of the clams were 8–13 years old, and therefore it will take many years to replace them.

The earthquake triggered many landslides and avalanches, and these destroyed much land vegetation. This destruction was minor, however, compared to the damage caused by the huge waves in some of the inlets. A solid wall of water nearly 100 ft high, and traveling at a terrific rate, will do unbelievable things. At one place, a barnacle-covered boulder estimated to weigh a half ton was deposited 80 ft above preearthquake sea level. Gravel, sand, and shells were deposited to an even greater height. Forests and soil in some places were swept completely clear to bedrock, and trees were ground into splinters (Hanna, 1971, this volume, Figure 12). At Whittier, a sawmill was washed away, and a 2-in. by 6-in. plank was driven through a giant tire of a lumber-moving machine (Kachadoorian, 1965, p. 19, Figure 20).

In the depressed areas, seawater now extends into the forest for distances varying according to the subsidence of the land. The vegetation in such areas had already turned brown in June 1964, and a new shoreline was being established when we were there. It seemed odd to a part-time beachcomber to be able to pick live sea shells, *Littorina* and *Acmaea*, from spruce trees.

A resident of the area (Mrs. Mildred O'Brien, oral communication, 1964) stated that birds of various species became very excited during the aftershocks of the earthquake and took to the air. Gulls would attempt to land on the quivering mud of Cordova harbor, touch their feet to the ground, cry and fly up a few feet, then try again and again to land.

Marine mammals were probably not adversely affected, with the exception of the sea otter, which feeds among kelp beds. The species is a very resourceful inhabitant of the area, and the population will probably survive, if not unduly persecuted by man.

There is no precedent upon which to base a prediction of the amount of time required to establish a new littoral life zone over such a vast area. Although earthquakes are of common occurrence, not often is a great body of land elevated as much as the Prince William Sound area was. Only one comparable uplift comes readily to mind—the rise accompanying the very violent earthquake of September 1899 in the general area of Yakutat, Alaska (Tarr and Martin, 1912). An uplift of 47½ ft was found 6 years later when the effects were first studied. At that time the new littoral zone apparently was not as completely occupied as had been the previous one.

## REFERENCES

Hanna, G Dallas, 1971. Biological effects of the earthquake as observed in 1965 *in* The Great Alaska Earthquake of 1964: Biology. NAS Pub. 1604. Washington: National Academy of Sciences.

Kachadoorian, Reuben, 1965. Effects of the earthquake of March 27, 1964, at Whittier, Alaska. U.S. Geological Survey Professional Paper 542-B. Washington: Government Printing Office. 21 p. Also *in* The Great Alaska Earthquake of 1964: Geology. NAS Pub. 1601. Washington: National Academy of Sciences, 1971.

Rigg, George B., and Robert C. Miller, 1949. Intertidal plant and animal zonation in the vicinity of Neah Bay, Washington. *Proceedings, California Academy of Sciences*, 26, Series 4 (No. 10), 323–351.

Tarr, Ralph S., and Lawrence Martin, 1912. The earthquakes at Yakutat Bay, Alaska, in September, 1899. U.S. Geological Survey Professional Paper 69. Washington: Government Printing Office. 135 p.

# I
# PRINCE WILLIAM SOUND SURVEY EXPEDITION

# G DALLAS HANNA
## CALIFORNIA ACADEMY OF SCIENCES

# Introduction: Biological Effects of the Earthquake as Observed in 1965

## INTRODUCTION

If the Alaska earthquake of 1964 be rated by its effect on human life and property, it does not rank high among other great tremors. However, if it be rated by energy expended or by destruction of animal and plant life in a short space of time, few comparable events have occurred during recorded history.

My brief observations in 1964 (Hanna, 1964, and this volume) were sufficient to inspire an attempt to discover and record, while the results were fresh, more details of what actually happened. This effort received the endorsement of the Committee on the Alaska Earthquake, its Panel on Biology, and others interested in ecology of nearshore animals and plants.

By 1965, seismologists had determined that the epicenter of the earthquake was near Unakwik Inlet (Figure 1). Geologists had found that a very large block of land had been tilted up on the southeast as much as 38 ft and down on the northwest as much as 7½ ft.

The project was essentially a study of ecology, and personnel with training in that phase of biology were chosen (Figure 2). H. William Johansen specialized in the marine algae, and Stoner B. Haven worked with the marine invertebrate animals. They ran transects both on beaches and near-vertical walls of rock (Figure 3). Walter J. Eyerdam, who had spent several summer seasons before the earthquake studying the plants of this area, collected and listed all the land plants that had become established on many square miles of uplifted sea bottom.

A mobile field headquarters was established on board the halibut purse seiner, M.V. *Harmony* (Figure 4), which had been chartered for the work with Captain Dan Forseth, Master (Hanna, 1967). During the period of field work (May 28–July 26, 1965), 33 field stations were occupied (Table 1). Various collections and transects were made at these stations by the investigators.

All the stations are in the Prince William Sound, Alaska,

ABSTRACT: The change in sea level caused by the tilting of a very large block of land during the Alaska earthquake of March 27, 1964, furnished a unique opportunity to study the effects of such an event on the animals and plants of the affected region. A field party spent the summer season of 1965 in the Prince William Sound area. The members were selected primarily because of their experience in the study of the ecology of shallow-water marine organisms. Records were also made of the various land plants that had become established on the land newly elevated above sea level by the earthquake. Reports have been prepared by the three specialists who made detailed studies.

The present report contains a brief account of the organization of the expedition, records of the 33 stations that were studied, and maps showing the locations of these stations.

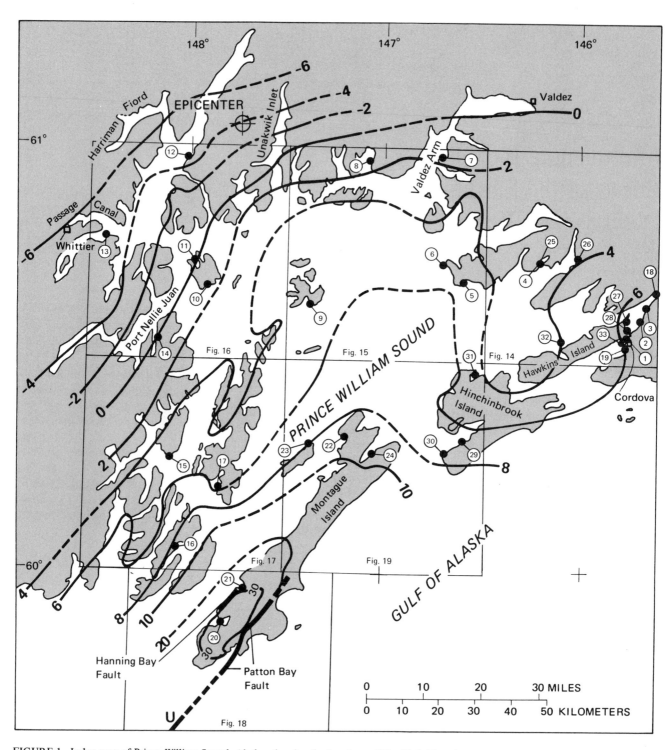

FIGURE 1   Index map of Prince William Sound, Alaska, showing the locations of the 33 field stations occupied during 1965 by investigators aboard M.V. *Harmony*. Larger-scale maps of the six sections indicated appear as Figures 14–19. Isobase contours by Plafker and Mayo (1965), U.S. Geological Survey, show land-level changes resulting from the March 27, 1964, earthquake. The contour interval is 2 ft between the −6-ft and +10-ft contours, and the interval is 10 ft between the +10-ft and the +30-ft contours. (Adapted from U.S. Geological Survey base map.)

FIGURE 2   Scientists and crew members aboard M.V. *Harmony* 1965 biological expedition in Prince William Sound, Alaska, left to right: Peter J. Barrett, geologist; Capt. Dan Forseth; G Dallas Hanna, expedition leader; Stoner B. Haven, zoologist; Walter J. Eyerdam, botanist; Harold Vadset, engineer; and H. William Johansen, phycologist.

area and are shown on the six portions of U.S. Geological Survey Alaska Topographic Series maps indexed on Figure 1. They also may be located readily on U.S. Coast and Geodetic Survey Sailing Chart 8551. As Plafker (1965) has pointed out, this area is a very small part of more than 170,000 km² that was uplifted or depressed. Observations in 1964 showed that earth and water movements on such a grand scale were catastrophic to marine plant and animal life.

The displacement of the sea floor probably was accompanied by violent shaking, which caused much of the silty substrate to go into suspension. Bottom sediments to a depth of at least 18 in. were similarly displaced in the intertidal zone. Very soon thereafter, strong waves and currents began to surge through many inlets. Some of these currents

were caused by giant submarine landslides, and others presumably were the result of the rapid uplift of the sea bottom. In any event, many square miles of an area were swept clean of soft sediment that was redeposited in deeper parts of the Sound. In some places, these deposits were thick enough to bury crab traps several fathoms deep, according to local reports.

## EFFECTS ON MARINE FAUNA AND FLORA

Shorelines were depressed or subsided as much as 6 or 7 ft on the north side of the zero hinge line of the tilted block. As might be expected, conditions in depressed areas were

FIGURE 3   Making a transect at Olsen Bay (Station 4), June 2, 1965.

FIGURE 4  The halibut purse seiner M.V. *Harmony* at Perry Island, Prince William Sound, June 1965.

TABLE 1  List of Stations

| Station | Location | Latitude (N) | Longitude (W) | Elevation Changes (ft) |
|---|---|---|---|---|
| 1 | Shipyard Bay, Hawkins Island | 60° 33.6′ | 145° 48.4′ | +5.4 |
| 2 | Orca, Orca Inlet | 60° 35.5′ | 145° 42.2′ | +6.4 |
| 3 | Shepard Point, Orca Inlet | 60° 37.8′ | 145° 40.2′ | +7.6 |
| 4 | Olsen Bay, Port Gravina | 60° 44.4′ | 146° 12.5′ | +3.6 |
| 5 | Knowles Head, Port Gravina | 60° 41.2′ | 146° 36.2′ | +5.7 |
| 6 | Goose Island, east side | 60° 43.5′ | 146° 43.2′ | +4.8 |
| 7 | Galena Bay, Valdez Arm | 60° 58.8′ | 146° 42.1′ | +2.0 |
| 8 | Heather Island, Columbia Bay | 60° 58.0′ | 147° 02.2′ | +1.7 |
| 9 | Bass Harbor, Naked Island | 60° 37.8′ | 147° 23.0′ | +4.7 |
| 10 | South Bay, Perry Island | 60° 40.4′ | 147° 55.5′ | +1.5 |
| 11 | West Twin Bay, Perry Island | 60° 42.2′ | 147° 58.5′ | 0 |
| 12 | Golden, Port Wells | 60° 57.8′ | 148° 00.2′ | −4.1 |
| 13 | Blackstone Point, Blackstone Bay | 60° 46.7′ | 148° 24.1′ | −5.2 |
| 14 | Port Nellie Juan, McClure Bay | 60° 32.9′ | 147° 09.9′ | 0 |
| 15 | Chenega, Chenega Island | 60° 16.7′ | 148° 04.6′ | +6.3 |
| 16 | Port Ashton, Sawmill Bay, Evans Island | 60° 03.4′ | 148° 02.5′ | +8.9 |
| 17 | Thumb Bay, Knight Island | 60° 12.6′ | 147° 49.4′ | +6.0 |
| 18 | Head of Orca Inlet | 60° 39.9′ | 145° 37.4′ | +7.0 |
| 19 | Cordova Flats, south of Cordova | 60° 32.2′ | 145° 45.2′ | +6.7 |
| 20 | MacLeod Harbor, Montague Island | 59° 53.4′ | 147° 47.8′ | +30.0 |
| 21 | Hanning Bay, Montague Island | 59° 57.1′ | 147° 42.9′ | +29.8 |
| 22 | Stockdale Harbor, Montague Island | 60° 19.5′ | 147° 11.3′ | +8.7 |
| 23 | Green Island, north end | 60° 18.1′ | 147° 21.6′ | +8.4 |
| 24 | Zaikof Bay, Montague Island | 60° 16.4′ | 147° 03.7′ | +8.8 |
| 25 | Olsen Bay, Port Gravina | 60° 44.4′ | 146° 12.6′ | +3.6 |
| 26 | Beartrap Bay, Port Gravina | 60° 44.8′ | 146° 01.7′ | +4.0 |
| 27 | Deep Bay, Hawkins Island | 60° 35.3′ | 145° 47.9′ | +6.8 |
| 28 | Hawkins Island, near Grass Island | 60° 34.3′ | 145° 46.5′ | +6.2 |
| 29 | Port Etches, Hinchinbrook Island | 60° 19.7′ | 146° 34.2′ | +3.8 |
| 30 | English Bay, Hinchinbrook Island | 60° 17.3′ | 146° 40.7′ | +7.1 |
| 31 | Anderson Bay, Hinchinbrook Island | 60° 28.3′ | 146° 31.1′ | +3.8 |
| 32 | Whiskey Cove, Hawkins Island | 60° 32.2′ | 146° 06.4′ | +4.2 |
| 33 | Spike Island, Orca Inlet | 60° 32.9′ | 145° 46.1′ | +6.1 |

FIGURE 5  Former harbor at Cordova. The upper 12 in. or more of bottom sediment has been swept away, leaving vast numbers of exposed clams to die. The *Verrucaria* zone is plainly visible on the rocks of the breakwater.

vastly different from those on the uplifted side. Destruction of animals and plants in the littoral zone was less extensive. By 1965, there had been a general upward migration of the various zone-forming organisms; a new barnacle line was being formed, although in the old zone the animals seemed still to be living despite being exposed to air for shorter periods than before the earthquake. *Fucus* and other algae had moved upward along with the grazing animals, by re-population and by crawling, respectively.

## CLAMS AND MUSSELS

Any disturbance as strong as the March 27, 1964, earthquake would certainly be fatal to countless marine organisms. The mortality of clams was especially noticeable (Figures 5 and 6). Because these mollusks were of much economic importance in the area, additional information was not difficult to obtain. The Alaska Department of Fish and Game estimated that at least 36 percent of the clams in Prince William Sound had been destroyed (Baxter, 1971, this volume). Clam mortality was observed to be as high as 90 percent at some of our field stations, but much lower at others.

The life-span of these mollusks is not known and probably depends to some extent on the species. However, it is common to find shells with 15 or more annual-growth rings. Fortunately, one of the most valuable species, the razor clam *Siliqua patula*, is confined mostly to open ocean beaches and was not as greatly affected as those species living in narrow inlets.

Mussels (*Mytilus edulis*) live in the intertidal zone in the

FIGURE 6  An uplifted former clam beach on Hawkins Island (Station 1), May 30, 1965, across the channel from Cordova; dead clams are visible in foreground.

FIGURE 7  Dense beds of mussels (*Mytilus edulis*) at Cordova, June 15, 1964, occupying a very definite position in the intertidal zone. The beds are not continuous and therefore are not as useful as barnacles in the determination of different life zones.

Prince William Sound area and are attached to rocks by a byssus. Where the uplift was 10 ft or more, destruction of the attached stages of this species of mollusk was total. Where the uplift was less than 10 ft, there was some survival in 1965. However, these mollusks (Figure 7) occupy a certain narrow zone between tides, and any appreciable change of this position because of change of sea level or uplift of land will probably result in the destruction of such beds. In 1965, we found a new set of young mussels in several places in the position where they should be in relation to the depth of the water.

The tidal range in Prince William Sound is approximately 10 ft. A small change in sea level was found to have disturbed the balance of the biological zonation (Figure 8). Obviously, where the land rose more than 10 ft, all life in the littoral zone was destroyed. Generally, intertidal species of animals and plants in most oceans are adapted to certain definite depths below mean high tide. If the water depths to which these animals and plants have become adapted are changed, the organisms often die because they are unable to move or to adapt to the changed environment; this earthquake caused such changes to an extent and on a scale never previously studied.

### FISHES

The best known immediate effect on fishes was the sudden destruction of many thousands of large red rockfish (*Sebastes* sp.) near Chenega Island, in Valdez Arm, and in Passage Canal (Kachadoorian, 1965). Some biologists have suggested that the fishes floated to the surface because submarine slides produced such large and sudden hydrostatic pressure changes that uncontrollable expansion of the swim bladders resulted.

Several groups of small fishes that live among the rocks and algae of the littoral zone were destroyed over the large areas where the sudden change in elevation was greater than the tidal range.

### BARNACLES

Probably the most impressive of all the biological effects involved the barnacles. These organisms attach themselves in astronomical numbers to rocks and other objects from the mean high-tide line down to a depth of about 4 ft. When the land rose that much or more, the entire population of the zone was killed. However, because barnacles, except for one species, cement themselves permanently to a base substance, their remains are mute evidence of land uplift. Their bleached shells formed a conspicuous white band throughout the upraised areas of Prince William Sound. Several species were involved.

Six years after the severe earthquake at Yakutat, Alaska, in 1899, where a section of the beach was elevated 47.5 ft, Tarr and Martin (1912) were able to use the top of the previous barnacle zone as a datum plane for measuring uplift. The same method was used by Plafker (1965) in preparing his contour map of the areas affected by the earthquake of March 27, 1964 (Figure 9). The contrast at the top of the barnacle zone is made even greater by a band of black lichen attached to the rocks immediately above. This band is the *Verrucaria* zone (Figures 5 and 10). (Unfortunately, this lichen was listed as the alga *Ralfsia* in some early reports.)

*Balanus balanoides*, *Balanus glandula*, and *Chthamalus dalli* are the most abundant barnacles in this upper zone. Evidently, they are able to survive with less time of immersion in seawater than species found in deeper water. How long they can live exposed to air and rain is uncertain, and

FIGURE 8  Piledriver Rock, Whiskey Cove, Hawkins Island (Station 32), July 15, 1965. Lines of demarcation of zones of pre- and postearthquake life are visible.

this probably depends to some extent on temperature and humidity. Of the other species of *Balanus* found at lower tidal levels, the most abundant is *Balanus cariosus*. Its upper limit almost reaches the lower limit of *Balanus balanoides*. Still lower—that is, below former low tide—there dwelt the very large *Balanus nubilis*. All the latter were killed in those places where the uplift of land was greater than 10 ft.

MARINE PLANTS

Under normal and stable conditions, the marine plants grow in well-defined horizontal bands that, in part, correspond to the zones of animal life. Most of these plants are green, brown, and red algae. Many of the species are annuals, but in Prince William Sound the annuals do not all die down at the same time.

The habitat of *Fucus distichus*, a brown alga with elongated floats, coincides in part with the lower band of the barnacle zone. Both the top and bottom of the zone are somewhat irregular, depending to some extent on the exposure. That is, on an exposed, rocky shoreline, where the surf is high, *Fucus* may extend up very nearly or entirely to the top of the barnacle zone.

Below the *Fucus*, the green algae *Enteromorpha* and

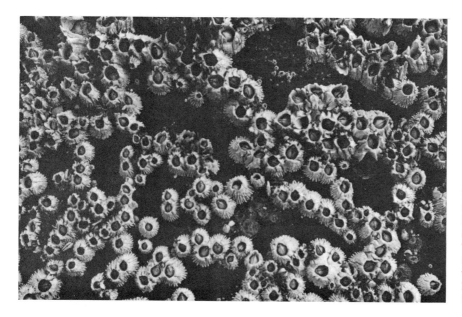

FIGURE 9  A typical rock surface with acorn barnacles (*Balanus* sp.), Latouche Island, May 28, 1964. These grew in a zone a few feet below former mean high water. The top of this zone was so widely recognizable that it enabled U.S. Geological Survey geologists to measure the uplift of the land above former sea level very soon after the earthquake.

FIGURE 10  MacLeod Harbor, Montague Island (Station 20), June 26, 1965. The uplift here was more than 30 ft. Former zones of life are clearly shown, from the *Verrucaria* black band above, to far below the former low-tide line.

*Ulva* form a conspicuous bright green zone with the red alga *Rhodymenia* below them. At mean low water, eelgrass, *Zostera*, a flowering plant, forms a green zone also; at extreme low water, the brown kelps are exposed. The *Zostera* and kelps cannot withstand much extension beyond the normal low tidal period during which they are exposed to air. They seem to be sensitive to as little as a foot of change in water level.

Grazing animals, especially Gastropoda, tend to limit excessive spreading of the algae beyond the upper and lower limits of their normal zones. The earthquake decimated the population of grazing animals, so that algae became unusually abundant and tended to spread beyond their normal depth limits. In some places the general mixture of healthy young plants of many shades of color formed beautiful gardens.

The great abundance of marine life below the intertidal zone was best displayed on the open shores of Montague Island at Cape Clear and Patton Bay (Figures 11 and 18). Dense festoons of calcareous algae and many forms of animal life covered hundreds of acres in 1964 soon after the earthquake where the former bottom had been 25–30 ft deep. Much of this fragile material had disappeared by 1965.

## WAVE EFFECTS ON TERRESTRIAL FAUNA AND FLORA

In those inlets where there had been extensive wave damage and wave flooding, the entire ground fauna and flora were killed. For example, in the vicinity of Lowell Point, 2 mi south of Seward on Resurrection Bay, a wave that swept inland, a hundred yards in places, covered the forest floor with gravel and debris. Boats, automobiles, trucks, and parts of wharves and buildings formed a tangled mass with the spruce and hemlock. Debris caught in the trees indicated that the wave had been about 20 ft high. A barrier of gravel was built up at the outer edge of the forest as the water velocity slackened, and this retained some of the saltwater behind the beach long enough to kill most of the vegetation, including the conifers. The water velocity had been so great that it cleared all the soil and gravel from the roots of the outermost trees, toppling them inward and tangling them with other flotsam (Figure 12).

The nature of bodies of water in some freshwater basins behind barrier beaches was changed radically by sea flooding as a result of subsidence. Also, because the forest edge around the basins was flooded by every high tide, the change killed all the land plants thus submerged.

Evidence of an earlier depression of the earthquake zone was found over an area extending along the coast on both sides of Prince William Sound (Plafker, 1965). Scouring and exposure by the tsunamis associated with the 1964 earthquake exhumed stumps of old trees still embedded in the peat of the former forest floor, which at one time had stood at least 12 ft higher (Figure 13). Specimens of the woods were collected and turned over to the U.S. Geological Survey for dating and further elucidation of the region's tectonic history.

## FIELD STATIONS OCCUPIED DURING 1965

The field stations were selected to cover as many types of habitat as possible. Some stations were near the heads of bays, adjacent to glacial and other freshwater streams;

FIGURE 11   Dead hanging calcareous algae on rocks at the south end of Montague Island in May 1964. These plants were red when alive but have bleached white in the sun and rain.

others presented a variety of shoreline environments from the protected to intermediate and open ocean beaches. Station 20 at MacLeod Harbor, Montague Island, exhibited the greatest land uplift above sea level, approximately 30 ft; Station 13 at Blackstone Bay showed the greatest subsidence, approximately 5 ft. Stations 10 and 11, on Perry Island, were very close to the zero hinge line of the tilted block of land.

Uplift or subsidence of the land surface at the various stations is based on measurements made in 1964 by a U.S. Geological Survey party under George Plafker and incorporated in a tectonic map (Plafker, 1969, Plate 2); Plafker used the top of the barnacle zone as the mean high tide datum plane as a reference from which to measure the amounts of tectonic change.

*Station 1* (Figure 14): Shipyard Bay, Hawkins Island, Orca Inlet, 2 mi northwest of Cordova, May 30, 1965. Uplift approximately 5.4 ft.

The transect was run across a solid-rock outcrop at the north end of what had been a heavily populated clam bed before the earthquake. Most of the soft sediment had been washed away. No live clams, young or old, were found. It was too early in the season to find, in the newly exposed terrace, plants sufficiently developed for identification, although numerous clumps of grasses had started. One large

*George Plafker*

FIGURE 12   Forest destruction caused by a tsunami in a Prince William Sound inlet (1964 photo). Some of these waves were nearly 100 ft high.

FIGURE 13   Stump of an ancient tree that grew when land was at least 12 ft higher than it was at the time of the 1964 earthquake, exposed by tsunami scour at Anderson Bay, Hinchinbrook Island (Station 31), July 14, 1965. The U.S. Geological Survey has determined that some of these trees range in age from less than 200 to more than 500 years.

outlying rock, formerly in the intertidal zone, was densely covered with dead shells of *Balanus cariosus*.

*Station 2* (Figure 14): About 1 mi north of Orca on Orca Inlet, May 31, 1965. Uplift approximately 6.4 ft.

The transect was run across a rocky headland at the north end of a clam bed that formerly had been heavily populated. Very few living mollusks were found below present high tide, but a new set of young barnacles was well established near mean high tide. There were many dead clams on the former bed, some still partly embedded in the former bottom sediment; this observation indicated that the softer material above them had been removed by sea waves accompanying the earthquake.

*Station 3* (Figure 14): Shepard Point, Orca Inlet, May 31, 1965. Uplift approximately 7.6 ft.

The station was at the site of a burned-out salmon cannery. Johansen attached previously prepared plastic strips to lines hung on some pilings that were still out beyond low-water mark; the weighted lines were long enough to cover more than the tidal range. His objective was to learn the settling rate of sessile organisms, especially algae, in this very favorable location. The strips were retrieved and studied after 45 days, at the end of the work season (Johansen, 1971, this volume).

*Station 4* (Figure 14): Olsen Bay, Port Gravina, June 2, 1965. Uplift approximately 3.6 ft.

At the head of the bay is a field research station of the U.S. Bureau of Commercial Fisheries Auke Bay Laboratory. This well-equipped branch station makes detailed studies of

salmon ascending Olsen Creek to spawn. About a mile from the head of the bay there is a small, unnamed, heavily timbered rocky island, which is an excellent place for a transect (Figure 3). Station 4, which was located on the west side of the island, furnished important biological data; additional studies were made on the east side along the vertical wall and at the wave-swept outermost point, where the uplift of the land had been such that zones of old and new biota overlapped to some extent. New zonation was definitely evident. For instance, the old eelgrass zone, which is normally located at very low tide, was represented by old dead rhizomes in the preearthquake low-tide zone. The new growth had become well established at the low-water mark. Old and new mussel beds (Figure 7) were almost in contact on a vertical east wall but did not overlap. The new shells were 1/4 to 3/8 in. long and were attached to algae, rocks, and old shells.

This station was so interesting that we visited it again later in the growing season to gather information on the establishment of plants on the newly exposed land (see Station 25).

*Station 5* (Figure 15): Knowles Head, Port Gravina, June 4, 1965. Uplift approximately 5.7 ft.

The bold promontory was chosen because of its exposure to southwest storms that sweep nearly the full length of Prince William Sound. The rocky beach had a very gentle slope seaward, which afforded the first good opportunity to note how some of the algae cover wide areas of such rocks both laterally and vertically. Although some species of animal life were exceedingly abundant, especially starfishes and sea cucumbers, there was a notable scarcity of grazing

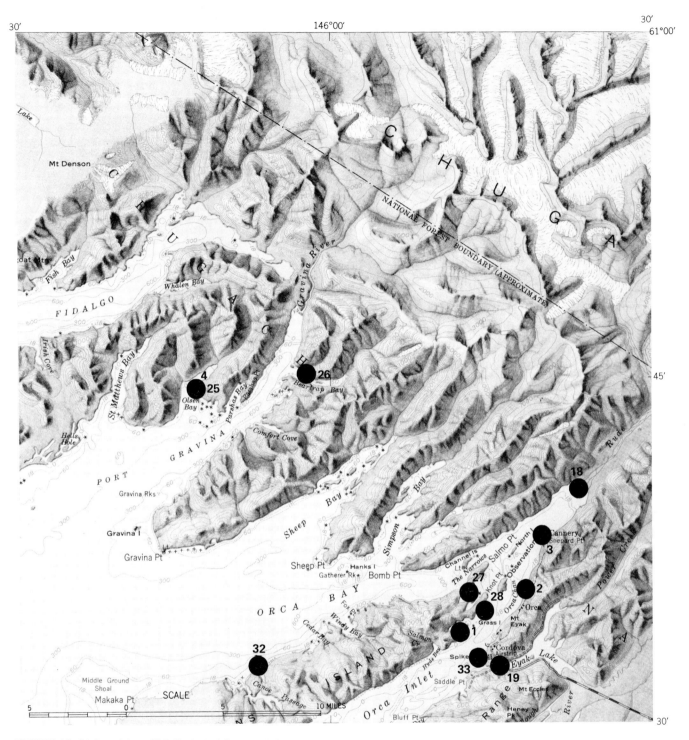

FIGURE 14    [Adapted from U.S. Geological Survey Alaska Topographic Series, Cordova (1948)].

Station Numbers and Names

| | | |
|---|---|---|
| 1. Shipyard Bay | 18. Orca Inlet | 27. Deep Bay |
| 2. Orca | 19. Cordova Flats | 28. Hawkins Island |
| 3. Shepard Point | 25. Olsen Bay | 32. Whiskey Cove |
| 4. Olsen Bay | 26. Beartrap Bay | 33. Spike Island |

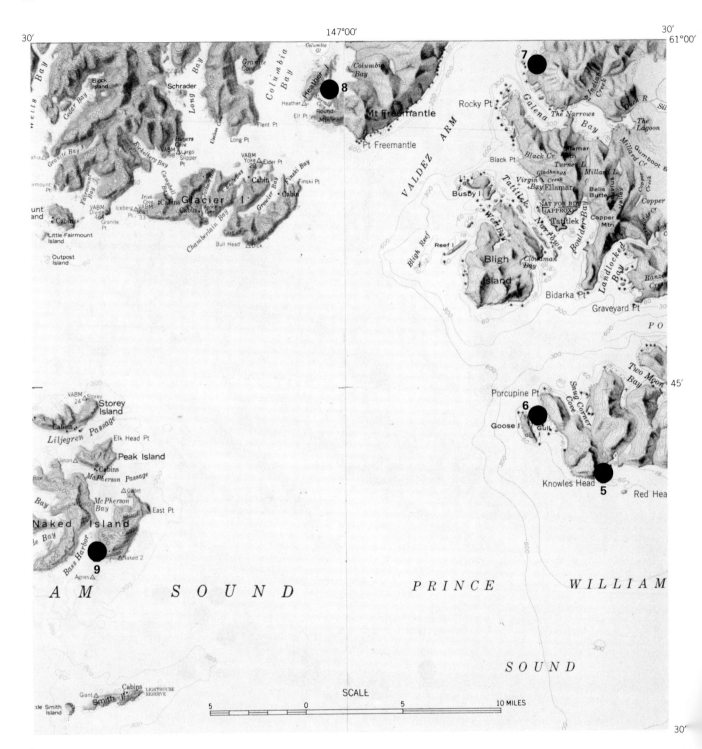

FIGURE 15   [Adapted from U.S. Geological Survey Alaska Topographic Series, Cordova (1948) and Seward (1953)].

Station Numbers and Names

5. Knowles Head          7. Galena Bay          9. Bass Harbor
6. Goose Island          8. Heather Island

mollusks, limpets, and *Littorina*. These forms obviously had not been able to follow the receding waters during the rapid uplift of the land.

*Station 6* (Figure 15): The east side of Goose Island, June 5-6, 1965. Uplift approximately 4.8 ft.

On the lee side of the island there is a long, steep boulder beach with solid outcrops of argillite and graywacke at the north end. Near the south end there are buildings of a very old fish saltery. The transect was located approximately a quarter of a mile north of the boulder beach. Individual barnacles of *Balanus cariosus*, a species that grows in a deeper intertidal zone than *Balanus glandula* and *Balanus balanoides*, were nearly all destroyed by the uplift. Only a few of those at the lower limit of their former range had survived at the time of our observation.

*Station 7* (Figure 15): Galena Bay, Valdez Arm, June 7, 1965. Uplift 2 ft.

The transect was located in Valdez Arm in the first small cove north of the mouth of Galena Bay. Because the uplift had been moderate at this point, it was not expected that there would be extensive change in the zonation of the plants and animals. The uplift was obvious, however, from the dead barnacles below the former high-tide line.

*Station 8* (Figure 15): Heather Island, Columbia Bay, June 7, 1965. Uplift approximately 1.7 ft.

The island forms part of the east side of Columbia Bay, into which the Columbia Glacier discharges vast quantities of ice. As expected, the fauna and flora had been affected by the freshening of the water. The only bivalve mollusks noted as common were *Mytilus* and *Cardium*, both of which are quite tolerant of some dilution of marine waters. Barnacles were not nearly as abundant as at those locations previously studied where the uplift had been greater.

*Station 9* (Figure 15): Bass Harbor, Naked Island, June 8, 1965. Uplift approximately 4.7 ft.

This location, exposed to southwest storms, was chosen because some intertidal organisms are adapted to such severe conditions. One of these is the limpet, *Acmaea digitalis*, which is normally restricted to the open coast.

*Station 10* (Figure 16): South Bay, Perry Island, June 13-14, 1965. Uplift 1.5 ft.

As the north end of the island is nearly on the zero hinge line of the tilted block, it was expected that the marine organisms of the littoral zone would not have been greatly affected by the earthquake. Because conditions seemed to be normal, this location was given special study. The first transect (10) was made on the west side of the bay near the entrance. Directly across the bay, on the east side, another

transect (10a) was run. It became obvious that detection of uplifts of as little as 1 ft would not be difficult within the first year following the change.

*Station 11* (Figure 16): West Twin Bay, Perry Island, June 15, 1965. Uplift undetectable from the biological evidence.

Two useful transects were run on the west side: no. 11 near the head of the bay and 11a ½ mi north toward the entrance to the bay. Studies of the intertidal zone at the stations on Perry Island by Haven and Johansen (1971, this volume) show how extremely abundant marine life is in Prince William Sound. A third transect, 11b, was run on the east side of the bay, ½ mi northeast of transect 11a.

*Station 12* (Figure 16): Golden, Port Wells, June 15, 1965. Subsidence approximately 4.1 ft.

Many glaciers discharge ice into various parts of Port Wells, especially College Fiord. The freshening of the water limits the fauna and flora, but very obviously a new barnacle zone was being formed about 4 ft above the top of the old zone. The animals in the old zone were still living, although they were getting considerably less exposure to air than before the earthquake.

*Station 13* (Figure 16): Blackstone Point, Blackstone Bay, June 16, 1965. Subsidence approximately 5.2 ft.

Three transects were run near Blackstone Point. New barnacle and *Fucus* zones were being formed, but the sinking of the land had not yet altered the old zonation to any great extent. Because the old *Verrucaria* lichen zone is now submerged during parts of each tidal cycle, it is probably dead. No evidence of the establishment of a new zone of this lichen was found anywhere in Prince William Sound. A very large and apparently violent wave had come into the cove there and must have reached almost to the foot of Tebenkof Glacier. Eyerdam found much damage to the vegetation on the terminal moraine.

*Station 14* (Figure 16): Port Nellie Juan, McClure Bay, June 17, 1965. Uplift or subsidence negligible.

The transect was run on a solid-rock exposure 100 yd north of a very large abandoned salmon cannery.

*Station 15* (Figure 17): Chenega, Chenega Island, June 17, 1965. Uplift approximately 6.3 ft.

A brief stop was made at the tsunami-destroyed and abandoned village of Chenega. Eyerdam (1971, this volume) collected a series of plants in the uplifted zone.

*Station 16* (Figure 17): Port Ashton, Sawmill Bay, Evans Island, June 18, 1965. Uplift approximately 8.9 ft.

The transect was run on a rock wall on the small island just opposite the Port Ashton Cannery. The wave that had

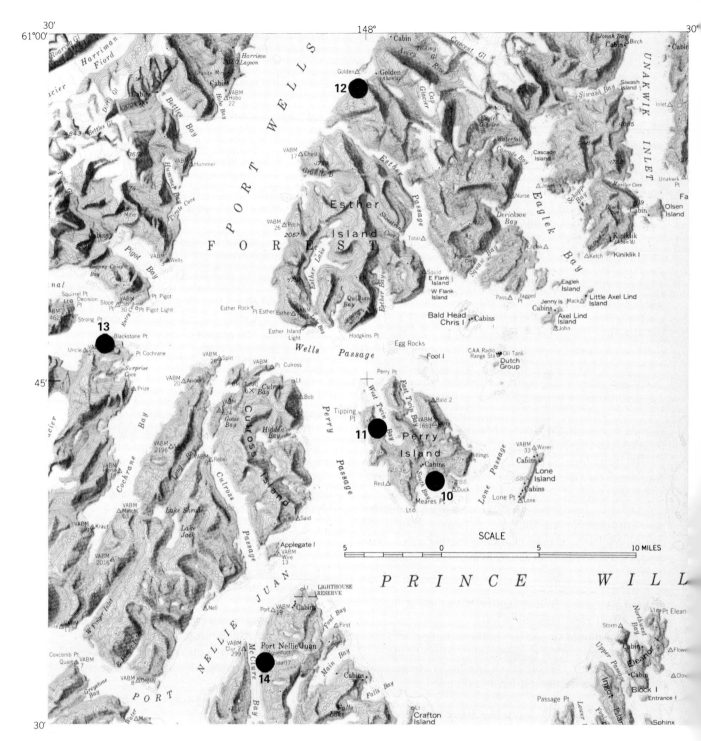

FIGURE 16 [Adapted from U.S. Geological Survey Alaska Topographic Series, Seward (1953)].

Station Numbers and Names

10. South Bay          12. Golden          14. Port Nellie Juan
11. West Twin Bay      13. Blackstone Point

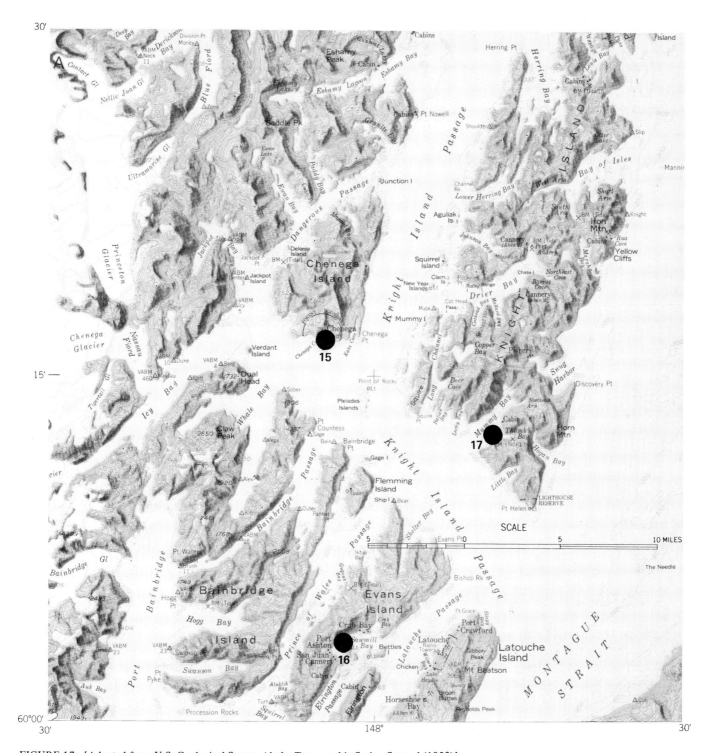

FIGURE 17   [Adapted from U.S. Geological Survey Alaska Topographic Series, Seward (1953)].

Station Numbers and Names

15. Chenega                    16. Port Ashton                    17. Thumb Bay

entered Sawmill Bay did a great deal of damage to the animals and plants as well as to various structures. An investigation was made to determine whether various burrowing organisms survived. Suitable bottom was found at several places in the bay, but very few survivors were found.

*Station 17* (Figure 17): Thumb Bay, Knight Island, June 20, 1965. Uplift approximately 6 ft.

The transect was run near the outer entrance to the bay nearly ½ mi north of an abandoned herring plant.

*Station 18* (Figure 14): Head of Orca Inlet, June 21–22, 1965. Uplift approximately 7 ft.

The new land exposed between former and present high-tide lines was occupied by a dense growth of sedge. The heavy influx of fresh water made this station less profitable for study of marine organisms.

*Station 19* (Figure 14): Cordova Flats, south of Cordova, June 23, 1965. Uplift 6.7 ft.

Eyerdam found several species of plants that had become established on the flats just south of Cordova.

*Station 20* (Figure 18): MacLeod Harbor, Montague Island, June 26–27, 1965. Uplift approximately 30 ft.

The amount of uplift within short distances seemed irregular because of pronounced vertical faulting. Transects were run on a steep rocky outcrop at the north entrance to the bay. Obviously, with the tidal range only about 10 ft, an uplift of 30 ft presents biological conditions far different from those found on any of the previous transects. The reports of the zoologist (Haven, 1971, this volume) and the phycologist (Johansen, 1971, this volume) should be consulted for details on the destruction of the great beds of giant kelp by continuous exposure to the atmosphere and the numerous forms of life that perished with them. The topography of the inner bay was greatly changed, and vast deposits of sand and silt were shifted or removed.

*Station 21* (Figure 18): Hanning Bay, Montague Island, June 28–29, 1965. Uplift approximately 29.8 ft.

A transect was run across a broad beach of large boulders on the south shore of the bay near the entrance. Among the boulders, there were large areas covered with shells that, before the earthquake, had accumulated on the bottom below the range of tidal zone. Transect 21a was run on a large outcrop of solid rock 1.6 mi to the northeast, in the middle of the east shore of the bay. Before the earthquake, this outcrop was covered with water. At that time it was heavily populated with marine life, especially calcareous algae. At the time of this observation, it was far above high water, and flowering plants were well established at many local sites where conditions had permitted seed to germi-

nate. After much digging, Haven reported no trace of a new set of clams. Johansen reported that in the newly established littoral zone in this area of great uplift, the brown alga *Fucus* had lost its dominance to another form, the red alga *Porphyra*.

*Station 22* (Figure 19): North side of Stockdale Harbor, Montague Island, June 30, 1965. Uplift approximately 8.7 ft.

The transect was run across an outcrop of solid rock near the entrance to the bay. The inner bay has a slate and graywacke gravel beach with a windrow of dead eelgrass at the present high-tide line. On this windrow, *Atriplex* plants were growing vigorously. A 1964 crop of dead stems of the same species was found a little higher up on the same area, between the pre- and postearthquake high-water marks. Some of the most conspicuous objects on this beach were well-preserved conifer stumps in place, which had been uncovered by the raising of the land and sweep of waves. Many of these stumps were found to be as much as 8 ft below the level of preearthquake mean high tide. Their position indicates that sea level had been considerably lower or that the land had been depressed considerably during some previous disturbance.

*Station 23* (Figure 19): North end of Green Island, July 1, 1965. Uplift approximately 8.4 ft.

Johansen and Haven ran a transect across a steep, rocky outcrop not far south along the west side of the island. An examination of the shoreline a mile farther south showed it to be a gentle slope. There, newly set barnacles were abundant from the low-tide (brown kelp zone) to the high-tide line. Species so young were difficult to identify, but it will be valuable to learn how they fare in years to come. *Fucus* seemed to be distributed lower in the tidal zone than is usual where there is no elevation of the land, and *Enteromorpha* extended higher.

*Station 24* (Figure 19): Zaikof Bay, Montague Island, July 2–3, 1965. Uplift approximately 8.8 ft.

This location was chosen as an example of a station exposed to much foul weather. Haven searched for clams inside the conspicuous hook formed on the east shore of the bay and found a few of what appeared to be young *Macoma*, *Mya*, and *Paphia*. Johansen studied the algae on the outer side of the hook.

*Station 25* (Figure 14): Olsen Bay, Port Gravina, July 8–9, 1965. Uplift 3.6 ft.

Additional studies at this location (see Station 4) were profitable because they provided a much better idea of summer conditions than was available at the end of May. By July, many plants had matured and could be identified. Personnel at the U.S. Bureau of Commercial Fisheries field

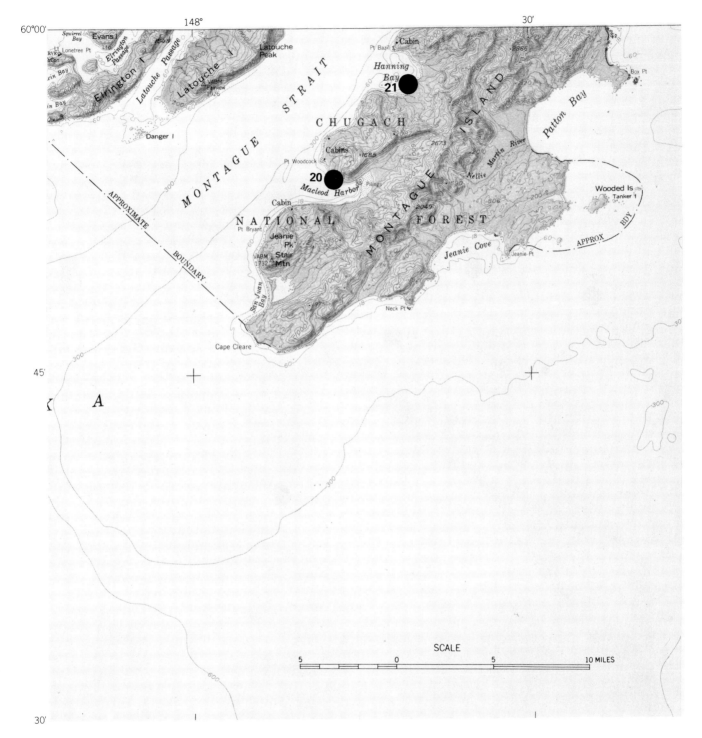

FIGURE 18 [Adapted from U.S. Geological Survey Alaska Topographic Series, Blying Sound (1953)].

Station Numbers and Names

20. MacLeod Harbor      21. Hanning Bay

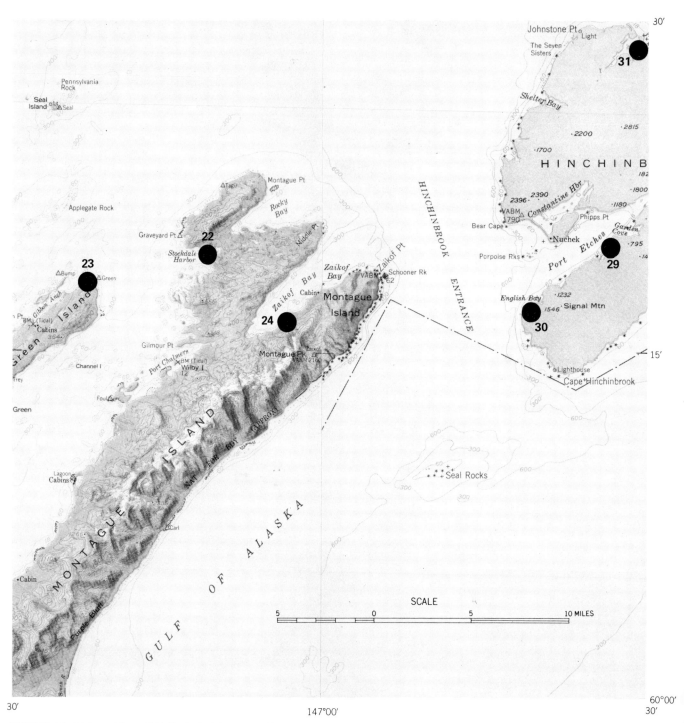

FIGURE 19 [Adapted from U.S. Geological Survey Alaska Topographic Series, Cordova (1948) and Seward (1953)].

Station Numbers and Names

22. Stockdale Harbor
23. Green Island
24. Zaikof Bay
29. Port Etches
30. English Bay
31. Anderson Bay

station provided considerable information through the interest of George Y. Harry, Jr., and Fredrik V. Thorsteinson.

*Station 26* (Figure 14): Beartrap Bay, Port Gravina, July 9, 1965. Uplift approximately 4 ft.

From the Olsen Bay station a trip was made to Beartrap Bay, where important information was obtained by Haven and Johansen. (See their reports, this volume.)

*Station 27* (Figure 14): Head of Deep Bay at the north end of Hawkins Island, July 10, 1965. Uplift approximately 6.8 ft.

More species of terrestrial plants were found growing between present and former high-tide lines at this station than at any other during the study.

Haven and Johansen also made observations on the west (Orca Bay) side of Salmo Point.

*Station 28* (Figure 14): Hawkins Island, near Grass Island, July 11, 1965. Uplift 6.2 ft.

Plants were collected by members of the expedition from the uplifted zone across the channel from Cordova.

*Station 29* (Figure 19): Second small cove northeast of English Bay, Port Etches, Hinchinbrook Island, July 12, 1965. Uplift approximately 3.8 ft.

The transect was run across the rocky shoreline outside the cove. Within the cove, wave action had uncovered many acres of clams, leaving the shells standing on end in the same position they had occupied when alive. This location was chosen for a station because of its proximity to the open Pacific Ocean; there seemed to be some distinct differences in the zonation from conditions found within the Sound.

*Station 30* (Figure 19): English Bay, Hinchinbrook Island, July 13, 1965. Uplift approximately 7.1 ft.

Young living *Mytilus*, about ¼ in. long, covered great areas at this transect, and many were even attached to the red alga *Rhodymenia*. Long filaments of byssus laced the algae together like spider webs and formed a blanketlike bed. Thirty-six sea otters were counted inside the barrier bar of nearby Constantine Harbor. These animals did not seem to have been affected by the earthquake.

*Station 31* (Figure 19): Anderson Bay, Hinchinbrook Island, July 14, 1965. Uplift approximately 3.8 ft.

After a transect had been made across a rocky headland, the ancient forest that had been exposed by the land uplift was subjected to some study. A great many trees up to 3 ft in diameter had grown there (Figure 13); the lowest one measured was 12 ft below the level of preearthquake high tide. The peat that surrounded the trees seemed to be very pure: it contained no obvious sand, silt, gravel, or rocks.

*Station 32* (Figure 14): Whiskey Cove, Hawkins Island, July 15, 1965. Uplift approximately 4.2 ft.

The station was located in the small bay near Canoe Passage, and the transects were run on Piledriver Rock, at the end of the intervening peninsula. Along the shore of the bay a thick section of peat was exposed, in which were many ancient stumps 6 ft below the level of preearthquake high tide. Among some gravel along this shore, Haven found a few adult *Paphia* clams and some small *Saxidomus*, both of which had survived the earthquake.

*Station 33* (Figures 14 and 20): Spike Island, Orca Inlet, opposite Cordova, July 16, 1965. Uplift 6.1 ft.

*Margaret M. Hanna*

FIGURE 20   Spike Island at Cordova (Station 33), July 16, 1965. Preearthquake zonation is shown by the white band of dead barnacles, bordered above by the band of black lichen, *Verrucaria*. The junction of these two bands is very close to preearthquake mean high-tide line. The foreground is postearthquake filling from the newly dredged Cordova boat harbor.

Excellent zonation before the earthquake is readily observed from the city wharf of Cordova (see Johansen, 1971, this volume, Figure 11). The uplift at Cordova was 6.2 ft.

## ACKNOWLEDGMENTS

George E. Lindsay, Director, California Academy of Sciences, relieved me of other duty during the fieldwork and the time required for the preparation of reports. Paul Silva and Frank Pitelka of the University of California cooperated by suggesting H. W. Johansen and Stoner Haven to undertake studies of the marine plants and the shallow-water animal life, respectively.

Financial support for the investigation was provided by the National Science Foundation (60 percent, Grant GD3533) and the Atomic Energy Commission [40 percent, Contract AT(04–3)–654].

Assistance, advice, and information were received from the staffs of the U.S. Geological Survey, the U.S. Coast and Geodetic Survey, the U.S. Bureau of Commercial Fisheries, The Alaska Department of Fish and Game, and local residents of the area around Prince William Sound.

## REFERENCES

Baxter, Rae E., 1971. Earthquake effects on clams of Prince William Sound *in* The Great Alaska Earthquake of 1964: Biology. NAS Pub. 1604. Washington: National Academy of Sciences.

Eyerdam, Walter J., 1971. Flowering plants found growing between pre- and postearthquake high-tide lines during the summer of 1965 in Prince William Sound *in* The Great Alaska Earthquake of 1964: Biology. NAS Pub. 1604. Washington: National Academy of Sciences.

Hanna, G Dallas, 1964. Biological effects of an earthquake. *Pacific Discovery*, 17 (November–December), 24–26. Also *in* The Great Alaska Earthquake of 1964: Biology. NAS Pub. 1604. Washington: National Academy of Sciences, 1971.

Hanna, G Dallas, 1967. The great Alaska earthquake of 1964. *Pacific Discovery*, 20 (May–June), 25–30.

Haven, Stoner B., 1971. Effects of land-level changes on intertidal invertebrates, with discussion of postearthquake ecological succession *in* The Great Alaska Earthquake of 1964: Biology. NAS Pub. 1604. Washington: National Academy of Sciences.

Johansen, H. William, 1971. Effects of elevation changes on benthic algae in Prince William Sound *in* The Great Alaska Earthquake of 1964: Biology. NAS Publ. 1604. Washington: National Academy of Sciences.

Kachadoorian, Reuben, 1965. Effects of the earthquake of March 27, 1964 at Whittier, Alaska. U.S. Geological Survey Professional Paper 542-B. Washington: Government Printing Office. 21 p. Also *in* The Great Alaska Earthquake of 1964: Geology. NAS Pub. 1601. Washington: National Academy of Sciences, 1971.

Plafker, George, 1965. Tectonic deformation associated with the 1964 Alaska earthquake. *Science*, 148 (June 25), 1675–1687.

Plafker, George, 1969. Tectonics of the March 27, 1964, Alaska earthquake. U.S. Geological Survey Professional Paper 543-I. Washington: Government Printing Office. 74 p. Also *in* The Great Alaska Earthquake of 1964: Geology. NAS Pub. 1601. Washington: National Academy of Sciences, 1971.

Plafker, George, and L. R. Mayo, 1965. Tectonic deformation, subaqueous slides and destructive waves associated with the Alaskan March 27, 1964 earthquake: an interim geologic evaluation. U.S. Geological Survey Open-File Report. Menlo Park, California: U.S. Geological Survey. 34 p.

Tarr, Ralph S., and Lawrence Martin, 1912. The earthquakes at Yakutat Bay, Alaska, in September, 1899. U.S. Geological Survey Professional Paper 69. Washington: Government Printing Office. 135 p.

H. WILLIAM JOHANSEN
UNIVERSITY OF CALIFORNIA*

# Effects of Elevation Changes on Benthic Algae in Prince William Sound

## INTRODUCTION

### GENERAL REMARKS

In the present report the vertical distribution and growth of intertidal marine algae are correlated with changes in the elevation of the land resulting from the Alaska earthquake of March 27, 1964. Thirty-three stations were established between May 29 and July 16, 1965, during the investigation of the biological effects of the earthquake and the accompanying tsunamis. The stations are all located in Prince William Sound (Figure 1), approximately between latitudes 59°53′N and 60°59′N and longitudes 145°37′W and 148° 25′W. (See Table 2, p. 41, for list of stations and transects; see also the preceding paper by Hanna for descriptions of stations.) Study at a station for 1 to 2 days gave one sufficient time to survey, take certain measurements regarding zonation, and collect representative specimens, but not much more. It was deemed most profitable, however, to limit ourselves to a brief stay at each station to make possible the sampling of a greater variety of localities in the earthquake-affected intertidal zone.

The purpose of the shore visits was mainly to determine the levels at which the more conspicuous zone-forming algae were growing and to discover any effects that the earthquake may have had on these algae. Where possible, the age and condition of the plants present were ascertained, and this information was correlated with the movement of the shore caused by the earthquake as measured by George Plafker of the U.S. Geological Survey in the summer of 1964 (Plafker, 1965; 1969, Plate 2). The measurements of elevational change were determined by tide-gage readings or by assuming the upper levels of the preearthquake barnacle zone or the *Fucus* zone to be at preearthquake mean high water. This level was correlated with the postearthquake water level and a difference obtained. At most stations, algal growths at preearthquake as well as postearthquake levels were very much in evidence.

ABSTRACT: Fifteen months after the Alaska earthquake, either dead or surviving preearthquake algae as well as postearthquake algae were present in areas where shorelines had been raised or lowered. In extensively elevated areas such as the southwest coast of Montague Island (30 ft) the preearthquake littoral zone was completely separate from the postearthquake littoral zone. The preearthquake littoral and upper sublittoral zones were marked by bleached coralline algae, dead specimens of *Fucus*, desiccated plants belonging to the Laminariales, and an uppermost band of the lichen *Verrucaria*, as well as the remains of animals. Surprisingly, at Montague Island the newly established littoral zone was dominated by *Porphyra* rather than by *Fucus*, the dominant algal constituent of unaltered or slightly altered littoral zones.

The 33 shoreline stations established in Prince William Sound are divided into four categories: (a) unaltered, (b) subsided, (c) moderately elevated, where preearthquake and postearthquake littoral zones were incompletely separated, and (d) extensively elevated, where the littoral zones were separated. The zone-forming algae and other marine plants belonging to *Verrucaria, Fucus, Gloiopeltis, Porphyra, Rhodymenia, Polysiphonia, Pterosiphonia, Zostera,* Laminariales, Corallinaceae, and also green algae were all affected if they were growing at stations in categories b–d above. The study of new postearthquake littoral zones revealed the strict relationship that many of these plants have to the level of the ocean and the effect that the elevational change had on the type of algae present in May to July of 1965.

The results of a settling-surface study showed that the first colonizers of littoral zones provided by the earthquake were probably small filamentous algae, such as *Ulothrix* and *Urospora*, as well as diatoms. One hundred and twenty taxa of macroalgae were collected during our visit to Prince William Sound, including 17 new records for the area.

*Now at Clark University.

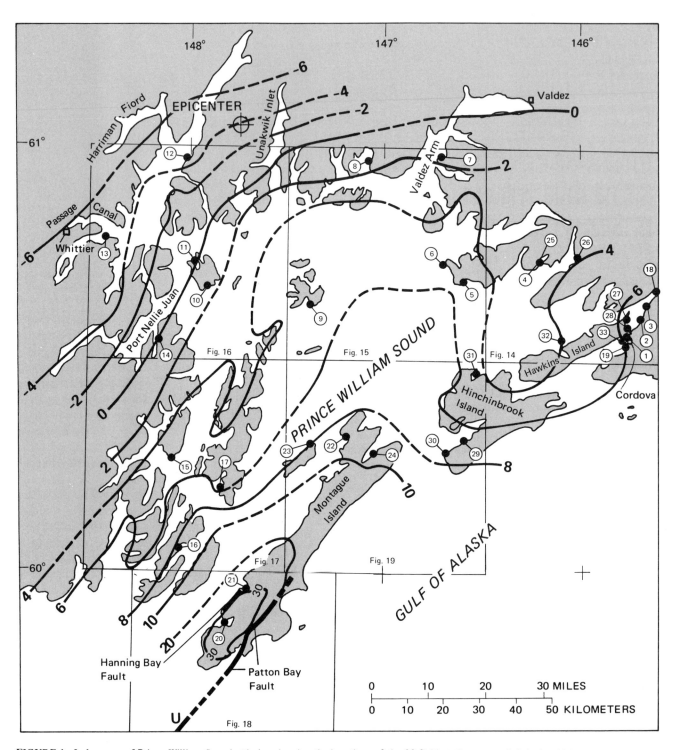

FIGURE 1 Index map of Prince William Sound, Alaska, showing the locations of the 33 field stations occupied during 1965 by investigators aboard M.V. *Harmony*. Isobase contours by Plafker and Mayo (1965), U.S. Geological Survey, show land-level changes resulting from the March 27, 1964, earthquake. The contour interval is 2 ft between the −6-ft and +10-ft contours, and the interval is 10 ft between the +10-ft and the +30-ft contours. Larger-scale maps of the six sections indicated appear as Figures 14–19 in the preceding paper by Hanna. (Adapted from U.S. Geological Survey base map.)

## METHODS

The major logistics involving the present expedition are outlined in the introductory report by Hanna (1971) in this volume.

Transects and measurements of the algal zones were made at nearly every station. A 40-ft-long ¼-in. nylon cord marked at 1-ft intervals was placed from the top to the bottom of the area to be transected. Pitons at either end facilitated placement of this line. Vertical elevations were established by using a hand-held level and a 15-ft stadia rod marked at 1-ft intervals. Slope and compass heading were determined with the aid of a Brunton compass. Sea-level datum was established, and later, on board the *Harmony*, the levels of algal zones previously measured on the shore were calculated with reference to mean lower low tidal level (=0.0-ft level). Measured algal levels may be inaccurate by as much as ±0.5 ft, and even more where the measurements were obtained on gently sloping shores.

Collections of algae were made to provide specimens needed for the type of identification that can be made only in a laboratory. Most of the specimens collected were preserved in a 5 percent formalin–seawater solution, and some were later pressed and dried. Voucher specimens are deposited in the University of California Herbarium in Berkeley and the Duke University Herbarium, Durham, North Carolina.

## HISTORY

### Previous Studies of the Effects of Earthquakes on Algae

Geological aspects of the March 27, 1964, earthquake have been presented by Plafker (1965). The area shaken by the earthquake is part of a seismically active arc extending from Kamchatka to south central Alaska. Unakwik Inlet, near the epicenter of the earthquake, and Montague Island, the area of the greatest uplift on land, are both in Prince William Sound and are less than 600 mi west of Yakutat Bay, the center of a severe earthquake in 1899 (Plafker, 1965).

Reports of death to marine organisms attributable to earthquakes of tectonic origin are indeed rare, and rarer yet are data on mass algal extermination. The great Kwanto earthquake of 1923, which devastated much of Tokyo and Yokohama, prompted studies of its effect on marine organisms by biologists: Kaburaki (1928) reported on the extent of mass destruction of invertebrates and algae by the uplift and the waves and by effluents resulting from fire and damage to man-made structures; Gislén (1931) in 1930 observed the remains of 34 animal and plant species that were uplifted and killed by the earthquake and found that 11 of these species were still rare or missing altogether.

Other earthquakes mentioned in the literature as resulting in the death of marine organisms by uplifting the shore are those that occurred at Valparaiso, Chile, in 1822; Concepción, Chile, in 1835; and Yakutat Bay, Alaska, in 1899 (Brongersma-Sanders, 1957). The Yakutat Bay earthquake, as well as the 1964 Alaska earthquake, resulted in vast uplifted and subsided coastal regions; a maximum uplift of 47⅓ ft was reported by Martin (1910). The effects of the uplift on marine organisms in the Yakutat Bay earthquake were given by Tarr and Martin (1912), who viewed the remains of barnacles, mussels, and bryozoa (for the most part, probably coralline algae) in 1905, 6 years after the earthquake. They also discussed the repopulation, or lack thereof, of rocks that comprised the pre- and postearthquake intertidal zones, mentioning the growth of alder and willow among the dead marine organisms and, at certain sites, the slow recolonization of the 6-year-old intertidal belt by those organisms that were prevalent before the earthquake.

### Previous Studies of Alaskan Benthic Marine Algae

In their classification of algal geographic regions on the west coast of North America, which was based mostly on water temperatures and algal distribution, Setchell and Gardner (1903, p. 167–171) included the coastline between Puget Sound and the Bering Sea in the "Boreal Region." This region contains an algal flora characterized by such species as "*Laminaria saccharina* in various forms, certain *Alariae*, certain digitate Laminariae, *Chorda*, *Rhodymenia pertusa* (P. & R.) J. Agardh, forms of *R. palmata*, *Agarum* etc., to say nothing of the large and conspicuous *Alaria fistulosa* P. & R." Setchell and Gardner also believed that when more information became available, it might be necessary to separate an Upper Boreal Region, just below the Aleutian Islands, from a Lower Boreal Region at the isocryme (mean seawater temperature minima for the coldest month) of 5°C and the isothere (mean maxima for the warmest month) of 10°C. Prince William Sound would then be situated in the Upper Boreal Region. Scagel (1957) considered the area along the Alaskan "panhandle" (probably in the vicinity of Sitka and north of Dixon Entrance) as an apparent distributional boundary between the algal flora of British Columbia and the more Arctic elements.

Other studies on the algae of Alaska have been limited to collecting expeditions and the subsequent study of the collections by various algologists. Setchell and Gardner (1903, p. 171–173) presented a historical survey of expeditions and publications dealing with the algae of northwestern North America before the twentieth century. The principal reports published as the result of algal collections in the Alaskan region have been those by Postels and Ruprecht (1840), Setchell (1899), Saunders (1901), and Wynne (1970).

## GENERAL ASPECTS OF PRINCE WILLIAM SOUND

### PHYSICAL ENVIRONMENT

The convoluted nature of the shoreline and the numerous islands in Prince William Sound dampen the heavy swells from the Gulf of Alaska. We did not visit shorelines fronting on the open gulf; most stations were established on calm shores within embayments. As far as we could determine during our 1- to 2-day visits and from reference to navigational charts, Knowles Head (Station 5) and English Bay in Port Etches, Hinchinbrook Island (Station 30), were two of the more exposed sites studied. These two stations, however, could only be classed as moderately exposed when compared to shores on the open Pacific Ocean, though inside the protecting Montague and Hinchinbrook islands gale winds will occasionally generate large waves.

Rain and fog are common throughout the Sound, and days when intertidal organisms receive direct sunshine are few. Low spring tides generally occur in early morning or late evening. Thus, the organisms inhabiting the lower intertidal zone receive very little, if any, direct sunlight.

According to Robinson's (1957) data, the monthly average temperature of surface water in the Gulf of Alaska immediately south of Montague Island from 1941 to 1952 varied as follows:

| Month | Temperature, °F (=°C) |
| --- | --- |
| January | 40 (=4.4) |
| February | 38 (=3.3) |
| March | 39 (=3.9) |
| April | 40 (=4.4) |
| May | 45 (=7.3) |
| June | 51 (=10.6) |
| July | 54 (=12.3) |
| August | 54 (=12.3) |
| September | 52 (=11.1) |
| October | 47 (=8.4) |
| November | 43 (=6.1) |
| December | 41 (=5.0) |

However, because most of our transects were made in more or less enclosed embayments, the water temperatures at transect sites were often more extreme than those in the open gulf. In such areas of shallow, quiet water the temperature would increase from the effects of insolation and decrease under the effects of cold air and glacier-fed stream runoff.

The meteorological data below, from Watson (1959), are based on records kept at Cordova Airport, but conditions there are not necessarily representative of all areas in Prince William Sound.

The following are data on air temperatures (January is usually the coldest month of the year, August the warmest):

| | | |
| --- | --- | --- |
| January 1957 | Maximum | 32.4°F |
| | Minimum | 17.6°F |
| | Monthly mean | 25.0°F |
| August 1957 | Maximum | 61.3°F |
| | Minimum | 45.5°F |
| | Monthly mean | 53.4°F |

The lowest recorded temperature at the Cordova Airport was –33°F in February 1947. The temperature drops below 32°F on an average of 193 days each year.

Precipitation is greatest in September, October, and November. The mean annual rainfall is 98.64 in., with 216 days per year receiving 0.01 in. or more of precipitation.

The prevailing direction of the wind is east.

In the average year, records of cloud cover at the Cordova Airport between sunrise and sunset indicate that 53 days are clear, 52 partly cloudy, and 260 cloudy.

In Prince William Sound, the ratio of the number of hours of darkness to the number of hours of daylight is high in the winter and relatively low in the summer. In June, the sun sets between 11 p.m. and midnight and rises between 3 and 4 a.m. The annual variation in day length plus the variation in water temperature as shown above indicates that the algal flora, as a whole, must show a high degree of seasonality.

The tidal cycle in Prince William Sound is of the semi-diurnal mixed type. When tidal levels are plotted against time, the result is a sinusoidal curve such as shown in Figure 2. During spring tides there is a great difference between the levels of the two lower tides and between the two higher

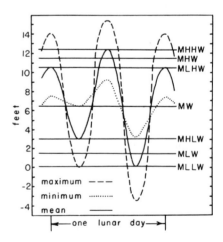

FIGURE 2  Diagram showing maximal, minimal, and mean tidal ranges at Cordova, Alaska.

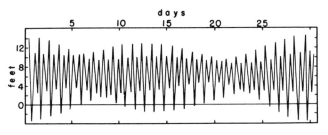

FIGURE 3 Marigram showing predicted tides for Cordova for June 1965.

TABLE 1 Tidal Levels and Abbreviations Used To Describe Them in This Report

| | |
|---|---|
| Highest Higher High Water | HHHW |
| Highest Lower High Water | HLHW |
| Mean Higher High Water | MHHW |
| Mean High Water | MHW |
| Mean Lower High Water | MLHW |
| Lowest Higher High Water | LHHW |
| Lowest Lower High Water | LLHW |
| Mean Water | MW |
| Highest Higher Low Water | HHLW |
| Highest Lower Low Water | HLLW |
| Mean Higher Low Water | MHLW |
| Mean Low Water | MLW |
| Mean Lower Low Water | MLLW |
| Lowest Higher Low Water | LHLW |
| Lowest Lower Low Water | LLLW |

tides of each day (Figure 3). For example, on June 1, 1965, there was a predicted difference of 3.4 ft between the two high tides and of 5.9 ft between the two low tides. The extreme tidal range in Prince William Sound is nearly twice as great as the mean tidal range. The greatest spring tides occur during the summer and winter solstices (Figure 4). The least neap tides occur during the vernal and autumnal equinoxes. The mean tidal range at Cordova is 10.0 ft, a range 6.0 ft greater than that at San Francisco and 16.7 ft less than that at Anchorage, Alaska.

All references to tidal level in this report are in feet from mean lower low water (MLLW), the 0.0-ft datum established by the U.S. Coast and Geodetic Survey. Tidal levels referred to and abbreviations used to describe them are given in Table 1. The highest tide in 1965 was 15.4 ft on January 18, and the lowest tide was –3.6 ft on June 30. The tidal data in this and the preceding paragraph are taken from the U.S. Coast and Geodetic Survey (1964) tide table, 1965, for Cordova, Alaska. Actual tidal level may fluctuate slightly from that given in a tide table according to the force of the wind and atmospheric pressure. However, as Kaye (1964) noted, because of the essentially harmonic nature of the tidal cycle, every level within the intertidal zone has a unique value for the ratio of time emersed to time im-

mersed. This ratio varies from zero at LLLW to infinity at HHHW; it reaches unity at about MW.

The maximal, minimal, and mean tidal levels predicted for Cordova for 1965 are shown in Figure 2. However, the U.S. Coast and Geodetic Survey tide table for 1965 (p. 182-183) shows that at some stations the heights of high and low water differ to some extent from those at Cordova. The greatest differences are the following:

| Station | | Height | |
|---|---|---|---|
| No. | Location | High Water | Low Water |
| 29 | Port Etches, Hinchinbrook Island | –1.2 | –0.2 |
| 20 | MacLeod Harbor, Montague Island | –1.1 | –0.1 |
| 21 | Hanning Bay, Montague Island | –0.9 | –0.1 |
| 16 | Port Ashton, Sawmill Bay, Evans Island | –1.1 | 0.0 |

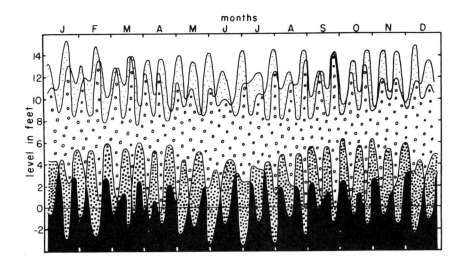

FIGURE 4 Graphic representation of the tidal cycles at Cordova, 1965, computed from tide tables of the U.S. Coast and Geodetic Survey (1964). The black represents the levels not exposed on any given day; the heavy stipples represent those levels exposed by one low tide per day; the circles represent those levels exposed by receding tides twice a day; the light stipples represent those levels covered by one rising tide per day; and white indicates those levels not reached by the tides on any given day.

## ALGAL ZONATION

Fluctuation in water level resulting from tidal action is the principal factor influencing the vertical distribution of intertidal marine organisms. However, as Lewis (1961) has stressed, to define biological zones on the basis of tidal level only disregards the complex of actual limiting factors such as desiccation, light intensity, temperature, and rainfall, not to mention the modifying factors such as wave action, aspect and configuration of the shore, nature of the substratum, and the time of day or season of low spring tides (Russell, 1963). Additionally, complex biological interactions, largely unrecognized, undoubtedly are at work in modifying intertidal zonation.

At many stations the algal zones were very clearly delimited, and it was possible to determine boundaries to the nearest inch. The relatively calm water and the large tidal amplitude of the mixed tides in Prince William Sound make the area ideally suited to the study of littoral zonation. Most of the vegetational layers are well defined, and the edges of those layers in relation to water level can be determined readily. The zonational features in 1965 were, of course, complicated by the elevational changes engendered by the earthquake.

The literature describing intertidal zonation in various parts of the world and the number of schemes for classifying the zones is vast. In 1949, Stephenson and Stephenson devised their "Universal Scheme," which many subsequent workers have followed. Lewis (1961) modified the Stephenson and Stephenson concept somewhat, mostly on the basis of his observation that the nearly cosmopolitan black *Verrucaria* zone may be covered by the higher tides in calm waters and thus is not entitled to the appellation "supralittoral." (When only one species of a genus is mentioned in this work, the generic name alone is usually given. The specific or varietal names, with the authority, are listed in the Appendix at the end of this paper.) This observation is supported by our measurements of the *Verrucaria* zone in Prince William Sound adjusted to preearthquake levels. At every transect, the lower edge of *Verrucaria* was below HHHW for 1965 (15.4 ft), and at 65 percent of the transects this edge was below 11.5 ft (MHW at Cordova). (See Table 7, p. 49). These data indicate that *Verrucaria* is immersed during each spring-tide sequence in the area studied. Lewis (1961) also observed that some of the algae characteristic of the upper reaches of the ocean floor may, on some coastlines, extend above LLLW (his ELWST) and thus be subjected to occasional brief exposures to the air. These plants are of a subtidal element, however, extending upward only a short distance past LLLW, the physical boundary between the subtidal and intertidal zones. The upper boundary of the biological sublittoral zone varies from place to place. For example, despite the fact that LLLW is below the −3-ft level according to tide-gage measurements at Cordova, the sublittoral zone as measured by the tip of the main laminarians at Shipyard Bay (transect 1a) extends up to the −1.5-ft level, and at South Bay, Perry Island (transect 10), it extends to the −2.2-ft level. Thus the upper boundary of the sublittoral zone in Prince William Sound agrees with Lewis's extension of the upper level of this zone to a level significantly above LLLW in the British Isles.

In this report the terms "intertidal" and "subtidal" are not used in the biological sense because their connotation is a physical one—the intertidal region being covered by the highest higher high tides and uncovered by the lowest lower low tides, whereas the subtidal region is never exposed to the air (Southward, 1958).

The terms proposed by Lewis (1961) will be used to describe the major biological zones in the present report:

Maritime zone, near and obviously affected by the ocean but never reached by the tides; terrestrial lichens, mosses and certain angiosperms.

Littoral zone, inhabited by organisms that are alternately exposed to air and covered by seawater.

Littoral fringe, in Prince William Sound encompasses *Verrucaria* and sometimes *Prasiola* and those organisms that only rarely are covered by the tides.

Eulittoral zone, encompasses those organisms covered and uncovered by the tides daily or almost daily.

Sublittoral zone, encompasses those organisms that are always or almost always covered by water.

The subzones within this framework will be described with reference to the dominant alga in each subzone and its level above or below MLLW. As pointed out by Moore (1958), the advantage in this method of using biological indicators lies in the fact that the presence of certain organisms implies the presence of certain conditions within their particular tolerance ranges.

Stations established, transects made, and related data are given in Table 2.

### Algae in Earthquake-Affected Areas

The 33 stations established during the present cruise may be divided into four categories, according to the extent of elevational change incurred during the earthquake. These categories are listed in Table 3 and will be treated in turn on the following pages.

### Relatively Unaffected Shores

In the areas of Prince William Sound that were only slightly uplifted or depressed by the earthquake, the littoral fringe is conspicuous by the black coating imparted to it by the lichen *Verrucaria*. Dense growths of the alga *Prasiola borealis* may occur above *Verrucaria*, but its designation as a

TABLE 2  Stations Established during Alaska Earthquake Investigation, 1965

| No. | Location | Date | Transect | Elevational Change, (ft)[a] |
|---|---|---|---|---|
| 1 | Shipyard Bay, Hawkins Island, across Orca Inlet from Cordova | May 30 | 1, 1a | +5.4B |
| 2 | Orca Inlet, about 1 mi north of Orca | May 31 | 2 | +6.4B |
| 3 | Orca Inlet, Shepard Point | May 31 | 3 | +7.6B |
| 4 | Olsen Bay in Port Gravina. Barrier island near head of bay | June 2 | 4, 4a | +3.6B |
| 5 | Knowles Head | June 4 | 5 | +5.7B |
| 6 | Goose Island, on lee of island | June 5, 6 | 6, 6a | +4.8B |
| 7 | First small cove north of Galena Bay, in Valdez Arm | June 7 | 7 | +2.0B |
| 8 | Heather Island, near Columbia Glacier | June 7 | – | +1.7B |
| 9 | Naked Island, Bass Harbor | June 8 | 9 | +4.7B |
| 10 | South Bay, Perry Island | June 13–14 | 10, 10a, 10b | ca. +1.5B |
| 11 | West Twin Bay, Perry Island | June 15 | 11, 11a, 11b | +0.1F |
| 12 | Port Wells, south of Golden | June 15 | – | −4.1B |
| 13 | Terminal moraine of Tebenkof Glacier, Blackstone Bay | June 16 | 13, 13a, 13b | −5.2B |
| 14 | West Gable Cannery in McClure Bay, Port Nellie Juan | June 17 | 14 | −0.1TBM |
| 15 | Chenega | June 17 | – | +6.3B |
| 16 | Port Ashton, Sawmill Bay, Evans Island | June 18 | 16 | +8.9B |
| 17 | Thumb Bay, Knight Island | June 20 | 17 | +6.0B |
| 18 | Head of Orca Inlet | June 21–22 | – | +7.0B |
| 19 | Cordova flats (south of Cordova) | June 23 | – | +6.7B |
| 20 | MacLeod Harbor, Montague Island | June 26–27 | 20, 20a | +30.0B |
| 21 | Hanning Bay, Montague Island | June 28–29 | 21, 21a | +29.8B, +29.1B |
| 22 | Stockdale Harbor, Montague Island | June 30 | 22 | +8.7B |
| 23 | Green Island, northwest shore | July 1 | 23 | +8.4B |
| 24 | Zaikof Bay, Montague Island | July 2–3 | 24 | +8.8B |
| 25 | Olsen Bay | July 8–9 | 25 | +3.6B |
| 26 | Beartrap Bay, Port Gravina | July 9 | – | +4.0B |
| 27 | Hawkins Island, head of Deep Bay at north end of island | July 10 | 27 | +6.8B |
| 28 | Hawkins Island, near Grass Island | July 11 | 28 | +6.2B |
| 29 | Port Etches, Hinchinbrook Island, south shore | July 12 | 29, 29a | +3.8B |
| 30 | English Bay, Port Etches, Hinchinbrook Island | July 13 | 30 | +7.1B |
| 31 | Anderson Bay, Hinchinbrook Island | July 14 | 31 | +3.8B |
| 32 | Whiskey Cove, west shore Hawkins Island, north of entrance to Canoe Passage | July 15 | 32 | +4.2B |
| 33 | Spike Island, opposite Cordova | July 16 | – | +6.1B |

[a]"B" indicates that the uplift or subsidence was determined by assuming that the upper level of the preearthquake barnacle zone was at preearthquake MHW (11.5 ft) and correlating this level with the postearthquake water level; "F" indicates that the same was done with upper *Fucus* level; "TBM" indicates height of tidal bench mark. The elevations are from Pfafker (1969, Plate 2). Not all the readings are as precise as the levels, to tenths of a foot, would indicate.

TABLE 3  The Stations Grouped, by Station Number, According to the Amount of Vertical Displacement Caused by the Earthquake

| Displacement | Station Number |
|---|---|
| Subsided | 12, 13 |
| Slight vertical movement | 7, 8, 10, 11, 14 |
| Elevated; relation of pre- and postearthquake littoral zones: | |
| Confluent | 1–6, 9, 15–19, 22–33 |
| Separated | 20, 21 |

marine alga is questionable. Depending on one's viewpoint, either the upper or lower limit of occurrence of *P. borealis* may be designated as the demarcation between the maritime and littoral zones.

The lower edge of *Verrucaria* may be designated as the upper limit of the eulittoral zone, a zone usually dominated by dense growths of *Fucus* overlaying more or less dense populations of barnacles. At most stations the upper border of the *Fucus* zone extended up to the lower edge of the *Verrucaria* zone; a *Fucus* zone fringe was evident in some areas. This fringe is described in the discussion on *Rhodymenia* later in this report.

In determining the boundary between the sublittoral and

littoral zones, the rhodophycean and chlorophycean algae that so commonly form transient and variable belts in the lower part of the eulittoral zone must be disregarded. The top of the sublittoral zone should be marked by the upper limit of a group of consistently appearing and conspicuous zone-forming organisms, the majority of which always live completely immersed in the ocean. The laminarians, exclusive of *Alaria*, meet this requirement; the upper limit of the holdfasts of *Laminaria* may thus be considered to delineate the border between the eulittoral and sublittoral zones. *Alaria* sometimes forms a belt above *Laminaria*, and scattered individuals may occur to a depth of several feet, but the zonal features of *Alaria* are often irregular and its occurrence is so inconsistent as to negate its value in separating the eulittoral and sublittoral zones.

The zones described above provide the main guidelines in departmentalizing life on the seashore. However, in Prince William Sound, as on other shores, subzones of red and green algae especially complicate the picture in the eulittoral zone. Some genera that form subzones are *Spongomorpha, Blidingia, Enteromorpha, Monostroma, Ulva, Porphyra, Rhodymenia, Gloiopeltis, Alaria*, and, to a lesser extent, *Pterosiphonia* and *Polysiphonia*. Coralline algae and the phanerogam *Zostera marina* also may form dense local stands in the sublittoral zone.

Although the zonal aspects are discussed within the framework set forth by Lewis (1961), the occurrence of the zones and subzones in relation to tidal level is described in feet above or below MLLW. For example, the boundary between the sublittoral and eulittoral zones, as marked by the upper limit of *Laminaria*, usually occurs between −3 and −1 ft, depending on the locality. Figure 5 gives the approximate levels of most of the belt-forming algae encountered as they would occur in a typical vertically unchanged area in Prince William Sound. The largely unchanged areas are represented by Stations 7, 8, 10, 11, and 14 (Table 3). Figure 5 is a composite and does not take local variation into account.

Other algae, although not occurring in sufficient abundance to warrant inclusion among the zone-forming plants, were nevertheless restricted to certain levels in the sublittoral and eulittoral zones. The following list includes plants commonly present in the upper sublittoral zone in Prince William Sound in June and July 1965.

*Agarum cribrosum*
*Ahnfeltia plicata*
*Chordaria flagelliformis*
*Constantinea rosa-marina*
*Cymathere triplicata*
*Cystoseira geminata*
*Desmarestia intermedia*
*Dictyosiphon foeniculaceus*

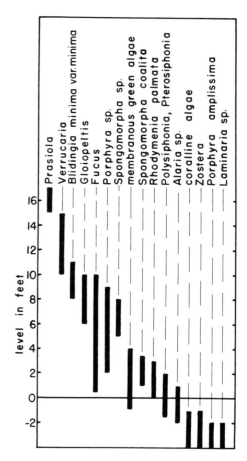

FIGURE 5 Approximate composite of levels of postearthquake zone-forming plants in Prince William Sound, based on data collected June–July 1965.

*Lithothamnia* (all encrusting epilithic coralline algae)
*Neoptilota asplenioides*
*Porphyra amplissima*
*Scytosiphon lomentaria* f. *lomentaria*

Most of these plants did not grow above the laminarians except where shade and moist draws or tide pools were available to them. The sea bottom below about −4 ft was not explored.

In addition to the algae mentioned as constituting subzones in the eulittoral zone, other algae occurring there seemed to have wide tolerance ranges or were too sparsely distributed to form zones. The following list includes species frequently encountered in the eulittoral zone of Prince William Sound.

*Bangia fuscopurpurea*
*Bossiella cretacea* (in tide pools)
*Cryptosiphonia woodii*

*Dumontia filiformis*
*Halosaccion glandiforme*
*Hildenbrandia occidentalis* var. *occidentalis*
Lithothamnia
*Melanosiphon intestinalis*
*Odonthalia* sp.
*Pilayella littoralis*
*Ralfsia fungiformis*
*Rhodochorton purpureum*
*Rhodomela* sp.

*Halosaccion glandiforme*, which formed one of the zones of Rigg and Miller (1949) in their study at Neah Bay, Washington, grew at many levels in Prince William Sound throughout the eulittoral zone and seemed to thrive in wetter areas. The coralline algae were restricted to the sublittoral zone or to very moist draws or tide pools in the eulittoral zone. At West Twin Bay, Perry Island (near transect 11b), *Rhodochorton purpureum* covered several square meters of a flat overhanging rock that never received the direct rays of the sun. *Odonthalia* usually grew in tide pools; at some sites (e.g., near Constantine Harbor, Port Etches, Hinchinbrook Island) it was heavily infected with *Soranthera ulvoidea*. *Pilayella littoralis* formed dark hairlike masses on rocks or preearthquake *Fucus* in the lower eulittoral zone. *Pilayella littoralis* may be the plant that comprises most of the "beard" of the "beard zone" at Vancouver Island, Washington (Stephenson and Stephenson, 1961a, b). The most abundant brown alga in the eulittoral zone in Prince William Sound was *Melanosiphon intestinalis*. The vertical ranges occupied by this alga were quite varied and generally broad.

## Subsided Shores

The only stations established during the cruise where subsidence had occurred are Port Wells, just south of Golden (Station 12), and the cove at the foot of Tebenkof Glacier (locally called Tebenkof Cove) in Blackstone Bay (Station 13). Much evidence of the recent depression of terrestrial organisms into the sea was noted at both sites. In Port Wells, dying mosses existed as low as the 11-ft tidal level (11.5 ft is MHW), dead terrestrial grass rhizomes were present at the 9-ft level, and *Verrucaria* could be seen at the 8-ft level. In one area, littorinids, barnacles, small fuci, and mosses all grew together on the same small rock surface.

In general, established algae seem more tolerant of increased immersion than of increased emersion. At both transects 13a and 13b, preearthquake *Fucus* thrived at least down to the −1- and −2-ft tidal levels, respectively, levels below the lower limits of most *Fucus* zones in Prince William Sound. There was no evidence of *Fucus* either dead or dying because of subsidence below its tolerance limits. On the other hand, the occurrence of young plants less than 8 cm long above preearthquake specimens that were gen-

TABLE 4  The Main Plants and Their Levels of Occurrence at Tebenkof Cove, a Subsided Area[a]

| Plant | Level[b] | |
|---|---|---|
| | Top | Bottom |
| Mosses | − | +9 |
| *Verrucaria* | +9 | +6 |
| Postearthquake *Fucus* | +8 | − |
| Preearthquake *Fucus* | +5 | below −2 |
| Scattered *Gloiopeltis* | +6 | +2 |
| *Polysiphonia* sp. | +2 | −1 |

[a]Compiled from transects 13, 13a, and 13b, June 16, 1965.
[b]Levels in feet above (+) or below (−) MLLW.

erally 10–26 cm long did give evidence of the upward extension of the *Fucus* zone.

*Verrucaria* that had been lowered into the present eulittoral zone was not growing well, if at all. The lower parts of the *Verrucaria* zone were at the 6- to 8-ft level, and the crusts there were being eroded from the rock.

A species of *Polysiphonia* formed subzones in the lower eulittoral zones at all three transect sites at Tebenkof Cove. Laminariales were not in evidence; perhaps the dense growths of *Fucus* in what would have been the upper sublittoral zone on preearthquake shores had as yet precluded the establishment and growth of laminarians. Table 4 indicates the main plants and their occurrence as observed at Tebenkof Cove.

The upper levels of preearthquake *Fucus* and the lower levels of *Verrucaria* indicate a subsidence of about 5 ft, in agreement with the −5.2-ft reading of Plafker (1969, Plate 2), which was based on the upper barnacle level.

## Uplifted Shores: Littoral Zones Confluent

At most of the stations we visited, the former intertidal area had not been elevated completely above the recently established one. Transects (Table 3) made in such areas passed downward through dead preearthquake plants into areas containing a mixture of dead and living preearthquake algae as well as species that had become established during the past 15 months (Table 5).

*Prasiola*, *Verrucaria*, and dead *Fucus* were usually the only preearthquake plants that could be recognized above the living *Fucus* zone. In some areas a brownish scum consisting of *Ulothrix* sp. and blue-green algae occurred in the area where postearthquake *Verrucaria* presumably will develop.

At some moderately uplifted stations, unhealthy *Rhodymenia palmata* and *Constantinea rosa-marina* exhibited color patterns characteristic of pigment loss in the distal parts of the blades. Both species generally are a deep magenta color,

TABLE 5    The Main Zones Recorded in Transect 17, Thumb Bay, Knight Island[a]

| Zones | Level[b] | |
|---|---|---|
| | Top | Bottom |
| *Verrucaria* | +20.8 | +17.1 |
| Preearthquake *Fucus* and barnacles | +17.1 | — |
| Decayed fleshy algae | +13 | — |
| Preearthquake lithothamnia and *Bossiella* sp. | +10.9 | — |
| *Fucus* zone fringe | +9.5 | +8.0 |
| Main *Fucus* zone | +8.0 | +0.6 |
| Zone of green algae such as *Ulva fenestrata*, and *Spongomorpha spinescens*; scattered plants of *Polysiphonia urceolata* and *Pterosiphonia bipinnata* | +3 | — |
| Zone of *P. urceolata* and *P. bipinnata* | +2.2 | — |
| Laminariales | −2.5 | — |

[a] The transect was made on June 20, 1965, near the mouth of the bay, an area uplifted 6.0 ft, according to Plafker (1969, Plate 2). The transect was made on a rock incline of 22° from the horizontal facing 50°W of S (230°).
[b] Levels in feet above (+) or below (−) MLLW.

but in afflicted plants (Figure 18) the distal parts of the blades showed a pale green to yellowish hue that indicated the death of tissue. Attempts to correlate levels at which the dying plants occurred with amount of uplift were unsuccessful. *R. palmata* is normally an inhabitant of the lower eulittoral zone, and *C. rosa-marina* lives in the upper sublittoral zone.

*Ahnfeltia plicata*, where uplifted from the sublittoral zone by the earthquake, bleached from the blackish color of living plants to white. The wiry consistency of this alga

was evident even in dead plants; it was the only noncalcified red alga except *Gloiopeltis furcata* that retained its shape and texture after death. Many of the branches were surrounded by bleached *Tenarea dispar*.

At Olsen Bay (Station 4), as well as at other stations, the crustose *Hildenbrandia occidentalis* var. *occidentalis* was in an advanced state of deterioration, but the peripheral young tissue of this alga was of the usual magenta color, whereas the older, more proximal parts of the crust were green-yellow and were sloughing from the rock (Figure 6). Again, the reasons for this occurrence may be related to the uplift, some 3 to 4 ft at Olsen Bay (Plafker, 1969).

Bleached lithothamnia occurred among the living algae comprising the eulittoral zone at most of the moderately uplifted stations.

### Uplifted Areas: Littoral Zones Separated

The earthquake elevated the shore 30 ft at MacLeod Harbor (Station 20) and 20 to 30 ft at Hanning Bay (Station 21), both of which are embayments on the southwest coast of Montague Island (Plafker, 1969). This uplift was great enough to carry all littoral organisms well above the reach of subsequent tides. As seen offshore from MacLeod Harbor, the most conspicuous indication of a change in elevation was a broad band of white bleached calcareous algae approximately 15 vertical feet broad, much broader when measured along the inclination of the rock surface (Figures 7 and 8). On closer approach, a narrow upper white band separated by bare rock from the broad lower band of coralline algae became visible (Figure 8). This narrow band consisted mostly of bleached barnacle tests. Below these white bands, a dark band of living algae, just

*G Dallas Hanna*

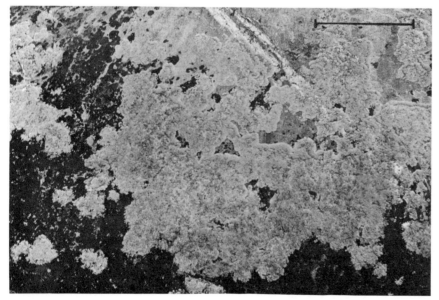

FIGURE 6    *Hildenbrandia occidentalis* var. *occidentalis*, dying as a result of the uplift at Olsen Bay (Station 4), June 2, 1965. The dark area is living, and the pale area is dead and sloughing from the rock. The scale is 10 cm long.

FIGURE 7  The uplifted shore at MacLeod Harbor, Montague Island (Station 20), June 26, 1965. The upper white belt consists of bleached barnacle tests; the lower white area consists mostly of bleached coralline algae. The bare rock between was the site of the littoral zone before the earthquake. A rope marked at intervals of 1 ft passes through the zones from the upper center to the lower left.

above water level, appeared, as well as clusters of dead kelp holdfasts and stipes that gave the coralline band a speckled appearance. The principal aspects of the shore at MacLeod Harbor and Hanning Bay as seen in June 1965 are listed in Table 6.

The lower edges of sublittoral dead preearthquake algae, such as kelp and corallines, merged into the upper parts of the zones of living algae. Some dead kelp stipes and holdfasts that persisted in the upper reaches of the new zones were overgrown with *Monostroma* sp. and *Blidingia minima* var. *minima*. Underneath the living *Porphyra*, dead crusts of lithothamnia in an advanced state of deterioration were visible. The erosive effects of moisture had obviously taken their toll of this crustose alga where it had not been uplifted above the present tidal range. Higher crusts above the zones of living algae were rather well preserved by desiccation.

Transects 20 and 20a, made at MacLeod Harbor, and transects 21 and 21a, made at Hanning Bay, represent two very different types of shoreline. The MacLeod Harbor transects were made on steeply sloping rocky cliffs (Figure 9), whereas the Hanning Bay transects cut through broad, gently sloping beaches of rounded boulders. The nature of the latter shoreline explains the deposition of debris that represents storm lines and high-tide lines, as well as other features

*G Dallas Hanna*

FIGURE 8  The site of transect 20 at MacLeod Harbor (Station 20), June 26, 1965. Patches of dead *Fucus* are visible among the barnacle tests near the top of the transect line. Bleached coralline algae give the white aspect to the rocks below. The rope is marked in feet.

TABLE 6 Principal Features of the Shore in the Extensively Uplifted Areas of MacLeod Harbor and Hanning Bay

| Main Zone | Dominant Feature[a] | Level (ft) (approximate)[b] Top | Bottom | Main Zone | Dominant Feature[a] | Level (ft) (approximate)[b] Top | Bottom |
|---|---|---|---|---|---|---|---|
| | Preearthquake | | | Eulittoral zone | Brown scum (MH) | +15 | +10 |
| Littoral fringe | *Prasiola* (MH) | +47 | +45 | | Zone of *Blidingia minima* var. *minima* on | | |
| | *Verrucaria* (MH, HB) | +45 | +42 | | cliffs (MH) | +12.5 | +10 |
| Eulittoral zone | *Fucus* (MH, HB) | +42 | +36 | | *Urospora penicilliformis* on tops of boulder | | |
| | Barnacles (MH, HB) | +42 | +36 | | (MH) | +12 | — |
| | Bare rock (MH, HB) | +36 | +32 | | *Ulothrix pseudoflacca*, highest living alga at | | |
| | Bleached coralline algae (MH, HB) | +32 | +15 | | HB | +11 | +10 |
| Sublittoral zone | Dried *Zostera* (HB) | +32 | +28 | | *Porphyra perforata* and other species | | |
| | Masses of dried algae (MH) | +30 | +29 | | (MH, HB) | +10 | +4 |
| | Patches of terrestrial grasses (MH, HB) | +30 | +20 | | *Spongomorpha coalita* (MH) | +5 | +3 |
| | Freshwater pools containing *Zygnema* sp. (MH) | +30 | +20 | | *Ulva fenestrata* (MH) | +4 | +2 |
| | Remains of *Laminaria* sp. (MH, HB) | +26 | +20 | | *Rhodymenia palmata* (MH, HB) | +2 | 0 |
| | Permanent pools containing decaying algae (MH) | +25 | +20 | | *Pterosiphonia bipinnata* (MH) | +1 | −1 |
| | Holdfasts of *Nereocystis* (MH) | +20 | +15 | | *Alaria* sp. (MH, HB) | +1 | — |
| | Postearthquake | | | Sublittoral zone | *Laminaria* sp. (MH, HB) | −1 | — |
| Littoral fringe | Storm line of driftwood (HB) | +15 | +14 | | Living coralline algae (MH, HB) | −1 | — |
| | | | | | *Rhodymenia pertusa* (HB) | −2 | — |
| | Windrows of kelp left by high tides (HB) | +13 | +12 | | *Nereocystis* sp. (MH, HB) | −10 | −40 |

[a]Where a feature is indicated as occurring at both MacLeod Harbor (MH) and Hanning Bay (HB), the approximate levels are based on measurements made at the former station.
[b]Levels in feet above (+) or below (−) MLLW.

FIGURE 9 Some of the zones of living algae at MacLeod Harbor (Station 20), June 26, 1965, at the site of transect 20a. The rope is marked in feet. P, *Porphyra*; B, brownish scum.

not present at MacLeod Harbor. On the other hand, the cliffs of MacLeod Harbor demonstrate more clearly the pre- and postearthquake zones of attached algae.

Nearly all traces of noncalcareous organisms that had occupied the preearthquake eulittoral zone had disappeared by June 1965. The only exceptions were the resistant fuci and dried masses of largely unrecognizable algae forming a loosely deposited layer just above the zone of dried kelp.

Interspersed among the bleached coralline algae were terrestrial plants such as grasses (Eyerdam, 1971, this volume) and freshwater pools containing green algae such as *Zygnema* sp.

The area of transition from the zones of dead preearthquake algae to the zones of living postearthquake algae is marked by such evidences of high-water activity as the storm line of driftwood and the windrows of decaying kelp left by the higher tides at Hanning Bay. On the steep cliffs at MacLeod Harbor this fringe is conspicuous because of the broad area of brownish scum that is largely comprised of *Ulothrix* sp. and blue-green algae (Figure 9). Below this scum occur the algal subzones outlined in Table 6.

In certain areas (e.g., south of Turner Glacier, Yakutat Bay) that were elevated 30–47 ft by the earthquake of 1899, Tarr and Martin (1912) saw very little repopulation of the new littoral zone when they viewed it in 1905, despite evidence that the preearthquake littoral zone had been extensively overgrown by seaweeds and animals. They explained this phenomenon on the basis of certain physical barriers such as sandbars, glaciers, and water currents. In contrast, all of the newly established littoral zones seen on shorelines uplifted by the 1964 earthquake were well populated by algae 15 months later. Differences in the composi-

tion and aspect of the algal flora were, however, manifest at MacLeod Harbor and Hanning Bay (Table 6). All perennial algae were in their first year of growth and, despite intensive search, no living specimens of *Constantinea rosa-marina*, *Ahnfeltia plicata*, or *Gloiopeltis furcata* were seen. The kelp zone at both stations was densely developed with crowded plants of young laminarias near the upper levels. Slow-growing algae such as lithothamnia, *Bossiella*, *Corallina*, *Ralfsia*, and *Hildenbrandia* were rare. The eulittoral zone was dominated by *Porphyra* instead of *Fucus*.

## ZONE-FORMING PLANTS

### VERRUCARIA

*Verrucaria*, probably *V. maura* Wahl. (Figure 10), forms a conspicuous black band along most of the rocky shores of Prince William Sound. The cosmopolitan distribution and universal zonational features of this ascolichen have been reported by numerous workers (see Southward, 1958, for a review of the universality of intertidal zonation). The *Verrucaria* zone is the uppermost of the three main zones of temperate seashores (the other two being the *Fucus*-barnacle–mussel zone and the laminarian zone) and, together with littorinids, characterizes the littoral fringe of Lewis (1961) and of the present report. The only "marine" alga growing higher than *Verrucaria* in Prince William Sound is *Prasiola borealis*.

All the *Verrucaria* bands seen during the present expedition represent preearthquake levels at which the organisms were growing (Figure 11). The lower level of the *Verrucaria*

*G Dallas Hanna*

FIGURE 10  Uplifted *Verrucaria* in Prince William Sound, June 1964. Note the perithecia. The scale is 1 mm long.

FIGURE 11 View of moderately uplifted shoreline at Spike Island, Cordova (Station 33). Photograph taken at low tide. Note the conspicuous *Verrucaria* zone, the bare pre-earthquake eulittoral zone, and the algae-coated postearthquake eulittoral zone.

*G Dallas Hanna*

zone and the upper level of the barnacle zone were utilized by Plafker in the summer of 1964 to establish elevational changes resulting from the earthquake (Plafker, 1965, 1969). The slow-growing nature of crustose lichens in general is recognized; no new zones of *Verrucaria* growing in the uplifted areas were detected. The elimination of uplifted *Verrucaria* and the reestablishment of new zones may take decades and may take longest in areas where a physical break occurs in the substratum between the former *Verrucaria* and the probable site of the new zones. Because most crustose lichens seem to spread best by vegetative means (Lewis, 1964, p. 161), a separation between old and new substrata would seriously impede recolonization. The possibility of dissemination by means of spores must not be discounted, however, inasmuch as crusts with perithecia were present in some areas.

At Port Etches (transect 29) and Anderson Bay (transect 31), both on Hinchinbrook Island, as well as at other sites, the littoral fringe at the level occupied by *Verrucaria* before the earthquake was devoid of macroscopic algae. Instead, the rocks in this area were coated by a brownish scum or film, which microscopic examination showed to consist of various species of *Ulothrix* and filamentous blue-green algae. Apparently, these minute algae were the only forms that could withstand the long periods of desiccation inherent in the littoral fringe, and they existed in these areas in lieu of *Verrucaria*.

The lower edge of the *Verrucaria* zone is often confluent with the upper limit of the barnacle zone and sometimes with the upper limit of the *Fucus* zone. Table 7 gives the levels delimiting the uplifted *Verrucaria* as obtained from measurements at various stations.

## FUCUS

In a comprehensive taxonomic work published in 1922, Gardner considered the genus *Fucus* on the west coast of North America as comprised of 5 species and 45 forms, 21 of which were reputed to occur in Alaska. Powell (1957a) suggested that this unwieldy array of taxa should be considered as belonging to the Linnaean species *F. distichus*, characterized by its monoecious condition and the presence of enclosed cavities, called caecostomata. He recognized two subspecies, *F. distichus* subsp. *edentatus* and *F. distichus* subsp. *evanescens*, from the Pacific coast of North America, but stated that certain identification of the two subspecies is often difficult. The only distinct character of *F. distichus* subsp. *evanescens* is its receptacle shape, the receptacle being "rather short and broad, rather flattened, and fairly distinctly delimited from the rest of the frond." Specimens answering the descriptions of both taxa, as well as intergrades between them, are present among my collections made in Prince William Sound.

At most of the stations it was possible to distinguish with certainty the *Fucus* plants that had begun their growth after the earthquake. Because the lower limits of most fucoid zones appeared to be slightly above MLLW, it was reasonably certain that fuci growing in the lower littoral zones in areas of moderate uplift were postearthquake plants (see also C in Figure 12). Only rarely did these plants exceed 15 cm by the end of June 1965; generally, they were less than 10 cm in length, and many were even less than 7 cm long. Other indications that these fuci were less than 15 months old were their lack of mature reproductive structures and their relative freedom from epiphytes (Figure 13).

TABLE 7  Levels of *Verrucaria* Correlated with Earthquake-Generated Elevational Changes[a]

| Transect | Lower Level of *Verrucaria* in 1965 | Elevational Change (approximate) | Preearthquake Lower Level of *Verrucaria* (approximate) |
|---|---|---|---|
| 4a | +13.5 | +3.6B | +9.9 |
| 8 | +10.1 | +1.7B | +8.4 |
| 9 | +15.2 | +4.7 | +10.3 |
| 10 | +13.0 | +1.5 | +11.5 |
| 10a | +9.5 | +1.5 | +8.0 |
| 10b | +10.8 | +1.5 | +9.3 |
| 11 | +10.0 | +0.1F | +9.9 |
| 11a | +14.0 | +0.1F | +13.9 |
| 11b | +10.7 | +0.1F | +10.6 |
| 13 | ca. +6.7 | −5.2 | +11.7 |
| 13a | +5.7 | −5.2 | +10.9 |
| 14 | ca. +13.5 | −0.4B | +13.9 |
| 16 | ca. +17.5 | +8.9B | +10.5 |
| 17 | +17.1 | +6.0B | +11.1 |
| 20 | +41.8 | +30.0B | +11.8 |
| 20a | ca. +39.0 | +30.0B | +9.0 |
| 21 | ca. +36.8 | +29.8B | +14.4 |
| 23 | +17.6 | +8.4B | +9.2 |
| 24 | ca. +15.0 | +3.6B | +11.0 |
| 27 | +18.5 | +6.8B | +11.7 |
| 29 | +15.9 | +3.8B | +12.1 |
| 29a | +16.5 | +3.8B | +12.7 |
| 32a | +15.1 | +4.2B | +10.5 |

[a]In feet above (+) or below (−) MLLW. See Table 2 for locality of transects and explanation of symbols.

At many places in these same zones of postearthquake fuci, plant length graded from shorter to longer from the top to the bottom of the main zone. This gradation was clearly observed at Thumb Bay, Knight Island (Station 17). Figure 14 shows representative plants arranged as they were found in a sequence from smallest to largest.

At stations such as Deep Bay (Station 27), where only moderate uplift had occurred, living preearthquake fuci still persisted in the upper parts of the new *Fucus* zone, as did dead plants above this zone (Figure 15). At Anderson Bay, Hinchinbrook Island (Station 31), as well as at some other sites, specimens of preearthquake *Fucus* were found to be surviving at a level slightly above the top of the zone of postearthquake *Fucus* and also within it. These preearthquake fuci were easily recognized by their mature condition and greater length (20–40 cm or more). The survival of these older specimens indicates that zygotes and/or germlings are more sensitive to environmental factors regulating the upper limit of survival than are older, well-established plants. If the young stages were as tolerant as the older ones, the new zone would have extended as high as the upper level of the surviving preearthquake plants when seen in June–July 1965.

Occasional dense zones of *Fucus* occurred on vertical and near-vertical rocky slopes, although at some sites such as South Bay, Perry Island (transect 10b), *Fucus* seemed to show a preference for the more horizontally oriented surfaces when both surface types were available. This preference was especially evident in an area consisting of large boulders where slopes of various inclination were present. Stephenson and Stephenson (1961a, b) reported that growth of *Fucus* on Vancouver Island, British Columbia, was usually more flourishing on less steep slopes than on vertical slopes, and Southward (1956) observed the same situation in the British Isles.

Living *Fucus distichus*, originating after the earthquake, constituted the most conspicuous algal zone at most stations, with the notable exceptions of MacLeod Harbor and Hanning Bay in the region of extensive uplift on Montague Island. The rock surfaces at sites of moderate uplift, such as Shipyard Bay (Station 1) and Shepard Point (Station 3), were completely hidden by the fronds of postearthquake *Fucus*. Counts indicated a density of 120 to 140 plants per 400 cm² in the upper parts of the zone and 60 to 80 plants

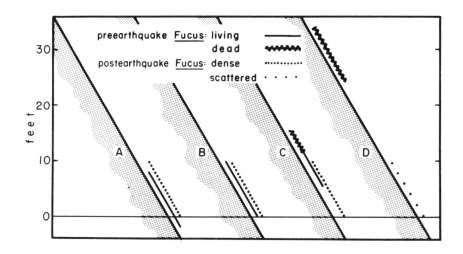

FIGURE 12  Diagrammatic representations of sections through the preearthquake and postearthquake *Fucus* zones at areas where the intertidal zone subsided (A), remained approximately the same (B), was moderately uplifted (C), and was extensively uplifted (D). For the sake of simplicity, new *Fucus* is indicated as occurring from the 0- to 10-ft tidal level.

*G Dallas Hanna*

FIGURE 13 Specimens of postearthquake (two small plants) and preearthquake (large plant) *Fucus* from Stockdale Harbor, Montague Island (Station 22), June 30, 1965. The scale is 10 cm long.

per 400 cm² in the lower parts. These data reflect the variation in density commonly noted in the higher and lower levels of the *Fucus* zone. From top to bottom of the zone the plants were progressively larger and farther apart. Thus, at stations such as Port Nellie Juan (Station 14) and Port Etches, Hinchinbrook Island (Station 29), the density of postearthquake *Fucus* was inversely proportional to plant length.

*G Dallas Hanna*

FIGURE 14 Postearthquake fuci from various levels within the *Fucus* zone at Thumb Bay, Knight Island (Station 17), June 20, 1965. The scale is 10 cm long.

FIGURE 15   Dried holdfasts of fuci that were uplifted at the northern end of Hawkins Island at Deep Bay (Station 27), July 10, 1965. The scale is 15 cm long.

*G Dallas Hanna*

The paucity of postearthquake *Fucus* at MacLeod Harbor (Station 20) and Hanning Bay (Station 21) was striking. These sites, near the southern end of Montague Island, were elevated approximately 30 ft during the earthquake (Plafker, 1965) and were the only areas we visited where the intertidal zone was lifted completely above the range of the subsequently formed intertidal zone. These two stations were also the only ones seen where the rocky shores lacked the typical coating of young *Fucus*. Density counts showed 2 to 16 plants per 400 cm² in areas of moderate uplift. The area normally occupied by *Fucus* was for the most part covered by dense growths of *Porphyra* sp. in the upper part and *Ulva fenestrata* in the lower part (Table 6).

Reasons for this phenomenon may only be guessed at. The speculation that *Fucus* has always been sparse here must be cast aside, because the physical environment seems not to differ to any significant extent from that of other stations and because the remains of dead fuci from the pre-earthquake intertidal zone were very much in evidence and certainly as copious in numbers of specimens as in similar zones at other stations. Thus, one comes to the conclusion that no viable fucoid reproductive bodies were available because the earthquake had lifted all the *Fucus* in the vicinity above the reach of salt water. This conclusion can be neither proved nor disproved, but a few supporting words are in order.

The earthquake occurred on March 27, 1964. Much indirect evidence points to the possibility that at that time the gametes of *Fucus* in Prince William Sound were immature. A boreal region such as Prince William Sound would have a fruiting time of summer and autumn for many algae.

Setchell (1920) observed that the perennial fucoid *Ascophyllum nodosum* fruits in the summer on the western coast of Greenland (Upper Boreal Region) and that fruiting occurs earlier and earlier southward. In general, many of the algae I saw in Alaska during the summer of 1965 gave the impression of young and vigorous growth, a condition that usually precedes fertility. Probably none of the fuci at the southern end of Montague Island had reached sexual maturity at the time of the earthquake, and hence begat no progeny for the next year.

Another possibility to consider is that zygote settlement and subsequent germination are dependent on special requirements. Lodge (1948) observed that after the removal of all the larger limpets and fucoid algae from a strip of rock passing through the intertidal zone at the Isle of Man, England, the initial repopulation was by species of *Enteromorpha* and *Ulva*, *Fucus* reappearing in the second year. Perhaps an analogy may be drawn between her observations and the repopulation of the *Fucus* zone at MacLeod Harbor and Hanning Bay by *Porphyra*, some species of which have been found to be very rapidly growing early colonizers (Bokenham and Stephenson, 1938). The few *Fucus* plants that were present in June of 1965 may well have been the offspring of plants from nearby areas, such as Latouche Island where the uplift of 3 m (Plafker, 1965) was not great enough to cause the death of plants in the lower reaches of the *Fucus* zone. In June 1965, we found many fertile specimens of *Fucus* floating in the open waters of Prince William Sound—an indication of a ready current-borne supply of reproductive cells.

Even at the termination of our cruise in the middle of

July, I had seen no undoubted postearthquake specimens that were exuding eggs and sperm. Powell (1957b), who studied the ecology of *Fucus* in the British Isles, observed that *F. distichus* subsp. *anceps* typically has a 2- to 3-year life-span. He stated that fertile specimens of this subspecies were found from April to August. A strong possibility then exists that *Fucus* in Prince William Sound does not fruit until its second year, and this possibility may explain the lack of fertile specimens in littoral zones initiated after the earthquake.

The *Fucus* zone is the most conspicuous littoral algal zone in Prince William Sound. The upper limit of this zone of postearthquake 10- to 15-cm-long plants is quite distinct and abrupt at most places, but in some areas its upper edge is rimmed by a band of shorter specimens (less than 5 cm long) extending ½ to 2 vertical feet higher. The upper limit of the longer plants is considered to be the top of the main *Fucus* zone and in 74 percent of the measurements we made was between the 7.5- and 11-ft tidal level (Table 8). Discussions of the upper limit of the *Fucus* zone in the present report pertain to this main zone. The narrow band of small fuci comprising the border above the main *Fucus* zone will be referred to as the "*Fucus*-zone fringe." The lower limit of *Fucus* was indistinct; usually it extended to the vicinity of MLLW on shorelines facing southward and somewhat higher on north-facing shores. This limit agrees with the observations of Gail (1918) in the Puget Sound, Washington, region. His experiments (1919) showed that reduced light intensity, and perhaps decreasing pH and oxygen concentration, determines the lower limit of *Fucus* growth. However, in Prince William Sound the bottom of the *Fucus* zone was irregular and could not be used as an indicator of tidal level. As stated above, we found the upper limit of the main *Fucus* zone to be usually between the 7.5- and 11-ft tidal level (Figure 12), but local factors such as degree of slope, exposure to waves, and the availability of a suitable substratum could extend this limit to the 13.3-ft level, as at Anderson Bay, Hinchinbrook Island (transect 31), or lower it to the 4.5-ft level, as at Olsen Bay (transect 4a). In 46 measurements, the mean of the top of the main *Fucus* zone was at the 9.16-ft tidal level.

As also mentioned above, at many sites the upper limit of the main zone of *Fucus* was bordered above by a ½- to 2-ft zone of very small fuci. At Port Etches, Hinchinbrook Island (transect 29a), the fuci below the 9.8-ft tidal level were as long as 13 cm, whereas immediately above this level, plant length suddenly decreased to 5 cm or less. From the 9.8- to the 11.2-ft tidal level, plants gradually decreased in length from 5 cm to less than 1 cm.

It is necessary to make two assumptions based on evidence available from related algal studies to explore a possible explanation for the existence of the *Fucus*-zone fringe: First, the *Fucus* in question sheds fertilized eggs only during

TABLE 8  Levels of *Fucus* as Recorded May–July 1965 in Prince William Sound[a]

| Transect | Preearthquake Upper Level | Postearthquake Upper-Level *Fucus* Fringe | Main *Fucus* Zone Top | Bottom |
|---|---|---|---|---|
| 1 | – | – | +11.7 | +5.7 |
| 1a | +17.2 | – | +6.5 | +3.7 |
| 3 | +17.0 | – | +8.8 | – |
| 3 | +17.7 | – | +8.7 | +4.0 |
| 4 | +14.8 | +12.4 | +11.2 | +5.6 |
| 4a | +13.5 | – | +4.5 | +1.0 |
| 5 | – | – | +7.7 | +0.5 |
| 6 | – | – | +9.0 | +4.9 |
| 6a | – | – | +7.1 | +0.4 |
| 7 | – | +12.5 | +8.0 | – |
| 8 | +9.2 | – | +8.5 | ca. +2 |
| 9 | +15.2 | – | +9.0 | +5.4 |
| 10 | – | – | +9.5 | ca. +0.5 |
| 10a | – | – | +8.8 | +0.2 |
| 10b | – | – | +8.5 | – |
| 11 | – | +11.5 | +10.5 | +0.3 |
| 11b | – | – | +10.8 | –1.0 |
| 13a | +4.9 | – | +7.8 | – |
| 13b | +4.5 | – | ca. +7.5 | below –1.8 |
| 14 | – | +12.9 | +12.2 | +3.1 |
| 16 | +16.9 | – | +9.0 | +2.0 |
| 17 | +17.1 | +9.5 | +8.0 | +0.6 |
| 20 | +42.0 | – | +10.2 | – |
| 20a | +38.9 | – | +10.9 | – |
| 21 | +36.8 | – | +8.3 | ca. +1.5 |
| 22 | – | – | +6.4 | –2.0 |
| 23 | +17.6 | – | +10.6 | – |
| 24 | +18.7 | +7.2 | +5.8 | –0.2 |
| 25 | +16.5 | – | – | – |
| 27 | +18.5 | +10.0 | +9.5 | +3.2 |
| 28 | – | – | +10.0 | – |
| 29 | +15.9 | – | +8.5 | – |
| 29a | +16.5 | +11.2 | +9.8 | – |
| 30 | +16.7 | – | +11.1 | +3.1 |
| 31 | +21.5 | – | +13.3 | – |
| 32 | +15.1–16.7 | – | +9.8 | – |
| 32 | +15.1 | – | +10.0 | – |

[a]In feet above (+) or below (–) MLLW. See Table 2 for locality of transects.

spring tides, and second, young plants of *Fucus* are able to survive long periods of exposure to air in a growth-arrested condition.

It has been demonstrated that certain marine plants, as well as animals, have life functions, especially the maturation and release of reproductive cells, that are regularly synchronized with tidal cycles. Williams (1905) showed that sexual plants of the brown alga *Dictyota dichotoma* growing in the Menai Straits, near Bangor, Wales, consistently discharged mature gametes 3 to 5 tides after the highest spring tide of a series during its reproductive period from the end of June until November. Later, Hoyt (1927) showed that *D. dichotoma* from Naples also fruits at fortnightly intervals during each series of spring tides, whereas the same morphological species (Hoyt's *Dictyota dichotoma* var. *menstrualis*) from North Carolina fruits at monthly intervals only during spring tides of the full moon. He showed further that wherever the tides are regular, the release of eggs and sperm is almost simultaneous, mostly occurring on the same day or even in the same hour, usually near daybreak. He also found that the larger the tidal range, the more regular the fruiting period. The advantage to the species of having large numbers of eggs and sperm released into the water at or about the same time is obvious. Sporangial plants, living under similar conditions, show no periodicity in fruiting behavior. Hoyt (1927, p. 618) concludes "that the periodic production of sexual cells may be much more common than is realized."

Since Hoyt's time, other marine algae have been shown to reproduce in sequence with the tides, but as yet no specific causal agent has been discovered. In fact, the organisms studied often continue their periodic behavior even when transferred into the laboratory. *Ulva lobata* (Kütz.) Setchell & Gardner has been shown by Smith (1947) to release gametes regularly during the beginning of each spring tide sequence on the Monterey Peninsula, California. Hollenberg (1936) established that *Halicystis ovalis* (Lyngb.) Aresch. in the Monterey area usually produces gametes near the end of a series of spring tides. My own observations indicate a mass discharge of carpospores by the red alga *Iridaea agardhiana* (Setchell & Gardner) Kylin during the morning of the lowest tide of a spring tide sequence in August at Bodega Head, California.

Many of the factors that seem responsible for the demonstrated periodicity of fruiting of various marine algae hold also for the *Fucus* in Prince William Sound. Furthermore, the tidal amplitude is great, a condition that Hoyt (1927) claimed went hand in hand with regularity in fruiting.

Knight and Parke (1950) observed a "dense carpet of young plants" (p. 447) in the upper part of the *Fucus vesiculosus* zone on shores in England and theorized that, despite the enhancing effect of increased illumination on germination, desiccation restricts the growth of these plants. They believe that the action of the two factors—illumination and desiccation—maintains a dwarf population at the top level of the zone. Plants 2–3 cm long were observed to be in a state of "protracted juvenility" for 2 years, but when they were transported to a lower level, they rapidly elongated.

The mass release of millions of fertilized eggs during a spring tide allows the zygotes to be spread on the rock surface as the water recedes from the high-tide mark—perhaps the 13- or 14-ft level. During the next few high tides, the uppermost young plants grow more slowly than their lower counterparts, which are under water for longer periods of time. When the spring tides give way to the lower neap tides, the fringe plants may be continuously emergent for several days until the onset of the next series of spring tides. The *Fucus*-zone fringe at Port Etches extends from the 9.8- to the 11.2-ft tidal level and, as may be seen in Figure 3, the tides may not come this high for 2 days at a time.

In this discussion I have discounted wave action that may wet these plants occasionally. As mentioned previously, this factor is negligible in many of the more sheltered areas of the Sound. During the unfavorable time of neap tides, the young plants may survive because the rain and fog, so prevalent in Prince William Sound, retard the desiccating action of direct sunlight. Growth of plants in the *Fucus*-zone fringe will then commence again at the onset of the next series of spring tides, but soon the plants form a distinct horizontal band because of their small size. Thus, in Prince William Sound a *Fucus*-zone fringe, comprised of *Fucus* plants 5 cm long or less, forms a distinct belt at Stations 4, 7, 11, 14, 17, 24, 27, and 29—a belt comparable to that seen by Knight and Parke (1950) in England.

## GLOIOPELTIS

At many places in the upper part of the *Fucus* zone, and at some places extending above it, were dense or patchy growths of the small rhodophycean alga *Gloiopeltis furcata*. The structure and reproduction of this alga were worked out by Sjöstedt (1926) and Kylin (1930), on the basis of specimens from Friday Harbor, Washington. The thallus is terete, 1 to 2 times dichotomously branched, and seldom attains a length of more than 4 cm. The axes are composed of densely packed thick-walled cells that surround a large-celled axial filament. Reproduction is by monoecious sexual plants and tetrasporangial plants, both of which were present in Prince William Sound.

The zonational aspect of this genus in Japan was mentioned by Segawa and Nakamura (1952) and Yendo (1914). It characteristically occupies an area in the upper eulittoral zone and is able to withstand long periods of desiccation. The chemical and physical properties of the thick confluent walls of the cortical tissue doubtless contribute to this ability.

On the west coast of North America, *Gloiopeltis furcata* and *Endocladia muricata* (both in the Endocladiaceae) are common inhabitants of the upper eulittoral zone. *Gloiopeltis furcata* is more conspicuous north of British Columbia but extends southward to Baja California, whereas *E. muricata* supplants it in quantity in Washington (Muenscher, 1915; Rigg and Miller, 1949) and southward. *Endocladia muricata* was only rarely seen in Prince William Sound.

At numerous transect sites, *Gloiopeltis* and *Fucus* grew intermingled on the same rocks. At South Bay, Perry Island (transect 10b), *Gloiopeltis* flourished on the vertical sides of boulders, but *Fucus* was restricted to the boulder tops. The ability of *Gloiopeltis* sporelings to become established on substrata unsuitable for many other algae has been noted by Yendo (1914). He observed that this faculty is probably due to the crustaceous nature of the sporeling.

The vertical distributions of *Gloiopeltis furcata*, as established from measurements made in Prince William Sound, are presented in Table 9. The variation in extent and height of the subzones formed by this alga from station to station was somewhat surprising. Perhaps the species is a fairly sensitive indicator of local environmental conditions, or, conversely, perhaps it has a wide range of tolerance. The sensitivity of *Gloiopeltis* to uplift was dramatically demonstrated at the site of transect 6 on Goose Island, an area uplifted 4.8 ft (Plafker, 1969). On a near-vertical rocky cliff, three distinct zones of this alga were in evidence (June 5, 1965):

| Zones | Feet |
|---|---|
| White, dead plants | 12.7 to 14.2 |
| Mixture of dead and living plants | 12.3 to 12.7 |
| Living plants | 10.4 to 12.3 |

Inasmuch as the dead and living plants were all of about the same size, they may all represent preearthquake specimens.

TABLE 9   Tidal Levels at Which *Gloiopeltis furcata* Was Seen during May–July 1965[a]

| Transect | Comments | Uplift or Subsidence (Plafker, 1969) | Level Top | Bottom |
|---|---|---|---|---|
| 4a | | +3.6B | +9.5 | +2.9 |
| 5 | Sparse | +5.7B | +11.5 | +7.5 |
| 6 | | +4.8B | +12.7 | +10.4 |
| 7 | | +2.0B | +7.5 | – |
| 10a | Distinct zone | ca. +1.5 | +10.5 | +6 |
| 10a | Upper plants small; lower plants large | ca. +1.5 | +8.8 | +3.2 |
| 10b | Occurs on more vertical slopes than *Fucus* | ca. +1.5 | +9.4 | +5 |
| 11 | Patchy growths | +0.1F | +8 | +7 |
| 11a | | +0.1F | +13 | +7 |
| 14 | Very scattered | –0.4B | +7.5 | +4.5 |
| 22 | Very sparse | +8.7B | +6.5 | – |
| 25 | Dying cystocarpic plants | +3.6B | +8.3 | – |
| 31 | | +3.8B | +16.8 | +14 |
| 32 | Beach of small boulders | +4.2B | +10 | +7 |
| 32a | | +4.2B | +11.6 | +6 |
| 32a | Dead and dying | +4.2B | +13 | +12 |

[a]In feet above (+) or below (–) MLLW. See Table 2 for locality of transects and explanation of symbols.

The uplift of nearly 5 ft elevated all the plants in the upper 1.5 ft of the zone beyond their limit of endurance, whereas only some of the plants between 12.3 and 12.7 ft succumbed. The plants in the lower part of the zone were elevated above the tidal level previously occupied by *Gloiopeltis*, but they survived, perhaps because they were beyond their sensitive young stages. In June 1965, 15 months after the earthquake, there was no evidence of new growths of *Gloiopeltis* below the well-developed plants then present. This absence is not surprising, because species of algae living high in the littoral zone are generally slow growers (Baker, 1909). For example, 2 years after denuding experiments on high intertidal rocks on the Monterey Peninsula in all seasons, Northcraft (1948) found no renewal of *Endocladia muricata*, a species very close to *G. furcata* in habitat, structure, and phylogenetic position, in spite of the fact that it was plentiful prior to denudation. For unknown reasons, however, this contrasts sharply with other experiments by Glynn (1965) who found that in 6 months new growth of *E. muricata* exceeded the initially harvested crop by 35 percent on a weight basis. Most of the *Gloiopeltis* seen in Prince William Sound appeared to be of preearthquake origin, but this can be said with certainty only of obviously uplifted or dead plants.

Uplifted and dead *Gloiopeltis furcata* was also reported by Kaburaki (1928) to be present after the Kwanto earthquake in Japan in 1923.

## PORPHYRA

Various species of the red alga *Porphyra* usually occurred scattered among other algae in the eulittoral and sublittoral zones, except at MacLeod Harbor and Hanning Bay, Montague Island. At these two highly elevated stations (20 and 21, respectively), densely populated and clearly delimited subzones of *Porphyra* occurred at levels ordinarily occupied by *Fucus*. Although no evidence is available, the rocks in the new littoral zone may have become covered by *Porphyra* in the summer of 1964 after an initial growth of diatoms and filamentous green algae, such as occurred on the settling surfaces at Shepard Point. At any rate, *P. perforata, P. tenuissima,* and *P. laciniata* had formed a dense subzone from +8.0 to +3.9 ft at MacLeod Harbor and from +8.9 to +1.3 ft at Hanning Bay when we visited the locality at the end of June 1965. As stated above, these levels are ordinarily dominated by *Fucus*; but at these two stations only scattered plants of this brown alga were present.

## GREEN ALGAE

At most transect sites the presence of large numbers of green algae lent a green aspect to the lower part of the eulittoral zone. The brown alga *Fucus*, which usually dominates the upper parts of the eulittoral, was often replaced in dominance lower in the zone by species of green algae, including *Ulva*, *Monostroma*, *Spongomorpha*, and *Enteromorpha* (Table 10). In addition, if a plentiful supply of moisture was available, it was not unusual to find *Blidingia*

TABLE 10  Levels at Which *Monostroma*, *Ulva*, *Enteromorpha*, and *Blidingia* Formed Subzones

| Transect[a] | Taxa | Level[b] Top | Level[b] Bottom |
|---|---|---|---|
| 1 | —[c] | +7 | +6 |
| 1a | — | +6.5 | +3.7 |
| 1a | *Enteromorpha linza* | +3 | 0 |
| 2 | — | +10.5 | +10.0 |
| 3 | *Enteromorpha* sp. | +4.7 | — |
| 3 | *Enteromorpha* sp. | +13 | +11 |
| 4 | *Monostroma* sp. overgrown by mussels | +1 | −1 |
| 4 | *Enteromorpha* sp. | +11.5 | — |
| 4 | *Enteromorpha* sp. | +6.8 | +3.0 |
| 4a | *Monostroma grevillei* var. *grevillei* | +4.5 | −1.9 |
| 4a | *Enteromorpha* sp. | 0 | — |
| 5 | *Blidingia minima* var. *minima* | +11.3 | +10.2 |
| —[d] | *Monostroma oxyspermum* | +3.2 | — |
| 6 | — | +7.2 | — |
| 6 | *Blidingia minima* var. *ramifera* | +7.7 | — |
| 9 | *Enteromorpha* sp. or *Blidingia* sp. | +11.4 | — |
| 9 | *Monostroma* sp. | +7 | — |
| 10 | *Blidingia minima* var. *minima* | +10 | — |
| 10 | *Monostroma areolatum* | +9 | +3 |
| 10b | *Ulva fenestrata* and *Monostroma* sp. | 0 | — |
| 11 | — | +3.8 | — |
| 11a | — | +6 | — |
| 11b | — | +2.0 | — |
| 13a | — | −1.0 | — |
| 14 | — | +3.1 | — |
| 16 | *Enteromorpha linza* | +2 | +1 |
| 16 | — | +2.8 | −1.5 |
| 17 | *Enteromorpha* sp. bearing mussels | +4 | 0 |
| 17 | *Enteromorpha intestinalis* in draws | +20 | +15 |
| 17 | — | +3.0 | — |
| 20a | *Ulva fenestrata* | +4.2 | — |
| 20a | *Blidingia minima* var. *minima* | +12.5 | — |
| 21a | Irregular zone | +10 | 9 |
| 21 | *Monostroma* sp. | +1 | — |
| 22 | *Monostroma fuscum* var. *fuscum* | −1.0 | −2.0 |
| 24 | *Monostroma grevillei* var. *lubricum* on the tops of boulders | +5 | +2 |
| 24 | *Blidingia minima* var. *minima* on the sides of boulders | +6 | +4 |
| 25 | — | +10.0 | — |
| 27 | — | +11.6 | — |

[a]See Table 2 for locality of transects.
[b]In feet above (+) or below (−) MLLW.
[c]Taxa observed but unidentified.
[d]Two Moon Bay, Port Fidalgo (no transect).

*minima* var. *minima* in the upper reaches of the eulittoral zone and *Enteromorpha intestinalis* in the littoral fringe. As many phycologists (e.g., Brown, 1915) have noted, the principal requirement of *E. intestinalis* seems to be moisture, regardless of whether it is fresh water or salt water. At Thumb Bay, Knight Island (transect 17), *E. intestinalis* grew in draws 15 to 20 ft above MLLW and was continually kept moist by freshwater seepage.

Many of the dense zones that were formed by green algae were clearly delimited, with at least the upper boundary forming a distinct horizontal line. However, the fact that these boundaries varied significantly at the different localities lent support to the supposition that local factors and local genetic races interact in determining upper levels of tolerance. Furthermore, the number of genera and species forming these green subzones was considerable. Each taxon and race probably interacts in its own characteristic way with environmental factors associated with the tides.

At Zaikof Bay, Montague Island (Station 24), dense growths of *Monostroma grevillei* var. *lubricum* were on the sides of boulders at the 4- to 5-ft tidal level. At transect 20a, which was made at MacLeod Harbor, Montague Island, *Blidingia minima* var. *minima* formed an irregular subzone immediately above the *Porphyra* subzone; it was therefore the highest living macroalga at this station except for *Prasiola*. The upper part of this *Blidingia* subzone merged into the brown scum subzone at the 12.5-ft level.

At this same transect, *Ulva fenestrata* formed a subzone in the lower eulittoral from 2 to 4.3 ft above MLLW. At Two Moon Bay, 35 mi northwest of Cordova, large specimens of *Monostroma oxyspermum* formed a dense subzone on a gravel slope in brackish water. The uppermost limit of this subzone was at the 3.2-ft level.

The most common algae occurring on mud were species of *Enteromorpha* and occasionally *Rhizoclonium*. The Cordova mud flats, which formerly were regularly covered by water, were rarely, if ever, covered in 1965, but patches of *E. ramulosa*(?), *E. prolifera*, *E. compressa*, and *R. tortuosum* occurred there and appeared to be healthy.

The green algae considered herein are seasonal and have therefore developed since the earthquake. Evidence that green algae had died as a result of the uplift was present only in the dried algal masses observed at MacLeod Harbor and in what appeared to be dead *Enteromorpha* among the dead *Fucus* at Green Island (Station 23). Large amounts of dead green algae were seen by Hanna (1964, and this volume) when he viewed the former littoral zone on Montague Island 3 months after the earthquake.

The main species of *Spongomorpha* forming subzones were *S. arcta* and *S. coalita*. As was true of the above-named membranous green algae, zones of *Spongomorpha* at times were well defined and dense, but their occurrence and elevation varied considerably at the different stations.

Young mussels, discussed in Haven's report (1971, this volume), grew at some stations (e.g., Station 4, Olsen Bay) in great profusion on *Monostroma* and *Spongomorpha*.

At South Bay, Perry Island (Station 10), and MacLeod Harbor, Montague Island (Station 20), the green alga *Prasiola borealis*, infected with the perithecial fungus *Guignardia alaskana* Reed, occurred above and within the upper reaches of *Verrucaria*. It was also seen at Two Moon Bay, Port Fidalgo. Despite the 30-ft uplift at MacLeod Harbor, *P. borealis* there appeared no different from that observed at South Bay and at Two Moon Bay. The effects of 15 months beyond the reaches of seawater had not altered its aspect in the least. The question arises of whether *P. borealis* is a marine alga. Even in nonelevated areas the species is immersed in seawater very rarely, if at all. Table 11 shows that *P. borealis* probably occurs at or above HHHW under normal circumstances. Highest higher high water in 1965 in Prince William Sound was 15.3 ft above MLLW.

## RHODYMENIA

The widely distributed rhodophycean alga *Rhodymenia palmata* was a conspicuous member of the algal flora at 12 of the 33 stations visited. The species is quite variable in form; attempts to distinguish between the formae purported to exist in Alaska (Setchell and Gardner, 1903, p. 314–316) were unsuccessful.

Scattered specimens of the perforate *Rhodymenia pertusa* occurred at Hanning Bay, Montague Island (near transect 21a), and English Bay, Port Etches, Hinchinbrook Island (Station 30). They were growing among the holdfasts of *Laminaria groenlandica* below the −2-ft tidal level. At some places, *R. palmata* formed dense belts slightly above MLLW,

TABLE 11    Levels of *Prasiola*, in Feet above (+) or below (−) MLLW

| Station | Lower Level of *P. borealis*, 1965 | Elevational Correction (Approximate, Plafker, 1969) | Preearthquake Level of *P. borealis* (Approximate) |
|---|---|---|---|
| Two Moon Bay, Port Fidalgo | +16.2 | − | − |
| South Bay, Perry Island | +17.0 | −1.5 | +15.5 |
| MacLeod Harbor, Montague Island | +45.3 | −30.0 | +15.3 |

growing most profusely on the tops rather than the sides of boulders (Figure 16). In those places where an *Alaria* subzone was present, the *Rhodymenia* extended one vertical foot or less above the kelp. This zone was obviously the same as that referred to by Setchell and Gardner (1903, p. 315), who mentioned the fact that *R. palmata* f. *mollis* often forms a zone at the low-water mark.

Table 12 indicates the tidal levels of the zone dominated by *Rhodymenia palmata*. The denser, more luxuriant growths of this red alga seemed to occur on the more wave-exposed faces of rocks and boulders (Figure 16). However, Southward and Orton (1954) noted no differences in abundance and zone width between *R. palmata* on wave-exposed and sheltered sides of a breakwater in England. A gradual increase in plant size from the top to the bottom of the zone, as is also true of *Fucus*, was clearly evident on smoothly sloping cliffs, such as at Port Etches, Hinchinbrook Island (Station 29). In the newly populated littoral zone at

*G Dallas Hanna*

FIGURE 16    A *Rhodymenia palmata* subzone at English Bay, Port Etches, Hinchinbrook Island (Station 30), July 13, 1965. A 15-cm ruler is near the center of the photograph.

TABLE 12   Levels of *Rhodymenia palmata* as Recorded May–July 1965

| Transect[a] | Remarks | Level[b] Top | Bottom |
|---|---|---|---|
| 1a | – | ca. +1.5 | – |
| 4 | – | ca. +1.0 | ca.  0.0 |
| 6 | Discolored | +3.9 | +1.1 |
| 6a | Discolored | –1.0 | – |
| 7 | Discolored | +3.6 | – |
| 20 | – | +2.0 | 0.0 |
| 20a | Not discolored | ca. +2.0 | – |
| 21 | – | ca. +1.2 | 0.0 |
| 21a | – | ca. +2.0 | – |
| 23 | Discolored | – | – |
| 27 | – | +5.7 | – |
| 29 | Healthy and dense | +6.6 | – |
| 29a | Slightly discolored | +6.7 | – |
| 30 | Some covered with young mussels | +4.6 | +1.8 |
| 31 | Discolored | ca. +3.0 | – |

[a] See Table 2 for locality of transects.
[b] In feet above (+) or below (–) MLLW.

MacLeod Harbor, Montague Island (Station 20), *R. palmata* formed one of a complex of narrow but dense zones, each dominated by one species of alga. From the bottom to the top, these vertical bands of algae were *Alaria* sp., *R. palmata*, *Spongomorpha coalita*, and *Porphyra* sp. (Figure 17).

At a number of stations (e.g., 6, 7, 23, and 31), the *Rhodymenia* plants (Figure 18) were not of the healthy, rich magenta color usually seen but rather, entirely or in part, a yellowish to greenish hue. This color may have been caused by the increased elevation of the former littoral zone or by a period of unusually low temperatures that occurred during the winter of 1964–1965 or by a combination of the two factors. The relatively narrow belts just above MLLW seem to imply a narrow range of tolerance to environmental factors regulated by the tides.

At Hanning Bay, Montague Island (transect 21a), *Rhodymenia palmata* formed the principal substratum for beds of young mussels.

## *POLYSIPHONIA* AND *PTEROSIPHONIA*

*Polysiphonia urceolata* and *Pterosiphonia bipinnata* sometimes occurred in sufficient density to constitute an indistinct and irregular subzone in the lower part of the eulittoral zone. The upper and lower boundaries of such a rhodomelacean subzone were rarely clearly delimited or consistent even in a limited area. Many of the growths of *P. urceolata* and *P. bipinnata* formed rust-colored patches among the green algae occupying the lower part of the eulittoral zone such as those that occurred at Thumb Bay, Knight Island (see Table 5). *Pterosiphonia bipinnata* was abundant in the newly developed littoral zone at MacLeod Harbor, Montague Island (transect 20a); specimens up to 38 cm long were present.

Other unidentified species of *Polysiphonia* occurred in the upper part of the eulittoral zone; for example, patches occurred at 13 to 14 ft at transect 1, Shipyard Bay, and just above 11 ft at transect 9, Bass Harbor, Naked Island.

## LAMINARIALES

Living Laminariales were present at many transect sites, and evidence of uplifted dead kelps persisted at Stations 20, 21, and 30. The kelps noted belong to six genera: *Nereocystis*, *Laminaria*, *Alaria*, *Agarum*, *Cymathere*, and *Costaria*. Spe-

FIGURE 17   Dense subzones of *Porphyra* sp. (P), *Spongomorpha coalita* (S), and *Rhodymenia palmata* (R) in the new littoral zone at MacLeod Harbor (Station 20), June 26, 1965. Note the dead lithothamnia in the upper left.

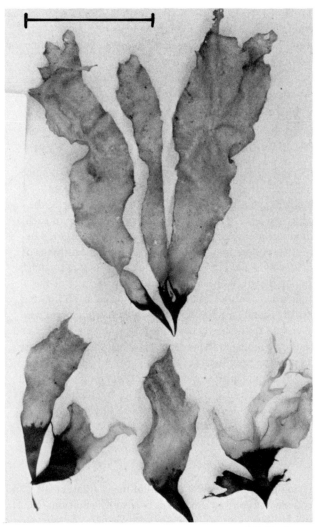

G Dallas Hanna

FIGURE 18   Bleached *Rhodymenia palmata* from Stockdale Harbor, Montague Island (Station 22), June 30, 1965. Note the dark un-bleached areas near the plant bases. The scale is 10 cm long.

cies of the first three genera at places formed distinct zones.

Extensive subtidal beds of *Nereocystis luetkeana* were present at MacLeod Harbor (Station 20), Hanning Bay (Station 21), and English Bay (Station 30). The holdfasts of those at MacLeod Harbor were attached at depths of from 10 to 40 ft below MLLW. Inside the harbor, in June, a distinct band of plants with small pneumatocysts was present along the north shore, and a group of plants with large pneumatocysts was present in the more wave-exposed water areas outside the harbor. Inasmuch as blades of *Nereocystis* ordinarily become sporogenous in summer (Rigg, 1917), the young sporophytes that were fringing the deeper edge of the zone in March 1964 must have survived the 30-ft uplift to produce spores in the summer of 1964.

Of the three species of *Laminaria* collected during our Alaska earthquake investigation (*L. yezoensis*, *L. groenlandica*, *L. saccharina*), *L. yezoensis* is easily recognized by its discoid holdfast, which at some places seemingly gives rise to several plants but usually lacks any evidence of haptera. The blades of old plants were more or less laciniate and smooth. Some forms of *L. groenlandica* superficially resemble *L. yezoensis* but are readily distinguished from it by the fact that they form haptera. The specimens of *L. groenlandica* were more or less bullate with blades entire or split from their apices one to several times. Several specimens were seen that exhibited longitudinal ribbing reminiscent of *Costaria costata*. *Laminaria saccharina* could be recognized by its longer, narrower blade, short stipe, and conelike holdfast composed of long, thin, branched haptera. This species is usually tan to yellow in color, as compared to the rich mahogany brown of the other species of *Laminaria*.

The upper sublittoral kelp flora, when present, was characteristically dominated by either *Laminaria groenlandica* or *L. saccharina*. The first species occurred on more open shorelines, at places forming dense stands resembling the *L.*

TABLE 13   Upper Levels Recorded for Living *Alaria* and *Laminaria* Subzones, in Feet above (+) or below (–) MLLW

| Transect | | | Laminaria | |
|---|---|---|---|---|
| No. | Location | Alaria | Small Plants | Large Plants |
| 1a | Shipyard Bay | +1.0 | – | –1.5 |
| 2 | Orca Cannery | – | – | –3.1 |
| 4 | Olsen Bay | – | – | –1.9 |
| 4a | Olsen Bay | – | – | –3.1 |
| 6a | Goose Island | –0.6 | – | – |
| 10 | South Bay, Perry Island | – | – | –2.2 |
| 11 | West Twin Bay, Perry Island | – | – | –2.2 |
| 17 | Thumb Bay, Knight Island | – | – | –2.5 |
| 20a | MacLeod Harbor, Montague Island | +2.7 | –1.0 | –2.2 |
| 21 | Hanning Bay, Montague Island | – | 0.0 | –2.0 |
| 21 | Hanning Bay | +1.5 | –1.0 | –1.5 |
| 22 | Stockdale Harbor, Montague Island | – | – | –2.0 |
| 23 | Green Island | – | +0.4 | –1.4 |
| 24 | Zaikof Bay, Montague Island | – | – | –2.8 |
| 29 | Port Etches | 0.0 | – | –1.0 |
| 30 | English Bay, Hinchinbrook Island | +2.8 | – | –0.2 |
| 31 | Anderson Bay | – | – | –0.2 |
| 32 | Whiskey Cove | – | +0.2 | –1.2 |
| 33 | Spike Island | ca. +3.5 | – | – |

: eastern Pacific
1 more protected
rkable tolerances
. specimens of *L.*
a freshwater stream
24). This species
produced by *L.*
*ezoensis* did, how-
ocky shores.
*landica* formed
smaller than the
ems to prevail
vas clearly demon-
th-old upper sub-
Hanning Bay region
23). This type of
eply sloping rocks
n beaches where
avel and small
become established
ne. The result was
rked by large plants
. At sheltered sites,
ough growing on
. *groenlandica*

dredged from 6 fathoms at Goose Island (Station 6) was
nearly 3 m long, yet was attached to a pebble only 6 cm in
diameter.

The upper limit of the main *Laminaria* zone (exclusive
of the small fringing plants) generally occurred between 1
and 3 ft below MLLW (Table 13). The lower edge of the
*Laminaria* zone could not be discerned (see the discussion
of the uplifted southern end of Montague Island earlier in

this report). Laminarias are therefore rarely exposed to air,
those at the –2-ft level being continually submerged, even
throughout the spring tides, unless exposed by the backwash
of waves (see also Figure 3). As with the fuci in the *Fucus*
zone fringe, small laminarias growing above the –2-ft level
will, in all probability, never reach maturity.

Evidence of kelps that perished after the uplift was seen
at Stations 20, 21, and 30; the most striking display still
present 15 months later was at MacLeod Harbor and Hanning Bay. All that remained of the laminarias that were
lifted above the postearthquake intertidal zone were dried
holdfasts, some with the stipes still attached (Figure 19).
The holdfasts were very loosely attached to the rock, coming free at a touch. At MacLeod Harbor the upper limit of
the dead plants formed a fairly distinct line 27 ft above
present MLLW. The holdfasts in the upper 2 to 4 ft of this
zone were smaller than the lower ones, and some of the
stipeless ones may represent the remains of *Alaria*, plants
not forming such robust "woody" holdfasts and stipes as
those of *Laminaria* and *Nereocystis. Alaria* grew profusely
in the lower parts of the new littoral zone and in the upper
reaches of the sublittoral zone at MacLeod Harbor and
Hanning Bay. At MacLeod Harbor some large dead holdfasts just above the present high-tide mark (15–20 ft above
MLLW) were doubtless the remains of *Nereocystis* (Figure
20). These holdfasts would have been at a depth of approximately 10 to 15 ft below MLLW prior to the earthquake.
None of the *Laminaria* holdfasts appeared to be of the
*L. saccharina* type, nor were specimens of this species seen
in the areas of transects 20 and 20a.

Epiphyte-covered bladeless laminarias that died as a result of the uplift were also present at the –1- to +1-ft tidal
level at English Bay, Port Etches, Hinchinbrook Island

FIGURE 19 Dead uplifted kelps at
MacLeod Harbor (Station 20), June 26,
1965. The scale is 30 cm long.

FIGURE 20   An uplifted holdfast, probably of *Nereocystis,* at MacLeod Harbor (Station 20), June 26, 1965. The scale is 10 cm long.

FIGURE 21   Stipes of uplifted laminarias (one indicated by arrow) projecting above the postearthquake alarias at English Bay, Port Etches, Hinchinbrook Island (Station 30), July 13, 1965.

(Station 30; see Figure 21). The uplift of 7.1 ft at this site (Plafker, 1969), indicated that the *Laminaria* stipes represent remains of plants formerly living 6 to 8 ft below MLLW. Apparently, the plants died slowly, following periods of emergence that were longer than their tolerance limits. They still were firmly attached, and specimens had to be cut loose. *Porphyra* sp., *Pterosiphonia bipinnata, Rhizoclonium* sp., *Monostroma* sp., and *Spongomorpha* sp. grew on them in dense profusion.

## CORALLINE ALGAE

Coralline red algae form extensive growths along shores in many parts of the world. Most coralline algae require nearly continuous submergence and are, therefore, restricted to permanent tide pools or the sublittoral zone, where they sometimes occur at the lower limits of submarine algal growth. In temperate and boreal regions, coralline algae form dense understories in the kelp forests. The large area of rocks once covered by living corallines, especially the encrusting forms, is indicated by the extensive, greatly uplifted former sublittoral areas of Montague Island. In these areas the kelps have dried and shriveled, revealing the stark white-coated rocks (Figure 8).

Articulated and crustose corallines are well represented in Prince William Sound. The latter form thin ($150 \mu$) to thick (2 cm) crusts on rocks, molluscan shells, and other marine vegetation. These crusts may be smooth, as in *Clathromorphum circumscriptum* (Figure 22), or warty, as in *Lithothamnium* sp. The articulated species (see Johansen, 1969) grow from crustose bases and consist of calcified segments (intergenicula) 1–4 mm long and 1–3 mm broad, which are connected by noncalcified nodes (genicula). The erect parts are pinnately or irregularly branched and in Alaska usually grow no taller than 13 cm.

Living plants are deep pink to purple. On exposure to air

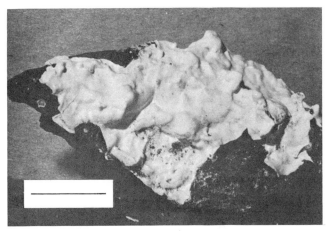

*G Dallas Hanna*

FIGURE 22   A bleached specimen of *Clathromorphum circumscriptum* from the uplifted sublittoral zone at MacLeod Harbor (Station 20), June 26, 1965. The scale is 2 cm long.

for a sufficient period of time, the plants die and bleach to pure white. The effect of emersion on crustose corallines was strikingly exemplified in certain permanent tide pools at English Bay, Port Etches, Hinchinbrook Island (Station 30), where the earthquake-altered topography caused a lowering of the water level in a tide pool. The new water level was marked by the corallines as if a water line had been painted on the rock. The calcareous coating below the water level was pink, and that above, white.

The greater part of the crusts lifted by the earthquake and bleached at MacLeod Harbor and Hanning Bay consisted of *Clathromorphum circumscriptum* (Figure 22) and *Lithothamnium* sp. Patches of *Lithothamnium* covered uplifted rock surfaces to the extent of about 50 cm$^2$. Hanging from the rocks in clusters were bunches of whitened *Bossiella orbigniana* ssp. *dichotoma* (Figure 23), *Corallina frondescens*, and *Corallina vancouveriensis*, the latter two species sometimes overgrown by *Neopolyporolithon reclinatum*. At some places, the articulated coralline algae were interspersed with jointed bryozoans.

At MacLeod Harbor the bleached coralline zone extended to 32 ft above MLLW, a level that would have been approximately +2 ft before the earthquake. The lower edge of the zone faded out in the upper reaches of the present intertidal zone where periodic wetting and new growths of seaweed were eroding the dead corallines away.

Living crustose corallines occurred sparsely among the kelp holdfasts below the −1-ft level at MacLeod Harbor. All specimens examined appeared thin and sterile, and they covered areas no greater than 4 cm$^2$. These small specimens might have been supposed to be of postearthquake origin, but there is no proof of this; living specimens are often

FIGURE 23   Bleached uplifted specimens of *Bossiella* sp. on a vertical rock face at MacLeod Harbor (Station 20), June 26, 1965. The scale is 5 cm long.

found deeper than 5 fathoms, and some were dredged from a depth of about 20 fathoms at South Bay, Perry Island (Station 10).

Coralline algae raised above their level of tolerance were also seen by Tarr and Martin (1912) after the Yakutat Bay earthquake of 1899. The "bryozoans" on uplifted rocks mentioned by them (p. 23) as forming a "broad horizontal band of whitewashed rock" and illustrated in their plate VI (p. 18) clearly were mostly the bleached remains of coralline algae. Their description of "a pink bryozoan that normally grows in permanent tide pools and below the low-tide mark" obviously referred to members of the Corallinaceae. After the earthquake of 1899, the white calcareous plants formed such a conspicuous belt where the change in elevation had exposed 30 to 40 vertical feet of the sea bottom that the natives, when they first saw it during the seal-hunting season of 1900, related it to the earthquake of the previous autumn. According to Tarr and Martin, the white belt extended for miles and was, in many places, 10 or more feet wide, at some places being more or less obscured by new growths of land plants.

*ZOSTERA*

The only marine phanerogam seen in Prince William Sound was *Zostera marina*. Living or dead specimens of this grass were obtained at 10 stations (Figure 24).

*Zostera marina* is able to grow in areas of thick mud or in a mixture of gravel and mud. Virtually every muddy area visited contained *Zostera*; its euryhaline nature was well demonstrated at Olsen Bay (Station 4) where it was kept moist by a freshwater stream at the unusually high level of 5 ft. The fact that the elevation increase here due to the earthquake was 3.6 ft (Plafker, 1969) indicates that this growth of *Zostera* had existed below MLLW prior to the earthquake—a level below which *Z. marina* normally lives. The short narrow leaves of the Olsen Bay plants show that the environment was not ideally suited to their requirements (see Phillips and Grant, 1965). The eurythermal characteristics and cosmopolitan distribution of *Z. marina* have been described by Setchell (1929).

Although no measurements were made, a gradation in leaf length and breadth in relation to tidal level in *Zostera*, occurring in its normal habitat, was strikingly evident at Olsen Bay. The leaves of the uppermost plants (upper limit of occurrence at the −0.3-ft tidal level) were considerably shorter and narrower than those of the deeper plants. In most areas where healthy *Zostera* was found, its uppermost limit occurred just below the 0.0-ft tidal level.

Dead *Zostera* of preearthquake origin was seen at stations 1, 4–6, 21–24, and 32. In most instances this *Zostera* consisted of mats of dead rhizomes with no evidence of dead leaves. In some areas of moderate uplift (e.g., Ship-

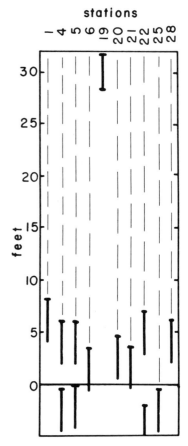

FIGURE 24 The levels of preearthquake and postearthquake *Zostera* at the 10 stations where they were measured. The plants above the 0.0-ft tidal level are dead preearthquake specimens; those below 0.0 ft are living.

yard Bay, Station 1), the rhizomes formed a favorable substratum for *Ulothrix pseudoflacca* and *Pilayella littoralis*. In the greatly uplifted Hanning Bay area (Station 21), dead *Zostera* leaves carpeted the former sea bottom, giving the appearance of mowed hay. Decay of the leaves was retarded there apparently because the tides did not reach them.

The uppermost levels of uplifted *Zostera* in relation to the present 0.0-ft tidal level are given in Figure 24. In some areas the great distance from the water to the plant remains made measurement difficult, and the data cannot therefore be given full credence.

SETTLING-SURFACE STUDY

In an effort to learn something about primary colonizers in the area of the earthquake, plastic settling surfaces were attached in the littoral and upper sublittoral zones at

Shepard Point, near Cordova. These surfaces were left in place 45 days.

To each of two 3.68-m (12-ft) lines were fastened eight plastic strips 20 by 4 cm and four strips 30 by 4 cm. These were attached 8 cm apart to a nylon cord. One surface of each strip was roughened with sandpaper. Similar plastic strips (but unsanded) placed in the ocean off Bodega Head, California, have been shown to serve as excellent substrata for many marine animals as well as a diverse array of seaweeds, including kelps. The lines were weighted and attached to pilings that leaned slightly and thus allowed the lines to hang freely. The relationship of the lines to tidal levels is shown in Figure 25. The lines were hung May 31, 1965, and recovered July 15, 1965; the strips were preserved whole in a solution of 5 percent formalin–seawater.

Aside from bacteria and diatoms, only green algae had settled on the Shepard Point strips after 45 days of exposure. Northcraft (1948), in an extensive study of denudation at Monterey, California, found that species of *Enteromorpha, Ulva,* and *Porphyra* were the prominent macroalgae in his group 1—the "rapidly growing, transiently-appearing group" (p. 397). These algae were evident 2 months after denudation and usually persisted anywhere from 3 weeks to 6 months. Northcraft also observed that green and brown algae tended to appear on his denuded rock surfaces before red algae (except *Porphyra*), and he theorized that spore motility was a factor in determining initial settlement; the spores of green and brown algae are flagellated and motile, whereas those of red algae are not. Rapidly growing seaweeds such as *Ectocarpus* sp. were found to be the primary macroalgal colonizers in southern California (Wilson, 1925).

The more conspicuous green and brown algae occurring on the rocks of Shepard Point were:

| Green Algae | Brown Algae |
|---|---|
| *Monostroma* sp. | *Melanosiphon intestinalis* |
| *Ulva fenestrata* | *Fucus distichus* |
| *Spongomorpha arcta* | *Pilayella littoralis* |
| *Enteromorpha linza* | |

Perhaps the lack of brown algae on the settling surfaces was due merely to the paucity of this group in the area. The spores necessary to effect establishment were produced by the green algae in the vicinity rather than by *Pilayella littoralis* or *Melanosiphon intestinalis* or other brown algae. The lack of *Fucus* on the strips may be explained by the need of this genus for moist crevices in which the relatively large nonmotile zygotes may lodge. As far as could be discerned, no laminarians were present within 100 yards of the test site.

For several reasons the identification of some of the settled algae could not be made with any great degree of certainty. The detailed structure and behavior of the reproductive organs, something that must be observed in living plants, is needed, in many instances, to make determination possible. The question mark in the following list of algae that had settled on the plastic strips denotes uncertainty of identification.

*Ulothrix implexa*
*Ulothrix flacca*
*Ulothrix pseudoflacca*
*Urospora penicilliformis*
*Enteromorpha groenlandica* (?)
*Enteromorpha* sp.
*Cladophora* or *Spongomorpha* sp.
*Schizonema* sp.
*Melosira* sp.
Unidentified colonial pennate diatoms attached side to side, forming bands many microns long

Figure 25 shows the distributions of the most abundant algae on the strips. Workers such as Northcraft (1948) have shown that algal swarmers settle both above and below the normal range of the parent species and that plants developing outside this range later tend to disappear. Thus, zonation is vague at the time of colonization, the critical zonational factors being most effective at some later time.

The algae recovered from the Shepard Point settling surfaces seem to belong to a transient group in the sense of Northcraft's group 1 (1948). The zones occupied by these filamentous greens and diatoms on the strips were at levels

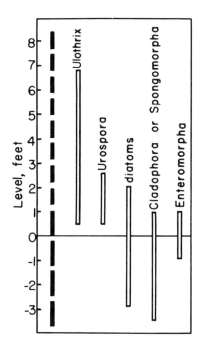

FIGURE 25  Diagram of one of the settling lines (left) and the tidal levels of the main algae occurring on both lines after 45 days in the ocean.

that were occupied by more permanent, robust algae on nearby rocks. If the strips had been left in place several more months, perennial algae, comparable to those belonging to Northcraft's groups 2 and 3, probably would have dominated the strips.

In essence, growth on the strips has shown that diatoms and filamentous green algae probably were the first algal colonizers of barren surfaces depressed or uplifted into the littoral and upper sublittoral zones by the earthquake.

Yendo (1914) noted that when twigs are planted in the ocean as a substratum for *Porphyra* in Japan, they first become coated with diatoms, then by *Ulothrix, Lyngbya,* or other microscopic filamentous algae, and that not until this occurs will *Porphyra* spores become attached. Very possibly, an analogous sequence of colonization took place on the rocks forming the newly established littoral zone at the southern end of Montague Island in the spring and summer of 1964.

The settling surfaces were remarkably devoid of animals, only molluscan egg masses and one young *Musculus* sp. being present, a sequence consistent with that found by workers who stated that algae precede animals in occupying new or denuded intertidal surfaces.

## SUGGESTIONS FOR FOLLOW-UP STUDIES ON THE ALGAE

Surveys of the algae in subsequent years at the same or different stations might give some indication of the sequence of algal repopulation. Most investigators (e.g., Bokenham and Stephenson, 1938; Northcraft, 1948) of algal succession in denuded littoral areas have observed that climax communities are reestablished within 1 to 3 years after denudation. Observations of the algal zones at the extensively uplifted MacLeod Harbor and Hanning Bay areas in 1969 and perhaps the following year or two would be rewarding, especially observation of the formation of the *Fucus* zone and the perseverance of *Prasiola borealis*.

In short, the value of follow-up investigations on the algae as they are related to the 1964 earthquake will decrease with time. Perhaps studies of a nature different from those reported herein could profitably be made (e.g., experimental growth of some of the zone-forming algae under controlled conditions or detailed quantitative sampling).

## SUMMARY

The zonal distribution and other ecological facets of the benthic marine algae in Prince William Sound as related to the earthquake of March 27, 1964, have been presented. Lit-

toral zones at the 33 stations established during May to July 1965 were either relatively unaltered in elevation, had subsided, were partly elevated above the preearthquake littoral zone, or were elevated above the reaches of subsequent tides. The marine plants present at these stations responded to the resultant change in environment by dying or surviving, apparently in accordance with the extent of the elevational change as well as with other factors such as plant age and microhabitat. Littoral zones at most stations are of the third category, but at MacLeod Harbor and Hanning Bay, where shores were elevated some 30 ft, the zones belong to the fourth category.

*Verrucaria, Zostera*, and the algae that occurred in sufficient abundance and within discrete levels with reference to the tides (i.e., those that formed zones) were studied with relation to the subsidence or uplift. The new littoral zone at MacLeod Harbor was dominated by *Porphyra* rather than *Fucus*, an alga that was prominent at the other stations. It is postulated that the elevation of the *Fucus*-inhabited littoral zone by the earthquake killed most of these plants in this area. Probably 2 to 3 years will pass before *Fucus* becomes established in its former luxuriance at MacLeod Harbor.

Results of the algal colonization of plastic strips left in the ocean 45 days show that small filamentous algae such as *Ulothrix* and *Urospora*, as well as diatoms, were probably the first colonizers in new littoral zones provided by the earthquake.

## ACKNOWLEDGMENTS

The work of the expedition was greatly aided by the cooperation of the captain and crew of the *Harmony*, fellow expedition members, and Mrs. G Dallas Hanna. In the months after the trip, Lloyd F. Austin, E. Kenneth Daniels, Charlotte Mentges, and Drs. Louis D. Druehl, James B. Jensen, Paul C. Silva, and Michael J. Wynne helped with the work of completing the report. I wish to thank Dr. George F. Papenfuss for reviewing the manuscript; Dr. G Dallas Hanna for preparing the photographs, along with his other activities as leader of the expedition; and my wife, Barbara Johansen, for carefully processing seaweeds.

Funds for this project were provided by the National Science Foundation, Grant No. GD 3533, and the Atomic Energy Commission, Contract No. AT(04-3)-654.

## APPENDIX: LIST OF ALGAE COLLECTED

Systematic phycologists are aware that, although some groups have recently been monographed and their specific limits clearly outlined, many groups have not been critically examined. Furthermore, as emphasized near the beginning of this report, very little algal exploration has been undertaken in Alaskan waters. For these reasons it has been impossible to identify many of the taxa collected during the 1965 expedition, some of which may represent undescribed entities. The difficulties in identifying the species of such filamentous green algal genera as *Ulothrix*, *Urospora*, *Rhizoclonium*, *Spongomorpha*, and *Cladophora* and of membranous forms such as *Monostroma*, *Ulva*, and *Enteromorpha* are numerous. A question mark in the following list indicates some degree of uncertainty in the determination. New records are noted with reference to the list by Dawson (1961) of algae from the eastern coast of the Pacific Ocean unless more recent records have been published.

Where the determination has been made by someone other than the writer, the initials of the person, in parentheses, follow the name of the alga: E. Kenneth Daniels (EKD), Louis D. Druehl (LDD), James B. Jensen (JBJ), Barbara J. Johansen (BJJ), Susan Loiseaux (SL), and Michael J. Wynne (MJW).

## RHODOPHYCOPHYTA

*Acrochaetium* species. Occasionally abundant on *Pterosiphonia bipinnata*.

*Antithamnion* species

*Ahnfeltia plicata* (Hudson) Fries. Bleached and dead at some uplifted stations; sometimes epiphitized by *Tenarea dispar*.

*Bangia fuscopurpurea* (Dillwyn) Lyngbye. *A301* from Shipyard Bay (Station 1) represents an extension of the known range of this species on the Pacific coast of North America northward from northern British Columbia.

*Bossiella cretacea* (Postels & Ruprecht) Johansen

*Bosiella orbigniana* ssp. *dichotoma* (Manza) Johansen

*Callophyllis* species

*Ceramium* species

*Clathromorphum circumscriptum* (Stroemfelt) Foslie. *A72* from Olsen Bay (Station 4) represents an extension of the known range of this species from Unalaska Island, Alaska.

*Constantinea rosa-marina* (Gmelin) Postels & Ruprecht

*Corallina frondescens* Postels & Ruprecht

*Corallina officinalis* var. *chilensis* (Harvey) Kützing

*Corallina vancouveriensis* Yendo

*Cryptosiphonia woodii* (J. Agardh) J. Agardh

*Delesseria decipiens* J. Agardh

*Dumontia filiformis* (Lyngbye) J. Agardh

*Endocladia muricata* (Postels & Ruprecht) J. Agardh

*Fauchea laciniata* f. *pygmaea* Setchell & Gardner(?)

*Gigartina papillata* (C. Agardh) J. Agardh (JBJ)

*Gigartina* species

*Gloiopeltis furcata* (Postels & Ruprecht) J. Agardh

*Halosaccion glandiforme* (Gmelin) Ruprecht

*Halosaccion tilesii* Kjellman(?)

*Hildenbrandia occidentalis* Setchell var. *occidentalis*. *A119a* from Bass Harbor (Station 9) represents an extension of the known range of species northward from northern British Columbia.

*Iridaea* species

*Lithothamnium* species

*Membranoptera dimorpha* Gardner. *A220* from Hanning Bay (Station 21) represents an extension of the known range of this species northward from British Columbia. (EKD)

*Neopolyporolithon reclinatum* (Foslie) Adey & Johansen. *A180*,

consisting of dead, uplifted specimens from MacLeod Harbor (Station 20), represents an extension of the known range of this alga northward from Vancouver Island, British Columbia. Occurs on *Corallina frondescens* and *Corallina vancouveriensis*.

*Neoptilota asplenioides* (Esper) Kylin (JBJ)

*Odonthalia dentata* (Linnaeus) Lyngbye

*Odonthalia floccosa* (Esper) Falkenberg

*Opuntiella californica* (Farlow) Kylin

*Phycodrys riggii* Gardner

*Platythamnion* species

*Polysiphonia mollis* Hooker & Harvey(?) (BJJ)

*Polysiphonia pacifica* var. *delicatula* Hollenberg (BJJ)

*Polysiphonia urceolata* (Lightfoot) Greville (BJJ)

*Porphyra amplissima* (Kjellman) Setchell & Hus

*Porphyra laciniata* (Lightfoot) C. Agardh

*Porphyra miniata* f. *cuneiformis* Setchell & Hus

*Porphyra nereocystis* Anderson

*Porphyra perforata* J. Agardh f. *perforata*

*Porphyra perforata* f. *segregata* Setchell & Hus. *A262* from Green Island (Station 23) represents an extension of the known range of this species northward from southern British Columbia.

*Porphyra tenuissima* (Stroemfelt) Setchell & Hus

*Pterosiphonia bipinnata* (Postels & Ruprecht) Falkenberg

*Ptilota tenuis* (Collins) Kylin. *A190f* from MacLeod Harbor, Montague Island (Station 20) represents an extension of the known range of this species northward from northern British Columbia. (JBJ)

*Rhodochorton purpureum* (Lightfoot) Rosenvinge

*Rhodoglossum* species

*Rhodomela larix* (Turner) C. Agardh

*Rhodymenia palmata* (Linnaeus) Greville

*Rhodymenia pertusa* (Postels & Ruprecht) J. Agardh

*Tenarea dispar* (Foslie) Adey. *A96c* from Knowles Head (Station 5) represents an extension of the known range of this species northward from northern Washington. Growing on *Ahnfeltia plicata*.

*Tokidadendron bullata* (Gardner) Wynne

## PHAEOPHYCOPHYTA

*Agarum cribrosum* (Mertens) Bory

*Alaria dolichorhachis* Kjellman (BJJ)

*Alaria pylaii* (Bory) Greville (BJJ)

*Chorda filum* (Linnaeus) Lamouroux (MJW)

*Chordaria flagelliformis* (Müller) C. Agardh. *A240* from Stockdale Harbor, Montague Island (Station 22), represents an extension of the known range of this species from Sitka, Alaska. (MJW)

*Chordaria gracilis* Setchell & Gardner, *A260* from Green Island (Station 23) represents an extension of the known range of this species from Unalaska Island, Alaska. (MJW)

*Coilodesme bulligera* Stroemfelt (MJW)

*Coilodesme cystoseirae* (Ruprecht) Setchell & Gardner (MJW)

*Colpomenia peregrina* (Sauvageau) Hamel (MJW)

*Compsonema sporangiiferum* Setchell & Gardner. *A143d* from West Twin Bay, Perry Island (Station 11), represents an extension of the known range of this species northward from Washington. (SL)

*Costaria costata* (Turner) Saunders

*Cymathere triplicata* (Postels & Ruprecht) J. Agardh

*Cystoseira geminata* C. Agardh (JBJ)

*Delamarea attenuata* (Kjellman) Rosenvinge. *A123r* from South Bay, Perry Island (Station 10), represents the first record of this species from the western coast of North America. (MJW)

*Desmarestia intermedia* Postels & Ruprecht (MJW)

*Desmarestia media* (C. Agardh) Greville (MJW)

*Desmotrichum undulatum* (J. Agardh) Reinke. *A161d* from

Thumb Bay, Knight Island (Station 17) represents the first known record of this species from the west coast of North America. (MJW)

*Dictyosiphon foeniculaceus* (Hudson) Greville (MJW)
*Ectocarpus* species
*Elachista fucicola* f. *lubrica* (Ruprecht) Rosenvinge (MJW)
*Eudesme virescens* (Carmichael) J. Agardh (MJW)
*Fucus distichus* subspecies *edentatus* (De la Pylaie) Powell
*Fucus distichus* subspecies *evanescens* (C. Agardh) Powell
*Giffordia* species
*Heterochordaria abietina* (Ruprecht) Setchell & Gardner (MJW)
*Laminaria groenlandica* Rosenvinge (LDD)
*Laminaria saccharina* (Linnaeus) Lamouroux (LDD)
*Laminaria yezoensis* Miyabe (LDD)
*Leathesia difformis* (Linnaeus) Areschoug (MJW)
*Melanosiphon intestinalis* (Saunders) Wynne (MJW)
*Nereocystis luetkeana* (Mertens) Postels & Ruprecht
*Petalonia debilis* (C. Agardh) Derbes & Solier (MJW)
*Pilayella littoralis* (Linnaeus) Kjellman
*Punctaria lobata* (Saunders) Setchell & Gardner (MJW)
*Punctaria* species (MJW)
*Ralfsia fungiformis* (Gunnerus) Setchell & Gardner
*Ralfsia pacifica* Hollenberg, in G. M. Smith
*Scytosiphon lomentaria* (Lyngbye) J. Agardh f. *lomentaria* (MJW)
*Soranthera ulvoidea* Postels & Ruprecht
*Sphacelaria subfusca* Setchell & Gardner

## CHLOROPHYCOPHYTA

*Blidingia minima* (Kützing) Kylin var. *minima*
*Blidingia minima* var. *ramifera* Bliding
*Chaetomorpha tortuosa* (Dillwyn) Kützing
*Cladophora* species
*Enteromorpha compressa* (Linnaeus) Greville var. *compressa*
*Enteromorpha groenlandica* (J. Agardh) Setchell & Gardner(?)
*Enteromorpha intestinalis* (Linnaeus) Link
*Enteromorpha linza* (Linnaeus) J. Agardh
*Enteromorpha prolifera* (Müller) J. Agardh
*Enteromorpha ramulosa* (J. E. Smith) Hooker(?)
*Lola lubrica* (Setchell & Gardner) A. & G. Hamel. *A118* from Heather Island (Station 8) represents an extension of the known range of this species northward from northern Washington.
*Monostroma areolatum* Setchell & Gardner. *A126* from South Bay, Perry Island (Station 10), represents an extension of the known range of this species from Sitka, Alaska.
*Monostroma fuscum* (Postels & Ruprecht) Wittrock var. *fuscum*.
*Monostroma grevillei* (Thuret) Wittrock var. *grevillei*. *A91* from Knowles Head (Station 5) represents an extension of the known range of this species from Unalaska Island, Alaska.
*Monostroma grevillei* var. *lubricum* (Kjellman) Collins
*Monostroma oxyspermum* (Kützing) Doty. *A82c* from Olsen Bay (Station 4) represents an extension of the known range of this species northward from southern British Columbia.
*Prasiola borealis* Reed. Infected with *Guignardia alaskana* Reed.
*Rhizoclonium riparium* (Roth) Harvey
*Spongomorpha arcta* (Dillwyn) Kützing
*Spongomorpha coalita* (Ruprecht) Collins
*Spongomorpha saxatilis* var. *chamissonis* (Ruprecht) Collins(?)
*Spongomorpha spinescens* Kützing
*Ulothrix flacca* (Dillwyn) Thuret, in Le Jolis
*Ulothrix implexa* Kützing
*Ulothrix pseudoflacca* f. *maxima* Setchell & Gardner
*Ulva fenestrata* Postels & Ruprecht
*Urospora penicilliformis* (Roth) Areschoug

## LICHEN

*Verrucaria maura* Wahlenberg

## ANGIOSPERM

*Zostera marina* Linnaeus

## REFERENCES

Baker, S. M., 1909. On the causes of the zoning of brown seaweeds on the seashore. *New Phytologist*, 8 (Nos. 5–6), 196–202.

Bokenham, N. A. H., and T. A. Stephenson, 1938. The colonisation of denuded rock surfaces in the intertidal region of the Cape Peninsula. *Annals of the Natal* [Union of South Africa] *Museum*, 9, 47–81.

Brongersma-Sanders, M., 1957. Mass mortality in the sea *in* Volume I: Treatise on marine ecology and paleoecology. J. W. Hedgpeth, editor. New York: Geological Society of America Memoir 67. p. 941–1010.

Brown, L. B., 1915. Experiments with marine algae in fresh water. Publications of the Puget Sound Marine Biological Station, v. 1. Seattle: University of Washington. p. 31–34.

Dawson, E. Y., 1961. A guide to the literature and distributions of Pacific benthic algae from Alaska to the Galapagos Islands. *Pacific Science*, 15 (No. 3), 370–461.

Eyerdam, Walter J., 1971. Flowering plants found growing between pre- and postearthquake high-tide lines during the summer of 1965 in Prince William Sound *in* The Great Alaska Earthquake of 1964: Biology. NAS Pub. 1604. Washington: National Academy of Sciences.

Gail, F. W., 1918. Some experiments with *Fucus* to determine the factors controlling its vertical distribution. Publications of the Puget Sound Marine Biological Station, v. 2. Seattle: University of Washington. p. 139–151.

Gail, F. W., 1919. Hydrogen ion concentration and other factors affecting the distribution of *Fucus*. Publications of the Puget Sound Marine Biological Station, v. 2. Seattle: University of Washington. p. 287–306.

Gardner, N. L., 1922. The genus *Fucus* on the Pacific coast of North America. Publications in Botany, v. 10. Berkeley: University of California. p. 1–180.

Gislén, Torsten, 1931. A survey of the marine associations in the Misaki district with notes concerning their environmental conditions. *Journal of the Faculty of Science*, Imperial University of Tokyo, 2 (Section 4: Zoology), 389–444.

Glynn, P. W., 1965. Community composition, structure, and interrelationships in the marine intertidal *Endocladia muricata-Balanus glandula* association in Monterey Bay, California. *Beaufortia*, 12 (No. 48), 1–198.

Hanna, G Dallas, 1964. Biological effects of an earthquake. *Pacific Discovery*, 17 (November-December), 24–26. (Reprinted in this volume as "Observations Made in 1964 on the Immediate Biological Effects of the Earthquake in Prince William Sound.")

Hanna, G Dallas, 1971. Biological effects of the earthquake as observed in 1965 *in* The Great Alaska Earthquake of 1964: Biology. NAS Pub. 1604. Washington: National Academy of Sciences.

Haven, Stoner B., 1971. Effects of land-level changes on intertidal invertebrates, with discussion of postearthquake ecological succession *in* The Great Alaska Earthquake of 1964: Biology. NAS Pub. 1604. Washington: National Academy of Sciences.

Hollenberg, G. J., 1936. A study of *Halicystis ovalis*. II. Periodicity in the formation of gametes. *American Journal of Botany*, 23 (No. 1), 1–3.

Hoyt, W. D., 1927. The periodic fruiting of *Dictyota* and its relation to the environment. *American Journal of Botany*, 14 (No. 10), 592–619.

Johansen, H. William, 1969. Morphology and systematics of coralline algae with special reference to *Calliarthron*. Publications in Botany, v. 49. Berkeley: University of California. p. 1–78.

Kaburaki, T., 1928. Effect of the Kwanto earthquake upon marine organisms. Proceedings of the Third Pan-Pacific Scientific Congress, Tokyo, 1926, v. 2. Tokyo: National Research Council of Japan. p. 1523–1527.

Kaye, C. A., 1964. The upper limit of barnacles as an index of sea-level change on the New England coast during the past 100 years. *Journal of Geology*, 72 (No. 5), 580–600.

Knight, M., and M. Parke, 1950. A biological study of *Fucus vesiculosus* L. and *Fucus serratus* L. *Journal of the Marine Biological Association of the United Kingdom*, 29 (No. 2), 439–514.

Kylin, H., 1930. Über die Entwicklungsgeschichte der Florideen. Lunds Universitet Årsskrift, Ny Foljd, avd. 2, bd. 26(6), p. 1–103.

Lewis, J. R., 1961. The littoral zone on rocky shores—a biological or physical entity? *Oikos* (Copenhagen), 12 (No. 2), 280–301.

Lewis, J. R., 1964. The ecology of rocky shores. London: English Universities Press. 335 p.

Lodge, Sheila M., 1948. Algal growth in the absence of *Patella* on an experimental strip of foreshore, Port St. Mary, Isle of Man. *Proceedings of the Liverpool Biological Society*, 56, 78–85.

Martin, Lawrence, 1910. Alaskan earthquake of 1899. *Geological Society of America Bulletin*, 21 (July 5), 339–406.

Moore, H. B., 1958. Marine ecology. New York: John Wiley & Sons. 493 p.

Muenscher, W. L. C., 1915. A study of algal associations of San Juan Island. Publications of the Puget Sound Marine Biological Station, v. 1. Seattle: University of Washington. p. 59–84.

Northcraft, R. D., 1948. Marine algal colonization on the Monterey Peninsula, California. *American Journal of Botany*, 35 (No. 7), 396–404.

Phillips, R. C., and S. Grant, 1965. Environmental effect on *Phyllospadix scouleri* and *Zostera marina* leaves (Abstract). *American Journal of Botany*, 52 (No. 6, Part 2), 644.

Plafker, George, 1965. Tectonic deformation associated with the 1964 Alaska earthquake. *Science*, 148 (June 25), 1675–1687.

Plafker, George, 1969. Tectonics of the March 27, 1964, Alaska earthquake. U.S. Geological Survey Professional Paper 543-I. Washington: Government Printing Office. 74 p. Also *in* The Great Alaska Earthquake of 1964: Geology. NAS Pub. 1601. Washington: National Academy of Sciences, 1971.

Plafker, George, and L. R. Mayo, 1965. Tectonic deformation, subaqueous slides and destructive waves associated with the Alaskan March 27, 1964 earthquake: an interim geologic evaluation. U.S. Geological Survey Open-File Report. Menlo Park, California: U.S. Geological Survey. 34 p.

Postels, A., and F. J. Ruprecht, 1840. Illustrationes algarum in itinere circa orbem. [Petropoli (Leningrad).] 22 p., 40 plates.

Powell, H. T., 1957a. Studies in the genus *Fucus* L. I: *Fucus distichus* L. emend. Powell. *Journal of the Marine Biological Association of the United Kingdom*, 36 (No. 2), 407–432.

Powell, H. T., 1957b. Studies in the genus *Fucus* L. II: Distribution and ecology of forms of *Fucus distichus* L. emend. Powell in Britain and Ireland. *Journal of the Marine Biological Association of the United Kingdom*, 36 (No. 3), 663–693.

Rigg, George B., 1917. Seasonal development of bladder kelp. Publications of the Puget Sound Marine Biological Station, v. 1. Seattle: University of Washington. p. 309–318.

Rigg, George B., and Robert C. Miller, 1949. Intertidal plant and animal zonation in the vicinity of Neah Bay, Washington. *Proceedings, California Academy of Sciences*, 26, Series 4 (No. 10), 323–351.

Robinson, M. K., 1957. Sea temperature in the Gulf of Alaska and in the northeast Pacific Ocean, 1941-1952. Scripps Institution of Oceanography Bulletin 7. La Jolla, California: Scripps Institution of Oceanography. 98 p.

Russell, G., 1963. Attitudes in intertidal ecology. *Biological Journal*, 3 (No. 2), 49–54.

Saunders, De Alton, 1901. Papers from the Harriman Alaska Expedition. XXV: The algae. *Proceedings of the Washington Academy of Sciences*, 3, 391–486.

Scagel, R. F., 1957. An annotated list of the marine algae of British Columbia and northern Washington (including keys to genera). Ottawa: National Museum of Canada Bulletin 150. 289 p.

Segawa, S., and M. Nakamura, 1952. Intertidal vegetation on the coast of Fukuyoshi, Fukuoka Prefecture. *Bulletin of the Society for Plant Ecology*, 1 (No. 4), 196–200.

Setchell, W. A., 1899. Algae of the Pribilof Islands. Contribution 7, Botany Laboratory. Berkeley: University of California. p. 589–596.

Setchell, W. A., 1920. Stenothermy and zone-invasion. *American Naturalist*, 54 (September–October), 385–397.

Setchell, W. A., 1929. Morphological and phenological notes on *Zostera marina* L. Publications in Botany, v. 14. Berkeley: University of California. p. 389–452.

Setchell, W. A., and N. L. Gardner, 1903. Algae of northwestern America. Publications in Botany, v. 1. Berkeley: University of California. p. 165–418.

Sjöstedt, L. G., 1926. Floridean studies. Lunds Universitet Årsskrift, Ny Foljd, avd. 2, bd. 22 (4), 95 p.

Smith, G. M., 1947. On the reproduction of some Pacific coast species of *Ulva*. *American Journal of Botany*, 34 (No. 2), 80–87.

Southward, A. J., 1956. The population balance between limpets and seaweeds on wave-beaten rocky shores. Annual Report, Marine Biological Station, Port Erin, Isle of Man, v. 68, p. 20–29.

Southward, A. J., 1958. The zonation of plants and animals on rocky sea shores. *Biological Reviews*, 33 (No. 2), 137–177.

Southward, A. J., and J. H. Orton, 1954. The effects of wave-action on the distribution and numbers of the commoner plants and animals living on the Plymouth breakwater. *Journal of the Marine Biological Association of the United Kingdom*, 33 (No. 1), 1–19.

Stephenson, T. A., and Anne Stephenson, 1949. The universal features of zonation between tide-marks on rocky coasts. *Journal of Ecology*, 37 (No. 2), 289–305.

Stephenson, T. A., and Anne Stephenson, 1961a. Life between the tide marks in North America, IV-A: Vancouver Island, I. *Journal of Ecology*, 49 (No. 1), 1–29.

Stephenson, T. A., and Anne Stephenson, 1961b. Life between the tide marks in North America, IV-B: Vancouver Island, II. *Journal of Ecology*, 49 (No. 2), 227–243.

Tarr, Ralph S., and Lawrence Martin, 1912. The earthquakes at Yakutat Bay, Alaska, in September, 1899. U.S. Geological Survey Professional Paper 69. Washington: Government Printing Office. 135 p.

U.S. Coast and Geodetic Survey, 1964. Tide tables, high and low water predictions, 1965, west coast North and South America, including the Hawaiian Islands. Washington: Government Printing Office. 224 p.

Watson, C. E., 1959. Climate of Alaska *in* Climatography of the United States. U.S. Weather Bureau, No. 60-49. Washington: Government Printing Office. 24 p.

Williams, J. L., 1905. Studies in the Dictyotaceae. III: The periodicity of the sexual cells in *Dictyota dichotoma. Annals of Botany*, 19 (No. 76), 531–560.

Wilson, O. T., 1925. Some experimental observations of marine algal successions. *Ecology*, 6 (No. 3), 303–311.

Wynne, Michael J., 1970. Marine algae of Amchitka Island (Aleutian Islands). I. Delesseriaceae. *Syesis*, 3, 95–144.

Yendo, K., 1914. On the cultivation of seaweeds, with special accounts of their ecology. *Economic Proceedings of the Royal Dublin Society,* 2, 105–122.

WALTER J. EYERDAM
SEATTLE, WASHINGTON

# Flowering Plants Found Growing between Pre- and Postearthquake High-Tide Lines during the Summer of 1965 in Prince William Sound

## INTRODUCTION

The uplift of the shoreline of the mainland and the islands of Prince William Sound (Plafker, 1965) was a feature of the Alaska earthquake of March 27, 1964. Along the hinge line of the crustal movement across the northwestern part of the Sound there was, of course, no elevation of the shores, but southward from that line the shorelines rose above their former level, and at the southwestern tip of Montague Island they reached a maximum of more than 34 ft. The length of the affected shorelines was many hundreds of miles (Figure 1).

Before the earthquake, the conifer forest extended from the upper limit of the splash zone of the sea to timberline. Sitka spruce and hemlock form the most conspicuous elements of this forest, but it contains more than a thousand additional species of plants. As the land rose during the earthquake, sea bottom became exposed to the atmosphere, and all marine life was exterminated. The area of this new land had not been computed by the time of this writing, but it was a significant amount. Its width varied with the amount of the elevation and the slope of the former sea bottom.

During the summer of 1965, my object was to learn the extent to which terrestrial plants had begun to occupy this newly created land after a year of exposure to the atmosphere. Seventy-five species of flowering plants had become established at the various stations where collections were made.

The stations were near transects run by the phycologist H. W. Johansen and the zoologist Stoner Haven. (See Hanna, 1971, this volume, for a complete list of stations and for maps.) Some of their transects were run on nearly vertical walls of rocks, unfavorable for growth of land plants. In such locations, I worked on nearby beaches. In the early part of the season, some of the species of plants were not sufficiently developed for positive identification. Plants found at each station were prepared by usual botanical

ABSTRACT: Land-level changes of considerable magnitude occurred in the Prince William Sound area during the earthquake of March 27, 1964. The uplift exposed wide areas of former sea bottom to atmospheric conditions. Because an early record of the establishment of land plants on this new land seems desirable, collections of land plants were made at 20 separate stations during the period May 30 to July 15, 1965. In approximately a year, 75 species of terrestrial flowering plants were found to have become established on this newly exposed land. The records should prove useful in the future to determine time required for mature forest development.

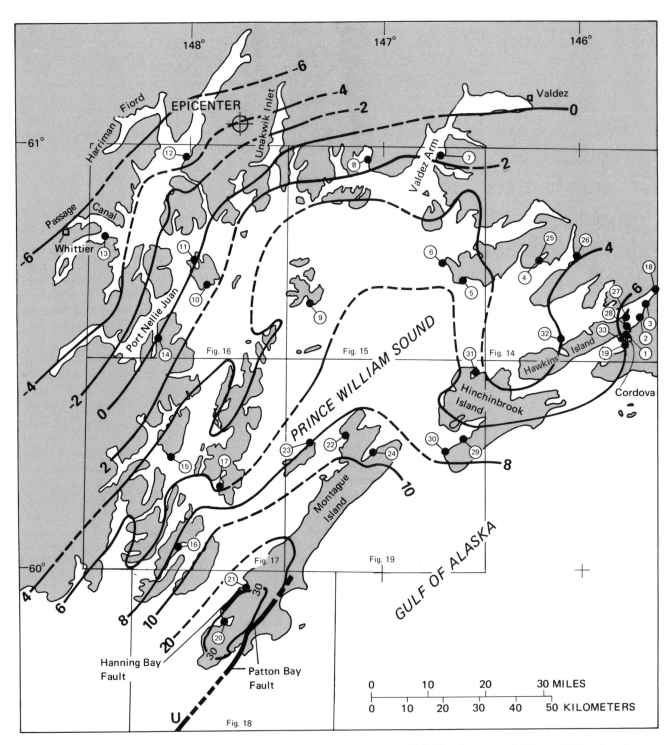

FIGURE 1 Index map of Prince William Sound, Alaska, showing the locations of the 33 field stations occupied during 1965 by investigators aboard M.V. *Harmony*. Isobase contours by Plafker and Mayo (1965) show land-level changes resulting from the March 27, 1964, earthquake. The contour interval is 2 ft between the −6-ft and +10-ft contours, and the interval is 10 ft between the +10-ft and the +30-ft contours. Larger-scale maps of the six sections indicated appear as Figures 14–19 in "Biological Effects of the Earthquake as Observed in 1965" (Hanna, 1971, this volume). (Adapted from U.S. Geological Survey base map.)

techniques, and after proper field data had been recorded, the specimens collected were deposited in the herbarium of the California Academy of Sciences.

Brief notes on habitat have been transcribed in the following station lists. Most of the scientific names used are according to Hultén (1941–1950). Plants tolerant of some salt were the most common, and at many localities they were the earliest to get started in the new land.

A few mosses, such as *Dicranum fuscescens* and *Grimmia maritima*, had become established in favorable places. Among the lichens were *Verrucaria*, *Leconora*, *Lecidia*, and *Atraria*, and there were a few hepatics. *Equisetum* was found at only one station.

An opportunity is seldom offered to study the time required for the establishment of a mature forest on land that has been cleared of unfavorable cover. The retreat of a glacier is probably comparable in some ways to the situation that resulted from the 1964 earthquake. The wave that cleared the forest off the mountainside at Lituya Bay, Alaska, on July 9, 1958 (Miller, 1960), to a height of 1,720 ft presented such an opportunity, but it was not followed up in later studies. Several studies have been based on the retreat of the glaciers in Glacier Bay, Alaska (Cooper, 1923, 1930, 1931, 1939a,b; Lawrence, 1958; Decker, 1966; Lawrence and others, 1967). Eight successive stages of vegetation development have been noted in that area, but only the first-generation stand of Sitka spruce forest has been attained within the first two and a half centuries since the neoglacial maximum. More than six centuries longer would be required to attain the ultimate sedge–sphagnum muskeg stage described by Dachnowsky-Stokes (1941), Zach (1950), and Lawrence (1950), except in very wet outwash sites where muskeg can develop within the first two centuries.

The development of terrestrial maritime strand vegetation on shores recently emerged from the sea in situations where the surfaces had previously supported littoral marine communities that died as a consequence of continuous exposure to the atmosphere must be quite different in species composition and in rate of development from primary succession on recently deglaciated terrestrial surfaces. Except where tsunamis left shores clean of preexisting biota and soils, the situation in the Prince William Sound study here reported is similar to a secondary succession; the decaying bodies of marine organisms, rich in organic matter and nutrients, provide conditions suitable for rapid establishment, growth, and reproduction of many land plants as soon as excess quantities of ocean salt have leached away. Crow (1971, this volume) has reported studies showing that precipitation of no more than 6 in. is enough under favorable conditions to remove salt rapidly from soils of land reclaimed from the sea in the Netherlands. In Prince William Sound the amount of precipitation is so great that, even in the driest months, it would reach this level in only a month or two.

We studied the first, or pioneer, stage in Prince William Sound in 1965 and hope that the lists in this report and the museum specimens that support them will afford an opportunity to study the succession of plants during the coming period of forestation. Such a study should involve reexamination of the terrain at intervals of no more than a decade for at least the next 100 years. Comparable situations exist along the shores of Glacier Bay, where rapid emergence of the land, amounting to ½ to 1 in. per year has resulted from rebound following the neoglaciation (Twenhofel, 1952; Lawrence, 1958). Strand vegetation development reported by Cooper (1936) at Glacier Bay and at Prince William Sound provide useful comparisons for the present study. The observations made by Tarr and Martin (1912) in 1905 and 1906 and in 1909 and 1910, 5–10 years after the Yakutat Bay earthquake of 1899, are, however, most similar to the results of the study reported here. Haven (1971, this volume) has indicated that they commented briefly (1912) on the organisms in the uplifted and postearthquake intertidal zones.

Some of our stations yielded only a few species of plants, whereas others yielded many. The amount of residual salt in the sand and gravel surely had a bearing on this yield (Crow, 1971, this volume). One of the pioneer plants found after glacier recession at Glacier Bay, Alaska, was *Dryas* (Cooper, 1939a, b; Crocker and Major, 1955; Lawrence and others, 1967), a genus that was not found at any of our stations.

The station names and numbers in the following list correspond with those in the accompanying papers by Hanna, Johansen, and Haven:

*Station 1:* Shipyard Bay, Orca Inlet, across the channel from Cordova, May 30, 1965. The land was uplifted 5.4 ft. Although early in the season, a surprising number of plants were found growing between the preearthquake and postearthquake high-tide lines. Obviously most of the salt water in the beach sand and gravel had been displaced by fresh water during the previous year. Seedling shrubs of *Sambucus*, *Ribes*, and *Rubus* were found growing in slate shingle. These species all produce edible berries, and their seeds are dispersed by birds.

*Station 4:* Olsen Bay, June 2, 1965. The uplift of the land was 3.6 ft. In 1964, Peter Moyle, working with the U.S. Bureau of Commercial Fisheries, prepared a manuscript list of plants found on the flats in front of the Biological Station, where he observed *Carex sitchensis*, *Cochlearia officinalis*, *Elymus arenarius mollis*, *Honckenya peploides*, *Poa eminens*, and *Potentilla pacifica*. These species and another grass (unidentified) had taken over the extensive flats in

FIGURE 2  U.S. Bureau of Commercial Fisheries Biological Station at the mouth of Olsen Creek, Olsen Bay (Station 25), July 9, 1965. In locations such as this, where abundant fresh water floods the former intertidal lands, dense populations of land plants have become established.

*G Dallas Hanna*

1964. Several other species were not well enough developed to be identified by June 2, 1965 (Figure 2). Therefore, the same area was examined later in the season. (See Station 25, July 8–9.)

*Station 5:* Knowles Head, June 4, 1965. The uplift of the land was 5.7 ft. At times, this station is exposed to heavy surf, which has created a beach composed of large boulders. The only flowering plant collected on the newly formed land area was *Potentilla anserina.*

*Station 13:* Blackstone Bay, June 16, 1965. The land was depressed 5.2 ft. The beach here is the flat seaward side of the terminal moraine of Tebenkof Glacier, a short distance inland. The flat was formerly covered with a dense growth of alder (*Alnus crispa* var. *sinuata*), spruce (*Picea sitchensis*), and undergrowth. As a result of the earthquake, a tsunami swept in and destroyed the vegetation far back from the former high-tide line. The dead vegetation was plainly visible from a distance at sea. What had not been physically wrecked by the rush of water and debris was killed by impounded salt water. Many individuals of the plant taxa of low stature had been buried by sand and gravel. A similar situation was found at some other places, such as Chenega Island, Pigot Bay, and Lowell Point near Seward, Alaska.

*Station 15:* Chenega Island, June 17, 1965. The uplift of the land was 6.3 ft. The beach area here, where a village had been washed away by a tsunami 60 ft high, is composed of slate shingle and solid rock. An unexpectedly large number of species of plants had become established in the narrow zone between preearthquake and postearthquake mean high-tide lines:

Common:
    *Arabis lyrata kamchatica*
    *Elymus arenarius mollis* (seaside ryegrass)
    *Galium aparine*
    *Heracleum lanatum* (wild rhubarb)
    *Rumex crispus* (?) (curled dock)
    *Sambucus racemosa* (red elder)

A few:
    *Barbarea orthoceras*
    *Circaea alpina* (?)
    *Epilobium latifolium* (fireweed)
    *Geum macrophyllum*
    *Glaux maritima*
    *Ligusticum hultenii*
    *Poa eminens* (?)
    *Rorippa palustris*
    *Rubus spectabilis* (salmonberry)
    *Stellaria humifusa*

One specimen:
    *Aquilegia formosa*

Frequency of occurrence not noted:
    *Alsine* sp.

*Station 16:* Port Ashton, Sawmill Bay, Evans Island, June 18, 1965. The uplift of the land was 8.9 ft. Beaches there range from graywacke and argillite cliffs to boulders and shingle. Violent tsunamis in the inlet destroyed much of the land vegetation for several feet above the former high-tide line, and rapid movement of water removed much of the biota of the littoral zone. At the time of our visit, 29 species of plants had moved into the zone between the former and the 1965 high-tide lines:

Very common:
  *Elymus arenarius mollis* (seaside ryegrass)

Common:
  *Atriplex drymarioides*
  *Carex limosa*
  *Carex sitchensis*
  *Cochlearia officinalis*
  *Epilobium angustifolium*
  *Galium aparine* (bedstraw)
  *Heracleum lanatum*
  *Honckenya peploides*
  *Mimulus guttatus*
  *Plantago juncoides*
  *Plantago maritima*
  *Poa annua*
  *Sambucus racemosa* (red elder)
  *Triglochin palustris*

Several:
  *Rubus spectabilis* (salmonberry)

A few:
  *Angelica genuflexa*
  *Chrysanthemum arcticum*
  *Ligusticum hultenii* (in slate shingle)
  *Poa eminens*
  *Potentilla anserina*
  *Sagina intermedia*
  *Stellaria humifusa*
  *Trifolium* sp.
  *Vaccinium* sp. (blueberry)

Two specimens:
  *Aquilegia formosa*

Frequency of occurrence not noted:
  *Arabis lyrata kamchatica* (stonecress)
  *Barbarea orthoceras* (beach mustard or winter cress)
  *Epilobium anagallidifolium*

*Station 17:* Thumb Bay, Knight Island, June 20, 1965. The uplift of the land was 6 ft. The shoreline in this bay is too abrupt and rocky to support many plants that otherwise might have moved into the new zone below the former high-tide line. This environment, together with the scouring effect of violent waves, had not left much fine sediment favorable for seedling establishment. The following species were found:

Very common:
  *Elymus arenarius mollis*

Common:
  *Honckenya peploides major*
  *Ligusticum hultenii*
  *Plantago juncoides*
  *Sambucus racemosa*

A few:
  *Cardamine umbellata*
  *Carex sitchensis*
  *Cochlearia officinalis*
  *Potentilla anserina*

*Station 18:* Head of Orca Inlet, June 21–22, 1965. The uplift of the land was 7 ft. At the head of this inlet, the sedge *Carex sitchensis* had occupied several square miles of the flat land that had been below high tide before the 1964 earthquake. Back of this stand of *Carex*, but still below the former high-tide level, were many species, including:

Very common:
  *Potentilla pacifica*

Common:
  *Arabis lyrata kamchatica*
  *Barbarea orthoceras*
  *Cardamine umbellata*
  *Cochlearia officinalis*
  *Elymus arenarius mollis*
  *Epilobium angustifolium*
  *Epilobium anagallidifolium*
  *Galium aparine*
  *Lathyrus maritima*
  *Plantago juncoides*
  *Poa eminens*
  *Potentilla anserina*
  *Ranunculus pygmaeus*
  *Salix barclayi*
  *Sambucus racemosa*

Abundant:
  *Carex sitchensis*
  *Honckenya peploides major*

Occasional:
  *Achillea borealis*
  *Conioselinum benthami*
  *Ligusticum hultenii*
  *Ribes bracteosum*
  *Senecio pseudo-arnica*

A few:
  *Heuchera glabra*

Rare:
  *Heracleum lanatum*
  *Mertensia maritima*
  *Oxyria digyna*
  *Picea sitchensis*
  *Rubus spectabilis*
  *Rumex crispus* (?)
  *Salix sitchensis*
  *Saxifraga aestivalis*
  *Stellaria humifusa*
  *Tiarella trifoliata*

*Station 19:* Cordova Flats, June 23, 1965. The uplift of the land was 6.7 ft. The former tidal flats south of Cordova had been swept clean of loose sand by tsunamis. Plant establishment on them after the uplift was slow. Only the following species were found:

Common:
  *Galium aparine*
  *Plantago juncoides*

Abundant:
  *Honckenya peploides major*

Scattered:
  *Elymus arenarius mollis*
  *Poa eminens*

Several:
  *Epilobium luteum*

A few:
  *Barbarea orthoceras*
  *Heracleum lanatum*
  *Luzula parviflora*
  *Poa annua*
  *Potentilla pacifica*
  *Sambucus racemosa*

*Station 20:* MacLeod Harbor, Montague Island, June 26–27, 1965. The uplift of the land was 30 ft. After the uplift in Prince William Sound, a subtidal zone of 24 ft was exposed. Because bottom slopes were gentle in the bay, the resulting zone of new land is very broad. Some of the new land, especially near the outer coast, is covered with large boulders. Toward the head of the bay there are extensive sand and gravel flats. Strong waves had swept the area clear of its rich marine fauna and flora. Land plants were slowly entering the areas of both boulders and gravel–sand: a clump here, a seedling there. The most common was the grass *Poa* (or *Puccinellia*), species not identified. In all, 26 identified species were growing on the new land:

Common:
  *Achillea borealis*
  *Angelica genuflexa*
  *Arabis lyrata kamchatica*
  *Carex sitchensis*
  *Claytonia sibirica*
  *Elymus arenarius mollis*
  *Honckenya peploides major*
  *Lathyrus maritima*
  *Luzula parviflora*
  *Mimulus guttatus*
  *Potentilla anserina*
  *Potentilla pacifica*

Abundant:
  *Galium aparine*

Occasional:
  *Ligusticum hultenii*

A few:
  *Aquilegia formosa*
  *Barbarea orthoceras*
  *Cardamine umbellata*
  *Epilobium anagallidifolium*
  *Heracleum lanatum*
  *Rubus spectabilis*
  *Sambucus racemosa*
  *Saxifraga aestivalis*
  *Stellaria humifusa*
  *Tellima grandiflora*

Rare:
  *Epilobium luteum*
  *Ranunculus bongardii*

*Station 21:* Hanning Bay, Montague Island, June 28 and 29, 1965 (Figure 3). The uplift of the land was 29.8 ft. Be-

*G Dallas Hanna*

FIGURE 3  Formerly submerged rocks of the center shore of Hanning Bay, Montague Island (Station 21), June 28, 1965. Scattered new bunches of grasses have started in what was formerly a dense bed of eelgrass (*Zostera*), now dead and bleached white.

FIGURE 4   Pebble beach at Stockdale Harbor, Montague Island (Station 22), June 30, 1965. The dead stems of 1964 *Atriplex* were about 2 ft high. New growth of the same species was abundant on windrows of dead eelgrass (*Zostera*). Ancient stumps from formerly submerged forest trees were abundant on this shore.

*G Dallas Hanna*

cause extensive areas in this bay are solid rock or boulder, the number of species of plants and individuals that had started in the newly exposed land area was limited. The most abundant species was a grass, probably *Poa eminens.*

Common:
> *Arabis lyrata kamchatica*
> *Carex sitchensis*
> *Galium aparine*
> *Mimulus guttatus*
> *Ribes bracteosum*
> *Sambucus racemosa*

Abundant:
> *Poa eminens*

A few:
> *Epilobium anagallidifolium*
> *Romanzoffia sitchensis*
> *Saxifraga aestivalis*
> *Senecio pseudo-arnica*

Rare:
> *Elymus arenarius mollis*
> *Ligusticum hultenii*

*Station 22:*  Stockdale Harbor, Montague Island, June 30, 1965 (Figure 4). The uplift of the land was 8.7 ft. The beach in this harbor is largely coarse gravel and shingle, but there is some solid graywacke and slate. Before the earthquake, the marine flowering plant *Zostera marina* (eelgrass) evidently grew in great abundance near the low-tide line. Naturally, all this growth had been killed by exposure to air and had washed ashore in windrows. A good stand of *Atriplex* was growing on these piles of dead eelgrass. A new and vigorous growth of *Zostera* had already become established

near the new low-tide line. The following species were also found:

Very common:
> *Galium boreale*

Common:
> *Arabis lyrata kamchatica*
> *Cochlearia officinalis*
> *Lathyrus maritima*
> *Ligusticum hultenii*
> *Sambucus racemosa*

Abundant:
> *Atriplex drymarioides*
> *Elymus arenarius mollis*
> *Galium aparine*
> *Honckenya peploides major*

Scattered:
> *Poa eminens*

A few:
> *Mertensia maritima*
> *Poa annua*
> *Rubus spectabilis*

*Station 23:*  Green Island, July 1, 1965 (Figure 5). The uplift of the land was approximately 8.4 ft. The collection was made on a coarse-gravel or shingle beach on the west side of the island. For some reason, fewer species of plants were found there than in other similarly uplifted zones. The species found were as follows:

Common:
> *Elymus arenarius mollis*
> *Galium aparine*

FIGURE 5  Green Island boulder area, formerly intertidal zone (Station 23), July 1, 1965. The black rocks are coated with encrusting calcareous algae, barnacles, and bryozoa, bleached white. New grasses have started among the debris of marine animals and plants.

*G Dallas Hanna*

*Honckenya peploides major*
*Lathyrus maritima*

A few:
*Ligusticum hultenii*
*Senecio pseudo-arnica*

*Station 24:*  Zaikof Bay, Montague Island, July 2-3, 1965. The uplift of the land was 8.8 ft. The beaches that were examined in this bay consisted of slate shingle. The following species of plants were collected:

Very common:
*Honckenya peploides major*
*Poa eminens*
*Potentilla pacifica*

Common:
*Arabis lyrata kamchatica*
*Barbarea orthoceras*
*Galium aparine*
*Ligusticum hultenii*
*Mertensia maritima*
*Plantago maritima*
*Ribes bracteosum*
*Sambucus racemosa*

Abundant:
*Atriplex gmelini*
*Carex sitchensis*
*Cochlearia officinalis*

A few:
*Aruncus sylvester*
*Chrysanthemum arcticum* (?)
*Epilobium angustifolium*
*Heuchera glabra*
*Rubus spectabilis*

*Station 25:*  Olsen Bay, July 8-9, 1965. The uplift of the land was 3.6 ft. On June 1, when this site was first visited, flowering plants were just starting, and most of them were too immature to be identified (see Station 4, June 2). Therefore, it was most rewarding to be able to visit the same locality later, when the following were collected:

Very common:
*Elymus arenarius mollis*
*Honckenya peploides major*
*Potentilla pacifica*

Common:
*Achillea borealis*
*Claytonia sibirica*
*Cochlearia officinalis*
*Ligusticum hultenii*
*Plantago maritima*
*Poa eminens*
*Stellaria humifusa*

Abundant:
*Carex sitchensis*

A few:
*Chrysanthemum arcticum*
*Puccinellia nutkaensis*
*Rubus spectabilis*

Rare:
*Hordeum brachyantherum*

*Station 27:*  Deep Bay, Hawkins Island, July 10, 1965. The uplift of the land was 6.8 ft. The bay is bounded outwardly by Salmo and Knot points. In this well-protected bay, more species had reached the newly exposed area than in any other station in Prince William Sound:

Very common:
  *Carex sitchensis*

Common:
  *Alnus crispa sinuata*
  *Arabis lyrata kamchatica*
  *Aruncus sylvester*
  *Atriplex gmelini*
  *Barbarea orthoceras*
  *Bromus sitchensis*
  *Cardamine umbellata*
  *Carex limosa*
  *Claytonia sibirica*
  *Cochlearia officinalis*
  *Deschampsia* sp.
  *Epilobium anagallidifolium*
  *Galium aparine*
  *Galium boreale*
  *Glaux maritima*
  *Heracleum lanatum*
  *Luzula parviflora*
  *Plantago maritima*
  *Puccinellia nutkaensis*
  *Ranunculus bongardii*
  *Rubus spectabilis*
  *Rumex crispus*
  *Sambucus racemosa*

Abundant:
  *Elymus arenarius mollis*
  *Honckenya peploides major*
  *Potentilla anserina*
  *Potentilla pacifica*

A few:
  *Carex circinnata*
  *Chrysanthemum arcticum*
  *Epilobium latifolium*
  *Lathyrus maritima*
  *Ligusticum hultenii*
  *Oxyria digyna*
  *Ranunculus pygmaeus*
  *Ribes bracteosum*
  *Sanguisorba sitchensis*
  *Tiarella trifoliata*

Rare:
  *Carex livida*
  *Chrysosplenium tetrandrum*
  *Fritillaria camschatcensis*
  *Heuchera glabra*
  *Sagina intermedia*
  *Saxifraga aestivalis*

Frequency of occurrence not noted:
  *Arabis hirsuta eschscholtziana*
  *Equisetum arvense*

*Station 28:*  Hawkins Island opposite Cordova, July 11, 1965. The uplift of the land was 6.8 ft. This area had been examined early in the season (May 30) before plants were well started, and only elderberry (*Sambucus*), currant (*Ribes*), and salmonberry (*Rubus*) were then recognized (see Station 1, Hanna, 1971, this volume). Therefore, the

following species, found generally in the vanguard, had reached this area also.

  *Bromus sitchensis*
  *Carex sitchensis*
  *Chrysanthemum arcticum*
  *Deschampsia* sp.
  *Elymus arenarius mollis*
  *Galium aparine*
  *Galium boreale*
  *Honckenya peploides major*
  *Lathyrus maritima*
  *Ligusticum hultenii*
  *Mertensia maritima*
  *Potentilla pacifica*
  *Rubus spectabilis*
  *Rumex crispus*
  *Saxifraga aestivalis*

*Station 29:*  Port Etches, Hinchinbrook Island, July 12, 1965 (Figure 6). The uplift of the land was 3.8 ft. This station is at the first cove southwest of Garden Cove. At the time of this observation, few plants had become established in the areas exposed by the uplift, chiefly because the severe tsunamis had cleared away most of the soft sediments. The following species had started:

Very common:
  *Carex sitchensis*
  *Elymus arenarius mollis*
  *Honckenya peploides major*

Common:
  *Mertensia maritima*

A few:
  *Hordeum brachyantherum*
  *Potentilla pacifica*

Rare:
  *Stellaria humifusa*

*Station 31:*  Anderson Bay, Hinchinbrook Island, July 14, 1965. The uplift of the land was 3.8 ft. Much damage had been done to the former intertidal zone in this vicinity by the strong tsunamis. Removal of fine silt had limited the sites favorable for new plant growth. The following species were found:

Very common:
  *Achillea borealis*
  *Carex sitchensis*
  *Glaux maritima*
  *Honckenya peploides major*

Common:
  *Atriplex gmelini*
  *Cochlearia officinalis*
  *Elymus arenarius mollis*
  *Galium aparine*
  *Hordeum brachyantherum*
  *Ligusticum hultenii*
  *Potentilla pacifica*

FIGURE 6   Port Etches, Hinchinbrook Island (Station 29), July 12, 1965. A large stump exposed by the elevation of the land and the scouring of large waves. This one had been submerged about 8 ft during a former catastrophe. Note the new plants growing at the base of the stump.

*G Dallas Hanna*

   *Ribes bracteosum*
   *Rubus spectabilis*
   *Senecio pseudo-arnica*

A few:
   *Hordeum nodosum*
   *Plantago maritima*
   *Rumex crispus*
   *Sambucus racemosa*
   *Stellaria humifusa*
   *Triglochin palustris*

*Station 32:* Whiskey Cove, Hawkins Island: the first inlet northeast of north entrance to Canoe Passage, July 15, 1965. The uplift of the land was 4.2 ft. The following species were found:

Common:
   *Achillea borealis*
   *Arabis lyrata kamchatica*
   *Atriplex gmelini*
   *Chrysanthemum arcticum*
   *Cochlearia officinalis*
   *Elymus arenarius mollis*
   *Galium aparine*
   *Galium boreale*
   *Hordeum brachyantherum*
   *Hordeum nodosum*
   *Lathyrus maritima*

   *Ligusticum hultenii*
   *Plantago maritima*
   *Poa eminens*
   *Potentilla anserina*
   *Potentilla pacifica*
   *Senecio pseudo-arnica*
   *Stellaria humifusa*
   *Triglochin palustris*

Abundant:
   *Carex sitchensis*
   *Glaux maritima*
   *Honckenya peploides major*

A few:
   *Alsine* sp.
   *Angelica lucida*
   *Barbarea orthoceras*
   *Epilobium luteum*
   *Heracleum lanatum*
   *Mertensia maritima*
   *Plantago juncoides*
   *Ranunculus pygmaeus*
   *Ribes bracteosum*
   *Rubus spectabilis*
   *Sagina intermedia*
   *Sambucus racemosa*

Rare:
   *Alnus crispa sinuata*
   *Atriplex drymarioides*

## APPENDIX: ALL SPECIES OF FLOWERING PLANTS FOUND BETWEEN PREEARTHQUAKE AND POSTEARTHQUAKE MEAN HIGH-TIDE LINES IN THE SUMMER OF 1965 IN PRINCE WILLIAM SOUND

| Species | Occurrence | Observed at Stations |
|---|---|---|
| *Achillea borealis* Bongard (northern yarrow) | Common on most beaches | 18, 20, 25, 31, 32 |
| *Alnus crispa* (Aiton) Pursh, ssp. *sinuata* (brush alder) | Seedlings were well started in gravel | 13, 27, 32 |
| *Alsine* sp. (chickweed) | Rare in slate rubble | 15, 32 |
| *Angelica genuflexa* Nuttall (angelica) | Not common | 16, 20 |
| *Angelica lucida*(?) Linnaeus (angelica) | Not common | 32 |
| *Aquilegia formosa* Fischer in De Candolle (columbine) | Found sparingly on many beaches | 15, 16, 20 |
| *Arabis hirsuta* (Linnaeus) Scopoli, ssp. *eschscholtziana* (hairy rock cress); (Androz) Hultenii | Common in beach gravel | 27 |
| *Arabis lyrata* Linnaeus, ssp. *kamchatica* Fischer (Hultén) (lyre-leaved rock cress) | Common in beach gravel | 15, 16, 18, 20, 21, 22, 24, 27, 32 |
| *Aruncus sylvester* Kostelsky (silvery goat's beard) | Rare | 24, 27 |
| *Atriplex drymarioides* Standley (orache) | Usually found on decaying eelgrass | 16, 22, 32 |
| *Atriplex gmelini* C. A. Meyer in Bongard (orache) | Common on decaying algae on most beaches | 24, 27, 31, 32 |
| *Barbarea orthoceras* Ledebour (winter cress) | Abundant on most gravel beaches | 15, 16, 18, 19, 20, 24, 27, 32 |
| *Bromus sitchensis* Trinius in Bongard (Sitka brome grass) | Common on some gravel beaches | 27, 28 |
| *Cardamine umbellata* Greene (bitter cress) | Common on some gravel beaches | 17, 18, 20, 27 |
| *Carex circinnata* C. A. Meyer (sedge) | Rare | 27 |
| *Carex limosa* Linnaeus (mud sedge) | Rare | 16, 27 |
| *Carex livida* (Wahlenberg) Willdenau (livid sedge) | Rare | 27 |
| *Carex sitchensis* Prescott in Bongard (Sitka sedge) | Abundant on newly exposed sand and mud flats | 4, 16, 17, 18, 20, 21, 24, 25, 27, 28, 29, 31, 32 |
| *Chrysanthemum arcticum* Linnaeus (Arctic daisy) | Found only in a few rock crevices | 16, 24, 25, 27, 28, 32 |
| *Chrysosplenium tetrandrum* (Lund) Fries (daisy) | Two specimens in gravel at the head of Deep Bay, Hawkins Island | 27 |
| *Circaea alpina*(?) Linnaeus (alpine enchanter's nightshade) | Only a few plants | 15 |
| *Claytonia sibirica* Linnaeus (Siberian spring beauty) | Vigorous plants on some gravel and rocky areas | 20, 25, 27 |
| *Cochlearia officinalis* Linnaeus (scurvy grass) | Common on most sand and gravel beaches | 4, 16, 17, 18, 22, 24, 25, 27, 31, 32 |
| *Conioselinum benthami* (Watson) Fernald (Bentham hemlock parsley) | Sparse | 18 |
| *Deschampsia* sp. (hairgrass) | Rare | 27, 28 |
| *Elymus arenarius* Linnaeus, ssp. *mollis* (Trinius) Hultén (seaside rye grass) | Abundant | 4, 15, 16, 17, 18, 19, 20, 21, 22, 23, 25, 27, 28, 29, 31, 32 |
| *Epilobium anagallidifolium* Lamarck (pimpernel willow herb) | A few small plants growing in crevices | 16, 18, 20, 21, 27 |
| *Epilobium angustifolium* Linnaeus (spiked willow herb) | Common on gravel beaches | 16, 18, 24 |
| *Epilobium latifolium* Linnaeus (broad-leaved willow herb) | Rare | 15, 27 |
| *Epilobium luteum* Pursh (yellow-flowered willow herb) | Common on some beaches | 19, 20, 32 |
| *Equisetum arvense* Linnaeus (common horsetail) | Rare | 27 |
| *Fritillaria camschatcensis* (Linnaeus) Ker-Gawl (Kamchatka lily) | Rare: only one specimen below former tide line at Olsen Bay | 27 |

APPENDIX: ALL SPECIES OF FLOWERING PLANTS FOUND BETWEEN PREEARTHQUAKE AND POSTEARTHQUAKE MEAN HIGH-TIDE LINES IN THE SUMMER OF 1965 IN PRINCE WILLIAM SOUND (Continued)

| Species | Occurrence | Observed at Stations |
|---|---|---|
| *Galium aparine* Linnaeus (bedstraw) | Common on many beaches | 15, 16, 18, 19, 20, 21, 22, 23, 24, 27, 28, 31, 32 |
| *Galium boreale* Linnaeus (Arctic bedstraw) | Common on sandy areas | 22, 27, 28, 32 |
| *Geum macrophyllum* Willdenau (large-leaved avens) | Rare: in gravel | 15 |
| *Glaux maritima* Linnaeus (black saltwort) | Abundant in beach gravel | 15, 27, 31, 32 |
| *Heracleum lanatum* Michaud (cow parsnip) | Common | 15, 16, 18, 19, 20, 27, 32 |
| *Heuchera glabra* Willdenau (smooth Heuchera) | Rare: in gravel and rock crevices | 18, 24, 27 |
| *Honckenya peploides* Linnaeus, ssp. *major* (Hooker) Hultén (sea-beach sandwort) | Abundant on sand and gravel beaches | 4, 16, 17, 18, 19, 20, 22, 23, 24, 25, 27, 28, 29, 31, 32 |
| *Hordeum brachyantherum* Nevski (wild barley) | Rare | 25, 29, 31, 32 |
| *Hordeum nodosum* Linnaeus (meadow barley) | Common in *Elymus* association at one station | 31, 32 |
| *Lathyrus maritima* (Linnaeus) Bigel (seaside vetch) | Rare | 18, 20, 22, 23, 27, 28, 32 |
| *Ligusticum hultenii* Fernald (Hultén's sea parsley) | Sparse: in gravel areas | 15, 16, 17, 18, 20, 21, 22, 23, 24, 25, 27, 28, 31, 32 |
| *Luzula parviflora* (Ehrhardt) Desvaux (small-flowered wood rush) | Common in crevices of slate | 19, 20, 27 |
| *Mertensia maritima* (Linnaeus) S. F. Gray (seaside cowslip) | Common in slate gravel | 18, 22, 24, 28, 29, 32 |
| *Mimulus guttatus* De Candolle (monkey flower) | Common in a few localities | 16, 20, 21 |
| *Oxyria digyna* (Linnaeus) Hill (mountain sorrel) | A few plants in sand | 18, 27 |
| *Picea sitchensis* (Bongard) Carr (Sitka spruce) | Several seedlings in gravel | 13, 18 |
| *Plantago juncoides* Lamarck (plantain) | A few in slate gravel | 16, 17, 18, 19, 32 |
| *Plantago maritima* Linnaeus (seaside plantain) | A few in slate gravel | 16, 24, 25, 27, 31, 32 |
| *Poa annua* Linnaeus (annual poa) | Only two plants | 16, 19, 22 |
| *Poa eminens* Presl (seaside meadow grass) | Common on gravel flats | 4, 15, 16, 18, 19, 21, 22, 24, 25, 32 |
| *Potentilla anserina* Linnaeus (seaside avens) | Very common on sand flats | 5, 16, 17, 18, 20, 27, 32 |
| *Potentilla pacifica* Howell (Pacific cinquefoil) | Very common | 4, 18, 19, 20, 24, 25, 27, 28, 29, 31, 32 |
| *Puccinellia nutkaensis* (Presl) Fernald and Weatherby (goose grass) | Sparse: with other grasses growing in sand | 25, 27 |
| *Ranunculus bongardii* Greene (Bongard's buttercup) | Rare | 20, 27 |
| *Ranunculus pygmaeus* Wahlenberg (pygmy buttercup) | Very common in slate gravel | 18, 27, 32 |
| *Ribes bracteosum* Douglas ex Hooker (wild gooseberry) | A few seedlings | 18, 21, 24, 27, 31, 32 |
| *Romanzoffia sitchensis* Bongard (saxifrage) | | 21 |
| *Rorippa palustris* (Linnaeus) Besser (yellow watercress) | Only one plant growing below the former high-tide line | 15 |
| *Rubus spectabilis* Pursh (salmonberry) | Seedlings common on slate gravel | 15, 16, 18, 20, 22, 24, 25, 27, 28, 31, 32 |
| *Rumex crispus* Linnaeus (broad-leaved dock) | Common in some slate–gravel areas | 15, 18, 27, 28, 31 |
| *Sagina intermedia* Fenzl (pearl wort) | One plant on slate gravel | 16, 27, 32 |
| *Salix barclayi* Andersson (Barclay's willow) | Seedlings common at the north end of Orca Inlet | 18 |
| *Salix sitchensis* Sanson (Sitka willow) | Seedlings rare at the north end of Orca Inlet | 18 |
| *Sambucus racemosa* Linnaeus (elderberry) | Seedlings with long roots in many places along the bases of cliffs | 15, 16, 17, 18, 19, 20, 21, 22, 24, 27, 31, 32 |
| *Sanguisorba sitchensis* C. A. Meyer (Sitka burnet) | A few specimens | 27 |

APPENDIX: ALL SPECIES OF FLOWERING PLANTS FOUND BETWEEN PREEARTHQUAKE AND
POSTEARTHQUAKE MEAN HIGH-TIDE LINES IN THE SUMMER OF 1965 IN PRINCE WILLIAM SOUND
(Continued)

| Species | Occurrence | Observed at Stations |
|---|---|---|
| *Saxifraga aestivalis* Fischer and Meyer (saxifrage) | Rare: growing in rock crevices | 18, 20, 21, 27, 28 |
| *Senecio pseudo-arnica* Lessing (sea-beach senecio, groundsel) | Common in coarse sand | 18, 21, 23, 31, 32 |
| *Stellaria humifusa* Rootboell (low chickweed) | Common in some areas | 15, 16, 18, 20, 25, 29, 31, 32 |
| *Tellima grandiflora* (Pursh) Douglas (false alumroot) | One plant in coarse sand | 20 |
| *Tiarella trifoliata* Linnaeus (astilbe) | Rare: growing in rock crevices | 18, 27 |
| *Trifolium* sp. (clover) | One plant at Port Ashton | 16 |
| *Triglochin palustris* Linnaeus (marsh arrowgrass) | Common in gravel | 16, 31, 32 |
| *Vaccinium* sp. (blueberry) | Rare | 16 |

# REFERENCES

Cooper, W. S., 1923. The recent ecological history of Glacier Bay, Alaska. *Ecology*, 4 (April), 93–128; (July), 223–246; (October), 355–365.

Cooper, William S., 1930. The seed-plants and ferns of the Glacier Bay National Monument, Alaska. *Bulletin of the Torrey Botanical Club*, 57, 327–338.

Cooper, W. S., 1931. A third expedition to Glacier Bay, Alaska. *Ecology*, 12 (No. 1), 61–95.

Cooper, W. S., 1936. The strand and dune flora of the Pacific Coast of North America: A geographic study *in* Essays in Geobotany in Honor of William Albert Setchell. Berkeley: University of California Press. p. 141–187.

Cooper, W. S., 1939a. A fourth expedition to Glacier Bay, Alaska. *Ecology*, 20 (No. 2), 130–155.

Cooper, W. S., 1939b. Additions to the flora of Glacier Bay National Monument, Alaska, 1935-1936. *Bulletin of the Torrey Botanical Club*, 66, 453–456.

Crocker, Robert L., and J. Major, 1955. Soil development in relation to vegetation and surface age at Glacier Bay, Alaska. *Journal of Ecology*, 43 (July), 427–448.

Crow, John H., 1971. Earthquake-initiated changes in the nesting habitat of the dusky Canada goose *in* The Great Alaska Earthquake of 1964: Biology. NAS Pub. 1604. Washington: National Academy of Sciences.

Dachnowski-Stokes, A. P., 1941. Peat resources in Alaska. U.S. Department of Agriculture Technical Bulletin No. 769. Washington: Government Printing Office. 84 p.

Decker, Henry F., 1966. Plants *in* Soil Development and Ecological Succession in a Deglaciated Area of Muir Inlet, Southeast Alaska. A. Mirsky, Editor. Institute of Polar Studies Report 20. Columbus: The Ohio State University. p. 73–95.

Hanna, G Dallas, 1971. Biological effects of the earthquake as observed in 1965 *in* The Great Alaska Earthquake of 1964: Biology. NAS Pub. 1604. Washington: National Academy of Sciences.

Haven, Stoner B., 1971. Effects of land-level changes on intertidal invertebrates, with discussion of postearthquake ecological succession *in* The Great Alaska Earthquake of 1964: Biology. NAS Pub. 1604. Washington: National Academy of Sciences.

Hultén, Eric, 1941-1950. Flora of Alaska and Yukon. Lunds Universitet Arsskrift, Ny Foljd, avd. 2, bd. 37–46; Kunglige Fysiografiska Sällskapets Handlinger, Ny Foljd, bd. 52–61. 1902 p.

Lawrence, Donald B., 1950. Glacier fluctuation for six centuries in southeastern Alaska and its relation to solar activity. *Geographical Review*, 40 (No. 2), 191–223.

Lawrence, Donald B., 1958. Glaciers and vegetation in southeastern Alaska. *American Scientist*, 46 (No. 2), 89–122.

Lawrence, Donald B., R. E. Shoenike, A. Quispel, and G. Bond, 1967. The role of *Dryas drummondii* in vegetation development following ice recession at Glacier Bay, Alaska, with special reference to its nitrogen fixation by root nodules. *Journal of Ecology*, 55 (No. 3), 793–813.

Miller, Don J., 1960. Giant waves in Lituya Bay, Alaska. U.S. Geological Survey Professional Paper 354-C. Washington: Government Printing Office. p. 51–86.

Plafker, George, 1965. Tectonic deformation associated with the 1964 Alaska earthquake. *Science*, 148 (June 25), 1675–1687.

Plafker, George, and L. R. Mayo, 1965. Tectonic deformation, subaqueous slides and destructive waves associated with the Alaskan March 27, 1964 earthquake: an interim geologic evaluation. U.S. Geological Survey Open-File Report. Menlo Park, California: U.S. Geological Survey. 34 p.

Tarr, Ralph S., and Lawrence Martin, 1912. The earthquakes at Yakutat Bay, Alaska, in September, 1899. U.S. Geological Survey Professional Paper 69. Washington: Government Printing Office. 135 p.

Twenhofel, W. S., 1952. Recent shore-line changes along the Pacific coast of Alaska. *American Journal of Science*, 250 (July), 523–548.

Zach, Lawrence W., 1950. A northern climax, forest or muskeg? *Ecology*, 31 (No. 2), 304–306.

STONER B. HAVEN
SIMON FRASER UNIVERSITY

# Effects of Land-Level Changes on Intertidal Invertebrates, with Discussion of Postearthquake Ecological Succession

ABSTRACT: Investigations were carried out in summer 1965 on the effects of land-level changes and other factors associated with the March 1964 earthquake on intertidal invertebrate populations in Prince William Sound, Alaska. Particular attention was paid to the process of community redevelopment in the postearthquake intertidal zone. Intertidal communities on shores unaffected by land-level changes were studied to provide a control for assessing the effects of the earthquake; additional evidence on preearthquake conditions came from in situ remains (dead or living) of vertically displaced populations. On rocky shores, three major preearthquake intertidal zones were usually recognizable: Verrucaria zone (above mean high-water level); midlittoral zone; and Laminaria zone (below mean lower low water). The sharp upper limit of midlittoral barnacles (mainly Balanus) and of Fucus provided a biological criterion for measuring land-level change. Factors affecting the vertical height and distinctness of this "barnacle line" were studied and were found generally to have relatively little effect within the Sound. Our vertical-displacement measurements agreed well with those made previously by U.S. Geological Survey personnel.

Effects of the earthquake varied with type of habitat and organism and with the amount and direction of land-level change. In general, organisms lifted above their normal vertical ranges were killed. On rocky shores with moderate uplift (2–9 ft), parts of most species populations survived, but with maximum uplift (as much as 30 ft on Montague Island), virtually total mortality extended throughout the intertidal and well into the subtidal zone. In the latter areas, extensive calcareous remains (many sessile forms; vast accumulations of mollusks) documented preearthquake populations. On downthrust rocky shores, sessile midlittoral populations (mussels, barnacles, Fucus) were alive at their new lower levels and apparently inhibited the establishment of normal Laminaria-zone species. Level-bottom populations died from the uplift, and there was additional extensive mortality of large bivalves at some stations caused apparently by removal of surface sediments by waves and currents generated by the earthquake.

Postearthquake community development (in terms of similarity to inferred preearthquake conditions) had in general proceeded most rapidly in the Laminaria zone and less rapidly upward and significantly less rapidly on maximally uplifted shores than on the less strongly affected shores elsewhere. With moderate uplift, most postearthquake animal populations contained both preearthquake survivors and abundant postearthquake recruitment. The postearthquake Verrucaria zone had a normal fauna (Littorina, Acmaea) but no new growth of the dominant lichen Verrucaria; at many places an algal film covered the rocks. With certain important exceptions (given below), the midlittoral zone appeared not to differ greatly from before the earthquake in species composition, vertical ranges, and relative abundance; however, some areas seemed sparsely or patchily populated. The Laminaria zone at all favorable sites supported dense Laminaria cover and a rich, virtually normal fauna.

In areas of maximum uplift, the postearthquake intertidal communities had to develop entirely anew. The fauna was greatly reduced—many species were absent, many others rare—compared to the time before the earthquake, except in the Laminaria zone, which supported a near-normal fauna. Much of the midlittoral zone was dominated by the alga Porphyra, whereas the normally dominant Fucus was uncommon; this distribution may have been related to a scarcity of grazing gastropods. The Verrucaria zone supported an algal film, no Verrucaria, and a strongly reduced gastropod fauna. In samples from a level bottom habitat, only one postearthquake clam was found.

Throughout the Sound, the postearthquake Balanus settlement in the upper midlittoral zone appeared to be nearly all B. balanoides, whereas before the earthquake both B. balanoides and B. glandula were present, with glandula probably the dominant species. Dense beds of postearthquake mussels (Mytilus) were widespread, but most were attached to underlying algae, rather than to rock surfaces, and were at somewhat lower levels than the preearthquake beds. Influence of grazing on vegetation during postearthquake community development was indicated by several examples of negative correlations between gastropod populations and algal density.

Evidence for ecological succession was provided by four main aspects of the postearthquake rocky shore communities that were significantly different from inferred preearthquake conditions: the dominance by algal films rather than Verrucaria in the uppermost zone; the dominance of Balanus balanoides in the midlittoral zone; the attachment of mussels to underlying algae; and, in the maximally uplifted area, the dominance of Porphyra rather than Fucus, correlated with scarcity of grazing gastropods. Additional aspects of succession in rocky shore and level bottom habitats are discussed.

## INTRODUCTION

The changes in land level (Figure 1) accompanying the Alaska earthquake of March 27, 1964, had profound effects on intertidal organisms and their habitats. In uplifted areas, intertidal populations were raised partially or completely above the reach of the tides, and former subtidal populations were brought into the intertidal zone. The converse occurred in downthrust regions. In addition, waves and rapid currents caused by the earthquake had destructive effects in some areas.

Dr. G Dallas Hanna led an expedition in May–July 1965 to investigate the biological effects of the earthquake in Prince William Sound, Alaska. This paper reports studies on intertidal invertebrate populations, including consideration of ecological succession in the newly developing postearthquake communities. Additional results from the expedition are reported in the three preceding papers: Hanna, "Biological effects of the earthquake as observed in 1965"; Johansen, "Effects of elevation changes on benthic algae in Prince William Sound"; and Eyerdam, "Flowering plants found growing between pre- and postearthquake high-tide lines during the summer of 1965 in Prince William Sound."

The studies of intertidal invertebrates were directed to three principal questions:

What was the species composition and general pattern of zonation in normal (preearthquake) intertidal communities in Prince William Sound?

What were the effects of the earthquake on these preexisting populations, i.e., how did mortality and survival vary with respect to animal group, habitat type, initial position in the intertidal zone, and amount of uplift or downthrust?

What was the nature of the new communities in the postearthquake intertidal zone; how did they compare with the preearthquake communities, how did the rate and other aspects of recolonization vary with respect to the factors mentioned in the preceding question, and what could be inferred regarding the process of ecological succession in these newly developing communities?

Investigations of the physical and biological effects of the earthquake were started immediately after the earthquake by the U.S. Geological Survey, U.S. Coast and Geodetic Survey, U.S. Bureau of Commercial Fisheries, and the Alaska Department of Fish and Game. Land-level changes and other physical effects have been reported by Grantz and others (1964), U.S. Coast and Geodetic Survey (1964a), Plafker and Mayo (1965), Plafker (1965, 1969), and the U.S. Coast and Geodetic Survey (1966). Biological effects as observed during the first summer after the earthquake are reported in Hanna (1964, and this volume), Alaska Depart-

ment of Fish and Game (1965), Plafker and Mayo (1965), and Plafker (1965, 1969). Talmadge (1966) reports observations made on mollusks in summer 1965.

Several previously recorded earthquakes have caused land-level changes and mass mortality of intertidal life (Kaburaki, 1928; Brongersma-Sanders, 1957). Of particular interest are the earthquakes of September 1899 at Yakutat Bay, Alaska, which caused a maximum shore uplift of 47 ft; Tarr and Martin (1912) comment briefly on the organisms in the uplifted and postearthquake intertidal zones. However, there has apparently never been a detailed study of the effects of an earthquake on intertidal animal populations, particularly with respect to the postearthquake recolonization process.

## STUDY AREA AND METHODS

### DESCRIPTION OF STUDY AREA

The present investigation was carried out entirely within Prince William Sound, on the south central coast of Alaska. As shown in Figure 1, the Sound lies largely within the zone of uplift and includes the site of maximum shore uplift, but it is also crossed by the line of zero land-level change and includes some downthrust areas as well (Plafker, 1965).

The land is rugged and mountainous and has a highly convoluted shoreline. There are many fiords and bays both on the mainland and on the numerous islands. Rivers and streams are frequent, and in the northern part of the Sound, several glaciers extend to or near to the sea. Most of the land is heavily forested down to the extreme high-tide or spray line.

The waters of Prince William Sound are protected from open-ocean surf by Montague and Hinchinbrook islands, which extend most of the way across the broad south-facing opening of the Sound into the Gulf of Alaska (Figure 1). Therefore, most of the Sound can be classified as a quiet-water area, similar to the Puget Sound–Strait of Georgia region rather than to the "protected outer coast" of Ricketts and Calvin (1962). However, wind-driven waves of considerable force, which frequently occur in the Sound, result in wave-action gradients from the most protected fiords to the exposed points. A slight ocean swell was encountered (even in calm weather) at our outermost stations on Montague and Hinchinbrook islands.

Most of the shoreline is rocky and more or less steeply sloping, but beaches or level-bottom habitats are also extensive. On these, the lack of strong wave action permits a wide variety of substrate types ranging from boulder and rock fields through shingle and gravel beaches to mudflats; no pure sand beaches were seen. At most places, several substrate types (e.g., solid rock, boulders, and gravel-mud

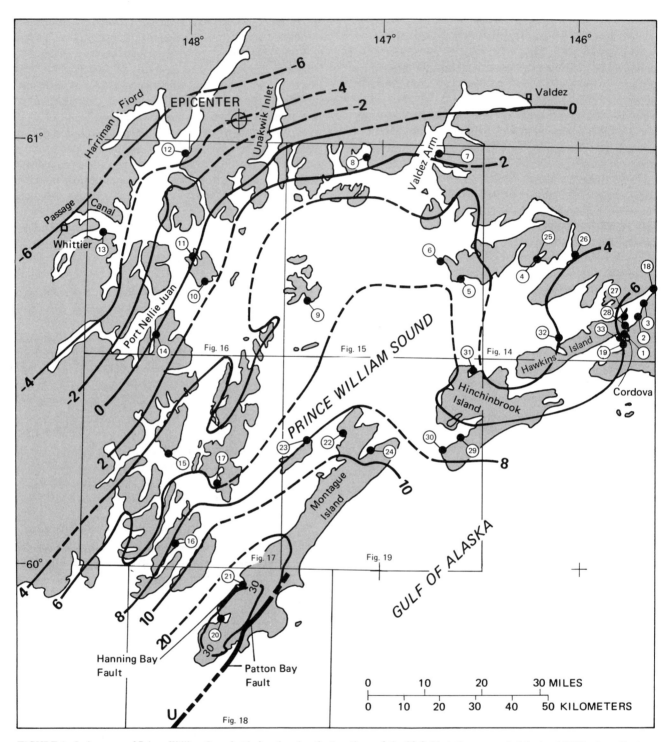

FIGURE 1    Index map of Prince William Sound, Alaska, showing the locations of the 33 field stations occupied during 1965 by investigators aboard M.V. *Harmony*. Isobase contours by Plafker and Mayo (1965) show land-level changes resulting from the March 27, 1964, earthquake. The contour interval is 2 ft between the −6-ft and +10-ft contours, and the interval is 10 ft between the +10-ft and the +30-ft contours. Larger-scale maps of the six sections indicated appear as Figures 14–19 in "Biological Effects of the Earthquake as Observed in 1965" (Hanna, 1971, this volume). (U.S. Geological Survey Base map.)

beach) are complexly interspersed along the shore.

Tides are of the mixed semidiurnal type, with two un-equal high and low tides daily (see Figure 2 in Johansen, 1971, this volume). The zero datum for tide measurements is mean lower low water. At Cordova (the tidal reference station for all the areas visited), mean tidal range is 10.0 ft, mean higher high water is +12.4 ft, and mean high water is +11.5 ft (U.S. Coast and Geodetic Survey, 1964b). During our fieldwork, tides ranged from −3.6 ft to +14.5 ft.

Water temperature in the Sound shows a strong seasonal cycle. Mean surface temperature at Cordova for the period 1949–1953 ranged from a maximum of $11°C$ in August to a minimum of $2°C$ in February (U.S. Coast and Geodetic Survey, 1956). Surface salinity is highly variable because of high rainfall and freshwater influx from streams and glaciers; detailed local data would be needed to give a valid picture for any given site. In general, lowest salinities are found at the heads of bays near the mouths of streams and in the vicinity of glaciers, whereas higher salinities occur along outer shores exposed to circulation from waves and cur-rents, particularly near the entrance to the Sound.

Aerial climate is typically maritime in character, with cool summers, relatively mild winters (for the latitude), and heavy precipitation (Watson, 1959). Average annual precipi-tation at Cordova is about 99 in., spread fairly evenly over the year (maximum in September–November, minimum in June). Highest normal daily maximum air temperature is $61°F$ in August, and lowest normal daily minimum tempera-ture is $17°F$ in February. Record high and low temperatures are $87°$ and $−33°F$, but deviations from normal are short and rare compared to inland conditions at this latitude (Watson, 1959).

METHODS

The expedition operated from a chartered 76-foot purse seiner, the M.V. *Harmony* of Seattle. Thirty-three stations were occupied in Prince William Sound. Studies of inverte-brates were carried out at 27 of these (see Table 3); loca-tions of the stations cited in the text are shown in Figure 1. The paper by Hanna (1971, this volume) contains a com-plete station list, maps, coordinates, and descriptions of the stations. We obtained land-level-change data from a map, provided by George Plafker, that showed the measure-ments made by the U.S. Geological Survey in 1964; this map has been published in Plafker (1969).

In order to cover as much of the Sound as possible within the time available, usually only 1 day (1 or 2 low tides) was spent at each station; up to 3 days were spent at some important stations. Most stations were in sheltered bays where there was anchorage for the *Harmony* and where landing could be made from a small boat. However,

a few stations on somewhat exposed points within the Sound were successfully occupied. An attempt to reach the outer coast of Hinchinbrook Island failed because of heavy swells.

Fieldwork consisted of general observations, transect surveys, collection of specimens, occasional quantitative sampling, and photography.

At most stations, one or more vertical transect surveys were made in the rocky intertidal zone at sites that appeared typical of the area after a general reconnaissance along the shore. The transects extended through both the displaced preearthquake intertidal zone (where accessible) and the postearthquake intertidal zone. Most of the transects were on vertical to gently sloping solid rock, but a few were on boulder fields or mixed boulder–rock areas. The transects were marked with a nylon rope divided into 1-ft intervals. Vertical heights of the principal zonal belts of preearth-quake and postearthquake organisms and the vertical ranges of important individual species were determined and mea-sured with a hand level or Brunton compass and a stadia rod. Heights were measured from water level and later cor-rected to heights above or below zero datum using tide-table data (U.S. Coast and Geodetic Survey, 1964b). The accuracy of the measurements is probably within ±½ ft, except at a few places where horizontal distances were great. Most of the transects were made in conjunction with H. W. Johansen and served to document both plant and animal distribution.

Photography was considered an important part of the field program, because it provided records of zonation and other aspects of population distribution and abundance that were impossible to obtain by other means (e.g., quantitative sampling) in the time available. Unfortunately, rain often hampered photography and caused the record to be less complete than desired. The photographs, all in color, will be retained by the author for comparison with any taken by future investigators; biological changes, particularly in the postearthquake zone, will thus be documented. Dr. Hanna was responsible for most of the photography, especially the close-up pictures.

Collection of specimens was limited primarily to ob-taining samples of zone-forming dominant or otherwise ecologically important species. For the upper and midinter-tidal regions, the collections represent a fairly complete sample of the dominant and conspicuous members of the fauna, but for the richer low intertidal zone, the collections are necessarily very incomplete. No special effort was made to sample small or otherwise inconspicuous organisms. Specimens were preserved on shipboard in "Whirl-Pak" plastic bags. A wad of cotton soaked in 10 percent formalin was placed in each bag. The bags, which were airtight when sealed, were packed in metal cans for shipment. No significant damage occurred to the specimens during shipment. The specimens have been deposited in the collection of the California Academy of Sciences, San Francisco.

## ROCKY SHORES: NORMAL (PREEARTHQUAKE) CONDITIONS

It was necessary to obtain information on the "normal" preearthquake intertidal ecology of Prince William Sound in order to assess validly the effects of the earthquake. Unfortunately, there were no published accounts of zonation or other aspects of general intertidal ecology for Prince William Sound. In fact, the 1963 quantitative study by Nybakken (1971, this volume) of the intertidal ecology of Three Saints Bay, Kodiak Island, is apparently the first such study on Alaskan shores. The closest previous investigations have been in Washington and in British Columbia (Shelford and Towler, 1925; Shelford and others, 1935; Rigg and Miller, 1949; Stephenson and Stephenson, 1961a, 1961b; Widdowson, 1965; Druehl, 1967). The work of Ricketts and Calvin (1962) contains ecological information on Alaskan species; MacGinitie's study at Point Barrow (1955) was on subtidal organisms. Intertidal zonation has received considerable attention on a comparative, worldwide basis; for discussions and references, see Stephenson and Stephenson (1949), Doty (1957), Southward (1958), Ricketts and Calvin (1962), and Lewis (1961, 1964).

We obtained data on normal preearthquake intertidal communities in Prince William Sound from areas unaffected or only slightly affected by the earthquake. Our principal station along the line of zero land-level change was West Twin Bay, Perry Island (Station 11). Four other stations (Stations 7, 8, 10, 14) had vertical displacement of 2 ft or less, which was considered negligible relative to the tidal range and the vertical ranges of most organisms.

We also obtained data on normal preearthquake intertidal communities from remains, dead or living, of preearthquake populations. On uplifted shores, abundant dead remains of calcareous sessile organisms such as barnacles, mussels, and bryozoans were still attached to the rocks. *In situ* remains of motile animals, particularly gastropods, were also common, lodged in cracks or attached by dried mucus. In downthrust and moderately uplifted areas, information was obtained from preearthquake organisms that were still alive and within the intertidal zone, although some of these were not definitely distinguishable from postearthquake individuals.

A generalized diagram of the principal vertical zones recognizable on rocky shores in Prince William Sound, together with the vertical ranges of some of the common species, is given in Figure 2. A list of all the species collected from both rocky shores and level-bottom habitats is given in Table 1 (some of the identifications are provisional or have not been made to the species level). Preearthquake conditions in level-bottom habitats are discussed later in this paper.

Three major zones were distinguishable on rocky shores: the *Verrucaria* zone; a broad midlittoral zone, usually divisible into an upper midlittoral or *Balanus–Fucus* zone and a lower midlittoral or "green" zone; and the *Laminaria* zone. These zones will be described later; plants will be mentioned when they are dominant species but in a very simplified manner; for a detailed account of plant distribution, refer to the paper by Johansen in this volume. The following is a generalized, composite picture of preearthquake conditions and therefore must be used with caution when interpreting the effects of the earthquake. There appeared to be considerable uniformity in the major pattern of intertidal zonation throughout the Sound, but the exact preearthquake conditions at any of the uplifted or downthrust stations are not known.

### VERRUCARIA ZONE

The *Verrucaria* is the uppermost zone and corresponds to the supralittoral fringe of Stephenson and Stephenson (1949), the littoral fringe of Lewis (1961), zone 1 of Ricketts and Calvin (1962), and zone A of Rigg and Miller (1949). The zone extends from a very sharp lower limit at, or slightly below, mean high water level upward for a variable distance averaging 2 to 5 ft. The upper boundary of the zone, above which terrestrial lichens occur, is usually irregular, probably because of local variations in substrate slope and aspect, freshwater runoff, and amount of wave splash. Most of the zone is covered regularly by higher high tides, only the uppermost portion being a true splash zone; thus the zone is considerably compressed compared to open coasts that experience heavy wave action.

The dominant species of this zone is the encrusting lichen *Verrucaria*, which usually exists in a dense cover and gives the rock a black appearance (Figure 3). The fauna is limited to only a few species, the most important of which are the gastropods *Littorina sitkana* and *L. scutulata*. The bulk of the populations of both species is found at and below the lower limit of the zone, at least at low tide. *Littorina scutulata* extends only sparsely into the zone (rarely more than 1 ft); *L. sitkana* extends in moderate numbers somewhat higher, but only a few individuals reach the top of the zone. Probably the littorines move up into the zone in greater numbers when it is covered by high tides.

The limpets *Acmaea persona* and *A. digitalis* have relatively narrow vertical ranges that center at the lower boundary of the *Verrucaria* zone and extend up into the zone for about 1 ft. Both species often occur in aggregations in cracks and crevices, *A. persona* being more strongly restricted to sheltered cracks than *A. digitalis*. Both range

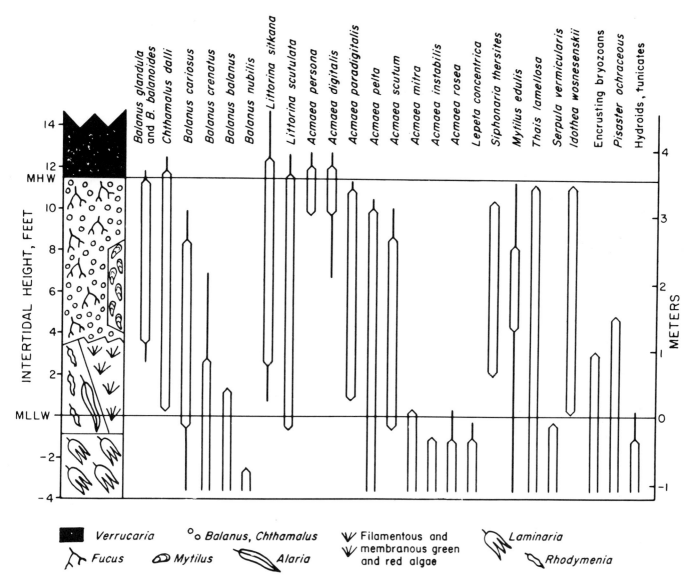

FIGURE 2   Simplified typical zonation on preearthquake rocky shore in Prince William Sound, with approximate vertical ranges of some common animal species. Principal zones, starting from the top, are *Verrucaria* zone; upper midlittoral zone, dominated by barnacles and *Fucus,* with mussel beds *(Mytilus)* in the lower part; lower midlittoral or "green" zone, dominated by filamentous and membranous algae or by larger algae such as *Alaria* and *Rhodymenia;* and *Laminaria* zone (based principally on transects at Station 11 and the other normal stations and on uplifted preearthquake populations elsewhere). MHW is mean high-water level; MLLW is mean lower low water, the zero datum.

more widely when grazing and may penetrate higher into the *Verrucaria* zone at high tide or at night. The dominant species of this pair throughout the protected part of the Sound is *A. persona;A. digitalis* is abundant only at the outer stations (Montague and Hinchinbrook islands), where it largely replaces *A. persona.*

The isopod *Ligia* sp. occurs occasionally in deep cracks near the bottom of the zone. Several species of small insects, mites, and spiders are common (none of these were collected). Many organisms typical of lower zones, for example, barnacles (particularly *Chthamalus dalli*), commonly

extend a foot or more into the *Verrucaria* zone, especially in sheltered cracks or depressions.

MIDLITTORAL ZONE

The midlittoral (midtidal) zone is vertically the widest of the three rocky shore zones. It corresponds to the midlittoral zone of Stephenson and Stephenson (1949), the eulittoral zone of Lewis (1961), zones 2 and 3 of Ricketts and Calvin (1962), and zones B and C of Rigg and Miller (1949). The clearly defined zone extends from the upper

TABLE 1   Species Collected in Prince William Sound

| Species | Occurrence of Living Specimens | | | | Principal Habitat[a] |
| --- | --- | --- | --- | --- | --- |
| | Normal | Mod. Uplift | Max. Uplift | Downthrust | |
| Porifera | | | | | |
| 3 species | + | + | | | 4 |
| Coelenterata | | | | | |
| Hydroids (several species) | + | + | + | | 4 |
| Haliclystus sp. | | | + | | 4 |
| Anthopleura artemisia | | + | | | L |
| Metridium senile | | + | | | 4 |
| 3 unidentified anemone species | + | + | | | 2–4 |
| Platyhelminthes | | | | | |
| Polyclad sp. | | + | | | 3 |
| Nemertea | | | | | |
| Cerebratulus sp. | + | | | | 4 |
| Emplectonema sp. | + | + | + | | 2–3 |
| Unidentified sp. | | + | | | 2–3 |
| Annelida | | | | | |
| Polynoid sp. | + | + | | | 4 |
| Nephthys sp. | | + | | | L |
| Glycera sp. | + | + | | | 3–4, L |
| Nereis sp. | + | + | | | 3–4, L |
| Cirratulid sp. | + | + | | | 3–4 |
| Thelepus sp. | | + | | | L |
| Sabellid sp. | | + | | | 4 |
| Serpula vermicularis | + | + | + | | 4 |
| Spirorbis sp. | + | + | | | 4 |
| Several unidentified Polychaetes | + | + | + | | 3–4, L |
| Oligochaete sp. | | + | | | 2–3, L |
| Sipunculida | | | | | |
| 1 species | + | + | | | 2–4 |
| Echiuroidea | | | | | |
| Echiurus echiurus alaskensis | + | + | | | 2–4, L |
| Mollusca: Polyplacophora | | | | | |
| Cryptochiton stelleri | + | + | | | 4 |
| Ishnochiton interstinctus | | + | | | 4 |
| Ishnochiton trifidus | | + | | | 4 |
| Katharina tunicata | + | + | | + | 2–3 |
| Mopalia ciliata | | + | | | 3–4 |
| Mopalia lignosa | | + | | | 3–4 |
| Mopalia sinuata | | + | | | 4 |
| Mopalia swani | + | + | | | 3–4 |
| Placiphorella rufa | | | + | | 4 |
| Tonicella insignis | + | + | | | 3–4 |
| Tonicella lineata | + | + | + | | 2–4 |
| Mollusca: Gastropoda | | | | | |
| Diadora aspersa | | | b | | 4 |
| Fisurella volcano | | | b | | 4 |
| Puncturella spp. | | | b | | 4 |
| Acmaea digitalis | + | + | | | 1–2 |
| Acmaea instabilis | | | b | | 4 |
| Acmaea mitra | + | + | + | | 3–4 |
| Acmaea paradigitalis | + | + | + | + | 2–3 |
| Acmaea pelta | + | + | + | + | 2–4 |
| Acmaea persona | + | + | + | + | 1–2 |
| Acmaea rosea | | + | + | | 4 |
| Acmaea scutum | + | + | + | + | 2–3 |
| Lepeta concentrica | | + | + | | 4 |
| Margarites pupilla | | + | + | | 2–4 |
| Margarites salmonella | | + | + | | 3–4 |

TABLE 1 (Continued)

| Species | Occurrence of Living Specimens | | | | Principal Habitat[a] |
|---|---|---|---|---|---|
| | Normal | Mod. Uplift | Max. Uplift | Downthrust | |
| *Margaritopsis pribiloffensis* | | + | | | 4 |
| *Littorina scutulata* | + | + | + | + | 1–3 |
| *Littorina sitkana* | + | + | + | + | 1–3 |
| *Lacuna* sp. | | + | + | | 4 |
| *Velutina* sp. | | + | | | 3 |
| *Trichotropis cancellatus* | | + | | | 4 |
| *Trichotropis insignis* | | + | | | 4 |
| *Fusitriton oregonensis* | | | b | | 4 |
| *Searlesia dira* | + | + | + | + | 2–4 |
| *Trophonopsis beringi* | | | b | | 4 |
| *Buccinium* sp. | + | + | | | 2–4 |
| *Ocenebra interfossa* | | + | + | | 4 |
| *Thais lamellosa* | + | + | + | + | 2–4 |
| *Thais lima* | | + | | | 2–4 |
| *Onchidoris bilamellata* | | + | | | 2–3 |
| Dorid sp. | | + | | | 3 |
| *Melibe leonina* | | + | | | 2 |
| Aeolid sp. | | + | | | 2–3 |
| *Siphonaria thersites* | + | + | | + | 2–3 |
| *Onchidella borealis* | + | + | | | 2–3 |
| Mollusca: Pelecypoda | | | | | |
| *Pododesmus macroschizma* | | | b | | 3–4 |
| *Musculus* sp. | | + | + | | 4 |
| *Mytilus edulis* | + | + | + | + | 2–4 |
| *Axinopsida* sp. | | + | | | L |
| *Diplodonta orbella* | + | + | + | | 4 |
| *Mysella* sp. | | + | | | L |
| *Clinocardium nuttallii* | + | + | + | | L |
| *Saxidomus giganteus* | + | + | | | L |
| *Humilaria kennerleyi* | | + | | | L |
| *Protothaca staminea* | + | + | | | 3–4, L |
| *Tellina lutea* | | | b | | L |
| *Macoma brota lipara* | | | b | | L |
| *Macoma inconspicua* | + | + | | | L |
| *Macoma irus* | + | + | | | L |
| *Macoma nasuta* | | + | | | L |
| *Tresus (Schizothaerus) capax* | + | + | | | L |
| *Mya arenaria* | | | b | | L |
| *Mya truncata* | + | + | | | L |
| *Hiatella arctica* | + | + | | | 3–4, L |
| Mollusca: Cephalopoda | | | | | |
| *Octopus* sp. | | + | | | 4 |
| Crustacea: Cirripedia | | | | | |
| *Balanus balanoides* | + | + | + | + | 2–3 |
| *Balanus balanus* | | b | + | | 4 |
| *Balanus cariosus* | + | + | + | + | 2–4 |
| *Balanus crenatus* | | + | + | | 3–4 |
| *Balanus glandula* | + | + | | + | 2–3 |
| *Balanus nubilis* | | | b | | 4 |
| *Chthamalus dalli* | + | + | + | + | 1–4 |
| Crustacea: Malacostraca | | | | | |
| *Exosphaeroma oregonensis* | + | + | + | | 2–4 |
| *Idothea ochotensis* | | + | | | 3 |
| *Idothea wosnesenskii* | + | + | + | + | 2–4 |
| *Ligia* sp. | | + | | | 1–2 |
| *Ampithoe* sp. and other Gammarids | + | + | + | + | 2–4 |
| *Cancer oregonensis* | + | + | + | | 3–4 |

TABLE 1 (Continued)

| Species | Occurrence of Living Specimens | | | | Principal Habitat[a] |
|---|---|---|---|---|---|
| | Normal | Mod. Uplift | Max. Uplift | Downthrust | |
| *Cancer magister* | + | + | | | 3–4 |
| *Hemigrapsus oregonensis* | + | + | + | | 2–4 |
| *Lophopanopeus bellus* | + | + | + | | 3–4 |
| *Pugettia gracilis* | | + | | | 3–4 |
| *Haplogaster grebnizkii* | + | + | | | 3–4 |
| Pagurid spp. | + | + | + | + | 2–4 |
| *Hyas lyratus* | | + | | | 4 |
| Ectoprocta | | | | | |
| Approx. 8 species | + | + | + | | 3–4 |
| Brachiopoda | | | | | |
| *Terebratalia transversa* | | + | + | | 4 |
| Echinodermata | | | | | |
| *Dermasterias imbricata* | + | + | + | | 3–4 |
| *Evasterias troschellii* | + | + | | | 3–4 |
| *Henricia leviuscula* | | + | | | 3–4 |
| *Leptasterias hexactis* | + | + | | | 3–4 |
| *Mediaster aequalis* | | + | | | 4 |
| *Orthasterias* sp. | | + | | | 4 |
| *Pisaster ochraceous* | + | + | | + | 2–4 |
| *Pycnopodia helianthoides* | + | + | | | 3–4 |
| 2 unidentified Asteroid species | | + | | | 4 |
| *Strongylocentrotus drobachiensis* | + | + | + | | 3–4 |
| *Amphipholis* sp. | | + | | | 4 |
| Amphiurid sp. | | + | | | 4 |
| *Ophiopholis aculeata* | + | + | | | 4 |
| *Cucumaria miniata* | + | + | | | 2–4 |
| *Eupentacta* sp. | | + | | | 4 |
| *Parastichopus californicus* | + | + | | | 4 |
| Chordata: Ascidiacea | | | | | |
| *Amaroucium* sp. | | + | + | | 4 |
| Botryllid sp. | | | + | | 4 |
| *Chelyosoma* sp. | | | + | | 4 |
| Didemnid sp. | | + | | | 4 |
| *Distaplia* sp. | | + | | | 4 |
| *Halocynthia aurantium* | | | + | | 4 |
| *Metandrocarpa* sp. | | + | | | 4 |
| *Styela* sp. | | + | | | 4 |
| *Synoicum* spp. | | + | + | | 4 |

[a] Habitat designations: 1, *Verrucaria* zone; 2, upper-midlittoral zone; 3, lower-midlittoral zone; 4, *Laminaria* zone; L, level bottom (mud flat) habitat.
[b] Found only as dead remains.

limit of barnacles and *Fucus* (the lower limit of *Verrucaria*) down to the upper limit of Laminarian algae (somewhat below the zero tide level). The boundary between the midlittoral and *Verrucaria* zones (Figure 3) is the sharpest and most conspicuous zonal boundary to be found in the Sound and is particularly important as the datum used for most of the land-level-change measurements; this is discussed later.

At most places in the Sound the midlittoral zone can be divided into upper and lower subzones. However, the boundary between these subzones is never as distinct as the upper and lower limits of the midlittoral zone as a whole, and sometimes consists only of a gradual transition. Nevertheless, the fauna and flora of the upper and lower parts of the midlittoral zone are different enough to justify separate discussion of the two subzones.

UPPER MIDLITTORAL OR *BALANUS–FUCUS* ZONE

The upper midlittoral zone is named for its dominant organisms, barnacles of the genus *Balanus* and the brown

G Dallas Hanna

FIGURE 3   Rocky shore zonation at West Twin Bay, Perry Island (Station 11), June 15, 1965, unaffected by the earthquake. Upper arrow: boundary between the *Verrucaria* (above) and upper midlittoral zones, at about mean high-water level. Lower arrow: boundary between the upper midlittoral and lower midlittoral zones.

alga *Fucus distichus* (Figure 3). This zone corresponds approximately to zone 2 of Ricketts and Calvin (1962) and zone B of Rigg and Miller (1949).

The most abundant barnacle species in the upper part of the zone are *Balanus glandula, B. balanoides,* and *Chthamalus dalli. Balanus cariosus* increases toward the lower part of the zone. Evidence that *glandula* was the dominant high-level *Balanus* species in the preearthquake communities, whereas *balanoides* was the dominant post-earthquake species, is discussed later. The conspicuous barnacle line at the upper limit of the midlittoral zone is formed principally by one or both of these *Balanus* species, with *Chthamalus dalli* present in smaller numbers but extending slightly higher. However, the distribution of *Chthamalus* is quite irregular; this species may be found in dense patches of varying size anywhere in the midlittoral zone, and at some stations (for example, Station 23) *Balanus* was unaccountably sparse and *Chthamalus* was the dominant high-level barnacle.

Barnacle and *Fucus* cover generally alternates in an irregular mosaic, although dense barnacle populations often occur under *Fucus.* Algae other than *Fucus* that frequently are dominant include *Gloiopeltis* and *Halosaccion.* At all the normal stations (with little or no change in elevation), both *Fucus* and *Balanus glandula* and/or *balanoides* extend up to virtually the same sharp upper limit; dead uplifted remains show that this condition prevailed throughout the Sound before the earthquake. At some places (Figure 3), *Fucus* cover is greater in the lower part of the zone, and barnacles are more important in the upper part. Evidence from uplifted remains as well as from the normal stations shows that *Balanus glandula* and/or *balanoides* populations are densest toward their upper limit and decrease irregularly downward; largest individuals also tend to be highest. Preearthquake barnacle populations appear to be sparser and composed of smaller individuals in the outer parts of the Sound (Montague and Hinchinbrook islands). Toward the heads of bays where stream inflow reduces salinity, all intertidal biota becomes reduced, but barnacles tend to persist farther and in greater numbers than *Fucus* and other algae.

Beds of the mussel *Mytilus edulis* are a conspicuous feature of the lower part of the *Balanus–Fucus* zone. Small mussels occur from the subtidal nearly to the top of the midlittoral zone, but dense beds occupy a fairly narrow vertical range (see Figure 16). The horizontal distribution of mussel beds is patchy and irregular; no correlation with environmental factors such as wave action is evident from our observations. Although the beds are best developed on solid rock, mussels are also common under boulders, nestled among gravel and small rocks on beaches, and attached to large algae. Mussels are discussed in more detail later in this paper.

The most abundant components of the rock-surface fauna in addition to barnacles and mussels are several species of herbivorous gastropods. Most common are *Littorina sitkana*, *L. scutulata*, *Acmaea paradigitalis*, *A. pelta*, *A. scutum*, *Siphonaria thersites*, and, in the uppermost part of the zone, *Acmaea persona* and *A. digitalis*. *Onchidella borealis* is characteristic but somewhat less common. Both littorines are abundant throughout the zone, although at some stations one or the other species was unaccountably rare. The small, recently described *Acmaea paradigitalis* (Fritchman, 1960) is probably the commonest limpet; it occurs mainly on bare rock among barnacles and *Fucus* in the upper part of the zone. Maximum population density of *A. pelta* and *A. scutum* is at lower levels; *A. scutum* prefers sheltered vertical surfaces and the undersides of boulders, whereas *A. pelta* is ubiquitous on and under algae and rocks. Activities of grazing gastropods and their relation to vegetation are discussed in the section on herbivorous gastropods and vegetation (p. 115).

The highly variable *Thais lamellosa* is the principal predatory snail of this zone, being common at low tide on open rock surfaces, in cracks, under algae, and under boulders. *Thais lima* is much less common and more scattered in distribution, but at one station it replaced *T. lamellosa* as the dominant species. Most asteroids are found at lower levels, at least at low tide, but the commonest, *Pisaster ochraceous*, frequently occurs well up into the *Balanus–Fucus* zone.

Of the chitons, only *Katharina tunicata* is common on open rock surfaces, the rest occurring largely under boulders. The isopod *Idothea wosnesenskii*, the nemertean *Emplectonema* sp., and hermit crabs (Paguridae), although most characteristic of the under-boulder habitat, are also numerous on open rock surfaces. Tidepools are relatively infrequent in most of Prince William Sound because of the steepness of the shore, but where found they have a similar fauna to the surrounding rocks, with some additions, notably two or more species of anemones (the anemones sometimes occur in cracks away from tidepools).

The under-boulder habitat in the *Balanus–Fucus* zone supports a fauna composed of a few species that are very abundant and widespread. Commonest are large gammarid amphipods of at least two species, the isopods *Idothea wosnesenskii* and *Exosphaeroma oregonensis* (the latter somewhat less numerous that *Idothea*), hermit crabs (Paguridae), the nemertean *Emplectonema* sp., the gastropods *Searlesia dira*, *Littorina sitkana*, *L. scutulata*, *Acmaea scutum*, *A. pelta*, *A. paradigitalis* (less common), *A. persona* (upper part of zone only), the chiton *Tonicella lineata*, and the mussel *Mytilus edulis*. Somewhat less common are several low intertidal species that reach their upper limits in the zone: the echiuroid worm *Echiurus echiurus alaskensis* (in shallow, mostly horizontal burrows under boulders), the barnacle *Balanus crenatus*, the large holothurian *Cucumaria miniata* (abundant at one station, scattered elsewhere), the asteroids *Evasterias troschellii* and *Leptasterias hexactis*, the nudibranch *Onchidoris bilamellata*, and the bivalve *Hiatella arctica*. Other clams, particularly *Protothaca staminea*, which occurred occasionally, are discussed in connection with level-bottom habitats.

## LOWER MIDLITTORAL OR GREEN ZONE

The lower midlittoral zone extends from an irregular line or transition area representing the lower limit of dense *Balanus* and *Fucus* cover down to the upper limit of laminarian algae (Figure 3). It is approximately equivalent to zone 3 of Ricketts and Calvin (1962) and zone C of Rigg and Miller (1949).

This zone is usually densely covered by many species of small membranous and filamentous algae that give rise to the term "green zone." However, the term is a misnomer, since red and brown as well as green algae are common. Evidence from the postearthquake intertidal zone in uplifted areas suggests that at some stations, particularly in the outer part of the Sound, the lower midlittoral is dominated by larger algae (*Rhodymenia*, *Alaria*). In level muddy areas, beds of eelgrass (*Zostera*) extend up into the lower part of the zone (to about the zero tide level).

Correlated with this general dominance of algae, there are no major animal dominants in terms of visible cover comparable to the barnacles and mussels of the upper midlittoral. There are, however, some locally dominant or otherwise conspicuous animals. The large barnacle *Balanus cariosus* occasionally forms dense beds to the exclusion of nearly all other sessile organisms. This species is widespread and common, but the factors favoring the development of these dense local aggregations are not known. *Balanus crenatus* also sometimes forms dense populations in the lower midlittoral and *Laminaria* zones, but since this was observed only in the new intertidal at uplifted stations, it may or may not be a normal situation. The large asteroids

*Pisaster ochraceous* and *Pycnopodia helianthoides* are abundant and conspicuous; *Dermasterias imbricata* is somewhat less common. Occasional large *Evasterias troschellii* are found, but this asteroid occurs more abundantly under rocks. A species of orange encrusting bryozoan is a common dominant on vertical or shaded rock surfaces, and the calcareous tube worm *Serpula vermicularis* extends in cracks up into the lower part of the zone.

Most of the fauna of the green zone occurs under boulders, hidden in cracks, or under algae. These habitats are considerably richer in species in the green zone than in the *Balanus–Fucus* zone. The fauna is a mixture of high and low intertidal species; no species were found that are restricted to the green zone. Among the common species are high intertidal forms that reach their lower limits at various levels within the green zone, including *Littorina sitkana*, *L. scutulata*, *Acmaea scutum*, *A. paradigitalis* (*L. scutulata* and *A. scutum* are the commonest of these in the green zone), *Chthamalus dalli*, *Katharina tunicata*, *Idothea wosnesenskii*, and the large gammarid amphipods. All these species decrease toward their lower limits, the exact levels of which are uncertain. Several other high intertidal species are common all the way through the green zone into the *Laminaria* zone, including *Acmaea pelta*, *Mytilus edulis*, *Balanus cariosus*, *Tonicella lineata*, *Thais lamellosa*, and pagurids.

The most characteristic animals of the green zone are the numerous low intertidal forms that reach their upper limits in the green zone or in the lower part of the *Balanus–Fucus* zone. Most extend down into the subtidal; in general, the number of species increases downward. The commonest of these species include *Searlesia dira*, *Evasterias troschellii* (small individuals very numerous), *Leptasterias hexactis*, *Pisaster ochraceous*, *Pycnopodia helianthoides*, *Tonicella lineata*, *T. insignis*, *Mopalia* spp. and several other chitons, *Haplogaster grebnizkii*, *Cancer oregonensis*, *Hemigrapsus oregonensis*, *Emplectonema* sp., several polychaetes (of which Nereids, Glycerids, and Cirratulids are the most conspicuous), *Diplodonta orbella*, and *Hiatella arctica*. Small urchins, *Strongylocentrotus drobachiensis*, are regular but uncommon.

## LAMINARIA ZONE

The *Laminaria* or kelp zone corresponds to the infralittoral fringe of Stephenson and Stephenson (1949), the upper sublittoral zone of Lewis (1961), zone 4 of Ricketts and Calvin (1962), and zone D of Rigg and Miller (1949). This zone is dominated by several species of the brown algal genus *Laminaria* where rocky substrates occur (Figure 4); many other species of algae are also common. The upper limit of the zone, defined by the upper limit of *Laminaria*, varies, according to our measurements, between about zero

and −2 ft at different stations. The average upper limit is clearly below zero. In muddy areas, the zone is often dominated by eelgrass (*Zostera*).

Because of insufficiently low tides, the *Laminaria* zone was barely accessible at the normal stations. However, the author's experience elsewhere along the North American coast indicated that in the postearthquake intertidal zone at many of the uplifted stations the zone was very rich and well developed. It is inferred, therefore, that the *Laminaria* zone was very rapidly repopulated after the earthquake and that a reasonably valid picture of the "normal" *Laminaria* zone can be constructed even though most of the data are from the postearthquake intertidal zone in uplifted areas.

The faunal richness of the *Laminaria* zone seems correlated (regardless of amount of uplift) with the degree of exposure to oceanic conditions. This correlation presumably involves good water circulation by waves and currents, low sediment content of the water, and relatively high salinity. Thus the richest stations, all having dense *Laminaria* cover with an abundant and diverse fauna, were Knowles Head (Station 5), Stockdale Harbor (Station 22), Green Island (Station 23), and English Bay (Station 30), all with moderate uplift; and MacLeod Harbor (Station 20) and Hanning Bay (Station 21) with maximum uplift. Our limited observations indicate that the principal normal station (West Twin Bay, Station 11) is typical of the more protected areas in the Sound, where there is more accumulation of fine sediment in the *Laminaria* zone, less dense *Laminaria* populations, and a less diverse fauna.

The *Laminaria* zone is richer in animal species than are any of the higher zones. Most of the animals are attached to sheltered vertical rock surfaces and are hidden under boulders, in cracks, or under algae. Among the most characteristic species are the ascidians, hydroids, bryozoans, and sponges. The ascidians and bryozoans are the most abundant and diverse of these groups, followed by hydroids, whereas sponges are rather rare. Other conspicuous species of the *Laminaria* zone include the gastropods *Acmaea mitra*, *A. rosea*, *Lepeta concentrica*, and *Lacuna* sp., the bivalve *Musculus* sp. (attached by byssal fibers to *Laminaria* fronds and stipes and to rocks), *Placiphorella rufa* and several other chitons, several polychaetes, the anthozoan *Metridium senile*, the brachiopod *Terebratalia transversa*, the barnacle *Balanus balanus*, and the holothurian *Parastichopus californicus*. In addition, the low intertidal species listed above for the green zone are also common in the *Laminaria* zone, as are the wide-ranging high intertidal species.

Additional species, principally mollusks, were found abundantly as dead remains in the uplifted preearthquake subtidal and *Laminaria* zones at the maximally uplifted stations on Montague Island. These include *Puncturella* sp., *Diadora* sp., *Acmaea instabilis* (only among dead *Laminaria* holdfasts, as expected from its stenotopic niche on this

FIGURE 4  Postearthquake *Laminaria* zone at Green Island (Station 23), July 1, 1965. Although this area was uplifted about 8 ft, the dense cover of *Laminaria* and the accompanying rich fauna are considered similar to preearthquake conditions.

alga), *Fusitriton oregonensis, Pododesmus macroschizma*, and *Balanus nubilis*. Although none of these were found alive anywhere in the Sound, they are undoubtedly a part of the normal fauna of the *Laminaria* zone on Montague Island and probably elsewhere.

It should be noted that in Table 1 there are many species that were collected only at uplifted stations (in the postearthquake intertidal zone). All of these are green-zone and *Laminaria*-zone species and can be assumed to be components of the normal fauna of the Sound. Many of them were collected at only one or two stations, and their absence from the normal stations is attributable to environmental variation, patchy distribution of rare species, or incomplete sampling.

## ROCKY SHORES: MODERATE UPLIFT

For the purpose of discussing the effects of the earthquake, our stations in Prince William Sound have been grouped into three categories—moderate uplift, maximum uplift,

and downthrust—in addition to the normal category (stations with little or no vertical displacement).

"Moderate uplift" includes 18 stations whose measured uplifts (Plafker, 1969) ranged from 3.6 to 8.9 ft (see Table 3, p. 112); at all these stations the preearthquake intertidal communities were only partly lifted above the postearthquake intertidal zone. There was considerable variability among these stations in the effects of the earthquake on preexisting organisms and in the state of the postearthquake communities, much of which was attributable to the varying amount of vertical overlap between the pre- and postearthquake communities (Figure 5). However, enough uniformity existed to justify pooling the stations for the following discussion.

### EFFECTS ON PREEARTHQUAKE POPULATIONS

In general, organisms that were lifted above the upper limits of their vertical intertidal ranges were killed. The most conspicuous evidence of this mortality was a white band formed by tests of barnacles in the uplifted *Balanus-Fucus* zone,

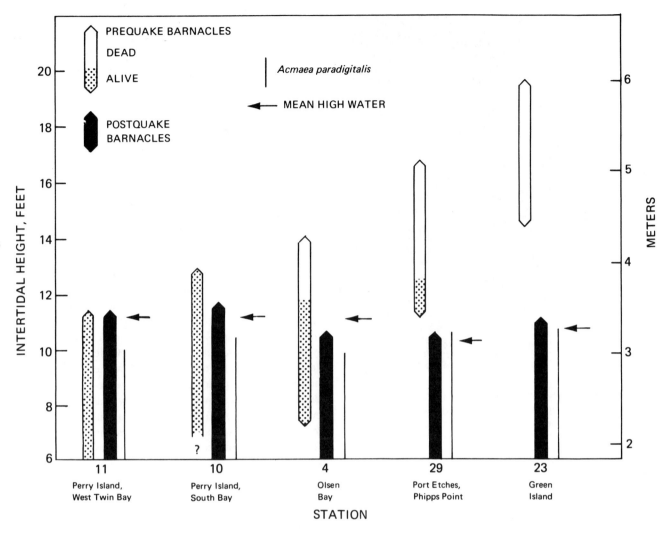

FIGURE 5  Varying overlap of pre- and postearthquake populations at moderately uplifted stations, compared with Station 11, which had no uplift. *Acmaea paradigitalis* is included as an example of a motile species, which was not found alive above its normal vertical range.

separated by a sharp line (the "barnacle line") from an overlying blackish band representing the uplifted *Verrucaria* zone (Figure 6; also illustrated in Hanna, 1964, and this volume; Plafker, 1965; Hanna, 1971, this volume; and Johansen, 1971, this volume). The vertical displacement of the barnacle line from its preearthquake position (at or near mean high water) provided the biological criterion that was used for measuring the amount of land-level change caused by the earthquake; this is discussed later.

The uplifted barnacle zone consisted mainly of tests of *Balanus glandula*, with varying mixtures of *Chthamalus dalli.* Dead *Fucus* plants were common among the barnacles. *Balanus cariosus* was moderately common in the lower part of the zone and below; it occurred occasionally in dense patches. No tests of *B. balanoides* were found, although it was apparently the dominant newly settled species in the postearthquake *Balanus–Fucus* zone (for further discussion

see "Aspects of Selected Animal Groups," later in this paper). Horizontal continuity and density of cover in the uplifted barnacle and *Verrucaria* zones varied considerably; both were least developed in the outer part of the Sound. However, whether this variation represents differences in preearthquake populations or differential removal of dead organisms by rain, frost, and waves is not known.

Dead gastropod shells, many still *in situ* in cracks and crevices or attached to rocks by dried mucus, were abundant above the reach of postearthquake waves. Scattered remains of sessile calcareous organisms from the preearthquake lower midlittoral and *Laminaria* zones were present, lifted above their preearthquake ranges but still within the postearthquake intertidal zone. Commonest of these were serpulid worm tubes, bryozoan tests, and coralline algae. Except for occasional clumps of sabellid worm tubes, no remains of noncalcareous animals were found; their absence

FIGURE 6   Moderately uplifted rocky shore at Deep Bay, Hawkins Island (Station 27), July 10, 1965. Arrows mark the pre- and post-earthquake barnacle lines, the distance between which represents the amount of uplift (about 7 ft). The dense postearthquake algal cover (mostly *Fucus, Halosaccion*) does not extend as high as the whitish barnacles, and there is no postearthquake equivalent of the black band of preearthquake *Verrucaria.*

showed that they had been removed by marine and terrestrial decomposers or by waves and rain within the first year after the earthquake.

At many stations, uplifted barnacles (*Balanus glandula, Chthamalus dalli*) were found alive above their preearthquake upper limit (Figure 5). Barnacles were considered alive if they moved in response to being touched; many other barnacles were found with the animal still inside the test but apparently dead. Living preearthquake barnacles ranged from about 1 to 3 ft above mean high water level and were therefore still within reach of higher high tides and waves. At Station 6, a dense aggregation of very large preearthquake *Balanus cariosus*, consisting mostly of living individuals, extended up to the postearthquake mean high water level, and thus provided another example of survival above the normal upper limit (the preearthquake upper limit of these barnacles was about 2 ft below mean high water). No other instances of this sort were observed.

In general, only the parts of the preearthquake populations that were still within their normal vertical ranges survived after the uplift. Since most of the common animals

had large vertical ranges, this survival was extensive, especially where the uplift was only a few feet. The presence of living preearthquake individuals in the postearthquake intertidal zone was well established for the following species on the basis of size, growth rings, and general appearance (e.g., shell erosion): *Mytilus edulis, Acmaea* spp., *Littorina* spp., *Thais lamellosa, Pisaster ochraceous, Pycnopodia helianthoides, Evasterias troschellii, Balanus cariosus, B. glandula,* and *B. balanoides.* Preearthquake survivors were probably present in most other species, but in the absence of reliable aging criteria they could not be distinguished satisfactorily from postearthquake individuals.

The question arises of whether any motile organisms survived by moving downward after being lifted out of their normal vertical ranges by the earthquake. The presence of abundant *in situ* dead gastropod shells up to their typical preearthquake upper limits on uplifted rocks showed that many did not. These animals apparently reacted to the uplift as they would to a low tide, by remaining in place and waiting for the water to return. However, evidence was obtained that the limpet *Acmaea persona* may have survived by downward movement at some sites. Collections from stations both affected and unaffected by the earthquake indicate that this species has a narrow vertical range, extending about 1 ft above and 2 ft below mean high water level (Figure 2). Size–frequency distributions of living *A. persona* from the species' normal vertical range in the postearthquake intertidal zone at several stations, together with a sample of dead *A. persona* found *in situ* on uplifted rocks at another station, are shown in Figure 7. Although growth rates of *A. persona* in Prince William Sound are not known, it is reasonable to conclude from size and shell erosion that at least the largest of the living limpets were survivors from preearthquake populations. At Station 27 the uplift of about 7 ft implies that the entire *A. persona* population was lifted above its preearthquake vertical range. Therefore, unless the preearthquake vertical range extended lower than indicated by our collections, the large preearthquake individuals must have survived by moving downward after the earthquake. The uplift at the other stations was not great enough to rule out *in situ* survival. Although this evidence is far from conclusive, downward movement of limpets might be expected. At high tide or when desiccation is not severe, *A. persona* moves actively out from sheltered cracks to feed, and other high intertidal limpets are known to make vertical movements in response to environmental changes (Abe, 1955; Frank, 1965; Haven, 1971).

POSTEARTHQUAKE INTERTIDAL ZONE

The fauna of the postearthquake *Verrucaria* zone was generally similar to the preearthquake fauna. *Littorina scutulata* and *L. sitkana* were abundant, with populations consisting

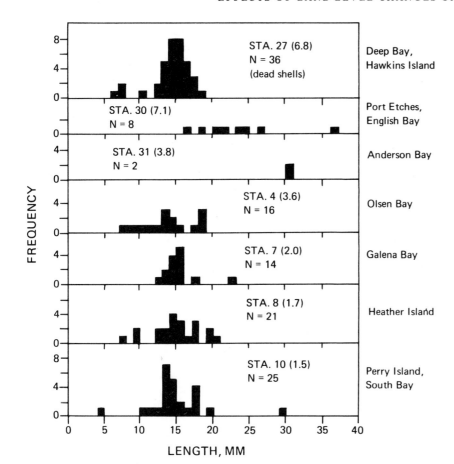

FIGURE 7 Size–frequency distributions of samples of live *Acmaea persona* from the postearthquake intertidal zone at several uplifted stations, together with a sample of *in situ* dead shells from Station 27.

both of preearthquake survivors and postearthquake recruitment. *Acmaea persona* and *A. digitalis*, both of which have narrow vertical ranges, were also common at some stations; however, at other stations the entire preearthquake populations of these species were killed, and postearthquake individuals were sparse or absent.

In contrast to the animals, no trace of postearthquake growth of the dominant lichen *Verrucaria* was found. At some stations the postearthquake *Verrucaria* zone was covered by a thin but conspicuous greenish or brownish film of encrusting microalgae consisting mainly of filamentous blue-green algae and the green alga *Ulothrix* (Johansen, 1971, this volume). At other stations this algal film was not evident, although inconspicuous algal cover was undoubtedly present in view of the observed grazing movements of the littorines.

Where the uplift was only a few feet, the postearthquake *Verrucaria* zone was often densely covered with barnacle tests (and some living barnacles) displaced from the pre-earthquake *Balanus-Fucus* zone (Figure 5). Depending on how long they remain, the barnacles could interfere with postearthquake growth of *Verrucaria*, which occurs only on rock surfaces. Where the uplift was greater (about 6 ft or

more), most of the preearthquake midlittoral barnacles were lifted above the postearthquake *Verrucaria* zone; largely bare rock was thus left for repopulation.

The postearthquake midlittoral zone was for the most part richly populated by both animals and plants. Most species populations included both preearthquake survivors and postearthquake recruitment. With several exceptions, species composition, vertical distribution, and relative abundance of invertebrates were similar to the inferred preearthquake conditions. As before the earthquake, *Balanus* and *Fucus* (and other algae) were usually the dominant organisms in the upper midlittoral zone (Figure 6), and a variety of algal species provided most of the cover in the lower midlittoral zone.

Except for *Balanus balanoides* and *B. glandula*, every dominant or common midlittoral species at the normal stations was also dominant in the postearthquake midlittoral at most of the uplifted stations. Conversely, comparison with preearthquake remains and with the normal stations indicated that most of the dominant animal species in the postearthquake midlittoral of the uplifted stations were also common before the earthquake. As previously mentioned, the many species found at uplifted but not at normal stations (Table 1) probably reflect the greater number of uplifted stations rather than differences between pre- and postearthquake faunas. Frequently one or more generally common species was not found in the postearthquake intertidal zone at a given uplifted station; some of these apparent absences (such as *Acmaea persona* and *A. digitalis*) may have been caused by the earthquake, but most were probably due to insufficient sampling.

Vertical ranges of the common animal species were in general not significantly different from those before the earthquake, though the ranges, especially the lower limits, were not determined for all common species at all stations. The data are best for the upper limits of barnacles and gastropods; as illustrated in Figure 5, both of these extended to their typical upper limits in the postearthquake midlittoral zone, except for the previously noted survival of uplifted barnacles above mean high water level.

Critical comparisons of pre- and postearthquake population densities could not be made. However, the average level of abundance of most postearthquake populations seemed about the same, or perhaps slightly lower, than in the preearthquake communities exemplified by the normal stations. At many individual stations one or more species appeared to be unusually rare, and a number of sections of shore were very sparsely populated. Interpretation of these situations would require definite knowledge of the preearthquake populations at these sites.

A distinctive characteristic of the postearthquake midlittoral populations was the presence of both pre- and postearthquake individuals. This presence resulted in complex population–age structures of sessile organisms such as barnacles, with the proportion of preearthquake individuals of course decreasing with increasing uplift (Figure 8). The preearthquake survivors contributed to the postearthquake population by their own presence, but, probably more importantly, served as reproductive stock. Successful postearthquake reproduction was indicated by the presence of abundant very small individuals and/or egg masses in the populations of most species.

The only example of preearthquake individuals causing

*G Dallas Hanna*

FIGURE 8  Overlapping pre- and postearthquake barnacle populations at Olsen Bay (Station 4), June 2, 1965; uplift about 3.6 ft. The approximate lower limit of large preearthquake barnacles (*Balanus glandula* and *B. balanoides*), made conspicuous by algae growing on them, is being pointed out. Below this is a dense settlement of postearthquake barnacles (probably all *B. balanoides*); the upper limit of postearthquake barnacles is near the top of the photograph but is not clearly discernible.

adverse effects was found at Goose Island (Station 6), where dense aggregations of very large *Balanus cariosus* (uplifted from the lower midlittoral) were still alive in the upper midlittoral zone. These *B. cariosus* were clearly competing for space with postearthquake barnacles, *Fucus*, and other organisms. The scattered calcareous remains of animals, such as serpulid worms and bryozoans uplifted from the *Laminaria*- and lower-midlittoral zones, were not extensive enough to have significant adverse effects.

The postearthquake midlittoral communities appeared to differ from preearthquake communities in several respects. Perhaps the most important of these was the previously mentioned dominance of *Balanus balanoides* in the postearthquake upper midlittoral zone, whereas *B. glandula* apparently was the commoner of the two before the earthquake. Another difference concerns postearthquake mussels (*Mytilus edulis*), dense beds of which had settled at many stations. Most of the dense aggregations of mussels were attached to algae rather than to rock, and the intertidal height of the new beds averaged lower than that of the preearthquake beds; this is discussed under "Mussels," p. 113.

The boundary between the upper and lower midlittoral zones was usually not as distinct as at the normal stations. It was sometimes virtually absent, as at Station 22 where dense *Fucus* extended throughout the midlittoral and into the *Laminaria* zone. Several instances of unusually extensive cover of membranous and filamentous algae, especially in the upper midlittoral zone, seemed to be correlated with sparsity of grazing gastropods. In the upper midlittoral zone, preearthquake *Balanus* and *Fucus* extended to virtually the same upper limit (mean high water), whereas the upper limit of dense postearthquake *Fucus* was often irregular and lower than that of the barnacles (Figure 6).

Several other differences concern barnacles. No dense settlements of *Balanus cariosus* were observed that were comparable to the very dense preearthquake aggregations of this species. Postearthquake *B. cariosus* were common but rather sparsely dispersed. Dense populations of postearthquake *B. crenatus* were found in the lower midlittoral and *Laminaria* zones at several uplifted stations, but this species was not collected at the normal stations. Whether or not these *B. crenatus* populations were unusually dense, to be later reduced, for example, by predators (Connell, 1961) cannot be determined without further study. The population density of postearthquake upper midlittoral barnacles (*Balanus balanoides*), although high, appeared to average less than preearthquake barnacle density (*B. glandula* and *B. balanoides*) in this zone, particularly in the upper part of the zone. Preearthquake population density was greatest near the upper limit (mean high water) and decreased downward, whereas postearthquake barnacles, although usually settling up to about mean high water, almost everywhere became less numerous in the upper 1 or 2 ft of their range.

Lower down, postearthquake settlement was locally dense enough at some stations to produce the elongated "hummock" growth form (Knight-Jones and Moyse, 1961).

The postearthquake *Laminaria* zone was densely populated, at favorable sites, with *Laminaria* and other algae and a rich fauna. This population indicated rapid and direct community redevelopment following the earthquake.

## ROCKY SHORES: MAXIMUM UPLIFT

The maximum amount of vertical displacement on land occurred on the southern part of Montague Island, where uplifts of as much as 10 m were measured (Plafker, 1965). The entire intertidal zone and a considerable part of the upper subtidal zone were lifted above the reach of the tides. There was virtually complete mortality of the uplifted intertidal and subtidal organisms, except possibly below the postearthquake zero level. Consequently, in contrast to the moderately uplifted shores, the postearthquake intertidal communities had to develop entirely anew.

We occupied two stations in the area of maximum uplift. At MacLeod Harbor (Station 20), most of our work was done on rocky and boulder shores along the point at the north entrance to the harbor; uplift here was 30 ft. At Hanning Bay (Station 21), uplifts varied because of faulting; at our study sites the uplift was about 30 ft. Our observations at Hanning Bay were made on the gently sloping boulder shore at the south entrance to the bay and on the rocky reef at the head of the bay. Both MacLeod Harbor and Hanning Bay (especially the former) were more influenced by open ocean conditions than any of our other stations except Station 30 on Hinchinbrook Island; a low ground swell occurred during our fieldwork.

### UPLIFTED PREEARTHQUAKE POPULATIONS

The horizontal and vertical extent of the uplifted zone was impressive, as was the magnitude of the mortality of the preearthquake intertidal and subtidal populations. The general appearance of the uplifted shore is shown by illustrations in Hanna (1964, and this volume), Plafker (1965), Plafker and Mayo (1965), Hanna (1971, this volume), and Johansen (1971, this volume).

The typical pattern of zonation of the dead uplifted organisms is shown in Figure 9. The most conspicuous single feature was an extensive zone dominated by remains of sessile calcareous organisms, chiefly coralline algae, bryozoans, serpulid worms, and certain barnacles (Figure 10). The upper limit of this calcareous zone was at about the preearthquake +3-ft level, in the lower midlittoral zone. The zone extended down past the postearthquake high-water line and through the entire new intertidal zone; therefore, preearth-

FIGURE 9 Dead remains of preearthquake populations on a steeply sloping rock surface at MacLeod Harbor, Montague Island (Station 20), June 26, 1965, in the maximally uplifted area. Upper arrow: upper limit of midlittoral barnacles (preearthquake mean high-water level) now about 30 ft above present mean high water. Middle arrow: top of "white" zone dominated by calcareous remains of bryozoans, coralline algae, and other species. Lower arrow: upper limit of *in situ* dead stipes and holdfasts of preearthquake kelp (mostly *Laminaria*).

quake dominance by calcareous organisms extended at least 30 ft below the zero tide level. The density of calcareous remains decreased downward. This decrease started at about 5 to 10 ft above postearthquake high-water level and was probably due largely to action of postearthquake storm waves. A general absence of fragile, nonsessile, or arborescent calcareous remains within the postearthquake intertidal zone was attributable to waves and currents. However, the possibility of a natural decline in preearthquake calcare-

ous populations at lower levels cannot be ruled out.

Coralline algae and encrusting bryozoans were the dominant organisms at the upper limit of the calcareous zone. Large serpulid worm tubes (*Serpula vermicularis*) were the most conspicuous remains in the middle part of the zone. Other characteristic animals, with varying upper limits in the preearthquake *Laminaria* or lower midlittoral zones, included *Balanus balanus*, *B. nubilis*, *Pododesmus macroschizma*, and several species of arborescent bryozoans.

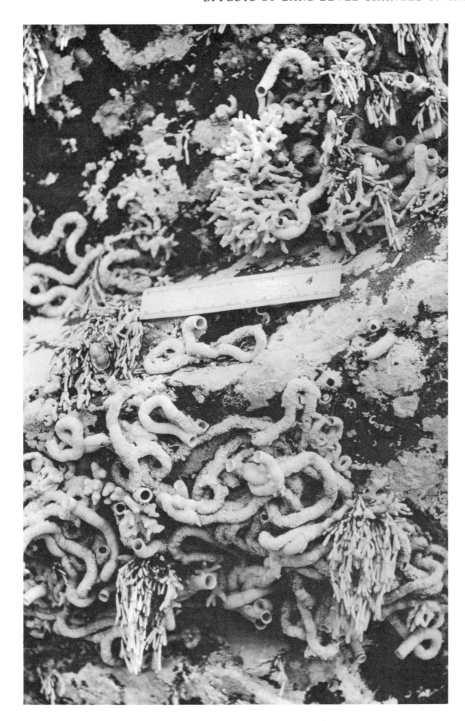

FIGURE 10  Calcareous remains in the preearthquake subtidal zone at MacLeod Harbor (Station 20), June 26, 1965; uplift 30 ft. Serpulid worm tubes, bryozoans, *Balanus balanus*, *Musculus* sp., and coralline algae are dominant.

Dead holdfasts and stipes of kelp formed a distinctive belt, within the calcareous zone, from about the preearthquake −2-ft level downward. They were most abundant in a band about 10 vertical ft wide and gradually decreased in number downward toward the postearthquake high-water level. The upper holdfasts undoubtedly belonged to *Laminaria*, whereas at least some of the lower holdfasts were

probably *Nereocystis*, although identification is not certain (Johansen, 1971, this volume).

Another conspicuous feature of the calcareous zone was the huge number of mollusk shells, aggregations of which occurred in practically every depression in the rocks or intervening patch of gravel. In some sand–gravel beach areas, apparently at the extreme upper limit of postearthquake wave wash, there were extensive windrows composed almost exclusively of masses of small mollusk shells, which could be be scooped up by the handful. In addition, many mollusks were still *in situ*; for example, the bivalve *Musculus* sp. was commonly still attached by "nests" of byssal fibers to bryozoans and rocks. Among the commonest species of dead mollusks were the following: *Diadora aspersa, Fisurella volcano, Puncturella* spp., *Acmaea instabilis* (among kelp holdfasts only), *A. mitra, A. pelta, A. scutum, Lepeta concentrica, Fusitriton oregonensis, Searlesia dira, Thais lamellosa, Musculus* sp. (small shells extremely common), *Saxidomus giganteus, Protothaca staminea, Macoma* spp., and the brachiopod *Terebratalia transversa.* Shells of about 130 species of mollusks were collected in the uplifted zone by W. J. Eyerdam (1971, this volume). Of course, the great abundance of shells in the uplifted zone was partly due to accumulation before the earthquake, but it undoubtedly indicates that there were very large mollusk populations that were destroyed by the uplift.

Remains of nonsessile organisms other than mollusks were much less common. A few carapaces of small canceroid crabs and a few poorly preserved remains of *Pisaster ochraceous, Pycnopodia helianthoides,* and *Strongylocentrotus* were observed, but no remains of soft-bodied organisms were found.

In the preearthquake upper intertidal zone, the *Verrucaria* and barnacle belts were much less conspicuous than in most of the normal and moderately uplifted areas (Figure 9). *Verrucaria* was particularly sparse; its presence was revealed by close examination, but a conspicuous black band was usually not visible at a distance. The upper midlittoral barnacle zone (mainly *Balanus glandula* and *Chthamalus dalli*) was patchy and discontinuous. However, the upper barnacle limit (i.e., the upper limit of the midlittoral zone) was a distinct line, not detectably more diffuse vertically than in the more protected parts of Prince William Sound. At several places in MacLeod Harbor, extensive aggregations of large *B. cariosus* were found in the preearthquake lower midlittoral zone. Uplifted mussel beds (*Mytilus edulis*) were also frequent. A zone largely devoid of sessile remains (populated by a few barnacles and gastropods) usually intervened between the upper midlittoral barnacles and the calcareous zone below (Figure 9). This zone was probably dominated by noncalcareous algae before the earthquake.

Large aggregations of shells of *Littorina sitkana, L. scutulata,* and *Acmaea digitalis* and smaller numbers of *A. persona* were found in cracks and crevices at and slightly above the upper barnacle limit. *Acmaea pelta, A. paradigitalis,* and *Thais lamellosa* were abundant at lower levels. Many gastropods and chitons were still attached to vertical rock faces by dried mucus. The vertical distribution of these midlittoral mollusks indicates that they died without making significant movements after the earthquake.

## POSTEARTHQUAKE INTERTIDAL ZONE

The newly developing communities in the postearthquake intertidal zone were significantly different in several respects from the preearthquake communities and from the postearthquake communities at the moderately uplifted stations. There were some similarities as well. Most of the differences are related to the absence, except possibly in the *Laminaria* zone, of any overlap with preearthquake populations. Initial colonization must have been by eggs, larvae, and spores that were brought in by currents or other means from areas less strongly affected by the earthquake. Of the uplifted, formerly subtidal organisms, only some encrusting calcareous remains were still present at the time of our observations, and there was no evidence of widespread interference with the postearthquake populations.

FIGURE 11 Zonation in the postearthquake intertidal zone at MacLeod Harbor (Station 20), June 26, 1965, on a maximally uplifted shore; uplift 30 ft. Arrow indicates the approximate upper limit of postearthquake barnacles, above which is a dark film of encrusting microalgae occupying the postearthquake *Verrucaria* zone. The dense algal zone below is dominated by *Porphyra.* Whitish preearthquake calcareous remains are visible in the upper right corner of the photograph.

A distinct pattern of vertical zonation was evident on smooth or steeply sloping surfaces (Figure 11). On boulder fields and mixed boulder–rock shores, the basic zonation was similar, but, especially in the midlittoral zone, plant and animal cover was patchy and variable.

The uppermost zone, as at many of the moderately uplifted stations, was covered by a layer of encrusting microalgae that from a distance appeared as a conspicuous dark band contrasting with the pale uplifted rock above. Although the upper limit was too indistinct to be measured accurately, this zone extended about 3 ft above the upper limit of midlittoral barnacles. There was no trace of the lichen *Verrucaria*.

In the upper midlittoral zone there was a dense settlement of postearthquake barnacles. Average abundance was not less than in the moderately uplifted areas. *Balanus balanoides* was the commonest species; apparently no *B. glandula* were present. The upper limit of *B. balanoides* was about +10 ft, only slightly less than the mean high-water level (for MacLeod Harbor) of +10.4 ft. Barnacles became sparse near their upper limit, where they were mixed with small numbers of the alga *Enteromorpha*. *Balanus cariosus* occurred from about +8 ft down into the *Laminaria* zone, but, as in the moderately uplifted areas, there were no dense aggregations similar to those found locally in the preearthquake intertidal zone. Small numbers of *Chthamalus dalli* were present throughout the midlittoral zone.

A principal difference from the moderately uplifted areas was the broad zone dominated by the alga *Porphyra* (Figures 11 and 12). At MacLeod Harbor this zone, ranging from about 8 ft to 3 ft, was largely restricted to the upper midlittoral, but at Hanning Bay it extended lower, to the 1-ft and zero levels in different transects. *Fucus* was usually the dominant alga of at least the upper part of this zone, both at the normal stations and in the postearthquake intertidal at the moderately uplifted stations. However, postearthquake *Fucus* was very sparse and patchy at the maximally uplifted stations, particularly at MacLeod Harbor. Other algal species occurred with the *Porphyra*, especially *Ulva* and *Enteromorpha*. Dense populations of *Balanus balanoides* were found under the *Porphyra*, seemingly unaffected by the algae (Figure 13). The dominance of *Porphyra* rather than *Fucus* may be related to the very low numbers of grazing gastropods, as discussed later.

Within or slightly below the *Porphyra* zone were dense patches of mussels (*Mytilus edulis*). As in the moderately uplifted areas, most of these were attached to algae rather than to rocks. Small numbers of mussels extended from the upper barnacle limit down through the *Laminaria* zone. Mussel populations were particularly dense at Station 21 (transect 21a). Between the *Porphyra* and *Laminaria* zones was a narrower but conspicuous zone dominated by the large alga *Alaria* and by other species, especially *Rhodymenia*. Inasmuch as the lower midlittoral zone at several moderately uplifted stations in the outer part of the Sound was also dominated by these algae, they were probably the typical preearthquake dominants.

The *Laminaria* zone was densely populated by *Laminaria* and other algae. The fauna was equally rich and typical of

FIGURE 12  *Porphyra* cover in the postearthquake midlittoral zone at MacLeod Harbor (Station 20), June 26, 1965; uplift 30 ft. Scattered *Fucus* is present (upper left). Removal of *Porphyra* reveals the underlying dense barnacle settlement (mostly *Balanus balanoides*), consisting of first and second postearthquake-year classes.

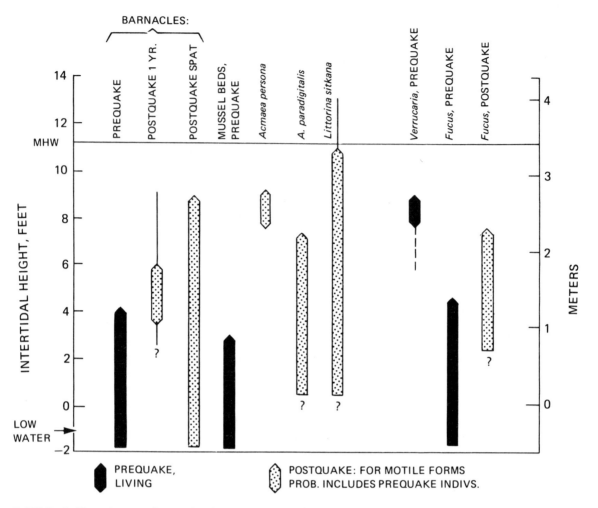

FIGURE 13   Vertical ranges of preearthquake and postearthquake organisms on a rocky shore in the downthrust area at Blackstone Bay (Station 13), June 16, 1965; subsidence about 5 ft.

the zone, with abundant tunicates and bryozoans, smaller numbers of hydroids, several common mollusks, including *Lepeta concentrica*, *Acmaea pelta*, *A. rosea*, *A. mitra*, *Thais lamellosa*, and *Musculus* sp.; the barnacles *Balanus crenatus*, *B. cariosus*, and a few *B. balanus*; and the asteroid *Dermasterias imbricata* (for other species collected, see Table 1). Except for the notable absence of several species (see below), the *Laminaria* zone was no less well developed than at several of the moderately uplifted stations; rapid and direct repopulation after the earthquake was thus indicated.

Living specimens were found, in the *Laminaria* zone, of several species whose remains were common in the uplifted calcareous zone. These species include *Lepeta concentrica*, *Thais lamellosa*, *Balanus balanus*, and arborescent bryozoans. Since the vertical ranges of many *Laminaria*-zone species extend well into the subtidal, it is possible that some of these living specimens, and perhaps individuals of other species, were preearthquake survivors, lifted from the subtidal into

the postearthquake *Laminaria* zone. However, although the size of many of the living specimens was similar to the larger of their dead uplifted counterparts, their age cannot be definitely determined. Another possible preearthquake survivor was an individual of the snail *Littorina sitkana* found in the lower midlittoral zone. Although growth rates are unknown, this snail seemed much too large to be a postearthquake individual. Perhaps some organisms were dislodged from the rocks during the uplift and by chance settled within the postearthquake intertidal zone.

Except for the *Laminaria* zone, the fauna of the post-earthquake intertidal zone was clearly impoverished in both species and numbers of individuals. During the fieldwork in the areas of maximum uplift, a strikingly smaller number and variety of animals was noted in the lower midlittoral zone than in the *Laminaria* zone, particularly in the under-boulder habitat. This sharp decrease constitutes a major difference from the moderately uplifted areas. Species that were not found alive in the postearthquake intertidal zone but that were common either in the uplifted preearthquake populations at the normal stations or in the postearthquake intertidal zone at the moderately uplifted stations, include *Acmaea digitalis, A. persona, A. instabilis, Pisaster ochraceous, Pycnopodia helianthoides, Leptasterias hexactis, Evasterias troschellii,* and *Lygia* sp. Several species were common as dead remains on the maximally uplifted rocks (subtidal and *Laminaria* zones) but were not found alive anywhere in the Sound: *Pododesmus macroschizma, Diadora aspersa, Puncturella* spp., *Fusitriton oregonensis,* and *Balanus nubilis.* Finally, several species were found in the postearthquake intertidal zone but in strongly reduced numbers, including *Acmaea pelta, A. paradigitalis, A. scutum, Littorina scutulata, L. sitkana, Thais lamellosa, Searlesia dira, Emplectonema* sp., *Pagurus, Idothea wosnesenskii, Exosphaeroma oregonensis,* and *Dermasterias imbricata.* The only species above the *Laminaria* zone whose abundance did not seem reduced compared to the postearthquake intertidal zone at the moderately uplifted stations were *Mytilus edulis, Balanus cariosus, B. crenatus, B. balanoides, Chthamalus dalli,* and the large upper midlittoral gammarid amphipods.

A contrast to the repopulation process at MacLeod Harbor and Hanning Bay was provided by observations made on Middleton Island, located in the Gulf of Alaska about 75 km southeast of Montague Island, by George Plafker and L. R. Mayo (communicated by G D. Hanna). Middleton Island was uplifted about 11 ft by the earthquake. During geological investigations in July 1965, Plafker and Mayo noticed that at none of the stations that they examined had any postearthquake barnacles become established in the midlittoral zone. The reason for the absence of both 1964 and 1965 barnacle settlement may be the distance of this isolated island from breeding stocks that survived the earthquake, perhaps combined with unfavorable currents for dispersal of larvae.

## ROCKY SHORES: DOWNTHRUST

In the area of land subsidence in the western part of Prince William Sound we occupied two stations (Stations 12, 13), both with a subsidence of 4 to 5 ft. We did not visit the area of maximum downthrust (over 6 ft) in the extreme northwest part of the Sound.

Our intertidal studies were done on moderately steep to vertical rocky shores. The postearthquake high tides did not reach much beyond the preearthquake zone of terrestrial mosses and lichens that begins above the *Verrucaria* zone; there was little penetration into the coniferous forest. There was greater penetration of terrestrial communities by postearthquake high tides along level shores at Station 13

(Eyerdam, 1971, this volume). Hanna (1964, and this volume) reported the occurrence of limpets and littorines on submerged tree limbs in the maximally downthrust region in the summer of 1964; this occurrence demonstrated a rapid colonization of formerly terrestrial substrates.

At Station 12 the tide was high during our fieldwork; only the upper 2 ft of the postearthquake midlittoral zone was accessible to observation. Postearthquake *Balanus* (probably *B. balanoides*) were sparse at their upper limit but became denser at lower levels. One-year-old *Balanus* (1964 settlement) were much less numerous than small spat (1965 settlement), in contrast to the situation in the uplifted areas, where both year classes were usually abundant. Other animal species found were *Littorina sitkana, L. scutulata, Acmaea paradigitalis, A. pelta,* and *A. persona;* all were patchily dispersed and in small to moderate numbers.

In some places, groups of littorines and *Balanus* spat were found intermingled with apparently still-living terrestrial mosses. The littorines were feeding on the moss, and there were irregular bare patches that were clearly the result of grazing. The moss extended only about 1 ft below the upper barnacle limit. There was no sign of new *Verrucaria;* its zone was still occupied by the moss and, in the uppermost part, by trees and shrubs.

Observations at low tide were carried out on the rocky shore at the northwest entrance to Tebenkof Cove in Blackstone Bay (Station 13). Three transect surveys were taken on moderately to steeply sloping surfaces. Because the lowest water level was −1 ft, the lowest parts of the downthrust preearthquake populations were not accessible. The vertical ranges of some of the dominant pre- and postearthquake organisms are shown in Figure 13. A notable feature was the overlap of pre- and postearthquake populations. For sessile species such as *Balanus, Mytilus,* and *Fucus,* the upper limits of the downthrust preearthquake populations were clearly distinguishable among the higher-ranging postearthquake settlers. Preearthquake barnacles were identified by their large size and their shell erosion, mussels by size alone. Gastropods and other motile forms were common and occurred in their normal vertical ranges relative to the postearthquake barnacle zone. Large preearthquake individuals were dispersed throughout the populations of motile species; thus there was probably some upward movement of these organisms to reestablish their proper vertical ranges after the earthquake.

The upper limit of postearthquake barnacles was considerably below mean high-water level (Figure 13). This apparent depression may be a measurement error due to a deviation of actual from predicted water level when the measurements were made (weather was stormy), or it may be related to the large amount of glacial outflow in this bay. On the other hand, it might have resulted from relative unsuitability of the formerly terrestrial surfaces for settlement of larvae. The latter possibility deserves further investigation, although the former explanations are favored by the correlation of upper gastropod limits with the upper barnacle limit. In general, 1-year-old *Balanus* were quite sparse except for a narrow belt of greater abundance in the central midlittoral zone; the current year's spat were somewhat more common but decreased sharply toward their upper limit.

Dense populations of large preearthquake sessile organisms (mussels, barnacles, *Fucus*) were downthrust into the lower midlittoral and *Laminaria* zones, where they appeared to be thriving. By means of competition for space, these downthrust populations were undoubtedly inhibiting the reestablishment of normal *Laminaria*-zone animals and plants. No postearthquake *Laminaria* were found (Johansen, 1971, this volume). Animal collections were not made in the *Laminaria* zone because it was under water. In contrast to the sessile midlittoral organisms, much of the preearthquake *Verrucaria* population did not survive the downthrust. *Verrucaria* showed a lack of tolerance for the physical or biological conditions below its typical vertical range by becoming patchy or disappearing below about 1 ft under the upper limit of postearthquake barnacles.

## LEVEL-BOTTOM HABITAT

Level-bottom habitats were widespread in Prince William Sound, both in the form of extensive mudflats, particularly in the vicinity of Cordova, and as smaller areas interspersed with rocky and boulder shores throughout the Sound. Most of the level bottoms were of mixed-particle composition, with considerable variability in the proportions of fine and coarse sediments. There were many beaches covered with small to medium rocks that supported a typical rocky-shore epifauna of barnacles, gastropods, *Fucus*, and other species and overlay a muddy or mixed substrate containing a characteristic level-bottom infauna.

We obtained data on level-bottom communities at 10 stations (Stations 1, 4, 6, 11, 16, 18, 21, 24, 29, 32) representing the normal, moderately uplifted, and maximally uplifted parts of the Sound. A limited amount of quantitative sampling was done using 20- by 20-cm quadrats, a ¼-in. wire screen, and a U.S. no. 20 sieve (opening 0.065 in.). Additional information on level-bottom communities may be found in the paper by Baxter (1971, this volume).

Our studies principally concerned bivalves, one of the dominant animal groups of the level-bottom habitat. Several species of another important group, the polychaetes, were found, but not enough sampling was done to assess their distribution and abundance. Small crabs (*Cancer*) were occasionally found on the surface of mudflats. A distinctive inhabitant of level bottoms was the echiuroid worm *Echiurus echiurus alaskensis*, which occurred in shallow horizontal or vertical burrows both in open mudflats and under boulders. It was not found at those uplifted stations where fine sediments had been removed. Another characteristic level-bottom dweller was the anemone *Anthopleura artemisia*; its base was usually attached to a rock well below the surface, and its oral disc when undisturbed extended up to the surface of the mud.

That the level-bottom environment in Prince William Sound supported very large populations of bivalves before the earthquake was demonstrated by piles and windrows of dead shells on uplifted shores, by populations of dead shells still *in situ* on uplifted mudflats, and by surviving living populations in some areas. Species composition was similar throughout the areas visited. Of the larger species, *Protothaca staminea* and *Saxidomus giganteus* were the most abundant, followed closely by *Mya truncata*, *Macoma irus*, *Clinocardium nuttallii* and *Tresus* (formerly *Schizothaerus*) *capax*. Found in smaller numbers were *Mya arenaria*, *Macoma brota lipara*, *Macoma nasuta*, and *Tellina lutea*. The main beds of the commercially important razor clam (*Siliqua patula*) on the Copper River flats were inaccessible to us because of shallow water; we did not find this species, dead or alive. The most abundant small clam was the whitish or pinkish *Macoma inconspicua*, frequently identified as *M. balthica*, but according to A. G. Smith (personal communication, 1965) best considered separate from the European *M. balthica*. This species was numerically the commonest bivalve at many places. Another common small clam was *Hiatella arctica*, which occurred equally as a nestler among algae, in cracks in rocks, and near the surface of mudflats, usually under small rocks or boulders. Many additional species of bivalves were found as dead shells only. Since some of these may have been intertidal and some subtidal before the earthquake, they are not considered here; a thorough collection of them was made by W. J. Eyerdam.

### EFFECTS ON PREEARTHQUAKE POPULATIONS

There was extensive mortality of bivalves following the earthquake in both the moderately and maximally uplifted parts of the Sound. The Alaska Department of Fish and Game (1965) has made preliminary estimates of clam mortality on the basis of the amount of uplift and assumed normal vertical ranges of −10 to +4 ft for several common species, including *Protothaca*, *Saxidomus*, *Tresus*, and others (some of the lower vertical limits may have to be revised: Rae Baxter, personal communication, 1965). Mortality estimates ranged from 11 percent with uplift of 3 ft to 100 percent with uplift above 15 ft. Species whose vertical intertidal ranges extended higher (e.g., *Clinocardium*, upper limit +8 ft), had proportionally greater mortality. Total loss of clam habitat in Prince William Sound, assuming an average land-level change of +6.3 ft, was estimated at 43 percent. Numerical estimates of mortality were also made (Alaska Department of Fish and Game, 1965) that reflect the large size of preearthquake clam populations: Mortality of commercial-size cockles (*Clinocardium*) at Cordova was 36 per m$^2$, and that of *Macoma balthica* (*M. inconspicua* of the present paper) reached 324 per ft$^2$.

The principal cause of clam mortality was the raising of populations above their normal vertical ranges. Associated factors such as reduced submersion time for feeding and increased exposure to terrestrial weather hazards probably caused most of the deaths (Alaska Department of Fish and Game, 1965). For example, freezing conditions on the mudflats in the winter (1964–1965) following the earthquake caused extensive mortality of uplifted but still intertidal clams (Rae Baxter, personal communication, 1965).

We found evidence that removal of surface sediments, caused presumably by the strong currents and waves associated with the earthquake, was another important cause of mortality on some mudflats. At several stations there were extensive beds of *in situ* dead clams, upright in what remained of their preearthquake burrows. Figure 14 is a closeup view of a large *Tresus capax* in one of these beds (Station 1), showing the typical upright position, the undisturbed condition of the two shell valves, and the rather

hard substrate, deficient in fine sediments and scoured by currents. For a general view of this clam bed, see Hanna (1971, this volume, Figure 6). The largest of these beds were in the vicinity of Cordova (Stations 1 and 18); the number of exposed clams in the area was a spectacular demonstration of both the size of the preearthquake populations and the extent of the mortality. In addition, populations of smaller, near-surface clams (*Protothaca, Macoma inconspicua,* and others) may have been washed away with the sediments, although some evidence suggests survival of *Macoma inconspicua*.

Sediment removal, where it occurred, apparently caused total mortality of large clams (at least within the postearthquake intertidal zone) where some survival of preearthquake populations was to be expected on the basis of the amount of uplift alone. Thus at Station 1 (uplift 5.4 ft), no large living preearthquake bivalves were found from the postearthquake zero level to the top of the mudflat (postearthquake 10.5 ft). Many holes were found, but digging proved them to be shallow and unoccupied; these holes may have been remains of preearthquake clam burrows. At Station 18, only limited observations could be made downward, but there was no sign of living bivalves.

In contrast to the total mortality on the mudflats where sediment had been removed, we found substantial populations of large living preearthquake clams in the lower inter-

*G Dallas Hanna*

FIGURE 14   *In situ* remains of a large *Tresus capax,* one of many such individuals apparently killed by removal of overlying sediments by earthquake-caused waves and currents on a moderately uplifted mudflat at Shipyard Bay (Station 1), May 30, 1965; uplift about 5.5 ft.

tidal zone at several moderately uplifted stations (Stations 4, 6, 16, 24, 29, 32). These bivalves represented the lower parts of preearthquake populations that were still within their vertical ranges after the uplift. At all places where we observed extensive survival of preearthquake bivalves, a large amount of fine sediment (mud with high organic content) was present. The substrate thus appeared to be normal soft muddy clam habitat. Although quantitative particle-size data were not obtained, this substrate clearly contrasted with the relatively hard-packed coarser sediments at the stations where *in situ* dead clams were abundant. The correlation of clam survival with presence of fine sediments is taken as evidence supporting the hypothesis that sediment removal was at least a major cause of the *in situ* mortality observed at Stations 1 and 18. Likewise, the presence of soft muddy bottoms containing large living bivalves is probably a valid biological indicator of the absence of abnormally strong postearthquake waves or currents. Most of our stations of this sort were, in fact, in relatively sheltered bays or coves.

That the above-mentioned living bivalves were preearthquake survivors was determined by size and by the annual-ring method of aging. The annual-ring method has been successfully used by Orton (1926) and Weymouth and Thompson (1931) for *Cardium* and by Fraser and Smith (1928) for *Protothaca*; it is reliable for most Prince William Sound clams because of a strong seasonality of growth (Rae Baxter, personal communication). Maximum age of *Protothaca staminea*, the commonest preearthquake survivor, was about 10 years (length, 40 mm); most were 6 to 8 years old. *Macoma irus*, another common species, had a maximum age of about 15 years (length, 61 mm); most were aged 4 to 8 years. *Saxidomus giganteus* and *Mya truncata* were less numerous. The largest *Saxidomus* (69 mm, age at least 8 years) was much smaller than the largest dead shells found; absence of larger living *Saxidomus* may have been due to the shallowness of our samples. At one station a few large siphons that probably belonged to preearthquake *Tresus capax* were seen below low-water level. *Macoma inconspicua* was abundant, but age determination was difficult because of its small size. No large *Clinocardium nuttallii* were found alive, although dead shells (maximum length collected, 96 mm) testified to their abundance before the earthquake; perhaps their shallow burrowing habits caused them greater mortality. Population densities of large living preearthquake clams were generally high. For example, a 1-ft$^2$ sample at Station 6 yielded 10 *Protothaca staminea*, 6 *Saxidomus giganteus*, and 14 *Macoma irus*.

## POSTEARTHQUAKE REPOPULATION

At the stations with surviving preearthquake clam populations, recovery to the normal condition will probably be rapid because the physical environment was not seriously altered. Furthermore, successful recruitment was occurring, at least for some species; small, probably postearthquake individuals were common at all these stations. Most numerous were *Protothaca staminea* (minimum length, 3 mm) and *Clinocardium nuttallii* (minimum length, 4 mm). These were undoubtedly postearthquake settlers, but the age of larger individuals (5 to 10 mm) could not be determined definitely without further data on growth rates and time of settlement. Small *Macoma* were common, but many could not be identified to species. Only a few juvenile *Saxidomus giganteus* were found.

At the stations more strongly affected by the earthquake, recovery of both the habitat and clam populations was, in general, proceeding more slowly, although there was much variation depending on local conditions. These stations include the moderately uplifted mudflats affected by sediment removal (Stations 1 and 18) and the maximally uplifted area (Station 21).

Station 18 appeared to be the least suitable for repopulation, although we made only brief observations on a poor low tide. The substrate consisted mainly of a blackish foulsmelling densely packed anaerobic clay. The bottom was much more steeply sloping than most mudflats, possibly because of postearthquake erosion by currents. It did not look suitable for life other than bacteria. A small amount of digging yielded no living clams. Dense *in situ* populations of dead *Mya truncata*, *Tresus capax*, and other species proved that this area was once a rich clam bed.

At Station 1, whose extensive beds of dead *in situ* clams have been discussed previously, more extensive data were obtained. Considerable numbers of small living clams were found. The substrate, although in better condition than that at Station 18 because of the absence of black anaerobic clay, was deficient in fine sediments. A 3- to 4-in. surface layer of densely packed sand with a little mud covered a still harder mixture of coarse sediments and rocks. Above the postearthquake zero level, the amount of fine sediment on the surface decreased, and the surface layer became irregular; at some places the gravelly lower layer was exposed. These irregularities and the surface ripples visible in Figure 14 indicated that erosion–deposition patterns were not yet stable. Small living clams were found only in the surface layer; considerable digging and sieving yielded none in the lower layer.

The living clams were sampled by a series of twentythree 20- by 20-cm quadrats, dug to a depth of about 4 in. and sieved through a no. 20 standard sieve. The quadrats were located by random tossing at five sites whose intertidal heights ranged from the postearthquake zero level to the top of the mudflat at +10 ft (since uplift was about 5 ft, the top of the mudflat was at about +5 ft before the earthquake).

TABLE 2   Population Density and Size Range of Bivalves from Sieved 20- by 20-cm Quadrat Samples, Postearthquake Intertidal Zone, Shipyard Bay, Hawkins Island (Station 1)

| Sample site | | Number per m$^2$ (Shell-Length Range, mm) | | |
| --- | --- | --- | --- | --- |
| Intertidal Height (ft) | Number of Quadrats | Macoma inconspicua | Clinocardium nuttallii | Protothaca staminea |
| 0 | 8 | 22 (6–10) | 25 (5–12) | 0 |
| 3 | 5 | 45 (5–11) | 35 (7–11) | 0 |
| 6 | 4 | 288 (3– 9) | 6 (6) | 0 |
| 7.5 | 3 | 325 (3–14) | 8 (7) | 25 (5–7) |
| 10 | 2 | 688 (4–14) | 0 | 13 (5) |

Results of the quadrat samples are shown in Table 2. Unfortunately, without knowledge of growth rates and time of settlement, the age of these small clams could not be determined satisfactorily, but at least the smallest, and perhaps most, of them were postearthquake settlers. The densities of up to 35 per m$^2$ of *Clinocardium nuttallii* appear to indicate a rapid rate of repopulation relative to the preearthquake adult population size of 36 per m$^2$ reported for Cordova by the Alaska Department of Fish and Game (1965); the vertical range was typical for *Clinocardium*. The other two species are more difficult to interpret. The abundance of small *Macoma inconspicua* indicated a high rate of postearthquake recruitment. However, the largest individuals (12 to 14 mm), which occurred only at the higher intertidal levels, were near the normal adult size, and some had two distinct growth rings. Therefore they may have been preearthquake survivors. This possibility is consistent with the increased population density toward the top of the mudflat, which at +10 ft was above the upper limit of +8 ft reported for this species by the Alaska Department of Fish and Game. Likewise, the smallest *Protothaca staminea* were probably postearthquake settlers, but their absence from lower levels is puzzling, and the possibility of preearthquake survival cannot be ruled out. On the other hand, an extensive survival of these small near-surface clams (*M. inconspicua* and *P. staminea*) would seem to be inconsistent with the total mortality of large clams on this mudflat, attributed to sediment removal. Perhaps the small clams were stirred up by currents but settled back down and survived. However, since the actual nature and extent of sediment removal is not known nor are the ages of the small clams certain, this problem cannot be resolved on the basis of the data at hand. A few small *Axinopsida* sp. and *Macoma irus* were the only living clams found in addition to the three species listed in Table 2.

In the maximally uplifted areas, where the entire intertidal zone was lifted above water level, there was no doubt that total mortality of preearthquake intertidal clams occurred, regardless of their size. A mudflat at the head of Hanning Bay (Station 21) was sampled to assess repopulation of clams in the postearthquake intertidal zone. In addition to random digging, 14 semiquantitative samples (one shovelful each) were taken between the −3-ft and +6-ft levels and were sieved. The only living clam found was one juvenile *Clinocardium nuttallii* (length, 5 mm) at the +2-ft level. The substrate appeared to be deficient in fine sediment. On the surface there was a thin layer (about 1 in. thick) of sand with some fine mud, the latter increasing below the zero level. Underneath was a densely packed mixture of rocks, shells, gravel, and sand, containing very little fine sediment. The minimal repopulation here, compared to the moderately uplifted Station 1, may be related to the greater distance from surviving breeding stock; the substrate did not appear significantly less favorable than at Station 1.

## ASPECTS OF SELECTED ANIMAL GROUPS

### BARNACLES: *BALANUS GLANDULA* AND *BALANUS BALANOIDES*

An apparent change in the dominant species of the upper midlittoral barnacle zone following the earthquake has been noted in previous sections. The barnacle species involved are *Balanus glandula* and *Balanus balanoides*. There were no significant differences in the relative numbers of the other two midlittoral barnacles, *Chthamalus dalli* and *Balanus cariosus*, before and after the earthquake, except for the postearthquake absence of dense aggregations of *B. cariosus*.

The available evidence indicates that the postearthquake settlement of upper midlittoral barnacles was all or nearly all *Balanus balanoides*, whereas both *B. balanoides* and *B. glandula* were present in the preearthquake populations, *B. glandula* probably being the dominant species. The two species were not distinguished during the fieldwork, and this difference was not recognized until afterward when specimens were identified. Conclusions must therefore be based on the limited number of specimens that were collected, together with observations and photographs.

The barnacles were identified by using descriptions of Henry (1940, 1942) and Cornwall (1955). My identifications were confirmed by Dr. William C. Newman of the Scripps Institution of Oceanography. The most obvious difference between the two species is that *Balanus glandula* has a calcareous base, whereas that of *B. balanoides* is membranous; there are also critical differences in the cover plates. The apparent lack of a calcareous base in the postearthquake barnacles was noticed in the field but was tentatively attributed to the young age of the barnacles.

All collections from the postearthquake barnacle zone at stations where there was no significant overlap with pre-earthquake populations yielded only *Balanus balanoides.* Comparison of specimens with photographs indicated that the postearthquake barnacle settlement at most other stations was likewise only *B. balanoides* (Figures 12 and 15). Barnacles that possibly were *Balanus glandula* were found in only one photograph (from a station where no specimens were taken). At most stations there were two distinct size classes of postearthquake barnacles (Figure 15): larger individuals representing settlement in the first season (1964) after the earthquake, termed the 1-year class, and very small individuals representing the current season's (1965) settlement. The latter appeared to be the same species (*B. balanoides*) as the 1-year individuals, but because of difficulties in identification, especially from photographs, the presence of some *B. glandula* cannot be ruled out.

All specimens collected from the dead uplifted preearthquake barnacle populations were *Balanus glandula.* Considerable searching in the field, prompted by the apparent absence of calcareous bases on the postearthquake barnacles, failed to reveal any dead uplifted barnacles without calcareous bases except for the easily recognizable *B. cariosus.*

On the other hand, collections of living barnacles from the normal stations and from stations where the uplift was small enough to allow extensive survival of large preearthquake barnacles yielded both *Balanus glandula* and *B. balanoides.* The most numerous of the two appeared to be *B. glandula*, but quantitative samples adequate to determine relative abundance or distributional differences were not obtained. A sample from the upper midlittoral barnacle zone at Station 11, the principal normal station, yielded both species, with *B. glandula* in the majority. A similar sample at Station 10 yielded 11 *B. glandula* and no *B. balanoides.* A collection of the large preearthquake barnacles shown in Figure 8 (Station 4, uplift about 4 ft) yielded 20 *B. glandula* and 6 *B. balanoides.* Both species had strongly eroded and pitted tests and were very similar externally. Small *B. glandula* found among these large barnacles were likewise heavily eroded and therefore may have been slow-growing preearthquake individuals. All the postearthquake *B. balanoides* (specimens and photographs) had smooth whitish relatively uneroded tests. Small collections of midlittoral barnacles made by Hanna in various parts of Prince William Sound in summer 1964 included large specimens of both *B. balanoides* and *B. glandula.*

Thus the living specimens demonstrate the presence of both species in the preearthquake populations, despite the apparent absence in 1965 of *Balanus balanoides* from the dead uplifted populations. A possible explanation for the latter is that the tests of *B. balanoides*, lacking firm attach-

*G Dallas Hanna*

FIGURE 15   View of postearthquake upper-midlittoral barnacles at MacLeod Harbor (Station 20), June 26, 1965, showing the two size classes. The large individuals, identified as *Balanus balanoides*, settled in 1964; the small ones in 1965.

ment by a calcareous base, may have been removed from the rocks more rapidly by rain runoff, frost, and wave splash.

A reasonable hypothesis to explain the dominance of *Balanus balanoides* in the postearthquake populations would seem to be that, at the time of the earthquake, *B. balanoides* had already spawned and therefore had a large crop of larvae in the plankton, whereas *B. glandula* had not yet spawned. The larvae of *B. balanoides* would then have been free to settle throughout the newly exposed postearthquake upper midlittoral zone. Mortality from the uplift would have prevented most *B. glandula* from breeding after the earthquake.

Spawning seasons for the two species in Prince William Sound are unknown. Highly seasonal breeding, with release of nauplii in March, has been reported for *Balanus balanoides* in Britain (Barnes, 1956). Breeding periods of *B. glandula* along the west coast of North America appear to be generally longer, but vary considerably at different places (Pierron and Huang, 1925; Rice, 1930; Barnes and Barnes, 1956; Glynn, 1965). Extrapolations to Prince William Sound are not warranted. However, only a small difference in spawning times of the two species in 1964 would be required by the hypothesis. Slightly earlier spawning by *B. balanoides* might be expected since it is a more northerly species than *B. glandula*.

The principal objection to the hypothesis is that, in areas of little or no land-level change, considerable numbers of *Balanus glandula* survived the earthquake. Perhaps their breeding was unsuccessful for other reasons. Much more investigation, including long-term studies of the future course of events in the postearthquake barnacle zone, is necessary before the situation can be properly understood.

## BARNACLES: UPPER LIMIT AND MEASUREMENTS OF LAND-LEVEL CHANGE

The upper limit of midlittoral barnacles (the barnacle line) is important because it was used by the U.S. Geological Survey (Plafker and Mayo, 1965; Plafker, 1965, 1969) and by ourselves as the principal criterion for measuring the amount of land-level change caused by the earthquake. Vertical land displacement was measured by determining the distance between the barnacle line and its assumed preearthquake position relative to water level or by determining the distance between the preearthquake and postearthquake barnacle lines. This method was used previously by Tarr and Martin (1912) after the Yakutat Bay, Alaska, earthquake of 1899; Kaye (1964) used the barnacle line as an index of long-term sea-level changes in New England.

Plafker (1965) has given evidence supporting the validity of the barnacle-line method, the most important of which was independent determination of land-level changes from

tide-gage data. We obtained data to further evaluate the method in Prince William Sound.

The species forming the upper midlittoral barnacle zone (and therefore the barnacle line) was identified by Plafker (1965) as *Balanus balanoides* on the basis of data obtained by G D. Hanna from students of *Balanus*. We found that three species were present in this zone, at least before the earthquake: *Balanus balanoides*, *B. glandula*, and *Chthamalus dalli*. *Balanus cariosus* and other species did not extend up to the barnacle line. Inasmuch as we found no evidence that *B. glandula* had a different upper limit from *B. balanoides*, the presence of these two species and the change in their relative abundance following the earthquake probably did not introduce any error into the land-level-change measurements. *Chthamalus dalli*, on the other hand, usually extended about 1 ft higher than the *Balanus* species. At most stations the conspicuous barnacle line was formed mainly by *Balanus*; only scattered *Chthamalus* extended higher. However, dense patches of *Chthamalus* were occasionally found whose upper limit was about 1 ft higher than the *Balanus* line of nearby rocks, and at a few stations (for example, Station 23) *Chthamalus* was the dominant barnacle and thus formed the barnacle line. Although an error of about 1 ft would be introduced into uplift measurements based on a *Chthamalus* line, such instances were too infrequent and the error too small to affect the overall pattern revealed by many measurements.

It is essential to know the normal preearthquake intertidal height of the barnacle line and the magnitude of the variations in this height caused by local environmental factors. Plafker (1965) found by using tide-gage data at several stations that in Prince William Sound the height of the barnacle line was at or no more than 15 cm below mean high-water level. This finding agreed generally with published results from other places: Moore (1935) reported upper limits for *B. balanoides* in Britain ranging from mean high water of neap tides to maximum high-water level, and for *B. glandula* in western North America upper limits of approximately mean high water have been reported (Rice, 1930; Ricketts and Calvin, 1962; Barnes and Barnes, 1956).

Our measurements of the upper limit of the postearthquake barnacle settlement in Prince William Sound (Table 3) showed an average deviation from mean high-water level of −0.3 ft, with a range of −2.2 ft to +0.9 ft (data from 19 stations). At 10 of these stations the new barnacle line was lower than mean high water (average, −1.0 ft) and at 9 it was higher (average, +0.5 ft). Some of the larger deviations may have been due to measurement errors. However, without repeated measurements over several seasons the possibility exists that at some sites the typical upper limit may differ significantly from mean high water, or that the postearthquake upper limit was not yet at its eventual stable position at the time of our measurements. Nevertheless, the

TABLE 3 Barnacle-Line Data (in feet)[a]

| Station No. | Location | Vertical Change Category[b] | Mean High Water[c] | Vertical Change (Plafker, 1969) | Our Measurements Top of Prequake Barnacles | Top of New Barnacles | Deviation of New Barnacles from MHW | Vertical Change Method 1[d] | Method 2[e] |
|---|---|---|---|---|---|---|---|---|---|
| 1 | Shipyard Bay, Hawkins Island | M | 11.5 | 5.4 | — | — | — | — | — |
| 4 | Olsen Bay, west side of islet | M | 11.1 | 3.6 | 14.8 | — | — | — | 3.7 |
| 4 | Olsen Bay, east side of islet | M | 11.1 | 3.6 | 14.0 | 10.6 | −0.5 | 3.4 | 2.9 |
| 5 | Knowles Head | M | 11.1 | 5.7 | — | — | — | — | — |
| 6 | Goose Island | M | 11.1 | 4.8 | 15.5 | 11.5 | 0.4 | 4.0 | 4.4 |
| 7 | Galena Bay | N | 11.1 | 2.0 | 12.6 | 10.6 | −0.5 | 2.0 | 1.5 |
| 8 | Heather Island | N | 11.1 | 1.7 | 10.2 | 8.6 | −2.5 | 1.6 | −0.9 |
| 9 | Naked Island | M | 10.9 | 4.7 | 15.3 | 11.5 | 0.6 | 3.8 | 4.4 |
| 10 | Perry Island, South Bay | N | 11.2 | 1.5 | 13.0 | 11.7 | 0.5 | 1.3 | 1.8 |
| 11 | Perry Island, West Twin Bay | N | 11.2 | 0.1 | 11.4 | 11.4 | 0.2 | 0 | 0.2 |
| 12 | Port Wells, near Golden | D | 11.2 | −4.1 | — | — | — | — | — |
| 13 | Blackstone Bay | D | 11.2 | −5.2 | 4.3 | 9.0 | −2.2 | −4.7 | −6.9 |
| 14 | Port Nellie Juan | N | 11.1 | −0.4 | 12.0 | 12.0 | 0.9 | 0 | 0.9 |
| 16 | Sawmill Bay | M | 10.5 | 8.9 | 17.0 | — | — | — | 6.5 |
| 17 | Thumb Bay | M | 10.8 | 6.0 | 17.2 | 9.6 | −1.2 | 7.6 | 6.4 |
| 18 | Orca Inlet | M | 11.5 | 7.0 | — | — | — | — | — |
| 20 | MacLeod Harbor, outer point | X | 10.4 | 30.0 | 40.8 | 10.0 | −0.4 | 30.8 | 30.4 |
| 20 | MacLeod Harbor, inner stack | X | 10.4 | 30.0 | 42.6 | — | — | — | 32.2 |
| 21 | Hanning Bay | X | 10.6 | 29.8 | 38.0 | 10.3 | −0.3 | 27.7 | 27.4 |
| 22 | Stockdale Harbor | M | 10.8 | 8.7 | 15.8 | 6.4 | −4.4 | 9.4 | 5.0 |
| 23 | Green Island | M | 10.8 | 8.4 | 19.7 | 11.1 | 0.3 | 8.6 | 8.9 |
| 24 | Zaikof Bay | M | 10.3 | 8.8 | 18.8 | 9.5 | −0.8 | 9.3 | 8.5 |
| 26 | Beartrap Bay | M | 11.1 | 4.0 | 14.8 | — | — | — | 3.7 |
| 27 | Deep Bay, Hawkins I., Point Salmo | M | 11.3 | 6.8 | 18.4 | 10.9 | −0.4 | 7.5 | 7.1 |
| 29 | Port Etches, Phipps Point | M | 10.3 | 6.0 | 16.8 | 10.6 | 0.3 | 6.2 | 6.5 |
| 30 | English Bay, Port Etches | M | 10.3 | 7.1 | 16.8 | 11.2 | 0.9 | 5.6 | 6.5 |
| 31 | Anderson Bay | M | 10.8 | 3.8 | 21.6 | 16.8 | — | 4.8 | — |
| 32 | Whiskey Cove, near Canoe Passage | M | 11.1 | 4.2 | 16.3 | 11.4 | 0.3 | 4.9 | 5.2 |
| 33 | Spike Island | M | 11.5 | 6.1 | 17.3 | 10.8 | −0.7 | 6.5 | 5.8 |

[a] Zero datum is mean lower low water.
[b] N, normal (little or no land-level change); M, moderate uplift; X, maximum uplift; D, downthrust.
[c] Calculated from tide tables (U.S. Coast and Geodetic Survey, 1965, p. 182–183), using locations nearest our stations.
[d] Top of new (postearthquake) barnacles subtracted from top of preearthquake barnacles.
[e] Mean high-water level subtracted from top of preearthquake barnacles.

bulk of our measurements were consistent with Plafker's finding that the upper barnacle limit in Prince William Sound is at or very close to mean high-water level.

Strong wave action, well known as a cause of elevation in the vertical ranges of intertidal organisms, was considered the most likely potential cause of local variations in the position and distinctness of the barnacle line. On outer coasts exposed directly to open ocean surf in western North America, the upper limit of *Balanus glandula* is strongly elevated and becomes poorly defined, with the population gradually decreasing into the splash zone rather than ending in a sharp line. We found no evidence of significant elevation nor indistinctness of the barnacle line due to wave action in Prince William Sound, even at our most exposed stations on Montague and Hinchinbrook islands.

The maximum displacement attributable to wave action that we found was at Stations 30 and 32, where the preearthquake barnacle line extended about 1 ft higher (with slightly sparser populations) on the most exposed rocks than on adjacent, more sheltered rocks. At Station 27 we looked for differences in desiccation attributable to northern versus southern exposures where rock surfaces were vertical and the barnacle line very sharply defined. The barnacle line was only about 3 inches lower on the south-facing rocks—an insignificant difference.

Plafker (1965) stated that the barnacle line can usually be resolved with an accuracy of 15 cm or less; Kaye (1964) measured it to the nearest 0.1-ft "field scale." Our estimate of resolution of the barnacle line (using a hand level or Brunton compass) was ±½ ft, which agreed with that of

Plafker. At close range the line was often less distinct, varying over a range of 1 ft or more, but at a distance of several feet the average height of the line could be more accurately resolved.

Land-level changes calculated by two different methods from our measurements are shown in Table 3. In method 1, land-level change is the distance between the pre- and post-earthquake barnacle lines, obtained by subtraction or by direct measurement; in either case the result is independent of the height of the water at the time of measurement. This method would be subject to error if the postearthquake barnacles had not settled with the same upper limit as that of the preearthquake barnacles relative to the tides. The small deviations of the postearthquake barnacle line from mean high water indicated that this source of error was not significant, except perhaps at a few stations. In method 2, land-level change is determined by the distance from the preearthquake barnacle line to its assumed preearthquake position, mean high-water level. Because this method depends on a measurement to water level, it is subject to error by deviation of actual water level from that predicted by the tide tables. Such deviations may be caused by meteorological or wave conditions (Brattegard and Lewis, 1964; Glynn, 1965). The seemingly anomalous barnacle-line heights at Stations 13 and 22 may have been due to this factor; the weather was very stormy when the measurements were made (none of our data were corrected for this error by tide-gage readings).

Results from the two methods differed by less than 1 ft at 16 of the 20 stations where both methods were used. At three stations the methods differed by 1.2 to 2.5 ft, and at one station by 4.4 ft; these measurements include those possibly affected by deviation of actual from predicted water level.

Differences between our land-level-change measurements and those of Plafker (1965) were calculated from Table 3; we used the nearest or the mean of the two nearest of Plafker's measurements to our stations. The average difference derived from our method 1 data was 0.6 ft (maximum difference 1.6 ft); from our method 2 data, the average difference was 1.0 ft (maximum difference 3.7 ft). The lower mean and maximum differences from our method 1 data are probably due to this method's independence from determination of water level.

In conclusion, our observations confirm the distinctness and uniformity of the pre- and postearthquake upper limit of midlittoral barnacles in Prince William Sound. The few complicating factors such as species variation and wave action could be significant for critical biological studies at particular sites, but not for determining a broad pattern of land-level change. Our measurements of vertical land displacement in general agree well with those made by the U.S. Geological Survey, relative to the precision of the technique.

Therefore the validity of using the barnacle-line method for determining land-level changes is fully supported.

MUSSELS

Characteristics of the preearthquake mussel populations (*Mytilus edulis*) in Prince William Sound have been described previously. Heavy mortality of mussels occurred in both the moderately and maximally uplifted areas. Many beaches were densely covered with mussel shells, and *in situ* beds of dead mussels were conspicuous on uplifted rocks, especially in the maximally uplifted areas. Although the vertical range of *Mytilus* extended from the subtidal zone up nearly to the barnacle line, dense adult beds occurred within a rather narrow band in the lower *Balanus–Fucus* zone (Figure 16). For this reason, percent mortality of the entire mussel population in the Sound was probably greater than that of the upper midlittoral barnacles. Total mortality of mussel beds apparently occurred wherever the uplift was greater than about 5 ft.

Dense patches of small postearthquake mussels were found in the midlittoral zone at most moderately and maximally uplifted stations. In addition, small mussels occurred in lesser numbers from the *Laminaria* zone (and below) up nearly to the barnacle line; abundance decreased toward their upper limit. Size distributions in the postearthquake mussel beds were variable, probably owing to different growth rates and times of settlement at different sites. Shell lengths of the mussels ranged from less than 1 mm to 20 mm (maximum lengths of preearthquake mussels ranged from 40 to 68 mm). Both 1964 and 1965 classes were probably present in the postearthquake settlement. However, without knowledge of growth rates, which are known to be labile in mussels (Field, 1921; Coe, 1945; Dehnel, 1956; Reish, 1964), the age of the larger individuals could not be determined with certainty; the smallest ones had doubtless settled very recently (1965). The highly successful postearthquake reproduction of mussels, despite the heavy mortality caused by the uplift, may have resulted in large part from spawning by the scattered but not uncommon adult mussels living in the lower intertidal and subtidal zones and therefore not killed by the uplift.

Two aspects of the postearthquake settlement of mussels were noteworthy: (a) the attachment of most of the mussels to algae rather than to rocks and (b) the somewhat lower average intertidal height of the postearthquake beds compared to their preearthquake counterparts.

Most or all of the individuals in the dense postearthquake mussel aggregations at most stations were attached to or nestled among algae (Figure 17). At only a few sites (for example, Station 5) were the bulk of the small mussels attached directly to rock surfaces. Attachment was usually to dense mats of filamentous or membranous types of algae

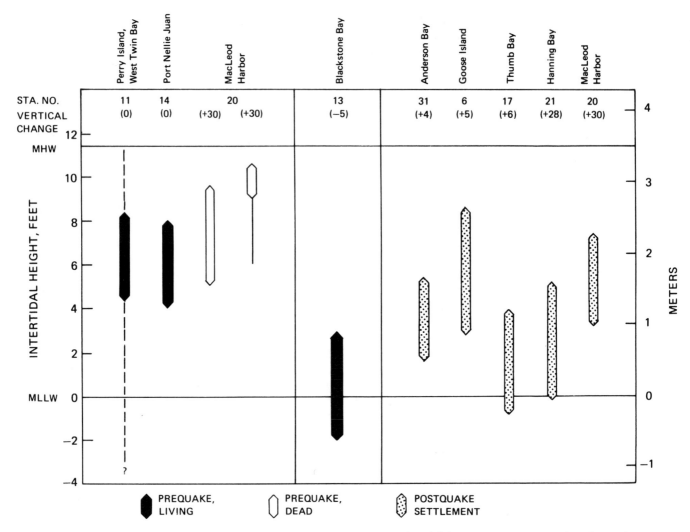

FIGURE 16 Vertical ranges of preearthquake and postearthquake mussel beds (*Mytilus edulis*). At all stations, scattered small mussels occurred above and below the main beds, as indicated by the dotted line for Station 11. The dead uplifted mussel beds at Station 20 have been plotted in their preearthquake positions.

such as *Enteromorpha*, *Polysiphonia*, and *Monostroma.* At some stations (as in Figure 17) dense mussel populations were attached to larger algae such as *Rhodymenia.*

Since mussels in the adult preearthquake beds were nearly always attached directly to rock surfaces (or nestled among gravel), the attachment of the postearthquake beds to algae would seem to be an abnormal, probably unstable situation related to the earthquake. One can postulate that after the earthquake, rapidly growing algal populations covered most of the available rock surface in the postearthquake intertidal zone before mussel spawning occurred. On the other hand, we found some evidence that settlement of young mussels on algae may occur normally in Prince William Sound. At Station 11 (no land-level change), a few aggregations of small mussels were found attached to filamentous algae just below the level of the main adult beds, but not

immediately adjacent to the latter. Although small mussels were also scattered elsewhere, mostly attached to rock, very few were found within the adult beds.

Bayne (1964) has provided evidence that *Mytilus edulis* larvae typically settle first on filamentous substrates away from adult beds. They then undergo a migratory phase in which they may successively attach to and detach from different filamentous substrates, being transported by currents, before finally settling within adult mussel beds. Bayne suggests that this behavior may be a mechanism to prevent competition between young and old mussels and to prevent mass ingestion of settling larvae by adults. Verwey (1954) found that mussel larvae generally do not settle on adult populations. These results provide a plausible, though untested, explanation for our observations at Station 11 and perhaps for the algal attachment of postearthquake mussels

G Dallas Hanna

FIGURE 17   Dense population of postearthquake mussels (*Mytilus edulis*) (maximum length about 20 mm) attached mainly to *Rhodymenia* and other algae rather than directly to the rock surface. Lower-midlittoral zone at English Bay (Station 30), July 13, 1965; uplift about 7 ft.

at the uplifted stations. On the other hand, the occurrence of scattered young mussels on rock surfaces at all stations and the few instances of dense postearthquake beds attached to rocks indicate that attachment of young mussels to algae is not mandatory in Prince William Sound.

Intertidal heights of the postearthquake mussel beds varied considerably. However, most of these beds occupied a somewhat lower position in the intertidal zone than did the preearthquake adult beds (Figure 16). Whereas the pre-earthquake beds were largely restricted to the upper mid-littoral zone, many of the postearthquake beds were largely within the lower midlittoral. This distribution may be related to their attachment to algae if the above-cited work of Bayne applies, but other factors may be involved.

Even if settlement of aggregations of mussel spat on algae and at lower levels than adult beds is a normal occurrence in Prince William Sound, there remains the question of how stable postearthquake adult beds attached to rock will eventually become established in the absence of preexisting beds. Algae-attached mussels, especially as they grow larger, may be subject to extensive mortality owing to removal of

the algae by storm waves and seasonal death. Algae-attached mussels may move to rock surfaces, or future settlements of mussels may attach directly to rocks. In either case, the eventual sites of rock-attached beds (not necessarily the same as the sites of the algae-attached beds) were at the time of our observations occupied by algae, barnacles, and other organisms. Therefore considerable competition for space may be involved during the establishment of the adult beds. Predation by asteroids, well-known predators of mussels, may also play a role in determining the eventual position of the adult beds, particularly their lower limits (Paine, 1966).

HERBIVOROUS GASTROPODS AND VEGETATION

An increasing amount of field experimental evidence from various parts of the world has shown that herbivores are often responsible for suppression of algal growth on rocky shores. Herbivore populations thus may strongly influence patterns of algal distribution and abundance—for example, by maintaining the bare appearance of rock surfaces in the upper intertidal zone (Conway, 1946; Lodge, 1948; Southward, 1956, 1964; Castenholz, 1961; Kitching and Ebling, 1961; Aitken, 1962; Haven, 1966). In the present study, particular attention was paid to herbivorous gastropods, the dominant intertidal grazers on rocky shores in Prince William Sound. Observations were made that suggested that grazing gastropods were having significant effects on the algal vegetation and therefore on the dynamics of development of the postearthquake communities.

All the observations to be reported involved negative correlations between density or distribution of gastropod populations and of certain types of algal cover. Speculations are made in light of the experimental evidence cited above that grazing activities were at least in part causally related to the observed distribution patterns.

The gastropod species involved were the common grazers of the midlittoral zone (some of which ranged beyond this zone): *Littorina scutulata*, *L. sitkana*, *Acmaea paradigitalis*, *A. pelta*, *A. scutum*, and, in lesser numbers, *A. digitalis*, *A. persona*, and *Siphonaria thersites*. Food habits of these species have not been thoroughly studied but can be described in general terms from published information and personal observations. The principal work on *Acmaea* is that of Test (1945). *Acmaea digitalis*, *A. paradigitalis*, and *A. persona* feed chiefly on epilithic microalgae, including young stages of larger algae. *Acmaea scutum* eats membranous macroscopic algae such as *Ulva* and *Enteromorpha* as well as encrusting microalgae. *Acmaea pelta* is the most euryphagous of the limpets; it consumes a wide variety of epilithic and epiphytic algae, both microscopic and larger forms. However, our observations indicated that neither *A. pelta* nor any other gastropod consumed *Fucus* to any great extent. Both species of *Littorina* are definitely scrapers of epilithic microalgae; *L. scutulata* also consumes larger algae (Dahl, 1964), and *L. sitkana* probably does so as well. *Siphonaria* has been reported to eat *Fucus* (Yonge, 1960), but we found it mostly feeding on microalgae on bare rock or, if on *Fucus*, feeding on epiphytes. The experiments of Castenholz (1961) in Oregon showed that natural populations of *L. scutulata* and *A. digitalis* prevent the growth of diatom cover in the upper intertidal zone, and similar results were obtained in California by Haven (1966) for two species of *Acmaea*, including *A. digitalis*.

Three types of negative correlations between grazers and algae were observed in the postearthquake intertidal zone at the uplifted stations: patches of relatively bare rock occupied by gastropods within areas densely covered with algae and containing few or no gastropods; a "grazing line" marking the upper limit of dense limpet and littorine populations and the lower limit of the encrusting algal film growing in the *Verrucaria* zone; and the dominance of *Porphyra*, rather than *Fucus*, at the maximally uplifted stations correlated with very low densities of grazers.

In the upper midlittoral zone at many moderately uplifted stations, we found more or less extensive areas covered mainly by membranous or filamentous algae. Within these areas were patches relatively bare of algae, ranging in size from a few square inches to many square feet, which contained varying numbers of limpets (particularly *Acmaea paradigitalis* and *A. pelta*) and littorines. Gastropods were sparse or absent in the surrounding algal cover. At several places the gastropods were seen to be feeding around the edges of the patches, and it was obvious that grazing was responsible for the bare patches. The most frequent type of cover in the upper midlittoral zone at the normal stations was a mosaic of *Fucus* and barnacles with abundant gastropods and scattered filamentous and membranous algae. Therefore it appeared that at least some of the situations just described represented greater than normal cover of the rapidly growing filamentous and membranous algae and that grazing activities may have been contributing to restoration of the typical population balance at these sites. Further observations would, of course, be necessary to test this possibility.

In the lower midlittoral zone, extensive cover by membranous and filamentous algae was the rule at both the normal and most of the uplifted stations. Nevertheless, several examples of bare areas correlated with dense limpet populations were found. Figure 18 shows a vertical rock in the lower midlittoral zone at Green Island, Station 23 (uplift 8 ft), densely populated by *Acmaea scutum* with a few *A. pelta* and *Siphonaria thersites* but having no macroscopic algae. A sharp line, apparently a grazing boundary, separated this bare surface from an adjacent area solidly covered by membranous algae but containing no limpets. The effects of grazing pressure were well demonstrated on this rock, but the factors favoring grazer versus algal dominance are unclear; for example, avoidance of established dense algal cover by gastropods may be involved.

It should be pointed out that negative distributional correlations between algae and grazers were far from universal. They did not apply to *Fucus* and other "hard" algae such as *Halosaccion* and *Rhodymenia*; gastropods were usually common on and among these algae but appeared to be eating encrusting epiphytes rather than the fronds themselves. *Acmaea paradigitalis*, *A. scutum*, *A. digitalis*, and *A. persona* were most closely restricted to bare areas on rocks, whereas littorines and *A. pelta* commonly occurred on and among algae as well as on bare rock.

The second type of situation interpreted as a grazing effect was observed at moderately uplifted stations where a conspicuous film of encrusting microalgae occupied the postearthquake *Verrucaria* zone. The lower limit of this algal film was often a rather sharp line, called here the "grazing line." This line was at or slightly below the upper limit of postearthquake barnacles (mean high-water level),

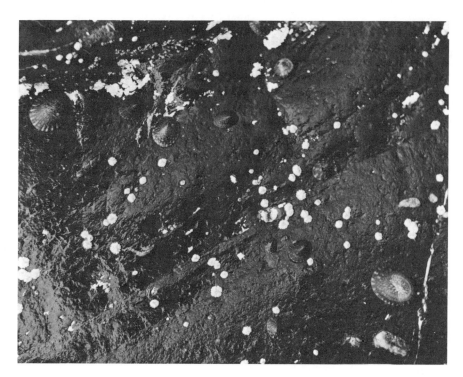

FIGURE 18 Vertical rock surface on Green Island (Station 23), July 1, 1965, in the postearthquake lower-midlittoral zone occupied by limpets (mostly *Acmaea scutum* and *A. pelta*) but having no macroscopic algae; uplift about 8 ft. An adjacent surface had dense algal cover but no limpets. Most of the white spots are barnacles.

and close examination showed that it was correlated with the upper limit of dense limpet and littorine populations. The best correlation was with the upper limit of *A. paradigitalis*, the commonest limpet; littorines were scattered above the line but the densest populations were below. Below the grazing line the rock surface was largely clear of a visible algal film. This difference was also noticeable on barnacles: Living or dead barnacle tests above the grazing line were darkened by an algal film, whereas those below the line were whitish, without visible algal cover. A conspicuous grazing line was found on some, but not all, rocks at all stations subsequent to Station 24, where it was first discovered.

If grazing was in fact responsible for the grazing line, such a line would be expected to be absent at the maximally uplifted stations (Stations 20 and 21), where postearthquake gastropod populations were very low. Examination under magnification of the original color slide for Figure 11 indicated that the algal film occupying the *Verrucaria* zone did extend down among the barnacles as far as open rock surface was visible.

The final instance of possible grazer effects concerns the dominance of the alga *Porphyra* in a broad band within the midlittoral zone at the maximally uplifted stations (Figures 11 and 12). *Fucus*, the presumed normal dominant alga of this zone, was uncommon and scattered. Although adequate quantitative samples were not taken because of time limitations, it was clear from extensive searching that at these stations, population densities of grazing gastropods were much lower after the earthquake than before, and lower than at the normal and moderately uplifted stations (Table 4). This was particularly true for the dominant midlittoral limpets and littorines and was undoubtedly a consequence of the total mortality of preearthquake breeding stock. Within the *Porphyra* zone, most of the small scattered groups of gastro-

TABLE 4 Relative Abundance of Herbivorous Gastropods[a]

| Species | Normal | Moderate Uplift | Maximum Uplift Prequake | Postquake |
|---|---|---|---|---|
| *Acmaea digitalis* | ++ | ++ | ++ | o |
| *Acmaea instabilis* | o | o | ++ | o |
| *Acmaea mitra* | + | + | + | + |
| *Acmaea paradigitalis* | +++ | +++ | +++ | + |
| *Acmaea pelta* | +++ | +++ | +++ | + |
| *Acmaea persona* | ++ | ++ | ++ | o |
| *Acmaea rosea* | o | + | o | + |
| *Acmaea scutum* | +++ | +++ | +++ | + |
| *Lepeta concentrica* | o | + | + | + |
| *Littorina scutulata* | +++ | +++ | +++ | + |
| *Littorina sitkana* | +++ | +++ | +++ | + |
| *Margarites* spp. | o | + | ? | ++ |
| *Siphonaria thersites* | ++ | ++ | o | o |
| *Onchidella borealis* | + | + | o | o |

[a] +++, abundant; ++, common; +, uncommon; o, not found.

pods that were found occupied small bare patches within the *Porphyra* cover.

The correlation between occurrence of a *Porphyra* zone and scarcity of grazing gastropods was strengthened by a demise of the *Porphyra* zone and an increase in gastropod populations northward on Montague Island. A well-developed *Porphyra* zone, with few grazers, was found at MacLeod Harbor (Station 20) and the outer boulder field at Hanning Bay (Station 21). However, the inner rocky reef at Hanning Bay (near transect 21a) was different, although the uplift was virtually the same. The *Porphyra* zone was recognizable but was clearly less well developed than at Stations 20 and 21. Bare patches were frequent in the *Porphyra* cover, and *Fucus* was more common, although still not dominant over large areas. Grazing gastropod populations were definitely larger; although overall densities were still less than normal, local patches—usually the bare areas within the *Porphyra*—contained substantial numbers of limpets and littorines. The trend was completed at Stockdale Harbor (Station 22), near the northern tip of Montague Island, which was within the moderately uplifted region (uplift about 9 ft). At this station a *Porphyra* zone was not present. *Fucus* was the dominant alga in the upper midlittoral zone, as at the normal and other moderately uplifted stations; in fact, *Fucus* was abundant throughout the midlittoral zone. *Porphyra* was present but was scattered in distribution. Grazing gastropods were very abundant; their populations included many preearthquake survivors. The situation was essentially the same at the nearby moderately uplifted Stations 23 and 24.

Thus, the three moderately uplifted stations closest to the maximally uplifted area were typical of the normal and moderately uplifted stations generally: no *Porphyra* zone, abundant *Fucus*, and abundant grazing gastropods. The intermediate situation at Station 21, transect 21a, supports the correlation between the *Porphyra* zone and scarcity of gastropods, but its difference from the other maximally uplifted stations is unexplained. No reason is apparent for the greater rate of settlement and/or survival of postearthquake gastropods at Station 21, near transect 21a, compared to the nearby Stations 21 and 20.

A hypothesis to explain the occurrence of the *Porphyra* zone at the maximally uplifted stations is that grazers normally limit the density of *Porphyra* (perhaps mainly by eating sporelings) and that the reduced grazing pressure due to total mortality and slow postearthquake repopulation of gastropods allowed the rapidly growing *Porphyra* to dominate the rocks newly exposed in the midlittoral zone after the uplift. The *Porphyra* may then have inhibited the establishment of *Fucus*. Increasing grazing pressure as gastropod populations approach their normal size may play a role in eventual establishment of dominance by *Fucus*. However, other factors may be involved. Johansen (1971, this volume)

cites evidence that *Fucus* was not yet in reproductive condition at the time of the earthquake and that the sparsity of *Fucus* may therefore have been due to a shortage of zygotes caused by the total mortality of preearthquake populations. He suggests that an initial scarcity of *Fucus* and its slow growth may have permitted the rapidly growing *Porphyra* to assume dominance.

## DISCUSSION: ECOLOGICAL SUCCESSION

The land-level changes caused by the earthquake in Prince William Sound had two major biological consequences for intertidal organisms: mortality of preexisting populations and initiation of the development of new communities on surfaces displaced into the intertidal zone from above or below.

By and large, the mortality of preearthquake organisms that were moved out of their normal intertidal ranges was to be expected and could be predicted as a function of the amount and direction of land-level change. For a marine animal, being uplifted, with the resulting greater exposure to atmospheric conditions, is worse than being downthrust. This principle is consistent with our finding of general mortality of organisms lifted above their preearthquake upper limits, but survival of many populations, such as mussels, barnacles, and *Fucus*, displaced downward (presumably, the latter will eventually be replaced by species typical of the lower levels). Thus, with a few exceptions such as the survival of some uplifted barnacles above their previous upper limit, the probable survival of uplifted *Acmaea persona* by downward movement, and the mortality of bivalves caused by sediment removal, the effects of the earthquake on preearthquake populations were generally according to expectation.

As for the second biological consequence of the earthquake, knowledge of ecological succession in intertidal communities is too incomplete for valid predictions of the nature of the recolonization process in the postearthquake intertidal zone. Although ecological succession is widely considered to be a fundamental characteristic of nonmarine communities, its nature and significance in marine benthic environments has been little studied, and the results have been conflicting. Discussions of succession, including its controversial aspects and references to its largely nonmarine literature, can be found in texts such as Oosting (1956), Odum (1959), Kendeigh (1961), and Kershaw (1964). Most of the evidence on marine benthic community development has come from studies of fouling or colonization of experimental settling surfaces and of artificially denuded shore plots; a few studies have been made on natural or artificial surfaces such as breakwaters, dredged harbor bottoms, and lava flows, newly exposed to marine conditions. A number of studies, mostly on hard substrates, have provided evidence for the occurrence of succession, that is, sequential dominance by various species or groups of species before the establishment of the relatively stable climax community typical of the environment being studied (Hewatt, 1935; Coe and Allen, 1937; Bokenham and Stephenson, 1938; Moore and Sproston, 1940; Scheer, 1945; Northcraft, 1948; Reish, 1962; Lawson, 1966; Clarke, 1967). On the other hand, several studies have reported no evidence for succession; the dominant species of the climax were present from the start, and no significant directional change in species composition or relative abundance was noted (Pierron and Huang, 1925; Shelford, 1930; Reish, 1963).

Several of our findings on rocky shores in Prince William Sound constitute evidence for the occurrence of succession, by indicating that at the time of our observations (over a year—i.e., in the second growing season—after the earthquake), the inferred climax community had not yet become established in the postearthquake intertidal zone. The four principal examples of this evidence are

1. Perhaps the best example, the widespread dominance of film-forming algae and the apparent absence of postearthquake growth of the lichen *Verrucaria* wherever new surfaces were displaced into the *Verrucaria* zone. Clearly, the preearthquake climax plant cover (solid *Verrucaria*) had not yet become established, and in its place was an entirely different type of cover. The absence of *Verrucaria* may have been due to its normally slow and largely vegetative means of reproduction (Johansen, 1971, this volume). Spores or minute new growth may have been present but undetected. In contrast to the plant cover, the similarity of the fauna of this zone (littorines and limpets) to that of the preearthquake situation, except at the maximally uplifted areas where the fauna was strongly reduced, showed that for animals the postearthquake surfaces in this zone were suitable for rapid recolonization.

2. The dominance of *Porphyra* in the midlittoral zone at the maximally uplifted stations, correlated with a paucity of grazing gastropods and of *Fucus*. This assemblage differed significantly in dominance relationships from the inferred preearthquake community, in which *Fucus* was probably the dominant alga, grazing gastropods were abundant, and *Porphyra* was sparse. The possible causal roles of grazing pressure, competition, and shortage of spores and larvae in the process of community development on these rocks have already been discussed.

3. The apparent dominance of *Balanus balanoides* and absence of *B. glandula* in the postearthquake upper midlittoral barnacle settlement, whereas *B. glandula* was probably the more abundant of the two before the earthquake. The dense barnacle settlement in the upper midlittoral zone during both the first and second seasons after the earthquake at most stations indicated that the new substrates were suitable for direct reestablishment of animals of the same lifeform (acorn barnacles) that dominated the preearthquake community. However, the reversal in dominance of the two *Balanus* species following the earthquake produced an important difference in the new barnacle zone from that before the earthquake and thus an example of succession. As discussed earlier, chance timing of the earthquake with respect to spawning of the two species may have caused this change. The rate of the presumed return to dominance of *B. glandula* and the possible mechanisms involved can hardly be predicted; considerable future study is required, especially in view of the paucity of currently available data.

4. The attachment of most of the dense postearthquake mussel beds to algae, rather than to rock surfaces, and at somewhat lower intertidal levels than the preearthquake beds. Possible explanations have already been discussed: rapidly growing algae may have preempted the available space before the mussels settled, or settlement of young mussels on algae may be a normal occurrence. In either case, evidence from the normal stations and from uplifted mussel beds showed that adult mussel beds were invariably attached to rock surfaces. Whether or not the eventual sites of adult rock-attached postearthquake mussel beds prove to be the same as the sites of the algae-attached beds, the former sites were dominated by algae, barnacles, and other organisms at the time of our observations. Competition, predation, and other factors, both internal and external to the community, may be involved in the takeover of these sites by mussels. Thus, except where postearthquake beds were found already directly attached to rock, the establishment of adult rock-attached mussel beds will probably involve a complex process of succession. Prolonged succession in mussel beds has been reported by Hewatt (1935) and Clarke (1967).

The survival of vertically displaced sessile populations outside their normal ranges constitutes another example of dominance by nonclimax species in the postearthquake intertidal zone. The principal examples were barnacle populations uplifted into the *Verrucaria* zone and upper midlittoral mussels, barnacles, and *Fucus* downthrust into the lower midlittoral and *Laminaria* zones. At least in the case of the downthrust populations, these displaced organisms were interfering with the establishment of species typical of the given levels. For example, downthrust mussels preempted space that should be recolonized by *Laminaria*. These seem to be special situations, associated with earthquake-caused land-level changes, that do not fit the usual concept of succession. Succession generally begins on a new substrate or upon destruction of a preexisting community, rather than with a thriving but abnormal community.

As for the level-bottom environment, those mudflats where preearthquake communities were destroyed, or nearly destroyed, by the uplift (maximally uplifted areas) and by sediment removal (some moderately uplifted areas) were still far from their normal climax condition at the time of our observations. On the one hand, the juvenile clams that had settled after the earthquake belonged to species that were dominant before the earthquake, and at least at one station (Station 1: moderate uplift, sediment removal) population densities of the new clams were high. This density would indicate that direct and rapid repopulation was occurring. However, postearthquake populations at Station 1 were deficient in numbers of species; at Station 18 (sediment removal, anaerobic mud) there were no new clams, and the maximally uplifted area was highly deficient in both numbers of species and numbers of individuals. Unfortunately, the extent to which these deficiencies were due to shortage of available larvae rather than unsuitability of the habitat for colonization cannot be determined without more extensive study. At Station 18, unsuitability of the habitat was doubtless the most important factor, whereas at the maximally uplifted stations, shortage of larvae was perhaps more important. However, at all these strongly affected stations, the deficiencies in fine muddy sediments of high organic content showed that the habitat was still quite different from what is inferred from less severely affected sites to be the condition in mature (preearthquake) mudflats. This difference indicates that a rather long period of habitat recovery will have to take place. Although external (allogenic) processes such as physical sediment deposition and settlement of planktonic detritus will probably be of major importance, activities of benthic organisms (for example, burrowing worms, clams, and particularly microorganisms) may play a significant role in modifying the physical substrate. Thus, autogenic biological succession (succession caused by internal community processes) may be important in the postearthquake redevelopment of mudflat ecosystems; this succession would not necessarily be revealed by data only on presence and abundance of the dominant macroinvertebrates.

Most aspects of the postearthquake communities other than the examples of evidence for succession discussed above indicated general similarity to the inferred preearthquake climax conditions. This similarity applies to the *Laminaria* zone throughout the Sound, the midlittoral zone and the fauna of the *Verrucaria* zone in the moderately uplifted and downthrust areas, and the moderately uplifted mudflats not affected by sediment removal. In these communities, the general similarity of species composition, abundance, and vertical ranges to conditions before the earthquake showed that for these aspects of the communities, sufficiently rapid and direct repopulation had occurred for essentially climax conditions to be established within about

a year, and probably mostly within the first growing season, after the earthquake. This condition, of course, does not rule out the occurrence of recognizable successional stages before the time of our observations, as will be discussed later.

Of all the postearthquake communities, the condition of the *Laminaria* zone was the most similar to the inferred preearthquake condition and was therefore judged to show the most rapid and direct redevelopment process up to the time of our observations. Although future observations may show that, especially at the maximally uplifted stations, the fauna and flora were still incomplete, the dense *Laminaria* cover and rich fauna at favorable sites was typical of this zone in western North America. Reasons for this rapid recolonization probably include favorable conditions for settlement and growth owing to minimal exposure to atmospheric climatic conditions; minimal interruption by the uplift of the supply of larvae and spores, because of the subtidal ranges of most *Laminaria* zone species; and *in situ* survival of individuals uplifted from the subtidal into the *Laminaria* zone, also resulting from the subtidal ranges of the species involved. The main exception to the above was in the downthrust area (Station 13), where displaced mid-littoral populations were occupying the *Laminaria* zone.

The overall rate of recovery in the midlittoral zone of the moderately uplifted and downthrust areas was less than that in the *Laminaria* zone. The midlittoral zone supported communities similar to the preearthquake climax in many aspects of species composition, abundance, and vertical ranges but at the same time exhibited two of the four major examples of succession: algae-attached mussel beds (not seen at downthrust stations) and dominance of *Balanus balanoides*. The *Verrucaria* zone in moderately uplifted areas showed a still slower rate of recovery to the time of our observations because, despite an essentially normal fauna at most stations, there was no new growth of *Verrucaria*. It should be pointed out that the moderately uplifted and downthrust areas did not provide altogether valid tests for the occurrence of succession, because the preearthquake communities were not completely destroyed. Surviving preearthquake individuals actually formed part of the postearthquake populations, in addition to acting as breeding stock.

Only the maximally uplifted stations provided an opportunity for community development to occur without contributions from preearthquake survivors, at least above the *Laminaria* zone. Some preearthquake survival may have occurred in the *Laminaria* zone, but at least the dominant laminarian algae were postearthquake colonizers (Johansen, 1971, this volume). Rocky shores at the maximally uplifted stations showed all four of the main examples of succession (absence of *Verrucaria*, the *Porphyra* zone, dominance by *Balanus balanoides*, and algae-attached mussel beds).

Another important characteristic of the new communities in the maximally uplifted area was the general reduction in numbers of both species and individuals compared to the numbers before the earthquake. This reduction was probably due mostly to a shortage of larvae and spores; these had to be dispersed from parts of the Sound where breeding stock survived the earthquake. Some of these cases of absence or rarity of species may have been due to unsuitability of the environment for colonization, thus providing additional examples of succession, but this causal factor could not be determined without further study. On maximally uplifted rocky shores, the *Laminaria* zone showed the most rapid overall rate of recovery toward the climax condition, followed by the midlittoral zone, which showed three of the four examples of succession, and then the *Verrucaria* zone, which had a depauperate fauna as well as an absence of *Verrucaria.* Decreasing rate of approach to climax conditions upward in the intertidal zone has been reported previously (for example, Lawson, 1966), but Moore and Sproston (1940) found the slowest rate of development in the midintertidal zone.

There are several ways in which succession might have been occurring in the postearthquake communities without being detected by our observations. Most important of these is the possible occurrence of recognizable successional stages before the time of our observations. Most of the studies cited earlier as providing evidence for marine benthic succession found that several successional stages, or at least successive dominance by several different species, occurred within a few weeks or months after the start of colonization. Sometimes the climax condition was reached within a year. On hard substrates, the first stage was frequently a film of encrusting microalgae, bacteria, and adsorbed molecules, followed by rapidly growing algae such as *Enteromorpha* and *Ulva,* and later by other algal or animal species. Some evidence exists that the initial "slime" film favors the subsequent settlement of larvae or spores (Coe and Allen, 1937); the apparent sparsity of first-year barnacle settlement on previously terrestrial surfaces in downthrust areas may be a consequence.

Second, instances of succession may have gone undetected or at best have been only suggested, because of the lack of detailed knowledge of the preearthquake communities at any of the stations, particularly with respect to small-scale variations in community structure. Thus, examples such as the frequently observed patches of membranous and filamentous algae being attacked by grazing gastropods, and the dense cover of *Balanus crenatus* found in the low intertidal at a few stations, may or may not represent differences from normal preearthquake conditions.

Third, the lack of emphasis on small, ecologically subordinate types of organisms in our fieldwork precluded any documentation of succession involving these nondominant

forms. Communities such as mussel and barnacle beds (Ricketts and Calvin, 1962; Glynn, 1965) are known to support a large number of small, relatively fragile species that would not be able to survive on the open rock surfaces without the protection (i.e., modification of the physical environment) afforded by the populations of the dominant species. It is reasonable to assume that this subordinate segment of the postearthquake barnacle and mussel communities in Prince William Sound (and perhaps of other intertidal communities as well) had achieved far less than its full complement of species and individuals at the time of our observations. Many of these species probably cannot become established, at least in any great numbers, until populations and individuals of the dominant species have reached a certain minimum size. Studies of marine benthic succession emphasizing these subordinate species would be very worthwhile.

Finally, the long-term, largely physical processes of shore formation need to be mentioned. The configuration of the shoreline within the intertidal zone was more or less drastically changed at many places by the vertical land displacement and other factors associated with the earthquake—for example, from a steep rocky shore to a gently sloping bottom. The processes of erosion by waves and currents, sediment deposition, and aerial erosion and weathering will take a very long time to reshape the shore to a state of geomorphological equilibrium. These gradual changes in the habitats will, of course, be accompanied by changes in the biological communities occupying them.

In conclusion, it should be emphasized that a series of general observations in a single season is not adequate to document properly an ongoing process such as community development in the postearthquake intertidal zone. All the examples of succession discussed above, and, in fact, most of our other findings, must be considered as interpretations whose validity needs to be tested by future investigations. It is unfortunate that we could not take maximum advantage of the natural experiment provided by the earthquake by carrying out detailed biological investigations during the months immediately following the earthquake. However, we hope that future investigations will be carried out in Prince William Sound so that the later stages of postearthquake community development can be documented.

## SUMMARY

• Land uplift (as much as 30 ft observed) in Prince William Sound, Alaska, caused by the earthquake of March 27, 1964, lifted intertidal organisms partly or completely above the reach of the tides. Subsidence (maximum, as much as 7 ft) had converse effects. Waves and currents generated by the earthquake also had destructive effects in the intertidal zone.

• Thirty-three stations were occupied in Prince William Sound in May, June, and July 1965. This paper reports investigations on effects of the earthquake on preexisting intertidal invertebrate populations and investigations on the development of new biotic communities in the postearthquake intertidal zone.

• Evidence on normal (preearthquake) intertidal zonation and community composition, for use as a control for assessing the effects of the earthquake, was obtained principally from stations where there was little or no land-level change. Additional evidence came from dead *in situ* remains of uplifted organisms (chiefly calcareous forms) and from surviving portions of populations only partly displaced out of their intertidal ranges.

• On rocky shores, three major preearthquake zones were recognizable throughout the Sound: (a) *Verrucaria* zone (above mean high-water level), dominated by the lichen *Verrucaria* and by gastropods, mainly *Littorina*; (b) midlittoral zone (from a sharp upper boundary at mean high water to mean lower low water or below), usually divisible into an upper midlittoral zone dominated by barnacles and *Fucus*, with mussel beds frequent in its lower part, and a lower midlittoral zone dominated by various algae; and (c) *Laminaria* zone (below mean lower low water), dominated by laminarian algae and a diverse fauna.

• On rocky shores with moderate uplift (2–9 ft) the preearthquake and postearthquake intertidal zones overlapped to varying degrees. In general, organisms that were lifted above their preearthquake upper limits were killed. However, the vertical ranges of most species were large enough to permit survival of parts of their populations. Some preearthquake barnacles were still alive up to 3 ft above their normal upper limit, and in at least one case (*Acmaea persona*) survival by downward movement may have occurred.

In the postearthquake *Verrucaria* zone, the fauna was similar to preearthquake fauna, but there was no postearthquake growth of *Verrucaria*; at many places, the rocks were covered by an encrusting algal film, and uplifted preearthquake barnacles were also present at many places. With some important exceptions, species composition, vertical ranges, and levels of abundance in the midlittoral zone were not greatly different from the inferred preearthquake conditions. Populations consisted of preearthquake survivors and postearthquake recruitment. The fact that the *Laminaria* zone (at favorable sites) was densely populated by *Laminaria* and a rich fauna indicates rapid and direct repopulation.

• On rocky shores with maximum uplift (30 ft or more) where all preearthquake intertidal organisms were lifted well above water level, virtually complete mortality occurred, as it did in the upper subtidal zone. Abundant dead remains documented these uplifted populations. Most prominent was an extensive white zone (preearthquake lower midlittoral downward) densely covered by calcareous remains of serpulids, bryozoans, coralline algae, and huge accumulations of mollusk shells.

The postearthquake communities had to start completely anew, at least above the *Laminaria* zone. In general, the fauna was greatly reduced from its preearthquake density, especially above the *Laminaria* zone; several species common before the earthquake were absent, and many others were rare. The *Verrucaria* zone was covered by an algal film, with no *Verrucaria*, very few littorines, and no limpets. Much of the midlittoral zone was dominated by *Porphyra* rather than *Fucus*, and grazing gastropod populations were very sparse; there was a dense barnacle settlement, and mussels were common. The *Laminaria* zone supported dense *Laminaria* cover and a rich fauna.

• On downthrust rocky shores, preearthquake and postearthquake populations overlapped vertically. Littorines were found grazing on terrestrial moss. Downthrust preearthquake populations of mussels, barnacles, and *Fucus* were alive at their new lower levels (i.e., the postearthquake *Laminaria* zone) apparently inhibiting the establishment of postearthquake *Laminaria* and the associated fauna.

• The postearthquake *Balanus* settlement in the upper midlittoral zone throughout the Sound appeared to be nearly all *Balanus balanoides*, whereas both *B. balanoides* and *B. glandula* were present before the earthquake, with *B. glandula* probably the commonest species.

• Most of the dense beds of postearthquake mussels (*Mytilus*) were attached to underlying algae rather than directly to rock surfaces and were at somewhat lower intertidal levels than the preearthquake rock-attached mussel beds.

• Factors affecting the upper limit of midlittoral barnacles have been discussed in relation to measurements of land-level change. In general, the validity of measuring land-level change by the displacement of this upper barnacle limit (Plafker, 1965) is supported. The average deviation of the upper limit of postearthquake barnacles from mean high water at our stations was −0.3 ft. Where *Chthamalus dalli* was dominant (only a few places), the upper limit was about 1 ft higher than where *Balanus balanoides* and/or *B. glandula* were dominant. Wave action and other factors had only minor effects on the upper barnacle limit within the Sound. Our measurements of land-level change by the barnacle-line method agreed well with those made by Plafker.

• Several examples of negative correlations between population densities of herbivorous gastropods and of certain algae were discussed as evidence that grazing activities were significantly influencing the vegetation during development of the postearthquake communities.

• In level-bottom habitats, uplifting caused extensive mortality of clams lifted above their normal upper limits. In addition, there was virtually total mortality of large clams at some stations, caused by removal of surface sediments by waves and currents associated with the earthquake. At one of these stations, postearthquake clams were absent; at another, they were moderately numerous but with only a few species present; and at the maximally uplifted stations, they were very sparse.

• The results were discussed in relation to ecological succession. On rocky shores, four main instances where postearthquake communities were significantly different from the inferred preearthquake communities provided evidence for relatively long-term (more than 1 year) ecological succession. These are the dominance by film-forming algae and absence of *Verrucaria* in the *Verrucaria* zone; the dominance of *Porphyra* rather than *Fucus* in the midlittoral at maximally uplifted stations, correlated with a scarcity of grazing gastropods (the reduced grazing pressure perhaps being related to the abundance of *Porphyra*); the dominance of *Balanus balanoides* in the upper midlittoral barnacle settlement; and the attachment of mussels to algae rather than to rock surfaces. Although many other aspects of the postearthquake communities appeared similar to the inferred climax condition, additional ways have been discussed in which succession may have been occurring without being detected by our observations. In the uplifted areas, the overall rate of postearthquake community development appeared to be fastest in the *Laminaria* zone and decreased upward.

## ADDENDUM

The author revisited Prince William Sound from August 23 to 28, 1968 (the fifth summer after the earthquake), to obtain followup data on the course of ecological succession in the postearthquake intertidal zone. The main findings from this trip are summarized below; they will be reported in more detail in a separate paper.

The following stations were visited, each for one low-tide period: Station 4, Olsen Bay (uplift 3.6 ft); Station 20, MacLeod Harbor (uplift 30 ft); Station 33, Spike Island (uplift 6.1 ft); and the breakwater in Cordova Harbor. Observations were largely confined to rocky shores.

Notable results include the following:

• *Balanus glandula*, probably the dominant barnacle in the preearthquake upper midlittoral zone, has partially or completely replaced *B. balanoides*, which dominated the initial postearthquake barnacle settlement.

• *Fucus* was the dominant alga in the upper midlittoral zone at MacLeod Harbor (maximum uplift). *Porphyra* and other membranous algae that dominated this zone in 1965 were very scarce. Grazing gastropods (*Acmaea*, *Littorina*), scarce in 1965, were abundant.

• Mussel (*Mytilus edulis*) beds were attached mainly to rock or to underlying barnacles, in contrast to the algae-attached beds observed in 1965. At least at MacLeod Harbor, the mussel beds were at a higher intertidal level than in 1965 (i.e., approximately at their preearthquake level), and their lower limits appeared to be controlled by asteroid predation.

• At MacLeod Harbor there was still no sign of postearthquake *Verrucaria*. Rather than supporting an algal film throughout, as in 1965, the *Verrucaria* zone had an algal film in its upper part but was relatively bare in its lower part. The presence of abundant gastropods (*Littorina*), mainly in the lower part, suggested grazing as the cause of the lower limit of the algal film. At Olsen Bay, small patches of *Verrucaria* below the preearthquake zone may have been postearthquake growth (this possibility may be verified or disproved upon completion of analysis of the collections).

• The fauna at MacLeod Harbor was much more diverse and abundant than the clearly depauperate fauna found in 1965 after the great uplift. At Olsen Bay, several species that were much more common than in 1965 (e.g., *Evasterias troschellii*) suggested that in moderately uplifted areas the earthquake caused greater mortality, at least for some species, than we suspected in 1965.

In general, the 1968 observations, although brief and made at only a few stations, confirmed the successional nature of several aspects of the postearthquake communities interpreted as such on the basis of the 1965 data and indicated that with some exceptions these communities have returned to essentially their preearthquake condition.

Finally, a note can be added on the progress of terrestrial succession of plants on the extensive uplifted rocky shores at MacLeod Harbor. There was patchy but dense cover of mosses, grasses, and some forbs, and considerable soil accumulation, particularly under the mosses. Alders were abundant, most about 2 ft tall but many up to about 5 ft. Spruce seedlings, most less than 1 ft tall, were moderately common and growing out of moss patches. There were numerous small freshwater ponds containing unidentified arthropods. Kelp remains were still numerous, but mollusk shells were sparse, and of the other calcareous marine remains, only a few patches of the most strongly attached forms (e.g., coralline algae, *Balanus nubilis*) were still present.

## ACKNOWLEDGMENTS

Fieldwork would not have been possible without the support of the captain of the *Harmony*, Daniel Forseth, and the crew, Harold Vadset and H. W. Daddian. The other members of the expedition collaborated closely in all aspects of the work: G D. Hanna (leader),

H. W. Johansen, W. J. Eyerdam, and P. J. Barrett. Margaret M. Hanna provided logistic support. Thanks are due Rae Baxter, James Nybakken, Frank A. Pitelka, and George Plafker for useful discussions and information.

Identifications of specimens were made by the following: Allyn G. Smith, Robert R. Talmadge, L. Andrews, S. R. Thorpe, Jr. (Mollusca); Dustin D. Chivers, William C. Newman, G. Streveler (Crustacea); William C. Austin (Ophiuroidea); Donald P. Abbott (Ascidiacea); and James Nybakken (general). Emily Reid prepared the line illustrations, and G D. Hanna processed most of the photography. An earlier version of the manuscript was critically read by G D. Hanna, H. W. Johansen, and F. A. Pitelka. I am grateful to my wife, Norine D. Haven, for assistance in preparation of the manuscript.

The expedition was supported by grants from the National Science Foundation and the Atomic Energy Commission to the California Academy of Sciences.

The 1968 trip was supported by a research grant from the National Research Council of Canada.

# REFERENCES

Abe, N., 1955. Colony formation of a limpet, *Acmaea dorsuosa* Gould, and variation of level of the colony. *Bulletin of the Marine Biological Station at Asamushi*, v. 7, p. 127–132.

Aitken, J. J., 1962. Experiments with populations of the limpet, *Patella vulgata* L. *Irish Nature Journal*, v. 14, p. 12–15.

Alaska Department of Fish and Game, 1965. Post-earthquake fisheries evaluation. An interim report on the March 1964 earthquake effects on Alaska's fishery resources. Juneau: Alaska Department of Fish and Game. 72 p.

Barnes, H., 1956. *Balanus balanoides* (L.) in the Firth of Clyde: The development and annual variation of the larval population and the causative factors. *Journal of Animal Ecology,* 25 (No. 1), 72–84.

Barnes, H., and M. Barnes, 1956. The general biology of *Balanus glandula* Darwin. *Pacific Science,* 10 (No. 4), 415–430.

Baxter, Rae E., 1971. Earthquake effects on clams of Prince William Sound *in* The Great Alaska Earthquake of 1964: Biology. NAS Pub. 1604. Washington: National Academy of Sciences.

Bayne, B. L., 1964. Primary and secondary settlement in *Mytilus edulis* L. (Mollusca). *Journal of Animal Ecology,* 33 (No. 3), 513–523.

Bokenham, N. A. H., and T. A. Stephenson, 1938. The colonization of denuded rock surfaces in the intertidal region of the Cape Peninsula. *Annals of the Natal [Union of South Africa] Museum,* v. 9, p. 47–81.

Brattegard, T., and J. R. Lewis, 1964. Actual and predicted tide levels at the Biological Station, Espegrend, Blomsterdalen. *Sarsia,* 17, 7–14.

Brongersma-Sanders, M., 1957. Mass mortality in the sea *in* Volume I: Treatise on marine ecology and paleoecology. J. W. Hedgpeth, editor. New York: Geological Society of America Memoir 67. p. 941–1010.

Castenholz, R. W., 1961. The effect of grazing on marine littoral diatom populations. *Ecology,* 42 (No. 4), 783–794.

Clarke, W. D., 1967. Discussion, part II, *in* Pollution and marine ecology. T. A. Olsen and F. J. Burgess, editors. New York: Wiley (Interscience). p. 47.

Coe, W. R., 1945. Nutrition and growth of the California bay-mussel (*Mytilus edulis diegensis*). *Journal of Experimental Zoology,* 99 (No. 1), 1–14.

Coe, W. R., and W. E. Allen, 1937. Growth of sedentary marine organisms on experimental blocks and plates for nine successive years at Scripps Institution of Oceanography. SIO Bulletin, v. 4. La Jolla, California: Scripps Institution of Oceanography. p. 101–136.

Connell, J. H., 1961. The effects of competition, predation by *Thais lapillus,* and other factors on natural populations of the barnacle *Balanus balanoides. Ecological Monographs,* 31 (No. 1), 61–104.

Conway, E., 1946. Browsing of *Patella. Nature,* 158 (No. 4021), 752.

Cornwall, I. E., 1955. Cirripedia. *Canadian Pacific Fauna,* Fisheries Research Board of Canada, No. 10e, p. 1–49.

Dahl, A. L., 1964. Macroscopic algal foods of *Littorina planaxis* Philippi and *Littorina scutulata* Gould (Gastropoda: Prosobranchiata). *Veliger,* 7 (No. 2), 139–143.

Dehnel, P. A., 1956. Growth rates in latitudinally and vertically separated populations of *Mytilus californianus. Biological Bulletin,* 110 (No. 1), 43–53.

Doty, M. S., 1957. Rocky intertidal surfaces *in* Volume I: Treatise on marine ecology and paleoecology. J. W. Hedgpeth, editor. New York: Geological Society of America Memoir 67. p. 535–585.

Druehl, L. D., 1967. Vertical distributions of some benthic marine algae in a British Columbia inlet, as related to some environmental factors. *Journal of the Fisheries Research Board of Canada*, 24 (No. 1), 33–46.

Eyerdam, Walter J., 1971. Flowering plants found growing between pre- and postearthquake high-tide lines during the summer of 1965 in Prince William Sound *in* The Great Alaska Earthquake of 1964: Biology. NAS Pub. 1604. Washington: National Academy of Sciences.

Field, Irving A., 1921. Biology and economic value of the sea mussel *Mytilus edulis. Bulletin, U.S. Bureau of Fisheries,* v. 38, p. 127–259.

Frank, P. W., 1965. The biodemography of an intertidal snail population. *Ecology,* 46 (No. 6), 831–844.

Fraser, C. M., and G. M. Smith, 1928. Notes on the ecology of the little neck clam *Paphia staminea* Conrad. *Transactions, Royal Society of Canada,* series 3, 22 (No. 2), 249–270.

Fritchman, H. K., II, 1960. *Acmaea paradigitalis,* sp. nov. (Acmaeidae, Gastropoda). *Veliger,* 2 (No. 3), 53–57.

Glynn, P. W., 1965. Community composition, structure, and interrelationships in the marine intertidal *Endocladia muricata-Balanus glandula* association in Monterey Bay, California. *Beaufortia,* 12 (No. 48), 1–198.

Grantz, Arthur, George Plafker, and Reuben Kachadoorian, 1964. Alaska's Good Friday earthquake, March 27, 1964: A preliminary geologic evaluation. U.S. Geological Survey Circular 491. Washington: U.S. Geological Survey. 35 p.

Hanna, G Dallas, 1964. Biological effects of an earthquake. *Pacific Discovery,* 17 (November-December), 24–26. (Reprinted in this volume as "Observations made in 1964 on the immediate biological effects of the earthquake in Prince William Sound.")

Hanna, G Dallas, 1971. Biological effects of the earthquake as observed in 1965 *in* The Great Alaska Earthquake of 1964: Biology. NAS Pub. 1604. Washington: National Academy of Sciences.

Haven, Stoner B., 1966. Ecological studies of coexisting limpet species (Gastropoda) in the high intertidal of central California (Ph.D. thesis). Berkeley: University of California, 355 p.

Haven, Stoner B., 1971. Niche differences in the intertidal limpets *Acmaea scabra* and *Acmaea digitalis* (Gastropoda) in central California. *Veliger*, 13 (No. 3), 231–248.

Henry, D. P., 1940. The Cirripedia of Puget Sound with a key to the species. *University of Washington Publications in Oceanography*, 4 (No. 1), 1–48.

Henry, D. P., 1942. Studies on the sessile Cirripedia of the Pacific coast of North America. *University of Washington Publications in Oceanography*, 4 (No. 3), 95–134.

Hewatt, Willis G., 1935. Ecological succession in the *Mytilus californianus* habitat as observed in Monterey Bay, California. *Ecology*, 16 (No. 2), 244–251.

Johansen, H. William, 1971. Effects of elevation changes on benthic algae in Prince William Sound *in* The Great Alaska Earthquake of 1964: Biology. NAS Pub. 1604. Washington: National Academy of Sciences.

Kaburaki, T., 1928. Effect of the Kwanto earthquake upon marine organisms. Proceedings of the Third Pan-Pacific Scientific Congress, Tokyo, 1926, v. 2. Tokyo: National Research Council of Japan. p. 1523–1527.

Kaye, C. A., 1964. The upper limit of barnacles as an index of sea-level change on the New England coast during the past 100 years. *Journal of Geology*, 72 (No. 5), 580–600.

Kendeigh, S. C., 1961. Animal ecology. Englewood Cliffs, New Jersey: Prentice-Hall. 468 p.

Kershaw, K. A., 1964. Quantitative and dynamic ecology. London: Edward Arnold. 183 p.

Kitching, J. A., and F. S. Ebling, 1961. The ecology of Lough Ine. XI. The control of algae by *Paracentrotus lividus* (Ech.). *Journal of Animal Ecology*, v. 30 (No. 2), p. 373–383.

Knight-Jones, E. W., and J. Moyse, 1961. Intraspecific competition in sedentary marine animals. *Society for Experimental Biology Symposia*, v. 15, p. 72–95.

Lawson, G. W., 1966. The littoral ecology of West Africa. *Oceanography and Marine Biology*, *Annual Review*, v. 4, p. 405–448.

Lewis, J. R., 1961. The littoral zone on rocky shores — a biological or physical entity? *Oikos* (Copenhagen), 12 (No. 2), 280–301.

Lewis, J. R., 1964. The ecology of rocky shores. London: English Universities Press. 335 p.

Lodge, Sheila M., 1948. Algal growth in the absence of *Patella* on an experimental strip of foreshore, Port St. Mary, Isle of Man. *Proceedings of the Liverpool Biological Society*, v. 56, p. 78–85.

MacGinitie, G. A., 1955. Distribution and ecology of the marine invertebrates of Point Barrow, Alaska. *Smithsonian Miscellaneous Collections*, 128 (No. 9), 1–201.

Moore, H. B., 1935. The biology of *Balanus balanoides*. IV. Relation to environmental factors. *Journal of the Marine Biological Association of the United Kingdom*, 20 (No. 2), 279–307.

Moore, H. B., and N. Sproston, 1940. Further observations on the colonization of a new rocky shore at Plymouth. *Journal of Animal Ecology*, 9 (No. 2), 319–327.

Northcraft, R. D., 1948. Marine algal colonization on the Monterey Peninsula, California. *American Journal of Botany*, 35 (No. 7), 396–404.

Nybakken, James W., 1971. Preearthquake intertidal zonation of Three Saints Bay, Kodiak Island *in* The Great Alaska Earthquake of 1964: Biology. NAS Pub. 1604. Washington: National Academy of Sciences.

Odum, E. P., 1959. Fundamentals of ecology (second edition). Philadelphia: W. B. Saunders Company. 546 p.

Oosting, H. J., 1956. The study of plant communities (second edition). San Francisco: W. H. Freeman and Company. 440 p.

Orton, J. H., 1926. On the growth rate of *Cardium edule*, part 1. Experimental observations. *Journal of the Marine Biological Association of the United Kingdom*, v. 14, p. 239–279.

Paine, R. T., 1966. Food web complexity and species diversity. *American Naturalist*, 100 (No. 910), 65–75.

Pierron, R. P., and Y. C. Huang, 1925. Animal succession on denuded rocks. Publications of the Puget Sound Biological Station, v. 5. Seattle: University of Washington. p. 149–158.

Plafker, George, 1965. Tectonic deformation associated with the 1964 Alaska earthquake. *Science*, 148 (June 25), 1675–1687.

Plafker, George, 1969. Tectonics of the March 27, 1964, Alaska earthquake. U.S. Geological Survey Professional Paper 543-I. Washington: Government Printing Office. 74 p. Also *in* The Great Alaska Earthquake of 1964: Geology. NAS Pub. 1601. Washington: National Academy of Sciences, 1971.

Plafker, George, and L. R. Mayo, 1965. Tectonic deformation, subaqueous slides and destructive waves associated with the Alaskan March 27, 1964 earthquake: an interim geologic evaluation. U.S. Geological Survey Open-File Report. Menlo Park, California: U.S. Geological Survey. 34 p.

Reish, D. J., 1962. A study of succession in recently constructed marine harbors in southern California. Proceedings, First National Coastal and Shallow Water Research Conference. Sponsored by the National Science Foundation and the Office of Naval Research, Washington, D.C. p. 570–573.

Reish, D. J., 1963. Further studies on the benthic fauna in a recently constructed boat harbor in southern California. *Bulletin of the Southern California Academy of Sciences*, 62 (No. 1), 23–32.

Reish, D. J., 1964. Studies on the *Mytilus edulis* community in Alamitos Bay, California: I. Development and destruction of the community. *Veliger*, 6 (No. 3), 124–131.

Rice, L., 1930. Peculiarities in the distribution of barnacles in communities and their probable causes. Publications of the Puget Sound Biological Station, v. 7. Seattle: University of Washington. p. 249–257.

Ricketts, Edward F., and Jack Calvin, 1962. Between Pacific tides. Stanford, California: Stanford University Press. 516 p.

Rigg, George B., and Robert C. Miller, 1949. Intertidal plant and animal zonation in the vicinity of Neah Bay, Washington. *Proceedings, California Academy of Sciences*, 26, Series 4 (No. 10), 323–351.

Scheer, B. T., 1945. The development of marine fouling communities. *Biological Bulletin*, 89 (No. 1), 103–121.

Shelford, V. E., 1930. Geographic extent and succession in Pacific North American intertidal (*Balanus*) communities. Publications of the Puget Sound Biological Station, v. 7. Seattle: University of Washington. p. 217–223.

Shelford, V. E., and E. D. Towler, 1925. Animal communities of the San Juan Channel and adjacent areas. Publications of the Puget Sound Biological Station, v. 5. Seattle: University of Washington. p. 33–73.

Shelford, V. E., A. O. Weese, Lucile Rice, D. I. Rasmussen, Archie MacLean, and H. C. Markus, 1935. Some marine biotic communities of the Pacific coast of North America. *Ecological Monographs*, 5 (No. 3), 249–354.

Southward, A. J., 1956. The population balance between limpets and seaweeds on wave-beaten rocky shores. Annual Report, Marine Biological Station, Port Erin, Isle of Man, v. 68, p. 20–29.

Southward, A. J., 1958. The zonation of plants and animals on rocky sea shores. *Biological Reviews*, 33 (No. 2), 137–177.

Southward, A. J., 1964. Limpet grazing and the control of vegetation on rocky shores *in* Grazing in terrestrial and marine environments. D. J. Crisp, editor. Symposia of the British Ecological Society, v. 4. Oxford: Blackwell Scientific Publications. p. 265–273.

Stephenson, T. A., and Anne Stephenson, 1949. The universal features of zonation between tide-marks on rocky coasts. *Journal of Ecology,* 37 (No. 2), 289–305.

Stephenson, T. A., and Anne Stephenson, 1961a. Life between the tide marks in North America, IV-A: Vancouver Island, I. *Journal of Ecology,* 49 (No. 1), 1–29.

Stephenson, T. A., and Anne Stephenson, 1961b. Life between the tide marks in North America, IV-B: Vancouver Island, II. *Journal of Ecology,* 49 (No. 2), 227–243.

Talmadge, R. R., 1966. Notes on the mollusca of Prince William Sound, Alaska. *Veliger,* 9 (No. 1), 82–86.

Tarr, Ralph S., and Lawrence Martin, 1912. The earthquakes at Yakutat Bay, Alaska, in September, 1899. U.S. Geological Survey Professional Paper 69. Washington: Government Printing Office. 135 p.

Test, A. R., 1945. Ecology of California *Acmaea. Ecology,* 26 (No. 4), 395–405.

U.S. Coast and Geodetic Survey, 1956. Surface water temperatures at tide stations, Pacific coast, North and South America and Pacific Ocean islands. U.S. Coast and Geodetic Survey Special Publication 280 (fifth edition). Washington: Government Printing Office. 74 p.

U.S. Coast and Geodetic Survey, 1964a. Preliminary report: Tidal datum plane changes, Prince William Sound, Alaskan earthquakes March-April, 1964. Office of Oceanography. Rockville [Maryland] : U.S. Coast and Geodetic Survey. 5 p.

U.S. Coast and Geodetic Survey, 1964b. Tide tables, high and low water predictions, 1965, west coast North and South America, including the Hawaiian Islands. Washington: Government Printing Office. 224 p.

U.S. Coast and Geodetic Survey, 1966. The Prince William Sound, Alaska, earthquake of 1964 and aftershocks. Fergus J. Wood, editor. Volume I: Operational phases of the Coast and Geodetic Survey program in Alaska for the period March 27 to December 31, 1964. Washington: Government Printing Office. 263 p.

Verwey, J., 1954. On the ecology and distribution of cockle and mussel in the Dutch Wadden Sea, their role in sedimentation and the source of their food supply. *Archives Néerlandaises de Zoologie,* 10 (No. 2), 171–239.

Watson, C. E., 1959. Climate of Alaska *in* Climatography of the United States. U.S. Weather Bureau, No. 60-49. Washington: Government Printing Office. 24 p.

Weymouth, F. W., and S. H. Thompson, 1931. The age and growth of the Pacific cockle (*Cardium corbis* Martyn). *Bulletin of the U.S. Bureau of Fisheries*, v. 46, p. 633–641.

Widdowson, T. B., 1965. A survey of the distribution of intertidal algae along a coast transitional in respect to salinity and tidal factors. *Journal of the Fisheries Research Board of Canada,* 22 (No. 6), 1425–1454.

Yonge, C. M., 1960. Further observations on *Hipponix antiquatus* with notes on North Pacific pulmonate limpets. *Proceedings, California Academy of Sciences,* 31, Series 4 (No. 5), 111–119.

# II
# SELECTED
# ECOLOGICAL
# EFFECTS

# Introduction

The subject of ecology is so all-encompassing that most other facets of biology, including human biological and economic problems, are inextricably included within it. Although the following papers deal directly with ecology, many other reports in this and in other volumes in the series are also on subjects of ecological importance. Awareness of ecological interrelationships becomes clearer and more acute after any cataclysmic disturbance in nature, especially when attempts are made to measure and evaluate effects of the disturbance. When whole populations of many species of organisms, including man, are dislocated, many effects may engender conditions that can contribute to the elimination of certain species.

In nature, ecological adjustments and niches are developed over great reaches of time, which explains the intricate involvement of ecological factors. When one factor in this balance is disturbed or removed, a ramifying and progressive series of interactions is set in motion. When several or many factors are simultaneously disturbed or rearranged, as they are in an earthquake, fire, flood, or volcanic eruption, the effects are so far-reaching that they can scarcely be evaluated. Evaluation is especially difficult because the waves of changes progress with time, multiplying their effects in countless ways throughout the natural world.

The following papers describe only a few of the earthquake's effects on only a few organisms. The small number of papers illustrates and emphasizes the tremendous disparity between the work that has been done and that which might be done to evaluate the effects of the Alaska earthquake; this disparity is explained in the introduction to this volume. It is hoped that these papers, though few, nevertheless will encourage future studies of the numerous ecological problems resulting from the earthquake.

Hubbard's detailed study of invertebrates deals with only one aspect of one affected area and illustrates the type of investigation that might well be extended to other groups of organisms. Plants and animals of the intertidal zone are perhaps the most severely affected by uplift and subsidence, and some immediate evaluations of effects can be made; it will be more significant if we can learn of the adjustments that are made by invertebrates during subsequent years.

Neiland's informative paper on forest–bog flora opens a research avenue, relating to water-level effects on development within coastal bogs, that should be followed for a number of years. The changes and effects that are implied can be measured only by patient, long-range studies.

The technique used by Crow in his study of the immediate changes in the habits of one species of bird illustrates the type of investigation that should and could be made of other species of aquatic fowl that are of interest both for conservation and preservation.

These papers on ecology will serve as guidelines for studies that should be made following another cataclysmic disturbance of the environmental balance.

G. W. PRESCOTT
Biological Station
on Flathead Lake
University of Montana

JOHN H. CROW *
WASHINGTON STATE UNIVERSITY

# Earthquake-Initiated Changes in the Nesting Habitat of the Dusky Canada Goose

ABSTRACT: The dusky Canada goose nests in a remarkably restricted area, a part of the Copper River Delta occupied by a plant community characterized by *Hedysarum alpinum americanum* and *Deschampsia beringensis*. This vegetation flourishes in the slightly saline soils at the tops of channel banks, where before the earthquake it was inundated by diluted seawater during occasional storm tides. As a result of uplift during the earthquake, however, the preearthquake channel-bank vegetation and the interchannel areas are no longer reached even by the highest tides, and the soil is being rapidly desalinized. Drier conditions and the removal of salt permit invasion of the *Hedysarum–Deschampsia* belt by plants characteristic of other belts, and hence the favored nesting habitat of the goose is deteriorating. Presumably the *Hedysarum–Deschampsia* community will eventually reestablish itself at a lower level on the tidal flats, but the area available is expected to be much smaller than the area occupied at present. Over the years the dusky Canada goose will find progressively more restricted nesting grounds, which will lead to a reduction in its numbers unless it can adapt to other kinds of vegetation.

*Now at Rutgers—The State University of New Jersey, Newark.

## INTRODUCTION

The Copper River Delta, Alaska, is the nesting ground of the dusky Canada goose (*Branta canadensis occidentalis*), which winters in the Willamette Valley, Oregon, but returns to the delta each year to breed. An interesting and important characteristic of this bird is that its nesting is restricted almost entirely to one kind of vegetation found on the Copper River Delta.

Because the delta was raised almost 2 m by the earthquake of March 27, 1964, serious concern arose for the well-being of the dusky Canada goose. As a result, this study was undertaken to ascertain whether there were changes in the principal nesting habitat of this bird and to describe the extant vegetation.

The uplift of 1.89 m (Reimnitz and Marshall, 1965) contrasts with elevation changes that had been taking place. Borings taken in the area have revealed the remains of vegetation at depths of from 6 to 12 m that have been silted over. This discovery led to the conclusion that the delta and adjacent Prince William Sound areas had been sinking with respect to the sea in the recent past (Tarr and Martin, 1914; Twenhofel, 1952).

The center of the study area was approximately 60°25′N and 145°25′E on the western half of the Copper River Delta, the center of maximum nesting of the dusky Canada goose. Additional information on this subject is given in another work (Crow, 1968).

## THE STUDY AREA

Four principal physiographic types can be distinguished on the delta: marsh, tidal flats, barrier islands, and dunes (Reimnitz and Marshall, 1965). Southeast of the delta lies the Gulf of Alaska and, except for penetration by the Copper River Valley, a near semicircle of mountains bounds

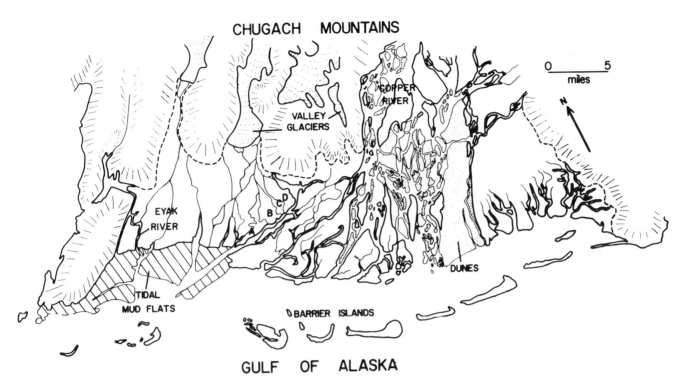

FIGURE 1   Map of the Copper River Delta showing the relative positions of belts characterized by: A, *Hedysarum–Deschampsia;* B, *Myrica–Poa;* C, *Salix–Festuca;* and D, *Picea–* and *Alnus*-dominated communities.

the delta, which stretches for about 50 mi along the coast (Figure 1).

Within the marsh, a complex reticulate system of distributaries and glacial channels covers this flat area of mainly alluvial deposits. The principal region of goose nesting was confined to an area dominated by fine-textured materials. Near the Copper River and in the areas bordering the Eyak River at the westerly end of the delta, sandy soil materials were to be found, whereas near the mountains, gravels dominate.

Four vegetation belts were identified from the seashore inland, each including a catena of communities associated with relief as well as soil texture. Each catena of communities consisted of a series of related zones paralleling the channels. The four belts were characterized and named according to the plant communities found at the highest elevation within the belt. From the seashore landward, the belts were the *Hedysarum alpinum americanum–Deschampsia beringensis* community, the *Myrica gale–Poa eminens* community, the *Salix* sp.–*Festuca rubra* community, with *Alnus fruticosa*- and *Picea sitchensis*-dominated communities both found in the last belt (Figure 1). Tidal influences, as would be expected, decrease in a landward direction.

Before the earthquake, only storm tides would cover the entire *Hedysarum–Deschampsia* belt with diluted seawater; otherwise, the *Hedysarum–Deschampsia* community was free of inundation, whereas associated zones of vegetation paralleling the channels would be covered regularly (Figure 2). The *Hedysarum–Deschampsia* habitat corresponds almost perfectly to the zone of drift accumulation under preearthquake conditions. In the belts farther inland, the tides rarely overflowed the channel banks. Ponds are common in the interchannel land surfaces.

In addition to the land surface being freed from inundation as a result of the earthquake, the uppermost layer of the water now flowing in the channels is not salty, even during the storm tides, apparently because the amount of fresh water flowing off the delta into the Gulf of Alaska is much greater than the amount of seawater that flows in during high tides. It may be that during winter months, seawater flows in the channels; extant vegetation would, however, remain unaffected because the tides no longer cover it.

Precipitation on the delta averages 369.7 cm yearly, with 166.4 cm falling from April to September (Fowells, 1965). This amount of precipitation will presumably facilitate desalinization of uplifted areas of the delta. In fact, Beekom and others (1953) have reported that rainfall of scarcely more than 15 cm is enough to cause rapid desalinization of the soil under suitable conditions.

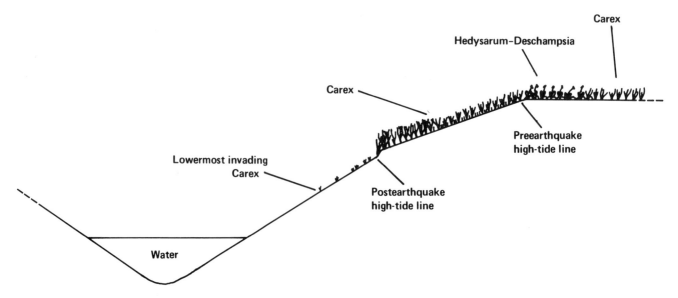

FIGURE 2 Cross–sectional diagram showing zonation of plant communities paralleling a channel. Notice the change in the high-tide lines. The postearthquake high-tide line corresponds approximately to the lowermost position of the preearthquake vegetation.

## GOOSE NESTING

The uplift of the western Copper River Delta is particularly interesting because the dusky Canada goose restricts its nesting to the delta area, and principally to the *Hedysarum–Deschampsia* community type. This plant community is dominated by forbs and grasses that grow along the uppermost portion of the channel banks over a restricted portion of the delta. C. E. Trainer (1959) reported that 97 percent of the dusky Canada goose nests (218 of 224) were located within the forb–grass vegetation and in small shrub fragments within the *Hedysarum–Deschampsia* belt. The limitation of nesting to this narrow strip may have been caused by the washing out of nests at lower sites (Hansen, 1961) and by the increased vulnerability to predation at sites higher and farther from the sea.

Other waterfowl found nesting in or near the *Hedysarum–Deschampsia* vegetation during the course of this investigation included the mallard (*Anas platyrhynchos*), pintail (*A. acuta*), gadwall (*A. strepera*), American widgeon (*Mareca americana*), and shoveler (*Spatula clypeata*) ducks. The mew gull (*Larus canus*), a predator on the eggs of the dusky Canada goose, and the glaucous-winged gull (*L. glaucescens*) were also common nesting birds in *Hedysarum–Deschampsia* vegetation. Still other birds nesting here included the short-eared owl (*Asio flammeus*), Arctic tern (*Sterna paradisaea*), short-billed dowitcher (*Limnodromus griseus*), and the savannah sparrow (*Passerculus sandwichensis*).

Voles (*Microtis* sp.) were also well confined to the *Hedysarum–Deschampsia* vegetation. The short-tailed weasel (*Mustela cicognanii*), the short-eared owl, and the marsh hawk (*Circus cyanens*) were often observed preying on the voles.

## METHODS OF ANALYZING VEGETATION

The principal objective of a thorough reconnaissance, begun in the summer of 1965, was the selection of representative sites for intensive study. At each reconnaissance site the vegetation was analyzed by means of a canopy-coverage technique (Crow, 1968; Daubenmire, 1959) that allows for relatively good approximations of the dominance of particular taxa within stands. This technique was useful in an initial appraisal of the presence of taxa both among stands of any one plant-community type and between stands of different plant-community types. Communities outside the *Hedysarum–Deschampsia* belt are discussed in another work (Crow, 1968).

Throughout the investigation, voucher plant specimens were collected. Nomenclature of vascular plants is according to Anderson (1959), except for the willows, which are named according to Hultén (1941-1950).

Quantitative details on selected stands were gathered to demonstrate the range of variation within any one kind of vegetation. Coverage techniques similar to those used during reconnaissance were applied to elongate macroplots 1.2 × 7.6 m. This method involved recording the percentage canopy coverage for each taxon, within a series of 20 × 50-cm microplots, from a choice of coverage classes. These were 0-5, 5-25, 25-50, 50-75, 75-95, and 95-100 percent. Summation of the midpoints of these classes gave a close approximation of the true canopy coverage. At the same time, the percentage occurrence of a taxon in a series of micro-plots within one stand of vegetation yields the frequency of occurrence. The presence of species found within the fixed area of the macroplot but not within the series of microplots was noted (Crow, 1968; Daubenmire, 1959).

These techniques were also used in transect studies wherein a series of 20 × 50-cm microplots were placed perpendicular to the zones of vegetation running parallel to the channels. Study sites were permanently marked so that precise relocation for future comparative studies would be possible.

Soil samples were collected at each study site and at appropriate points along transects. Samples approximately 0.7–1 dm in diameter and 1 dm in depth were obtained with a common garden trowel and placed in paper bags to dry. Laboratory determinations of pH and conductivity were made on material passing a 1-mm sieve by common procedures (Crow, 1968; Moodie and others, 1963). Twice-saturation percentage extracts from selected soil samples were analyzed for Na, K, Ca, and Mg by flame emission or atomic absorption spectroscopy.

## NESTING VEGETATION

A total of 32 species of vascular plants was recorded in ten stands of the *Hedysarum-Deschampsia* community type. Fourteen species were present in ten stands, and four additional species were found in 90 percent of the stands. The

TABLE 1 Plants Found in 90 percent or More of the Stands of the *Hedysarum-Deschampsia* Community

| Life Form | Species |
| --- | --- |
| Prostrate shrub | *Salix arctica* |
| Perennial forbs | *Chrysanthemum arcticum* |
| | *Dodecatheon macrocarpum* |
| | *Hedysarum alpinum americanum* |
| | *Iris setosa* |
| | *Lathyrus palustris pilosus* |
| | *Ligusticum hultenii* |
| | *Plantago macrocarpa* |
| | *Polygonum viviparum* |
| | *Potentilla pacifica* |
| | *Triglochin maritima* |
| Perennial graminoids | *Calamagrostis inexpansa* |
| | *Carex lyngbyei cryptocarpa* |
| | *Deschampsia beringensis* |
| | *Festuca rubra* |
| | *Poa eminens* |
| Annual forbs | *Parnassia palustris* |
| | *Rhinanthus minor groenlandicus* |

combinations of species and high constancy and the aforementioned percentage occurrence within a fixed area in a series of stands made this community easy to identify in the field. These 18 most common species usually accounted for more than 90 percent of the total coverage of all species in the *Hedysarum-Deschampsia* community type (Table 1).

Ecotones (transition areas) were found nearly always to be abrupt. This situation was especially conspicuous on the margin of the *Hedysarum-Deschampsia* vegetation nearest the channels (Figure 3). Apparently small changes in relief were very important in the maintenance of the well-defined parallel zones of vegetation.

Two channel-bank communities were recognized within the *Hedysarum-Deschampsia* belt: a pure *Carex lyngbyei cryptocarpa* zone and a *Carex lyngbyei–Eleocharis kamtschatica* zone, the former situated lower along the bank. These two communities were inundated regularly before the earthquake, but under postearthquake conditions they remain clear of the tides. The lower edge of the pure *Carex* community approximates the new uppermost level of the storm tides. The pure *Carex* community contained only the one species. *Carex-Eleocharis* vegetation was more diverse in species but was nevertheless conspicuously dominated by *C. lyngbyei*.

In addition to *C. lyngbyei* and *E. kamtschatica*, *Salix arctica*, *Triglochin maritima*, *Potentilla pacifica*, and *Ranunculus cymbalaria* were most common.

Interchannel depressions were poorly drained. In addition to the previously mentioned ponds, a set of *Carex*-dominated communities existed in these interchannel habitats. These communities were similar in appearance to the *Carex*-dominated channel banks, which made the zone dominated by *Hedysarum-Deschampsia* readily discernible, even from the air.

Important changes in the nesting area took place during the period of study. Soil samples revealed the expected marked desalinization. For example, samples taken in 1964, shortly after the uplift, by P. E. K. Shepherd (formerly of the Alaska Department of Fish and Game) contained high concentrations of salts. Samples taken by the author in 1967, as near as possible to Shepherd's sampling spots, showed salt removal and depression of pH values as indicated in Table 2. This table also gives data on the loss of sodium. These changes should allow a greater number of glycophytes (species that grow in nonsaline conditions) to invade.

One important question to be answered was whether the nesting vegetation would be displaced by communities dominated by trees or shrubs. Evidence strongly suggests that such a change will occur. One area approximately 250 × 60 m was carefully surveyed in 1965 and again in 1967 for shrub seedlings and small shrubs. This area included a channel bank and adjacent *Hedysarum-Deschampsia* vegetation. In 1965, only 14 *Salix* spp. and three *Alnus fruticosa*

FIGURE 3 A distinct ecotone in the area of maximum goose nesting. The *Hedysarum-Deschampsia* vegetation is to the left, and the *Carex* vegetation of the channel bank is to the right; notice the sharpness of the ecotone despite the very gentle slope of the channel bank. June 1965.

TABLE 2 Chemical Changes of Soil from 1964 to 1967

| Vegetation Zone | Year | Hydrogen-Ion Concentration (pH) | Concentration (meq/liter) | |
| --- | --- | --- | --- | --- |
| | | | Sodium (Na) | Total cations |
| *Hedysarum-Deschampsia* | 1964 | 7.2 | 5.9 | 16.0 |
| | 1967 | 7.0 | 0.2 | 2.5 |
| *Carex-Eleocharis* (high) | 1964 | 7.6 | 5.4 | 16.9 |
| | 1967 | 7.4 | 0.2 | 2.7 |
| *Carex-Eleocharis* (low) | 1964 | 7.8 | 113.0 | 163.9 |
| | 1967 | 7.1 | 0.2 | 2.7 |
| High-water line | 1964 | 7.8 | 34.6 | 47.6 |
| | 1967 | 7.8 | 15.4 | 22.1 |

seedlings were located, all in the pure *Carex* and *Carex-Eleocharis* zones, except for one *Salix* plant, which was growing in the ecotone near the *Hedysarum-Deschampsia*. The tendency for invasion seemed to be mostly correlated with the least dense vegetation. No *Myrica gale* plants were observed.

By 1967, the number of shrub plants located had increased to 381: 172 were *Myrica* plants, mostly seedlings; 151 were *Salix* plants; and 58 were *Alnus* plants. The height of each plant observed was measured in order to evaluate the success of the invasion. Specimens taller than 15 cm included 3 *Myrica* plants, 71 *Salix* plants, and 11 *Alnus* plants. None of the 381 plants located was found in the *Hedysarum-Deschampsia* vegetation. By far the largest percentage of invading shrubs was found in the previously pure *Carex* zone. This strongly suggests that competition is an important factor in invasion and establishment. Before the earthquake, the pure *Carex* vegetation would have provided the least suitable invasion sites for shrubs.

Storm tides now come to about the preearthquake lower boundary of the pure *Carex* vegetation. Because shrubs or trees developed before the earthquake in well-drained habitats free from tidal inundation, it seems reasonable to hypothesize that the bottom of the preearthquake *Carex* vegetation will approximate the lower boundary of shrub or forest invasion.

Although the *Hedysarum–Deschampsia* vegetation was not invaded by shrubs by 1967, other approaches revealed drastic changes. Perhaps the most conspicuous changes were brought about by vole populations. Such changes did not occur everywhere, but many places were affected. The population of voles became very large during the summers of 1965 and 1966 and caused a striking defoliation of some *Hedysarum–Deschampsia* stands by 1966. One of these stands was studied in 1967 after the vole population had virtually vanished from the site. The results appeared to be typical for affected areas. Specifically, the total coverage of plants had decreased in comparison with 1965 reconnaissance records and with other stands of the *Hedysarum–Deschampsia* community type. One species, *Stellaria humifusa*, had increased strikingly from a coverage of 0–5 percent of the site in 1965 to a coverage of 22 percent in 1967. The increase of *Stellaria* was a typical phenomenon associated with *Hedysarum–Deschampsia* areas heavily used by the voles. In contrast to this trend were the decreases of other species, including *Hedysarum alpinum americanum*. Reconnaissance records from 1965 showed *Hedysarum* covering between 25 and 50 percent of the ground surface, whereas in 1967 the coverage was only 2 percent.

Other successional changes within the *Hedysarum–Deschampsia* vegetation included coverage changes by constituent species. Care was taken to compare sites at the same times of the year. A detailed successional study at a representative site revealed that 14 out of 20 species recorded in 1965 had decreased by 1967. Three important constituent species of the nesting vegetation showed very great decreases: *Hedysarum*, *Triglochin*, and *Deschampsia* had coverage decreases of 44, 40, and 35 percent, respectively. Not only are these serious changes by major species, but the *Triglochin* is an important goose-forage species. Significant coverage increases were recorded for two important species associated with other vegetation belts. *Poa eminens* and *Festuca rubra* coverage increased by 15 percent and 38 percent, respectively. These changes perhaps reflect the shift in potential of the habitat.

To evaluate the degree of change in the *Hedysarum–Deschampsia* vegetation, several statistics were computed. The coverage sum of all species in 1965 was 377; by 1967 it had decreased to 265, a decreased net coverage of 112. Although a percentage decrease may be computed, it hides

the concept that it was yielded by the sum of coverage increases and decreases for all species. To avoid this pitfall, a so-called coefficient of change is calculated by adding the absolute values of coverage increases and decreases from 1965 to 1967; this yields a sum of 242. Comparison of this figure with the 1965 coverage sum of 377 gives a percentage absolute change of 64. In other words, the coverage of the *Hedysarum–Deschampsia* stand under consideration had changed 64 percent in terms of coverage from 1965 to 1967.

The diversity of plant species at the site also changed. The number of species increased from 20 to 23 over the period of study, the three new species being *Primula egalikensis*, *Lomatogonium rotatum*, and *Calamagrostis deschampsioides*. The increase is inconclusive because of the presence of these species in other *Hedysarum–Deschampsia* stands in 1965, but it does reflect some change in the stand.

Channel-bank zonal communities, pure *Carex* and *Carex-Eleocharis*, likewise changed greatly. Increases associated with the lateral migration of species down the channel banks, as well as the invasion of species from previously better drained vegetation belts, were recorded. Data documenting deterioration of interchannel-basin vegetation are discussed elsewhere (Crow, 1968).

The tidal flats were investigated to determine their potential for goose nesting in the near future. Because a very large percentage is still regularly covered by the tides, it seems unlikely that anything but a fraction of the present goose population might nest in the few suitable places. Indeed, if the land surface should in time build up from the deposition of fine particles being carried in the channel waters, then nesting might be possible. Such buildup might, however, take hundreds of years (Crow, 1968).

## CONCLUSIONS

Successional investigations have provided evidence of a rapid change in the biotic potential of the nesting ground of the dusky Canada goose. These changes are exemplified by significant invasion of shrub species such as *Myrica gale*, *Salix* spp., and *Alnus fruticosa*. Changes in dominance, as reflected by coverage, were also noted for constituent species of the *Hedysarum–Deschampsia* vegetation, the nesting vegetation. These data support the hypothesis that the preearthquake nesting vegetation is deteriorating as a result of the uplift. Desalinization data provide evidence of habitat change in addition to water-level changes resulting from the earthquake. At present, the tidal flats are mostly unsuitable for rapid development of *Hedysarum–Deschampsia* vegetation.

Successfulness of the dusky Canada goose in the future will probably depend on how well it adjusts to the deterioration of its nesting vegetation. Restriction of goose nesting to *Hedysarum–Deschampsia* vegetation would certainly be catastrophic should present trends continue. It is hoped that the behavior of this bird may be plastic enough to allow either a move elsewhere or successful use of other vegetation on the delta, but no such guarantees exist.

## ACKNOWLEDGMENTS

The author is grateful to the Alaska Department of Fish and Game for sponsoring this work from 1965 through 1967.

## REFERENCES

Anderson, J. P., 1959. Flora of Alaska and adjacent parts of Canada. Ames: Iowa State University Press. 543 p.

van Beekom, C. W. C., C. van den Berg, Th. A. de Boer, W. H. van der Molen, B. Verhoeven, J. J. Westerhof, and A. J. Zuur, 1953. Reclaiming land flooded with salt water. *Netherlands Journal of Agricultural Science*, 1 (August), 153-163; (November), 225-244.

Crow, John H., 1968. Plant ecology of the Copper River Delta, Alaska (Ph.D. thesis). Pullman: Washington State University. 120 p.

Daubenmire, R., 1959. A canopy coverage method of vegetational analysis. *Northwest Science*, 33 (February), 43-65.

Fowells, H. A., 1965. Silvics of forest trees of the United States. U.S. Department of Agriculture Handbook No. 271. Washington: Government Printing Office. 762 p.

Hansen, Henry A., 1961. Loss of waterfowl production to tide floods. *The Journal of Wildlife Management*, 25 (No. 3), 242-248.

Hultén, E., 1941-1950. Flora of Alaska and Yukon. Lunds Universitet Årsskrift, Ny Foljd, avd. 2, bd. 37-46; Kunglige Fysiografiska Sällskapets Handlinger, Ny Foljd, bd. 52-61. 1902 p.

Moodie, C. D., H. W. Smith, and R. L. Hausenbuiller, 1963. Laboratory manual for soil fertility. Pullman: Washington State University, Department of Agronomy. 198 p.

Reimnitz, Erk, and Neil F. Marshall, 1965. Effects of the Alaska earthquake and tsunami on recent deltaic sediments. *Journal of Geophysical Research,* 70 (May 15), 2363-2376. Also *in* The Great Alaska Earthquake of 1964: Geology. NAS Pub. 1601. Washington: National Academy of Sciences.

Tarr, R. S., and Lawrence Martin, 1914. Alaskan glacier studies of the National Geographic Society in Yakutat Bay, Prince William Sound, and Lower Copper River Regions. Washington: National Geographic Society. 498 p.

Trainer, C. E., 1959. The 1959 western Canada goose (*Branta canadensis occidentalis*) study on the Copper River Delta, Alaska. Annual Waterfowl Report, Alaska Bureau of Sport Fisheries and Wildlife. Henry A. Hansen, Supervisor. 11 p.

Twenhofel, W. S., 1952. Recent shore-line changes along the Pacific coast of Alaska. *American Journal of Science,* 250 (July), 523-548.

JOEL D. HUBBARD*
UNIVERSITY OF WISCONSIN AT SHEBOYGAN

# Distribution and Abundance of Intertidal Invertebrates at Olsen Bay in Prince William Sound, Alaska, One Year after the 1964 Earthquake

## INTRODUCTION

In the summer of 1965 the Bureau of Commercial Fisheries began a study of intertidal invertebrates at Olsen Bay, Prince William Sound, Alaska (Figure 1). The study was part of a long-term investigation into the intertidal ecology of pink salmon (*Oncorhynchus gorbuscha*) in Olsen Creek and was directed especially toward an evaluation of the effect on intertidal organisms of uplift associated with the 1964 Alaska earthquake. Specific objectives of the study included the following:

1. Determination of species composition of macroinvertebrate fauna on three types of intertidal habitats.
2. Determination of distribution, vertical zonation, and relative densities of these organisms with respect to substrate composition and tidal exposure.
3. Evaluation of any changes in community structure or distribution of species resulting from environmental changes accompanying the earthquake.

Uplift associated with the earthquake has been estimated to be about 3-4 ft in the Olsen Bay area (Plafker, 1969, Plates 1 and 2). Some of the effects of a vertical displacement of this magnitude are evident from even a superficial examination of the area—remains of barnacles and algae are present well above the upper limit of the region now occupied by living individuals; unusually large concentrations of empty mollusk shells litter the beaches; and large expanses of previously subtidal muds are exposed at low tides. Other effects of the earthquake may be inferred. These include changes in the substrate, such as disruption of permanent burrows, shifting of silt by earthquake-generated waves, and alteration of substrate stability along the shoreline; and changes in the microclimate, such as exposure of sedentary organisms to longer drying periods, concurrent longer periods of exposure to higher temperatures during summer months, and increased exposure to freezing in winter.

ABSTRACT: In the summer of 1965, the Bureau of Commercial Fisheries began a study of intertidal invertebrates in the Olsen Bay area of Prince William Sound; this included an evaluation of the effect on intertidal organisms of uplift caused by the 1964 Alaska earthquake. Intensive sampling of four areas representative of the three most common types of habitat in this protected bay revealed a vertical distribution and abundance of invertebrate species strongly influenced by substrate composition and tidal exposure. Mean tide level (+6.2 ft) exhibited particular importance as the upper limit of numerous organisms. It was found that the uplift produced measurable changes in the distributions of certain bivalve mollusk distribu-amount of uplift, approximately 3.0 to 3.5 ft in Olsen Bay, could be estimated by comparing the positions of some of these organisms before and after the earthquake. The most obvious and reliable quantitative index of the uplift was provided by pre- and postearthquake limits of barnacle populations, whereas supportive evidence was obtained from examination of certain bivalve mollusk distributions. Differential mortality, noted especially between different species of mollusks and between different age-classes of certain species, was apparently attributable to earthquake-related processes. While reproductive success of some species appeared unaffected by the earthquake, other species have apparently experienced little reproduction since the earthquake.

*Now at the University of Colorado.

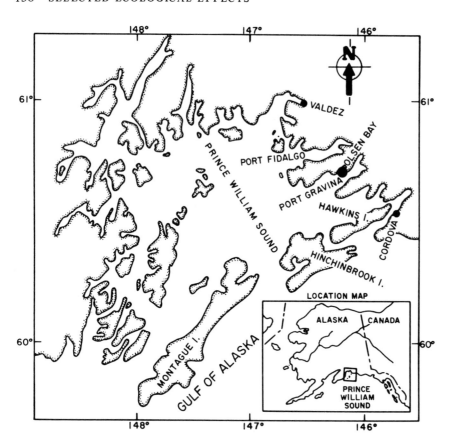

FIGURE 1   Index map of Prince William Sound, showing location of Olsen Bay detailed map (Figure 2).

## DESCRIPTION OF OLSEN BAY AREA

Olsen Bay is on the eastern shore of Prince William Sound and forms an indentation in the northern shoreline of Port Gravina at lat 60°45′N, long 146°12′W (Figure 1). Midway up this relatively small bay, its 2–3-mi-long axis turns from north to northeast, terminating in an alluvial silt–gravel tideflat that occupies the entire width of the bayhead. Olsen Bay is protected from any ocean swell or extreme wave action and fits the well-protected bay and estuary category of Ricketts and Calvin (1962); three large islands, Montague, Hinchinbrook, and Hawkins, shelter Prince William Sound from Gulf of Alaska storms.

The surrounding terrain is rugged and has steep, heavily timbered mountainsides that rise abruptly from the shoreline; deep valleys extend considerable distances inland from the bayhead. The tideflat is bounded by two streams: Olsen Creek on the west and Little Creek on the east; the former is by far the more important of the two, both in terms of flow and in numbers of spawning salmon. The central portion of the tideflat is cut by a third stream, Middle Slough. All three streams have eroded numerous interconnecting channels in the uniform mud region of the lower intertidal and subtidal zones (Figure 2).

The principal types of aquatic habitat in the bay are gravel-shingle beaches, silt-gravel tideflat, and freshwater streams at the bayhead—all of which grade down to homogeneous mud at the lower levels. There are no sandy beaches. The beach merges with the tideflat at the bayhead and extends around the perimeter of the bay, interrupted occasionally by streams and small rocky outcrops. Except for these outcrops and occasional large boulders, the only rocky intertidal habitat in the immediate area is on a small island near the mouth of the bay, where there are numerous tidepools, rocky ledges, and vertical faces. The island was not sampled in this study, but measurements of the vertical limits of barnacle populations were made in cooperation with another investigator who describes the island briefly (Haven, 1971, this volume).

Despite its location in the subarctic zone, Olsen Bay has a temperate maritime climate because of the warming effect of the Alaska Stream. It is characterized by high precipitation, frequent mist and fog, generally cool summer temperatures, and less severe winter conditions than one might expect at these latitudes. Surface temperatures of the bay from June to September ranged from 12° to 14°C. During the same period, Olsen Creek temperatures ranged from 4.5° to 10°C.

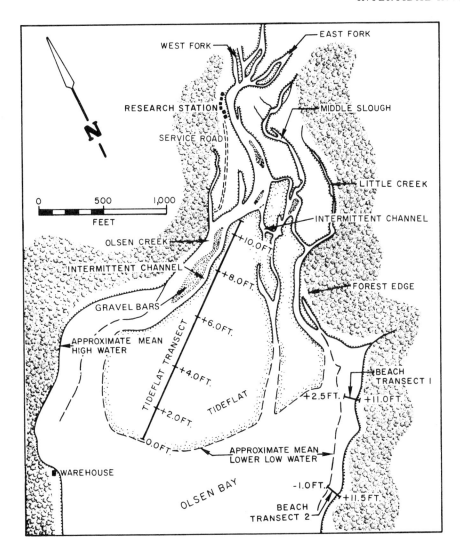

FIGURE 2 Detailed map of Olsen Bay, showing location of sample areas.

All tide-level data at Olsen Bay are based on daily predictions for Cordova, with time and height corrections applied for Snug Corner Cove, Port Fidalgo (60°44'N, 146°39'W), as tabulated by the U.S. Coast and Geodetic Survey (1964). The maximum tidal range in the Olsen Bay area in 1965 was 18.4 ft (15.4 high to –3.0 low); from June to September, the maximum range was 18.1 ft (14.7 high to –3.4 low).

Based on the tables of the U.S. Coast and Geodetic Survey (1964), certain standard levels have been computed for Olsen Bay that are useful in describing vertical zonation in the intertidal zone. These are mean higher high water (MHHW), +12.00 ft; mean high water (MHW), +10.95 ft; mean tide level (MTL), +6.20 ft; mean low water (MLW), +1.45 ft; and mean lower low water (MLLW), 0.00 ft. Mean tidal range, the difference between mean high and mean low water, is 9.5 ft. Mean tide level (6.20 ft), that point that is covered and uncovered by every tidal change, appears to be

of considerable significance as the upper limit of distribution for many organisms in Olsen Bay. The actual elevation of seawater at any given theoretical tidal elevation was established by surveying from a single reference point. This point was determined by driving stakes at the edge of the water at the highest point of a tide cycle and was verified by repeating the procedure on several dates.

## DESCRIPTION OF SAMPLING AREAS

Four areas representative of the three most common types of habitat in the bay were selected for intensive sampling: two gravel-shingle beaches along the east shore, the tideflat at the head of the bay, and Olsen Creek, the principal tributary to the bay (Figure 2). Detailed observations were made on each area along a transect perpendicular to the tidal waterline at Olsen Bay. Substrate materials were described by the following approximate particle size:

| Description | Particle size |
|---|---|
| Mud, silt | No individual particles felt between fingers |
| Sand | <2 mm |
| Gravel | 2–30 mm |
| Rock fragments | 3–6 cm |
| Shingle, cobble | 6–15 cm |
| Rock | 15–25 cm |
| Boulder | >25 cm |

Cobbles were waterworn and rounded, whereas shingle was rough and angular. Except for the mud, which was present at lower levels throughout the bay, all the substrates contained various amounts of fine to coarse particles.

BEACH TRANSECTS

Beach transect 1 was 150 yd seaward from the northeast corner of the bayhead, and transect 2 was 280 yd farther seaward along the shore (Figure 2). Transect 1, which extended from the +2.5-ft to +11.0-ft level, had a grade of 2.1 percent from +2.5 to +4.0 ft, and a grade of 14.4 percent from +4.0 to +11.0 ft. Transect 2, which extended from the −1.0-ft level to the +11.5-ft level, had a grade of 7.7 percent from −1.0 to +4.0 ft and a grade of 14.2 percent from +4.0 to +11.5 ft. An abrupt increase in grade was evident at the +4.0-ft level along much of the shoreline of the bay.

The upper levels of both beach transects had similar substrates, but the mud zone extended considerably higher on transect 1, where it reached +4.5 ft, than on transect 2, where it extended only to +1.0 ft. On transect 1, soft sticky mud with occasional subsurface rock fragments below +4.5 ft graded upward into sandy-silt gravel with increasing amounts of shell debris and rock fragments to +6.5 ft. From this level to +11.0 ft, the substrate was predominantly sand-gravel-shingle over sandy silt mixed with considerable shell debris. On transect 2, pure mud with scattered gravel and rock fragments at +1.0 ft graded into a mixture of silt and gravel with rock fragments between +1.0 and +2.0 ft and finally into sandy silt with gravel and rock fragments from +2.0 to +9.0 ft. A discontinuous surface layer of gravel, shingle, and rock fragments became more extensive toward the upper regions of the beach, and generally drier conditions prevailed. An important stabilizing influence along these gravel-shingle beaches is the mussel *Mytilus edulis*, which frequently occurs in large concentrations and binds together extensive patches of the substrate with its byssal attachment fibers.

TIDEFLAT TRANSECT

The tideflat transect extended from the 0.0-ft to the +11.0-ft level and was 1,835 ft long with an average grade of 0.6

percent. Below the +4.5-ft level, the substrate was moist, sticky mud, which extended seaward well beyond −3.0 ft, as evidenced by the extensive growth of eelgrass below this level. The mud substrate at the lower elevations (generally below +4.5 ft) was semifluid near the surface and became increasingly compact and sticky to a depth of 18–24 in. With increasing tidal elevation, the depth of this mud layer decreased and the underlying sand, gravel, and rock fragments became more evident. The proportion of the coarser materials increased from less than 5 percent at +1.0 ft to 25 percent at +4.0 ft and 50 percent at +5.0 ft. Above +5.0 ft, the substrate became more compact and more granular and had equal proportions of silty sand and gravel, and occasional rock fragments. Approaching the higher intertidal elevations, from +9.0 to +11.0 ft, the silty sand was still more compacted. In the upper half of the region sampled, from about +4.0 to +11.0 ft, shingle and larger rock fragments occurred sporadically on the surface.

Although the grade of the tideflat was slight, and its general appearance was flat, minor differences in elevation produced shallow pools and narrow channels that were covered by tidewater for longer periods than adjoining elevated areas. This allowed forms normally found only at lower levels to intrude into higher levels of the tideflat.

At all stations up to the +5.5-ft level, a dark subsurface layer of sulfide-impregnated silt emitted a sulfurous odor, indicating an oxygen-deficient condition below the surface.

OLSEN CREEK

Olsen Creek lies almost entirely within the intertidal zone at the head of Olsen Bay and is formed by the confluence of East and West Forks, which drain separate steep-sided valleys. Minimum flow is derived primarily from groundwater, whereas higher flows are primarily from surface runoff. In the lower intertidal region of the creek, meanders and interconnecting channels are numerous and form a moderately braided pattern along the extreme western side of the tideflat. Stream cutting in this recently exposed region has resulted in the formation of embankments 1 to 2 ft high at several points. A detailed description of Olsen Creek has been published by Helle and others (1964). Data relating to tide elevation in this earlier report must be corrected to take into account the 1964 uplift of 3–4 ft.

The streambed is composed chiefly of coarse gravel and cobble in the upper portion of the intertidal zone and has increasing amounts of sand, fine gravel, detrital material, and shell debris below the +5.0-ft tide level. Below +3.0 ft, silt and detritus predominate. Between +2.0 and +3.0 ft, numerous unbroken bivalve shells were found, primarily those of mature *Clinocardium nuttallii, Macoma nasuta,* and *Saxidomus giganteus.* The streambed is often disturbed in summer and fall by salmon digging redds in which to deposit their eggs. Some redds are found between +6.0 and +10.0 ft, but the most intensive digging is above +10.0 ft.

Vegetation in the stream is extremely sparse and is limited primarily to a brownish gelatinous alga that adheres to the substrate.

## METHODS OF DESCRIPTION AND CENSUS

The distribution and abundance of intertidal macrofauna were determined by counting numbers of organisms in quadrats along established transects. The first step in sampling each quadrat was to describe the surface in terms of substrate type, vegetation present, estimated percentage of cover provided by the vegetation, and presence of rock fragments or other attachment sites. Next, the more motile forms, such as *Pagurus* or *Hemigrapsus*, were counted, after which the organisms inhabiting the surface and under-rock habitats were counted. Finally, the entire quadrat was excavated and the material sifted to determine the numbers of each of the other species present. The sample quadrats were 0.25 m$^2$ on the tideflat and beach transects and 1 ft$^2$ in the stream. Quadrats on tideflat and beach transects were excavated to a depth of 10–12 in., or occasionally to greater depths when burrows of deeper-dwelling organisms were encountered. In Olsen Creek, quadrats were excavated to depths of 8–10 in.

Representative specimens of all species were preserved and are deposited in the museum of the Bureau of Commercial Fisheries Biological Laboratory, Auke Bay, Alaska.

### BEACH TRANSECTS

The belt- or strip-transect method, in which a series of contiguous quadrats on a line perpendicular to the water's edge make up the strip, was used in sampling the two beach transects. The transects began in the region of pure mud and continued up the beach to a level where no living aquatic invertebrates were observed. The tide level of each quadrat was determined by measuring the difference between its elevation and that of the previous quadrat or established reference point.

### TIDEFLAT TRANSECT

Two types of sampling were done in the tideflat transect—quantitative and qualitative. All sampling was done along the same transect line, which was approximately parallel to the intertidal portion of Olsen Creek. The quantitative-sampling stations were located at intervals of 0.5 ft of elevation, from 0.0 to the +11.00-ft level, and the average distance between stations was 83.4 ft. Stations for qualitative sampling were occupied at −1.0, −2.5, and −3.0 ft.

At each station a 5- by 5-m area, subdivided at 0.5-m intervals to yield a grid of coordinate points, was established to permit random selection of samples. From 5 to 10 sampling points were chosen randomly at each station. These points were taken as the midpoints of each 0.25-m$^2$ quadrat, the description and census of which were accomplished in the same manner as that described for the beach-transect quadrats.

### OLSEN CREEK

Olsen Creek was sampled with a 1-ft$^2$ Surber sampler at 1-ft tide-level intervals along the main channel from 0.0 to +11.0 ft. Five quadrats, chosen subjectively to include the available substrate types and current velocities, were excavated at each station. Specimens were separated from detritus and sediment by elutriation. Samples from each station were eventually combined because of the uniformity of fauna on all substrates sampled.

## DISTRIBUTION AND ZONATION OF INTERTIDAL ORGANISMS

### BEACH AND TIDEFLAT TRANSECTS

The vertical distribution of all the common flora and fauna in the tideflat and beach transects is shown in Figure 3, and the density of the conspicuous species (conspicuous in terms of size, numbers, or growth form) is shown in Figures 4–30. Density is expressed as the average number of individuals per 0.25 m$^2$ for the several samples taken at each station on the tideflat (solid lines) and for consecutive samples at different tide levels on beach transect 1 (dashed lines) and beach transect 2 (long and short dashed lines).

In some areas, principally on the lower pure-mud portions of the tideflat and beach transects, barnacles, limpets, and littorines were found in greater numbers than might have been expected. These anomalies resulted from the occurrence of rock fragments that provided stable attachment sites in the quadrats.

Because tideflats have a generally low grade and often contain areas of little or no elevation change, their vertical biological zones are often obscure. Frequently, communities occurring in association with particular combinations of substrate, tidal exposure, vegetative cover, and small topographic variations are more characteristic of tideflats. Although local concentrations of some species were marked on the relatively small Olsen Bay tideflat, vertical zonation of most species was also evident, reflecting the importance of differences in substrate composition at succeeding elevations.

The upper and lower limits of the observed zones on the tideflat were generally irregular, primarily because of differ-

142 SELECTED ECOLOGICAL EFFECTS

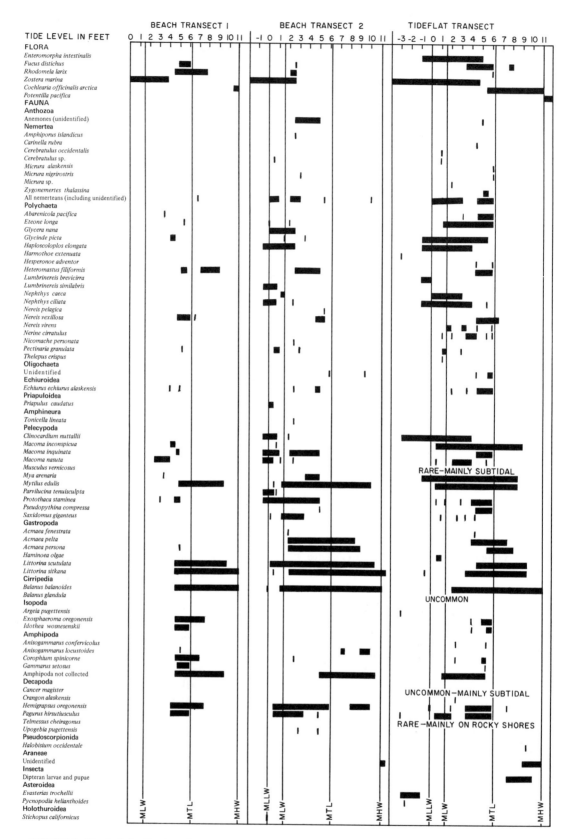

FIGURE 3  Vertical distribution of common fauna and flora on tideflat and beach transects at Olsen Bay in 1965.

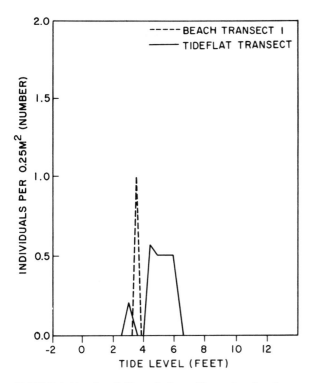

FIGURE 4 Density of *Abarenicola pacifica* on beach and tideflat transects.

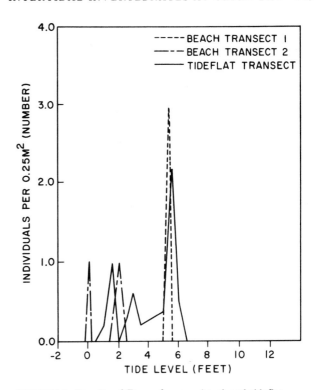

FIGURE 5 Density of *Eteone longa* on beach and tideflat transects.

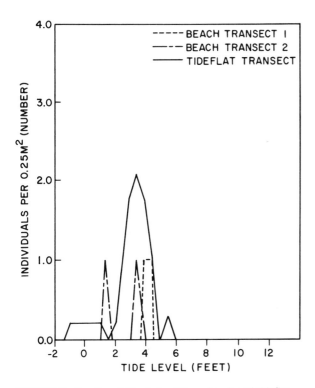

FIGURE 6 Density of *Glycinde picta* on beach and tideflat transects.

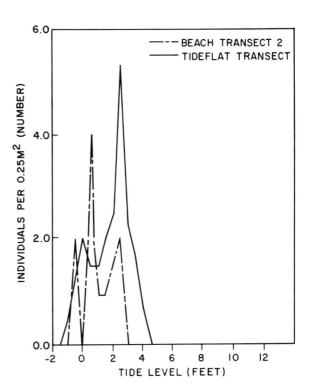

FIGURE 7 Density of *Haploscoloplos elongata* on beach and tideflat transects.

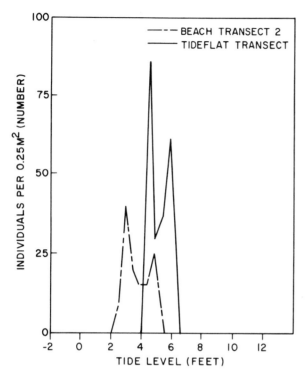

FIGURE 8   Density of *Heteromastus filiformis* on beach and tideflat transects.

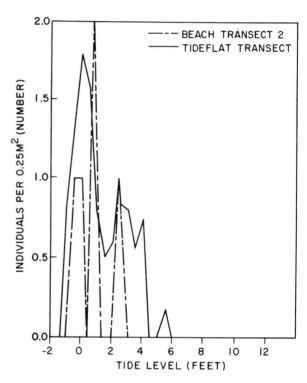

FIGURE 9   Density of *Nephthys ciliata* on beach and tideflat transects.

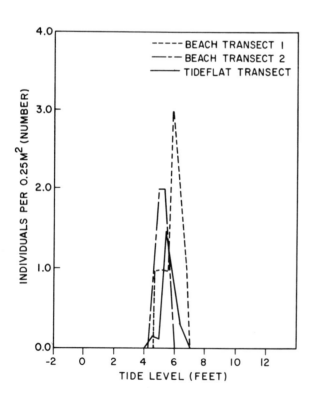

FIGURE 10   Density of *Nereis vexillosa* on beach and tideflat transects.

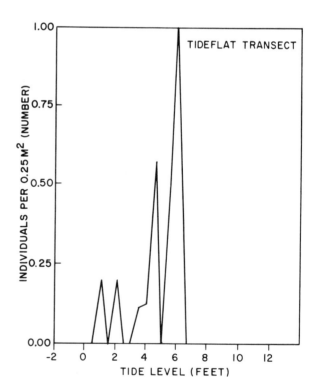

FIGURE 11   Density of *Nerine cirratulus* on tideflat transect.

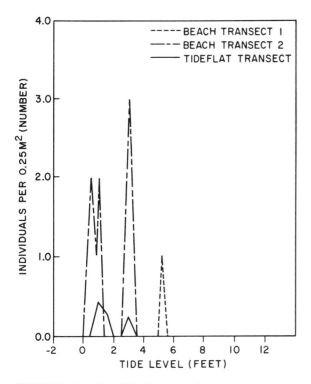

FIGURE 12 Density of *Pectinaria granulata* on beach and tideflat transects.

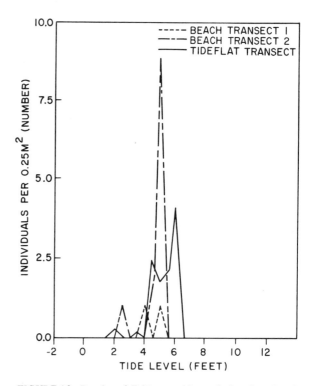

FIGURE 13 Density of *Echiurus echiurus alaskensis* on beach and tideflat transects.

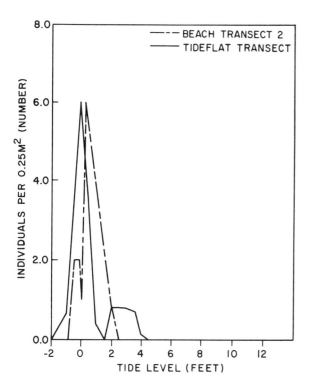

FIGURE 14 Density of *Clinocardium nuttallii* on beach and tideflat transects.

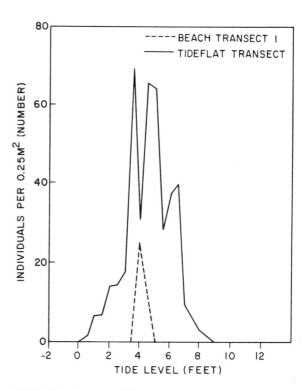

FIGURE 15 Density of *Macoma inconspicua* on beach and tideflat transects.

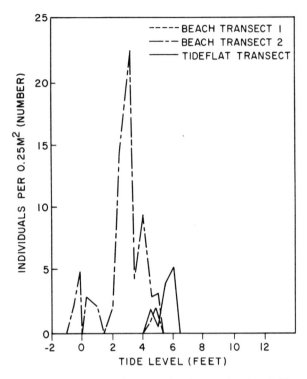

FIGURE 16   Density of *Macoma inquinata* on beach and tide-flat transects.

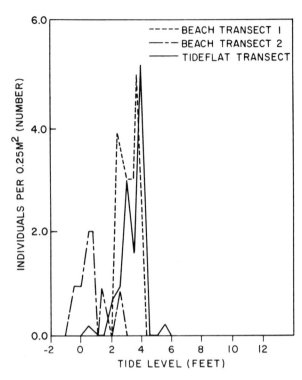

FIGURE 17   Density of *Macoma nasuta* on beach and tideflat transects.

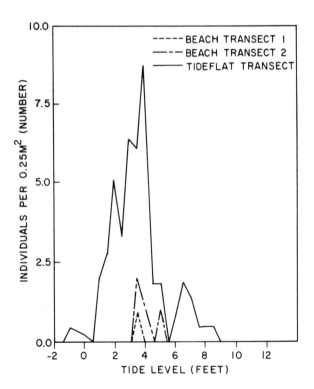

FIGURE 18   Density of *Mya arenaria* on beach and tideflat transects.

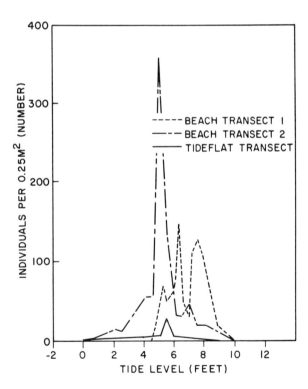

FIGURE 19   Density of *Mytilus edulis* on beach and tideflat transects.

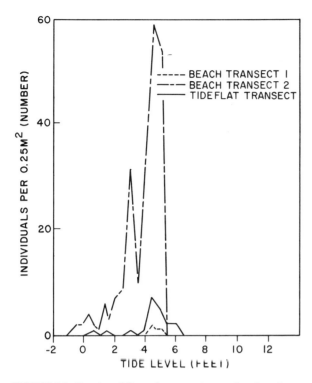

FIGURE 20   Density of *Protothaca staminea* on beach and tideflat transects.

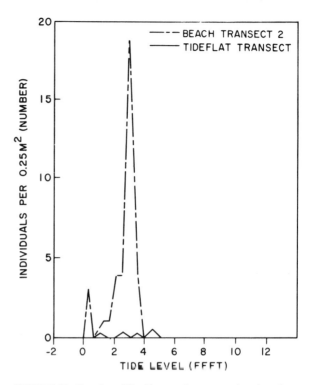

FIGURE 21   Density of *Saxidomus giganteus* on beach and tideflat transects.

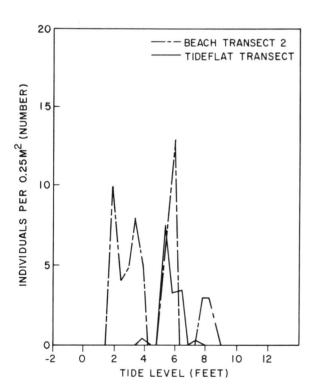

FIGURE 22   Density of *Acmaea pelta* on beach and tideflat transects.

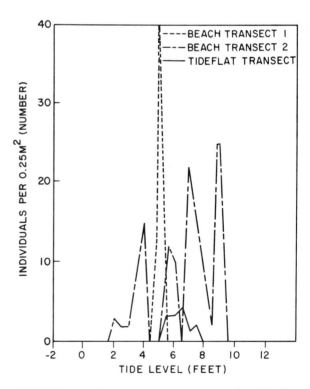

FIGURE 23   Density of *Acmaea persona* on beach and tideflat transects.

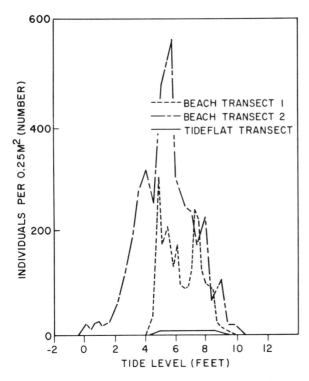

FIGURE 24   Density of *Littorina scutulata* on beach and tideflat transects.

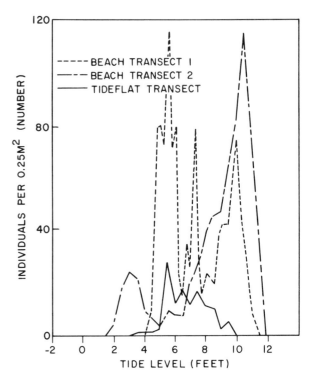

FIGURE 25   Density of *Littorina sitkana* on beach and tideflat transects.

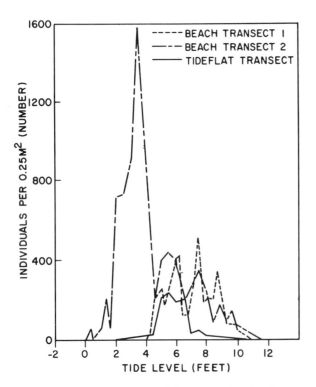

FIGURE 26   Density of *Balanus balanoides* on beach and tideflat transects.

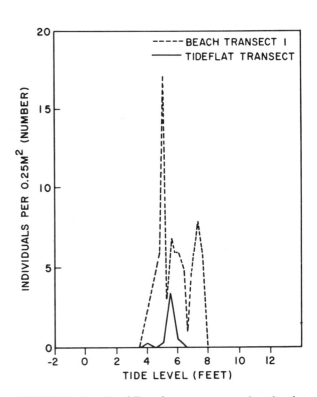

FIGURE 27   Density of *Exosphaeroma oregonensis* on beach and tideflat transects.

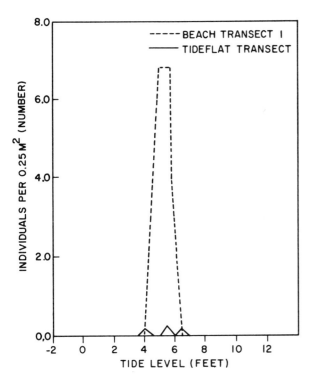

FIGURE 28 Density of *Idothea wosnesenskii* on beach and tideflat transects.

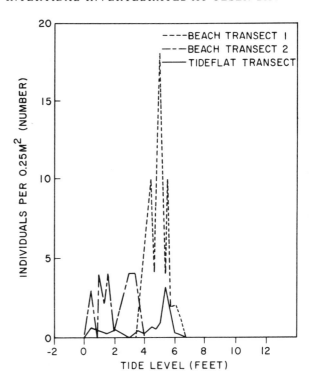

FIGURE 30 Density of *Pagurus hirsutiusculus* on beach and tideflat transects.

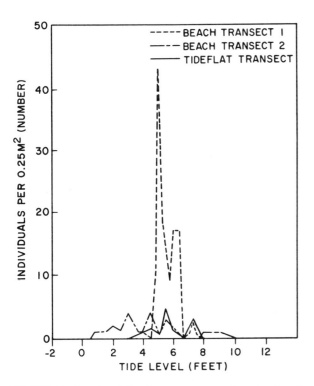

FIGURE 29 Density of *Hemigrapsus oregonensis* on beach and tideflat transects.

ences in tidal exposure resulting from small local variations in elevation caused by the presence of a series of low, broad gravel ridges separated by old stream channels. These shallow channels receive the tidal flow earlier and retain it longer than do adjoining elevated areas. Where the ridges were not completely separated, depressions formed by the old stream channels held water longer than adjacent higher ground. The effect of this prolonged submersion is similar to that observed in isolated tidepools, where organisms can exist above their usual upper limits. The total result is that some organisms penetrate farther landward than would be possible if the surface were more regular. The accumulation of fine sediment and detritus in the channels and depressions and the varying influence of freshwater runoff add to the irregularity of the distribution of the tideflat biota.

The intertidal shoreline of Olsen Bay was generally divisible into three bands or zones, each characterized by the dominance of certain organisms: the lower, eelgrass zone; the middle, *Balanus–Fucus* zone, where the greatest number of species was concentrated; and the upper, *Littorina* zone. The tidal elevation of the boundaries of the zones varied with location in the bay.

*Eelgrass Zone*

This lowest intertidal zone had a semifluid surface layer and a dense growth of eelgrass (*Zostera marina*) over most of its width and almost no surface-dwelling fauna, except for an occasional starfish, Dungeness crab (*Cancer magister*), or sea cucumber (*Stichopus californicus*). Most commonly observed in the eelgrass zone were those actively burrowing polychaete worms that do not require a firm substrate for maintenance of a permanent burrow and several of the bivalves, usually either shallow burrowers or those adapted to foul mud conditions.

The two dominant plants below the 4-ft level were eelgrass and *Enteromorpha intestinalis*. Dense growths of eelgrass extended from well below –3.0 ft to the +4.0-ft level on beach transect 1 and to the +2.0-ft level on beach transect 2, but were gradually supplanted by *E. intestinalis* on the tideflat above the 0.0-ft level. Above 0.0 ft on the tideflat, the eelgrass cover gradually decreased from an average of 25 percent per quadrat to 5–10 percent per quadrat at the upper limit of the eelgrass zone (Figure 31). This decrease was caused both by a reduction in the length of individual plants and the increasing distance between them—the length of plants on the tideflat decreased from 48 in. at –2.5 ft to 9–15 in. at +3.0 ft and 6–12 in. at +4.5 ft. *Enteromorpha* was found in patches at –1.0 ft; it increased to an average quadrat cover of 50 percent at +1.5 ft and then occurred more sparsely above this level (Figure 31). The upper limit of eelgrass descended as the mouth of the bay was approached, generally corresponding to the decreasing elevation of the upper limit of the mud substrate from +4.0 ft on beach transect 1 (nearest the tideflat, where it reached +4.5 ft) to +2.5 ft on beach transect 2.

Organisms associated with pure mud were restricted to lower elevations on beach transect 2 than on transect 1 or on the tideflat; this difference was greater than would be expected from a consideration of tolerance to exposure alone, because pure mud did not extend as high on beach transect 2 (to +1.0 ft) as it did on the tideflat transect or on beach transect 1 (to +4.5 ft). In addition to the reduced area of mud in transect 2, more compacted substrate materials replaced pure mud at all but the lowest elevations. Thus, in this protected area, the combination of tidal exposure time and substrate seem to be of primary importance in determining the occurrence and vertical distribution of organisms.

The eelgrass zone can be divided into a lower and an upper portion on the basis of species present. In the lower portion (from about –3.0 ft to 0.0 ft), the only two invertebrate species commonly encountered were *Nephthys ciliata* (Figure 9) and *Clinocardium nuttallii* (Figure 14). *Clinocardium* reached its greatest density in this lower portion on the tideflat and on beach transect 2. Most of these individuals were large and occurred near the surface, a position dictated by their rather short siphons. The starfish *Evasterias troschellii* was occasionally observed at these lower levels (Figure 3), presumably preying on *Clinocardium*. With few exceptions, fauna in the lower portion of the eelgrass zone on beach transect 1 was sparse, both in number of species and in number of individuals.

In the upper portion of the eelgrass zone, from about 0.0 to +4.5 ft (to +2.5 on beach transect 2), the number of

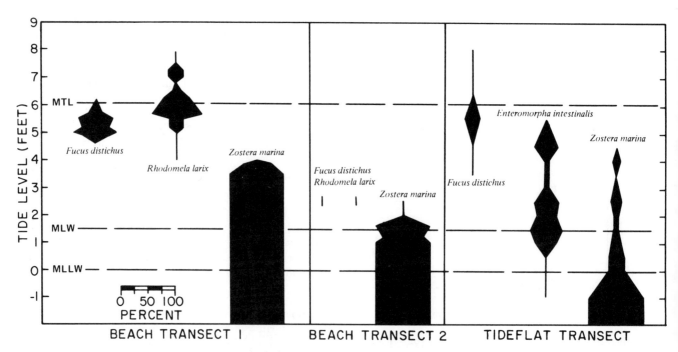

FIGURE 31 Percentage of substrate covered by principal plants on beach and tideflat transects at Olsen Bay, 1965. Single lines indicate less than 5 percent cover. Occurrence of *Zostera* continues below base line of graph in all cases.

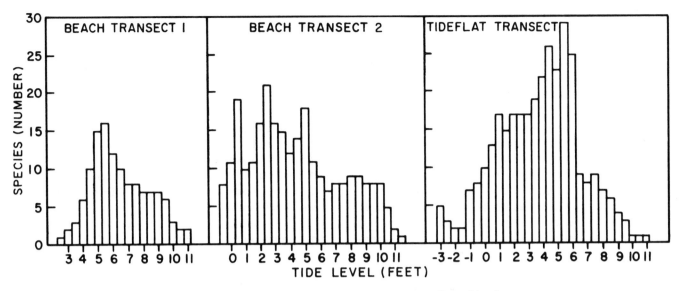

FIGURE 32 Numbers of species present per ½ ft of elevation on tideflat and beach transects.

species increased rapidly along the tideflat transect and beach transect 2, although the number of species remained relatively low on beach transect 1 (Figure 32). Polychaetes and bivalves continued to constitute the greater portion of the fauna here. The lugworm *Abarenicola pacifica* reached its greatest densities on beach transect 1 and on the tideflat transect (Figure 4); here it also occurred up into the midtide area, where the more compact substrate material tended to keep its burrows from collapsing. Typical sandy-mud-dwelling polychaetes represented were *Glycinde picta* (Figure 6) (which also occurred in the lower *Balanus–Fucus* zone), *Haploscoloplos elongata* (Figure 7), decreasing numbers of *Nephthys ciliata* (Figure 9), and the sand-grain tube-builder *Pectinaria granulata* (Figure 12). On beach transect 2, the priapuloid, *Priapulus caudatus*, occurred in small numbers around the +0.5-ft level (Figure 3).

*Macoma inconspicua* (Figure 15), *Macoma nasuta* (Figure 17), and *Mya arenaria* (Figure 18) were the most abundant bivalves in the upper portion of the eelgrass zone, even in the foul mud of the tideflat. *Macoma nasuta*, especially, appeared to be able to survive in substrates where oxygen concentration was very low. Although the surface material of this region is mud, small numbers of both common limpets, *Acmaea pelta* and *Acmaea persona*, occurred there (Figures 22 and 23), together with *Littorina scutulata* (Figure 24), *Littorina sitkana* (Figure 25), and *Balanus balanoides* (Figure 26). The presence of these organisms on a mud substrate is explained by the occasional occurrence on the surface of rock fragments and vegetation that provided stable grazing sites for the limpets and littorines and attachment sites for the barnacles. Concentrations of the mussel *Mytilus edulis* also extended into the upper fringe of this zone. The increasing amounts of gravel at these higher elevations enabled the mussels to bind together the substrate

with their byssal fibers, also forming relatively stable grazing and attachment sites for limpets and barnacles. Juvenile *Littorina scutulata* were found in large numbers among mussels and gravel, in crevices formed by barnacle aggregations on rock fragments, and on blades of eelgrass. All these places form the so-called "nurseries" for the young gastropods in the lower portions of their vertical ranges.

*Balanus–Fucus Zone*

The *Balanus–Fucus* zone extends from the eelgrass zone upward to about +10.0 ft. At Olsen Bay the growth of *Fucus distichus* was sparse and limited primarily to the lower part of this zone on beach transect 1 and on the tideflat and to areas influenced by freshwater runoff, such as Middle Slough. In the lower elevations of this zone, *Rhodomela larix* and *Enteromorpha intestinalis* contributed significant vegetational cover only on beach transect 1 and on the tideflat (Figure 31). Beach transect 2 generally lacked vegetation above the eelgrass zone. Areas covered by *Fucus* or *Rhodomela*, or by dense beds of *Mytilus*, appeared dark from a distance, whereas areas lacking these organisms were lighter because the gravel–shingle substrate and attached barnacles predominated. Because the relative abundance of these dominant organisms varied both horizontally and vertically along the shoreline, the net appearance of the *Balanus–Fucus* zone was a wide light-colored band with a darker mosaic of algae or *Mytilus* sporadically superimposed on the lower horizon.

The lower portion of the *Balanus–Fucus* zone, between the eelgrass zone and mean tide level (+6.20 ft at Olsen Bay), had the greatest diversity of species. It appeared to be an area of transition where the substrate was soft enough for burrowing worms but contained enough coarse material to support tube-dwelling worms or those forms unable to maintain themselves successfully in a pure-mud substrate. Compared with the eelgrass zone, there were more of the larger substrate materials in the lower part of the *Balanus–Fucus* zone, which provided attachment sites for surface dwellers; compared with the upper part of this zone, there was more protective vegetative cover and a substrate composition more favorable for subsurface organisms. Mean tide level appeared to be of considerable ecological significance, particularly on the tideflat, because it represented the upper limit of numerous species (Figure 35); this was especially noticeable in the worms, for which desiccation, a function of exposure time, is a special problem.

Several species that are especially active on the surface were found in greater abundance in the lower portion of the *Balanus–Fucus* zone than elsewhere—*Exosphaeroma oregonensis* (Figure 27), *Idothea wosnesenskii* (Figure 28), *Hemigrapsus oregonensis* (Figure 29), and *Pagurus hirsutiusculus* (Figure 30). The greater abundance of these four species is caused by the greater surface area covered by the vegetation and the favorable substrate of this zone. These four species were also found in the under-rock habitat, although *Idothea* was most often found crawling about on thalli of *Fucus*.

*Exosphaeroma* and *Idothea* were absent from beach transect 2, and *Hemigrapsus* and *Pagurus* were found there only in small numbers because of the general lack of vegetation. Greater numbers of these species were present on beach transect 1 than on the tideflat, probably because of the greater amounts of gravel and rock fragments composing the substrate on the beaches and the general lack of *Fucus* on the tideflat transect.

More gravel and rock fragments in the *Balanus-Fucus* zone than in the eelgrass zone provided increased surface area for attachment of *Balanus* and for grazing by the two littorines and the two common limpets and resulted in the greater densities observed (Figures 22-26). *Littorina scutulata* reached much greater densities than *L. sitkana* in the lower *Balanus–Fucus* zone, although the latter species was the more abundant form at higher levels.

A sharp decrease in numbers of *Balanus* occurred at the +4.0-ft level on beach transect 2 (Figure 26), corresponding to the abrupt increase in grade noted at this elevation here and along much of the Olsen Bay shoreline. Breaking wave action at this elevation would make this portion of the zone less favorable for settlement of barnacle spat and probably accounts for the sudden decrease in density observed. Similar abrupt changes in density were not observed on beach transect 1 or on the tideflat transect (Figure 26). This is probably because of lack of suitable substrate at the +4.0-ft level in these areas. It is also probable that some damping of wave action occurs at beach transect 1, which is further removed from the bay mouth than transect 2 and is more protected.

Subsurface fauna, primarily polychaetes and bivalves, was particularly diverse in the lower half of the *Balanus–Fucus* zone. *Abarenicola pacifica* maintained a uniform density from the eelgrass zone into the *Balanus–Fucus* zone only on the tideflat. *Eteone longa* reached its peak densities on the lower part of the *Balanus–Fucus* zone of beach transect 1 and the tideflat; lower densities of *E. longa* were observed on beach transect 2 below the *Balanus–Fucus* zone (Figure 5). Another of the polychaetes, *Heteromastus filiformis*, occurred in local concentrations on the lower portion of the *Balanus–Fucus* zone of beach transect 2 and of the tideflat, but it was not observed at this level on beach transect 1 (Figure 8). Not unexpectedly, greatest densities of the mussel worm *Nereis vexillosa* (Figure 10) were found in the areas of greatest densities of *Mytilus edulis* on all three transects. Small numbers of *Nerine cirratulus* occurred on the tideflat from the mean tide level downward into the eelgrass zone (Figure 11).

The echiuroid *Echiurus echiurus alaskensis* (Figure 13), which requires a fairly compact substrate for maintenance of its permanent burrows, was taken in considerable numbers below the mean tide level on beach transect 2 and on the tideflat. The polychaete *Hesperonoe adventor* occurred as a commensal with this species.

*Macoma inconspicua* (Figure 15), *Mytilus edulis* (Figure 19), and *Protothaca staminea* (Figure 20) were the most common bivalves encountered in the lower *Balanus–Fucus* zone on all transects. *Macoma inquinata* and *Saxidomus giganteus* also were most abundant near the lower margin of this zone (Figures 16 and 21).

The upper part of the *Balanus–Fucus* zone, which extends from +6.2 to +10.0 ft, showed a sharp decrease in number of species on beach transect 1 and on the tideflat transect (Figure 32). This decrease was primarily the result of nearly all polychaetes and bivalves reaching their upper limits at or slightly above mean tide level (+6.2 ft). The greater reduction in number of species in beach transect 1 and in the tideflat transect than in beach transect 2 may possibly be attributed to the slightly greater wave action at beach transect 2, allowing penetration of greater numbers of species to higher levels as a result of the more favorable moisture conditions.

Most of the animals found in the upper portion of the *Balanus–Fucus* zone were surface dwellers of a few species. The most common animals were *Mytilus edulis* (Figure 19), *Acmaea persona* (Figure 23), *Littorina scutulata* (Figure 24), *Littorina sitkana* (Figure 25), and *Balanus balanoides* (Figure 26). Animals occurring in smaller numbers were *Macoma inconspicua* (Figure 15), *Acmaea pelta* (Figure 22), *Exosphaeroma oregonensis* (Figure 27), and *Hemigrapsus oregonensis* (Figure 29). *Macoma inconspicua* were found up to +9.0 ft, while *Mytilus edulis* occurred to +10.0 ft. *Acmaea pelta* did not range as high up the beach as *A. persona*.

Although marine vegetation was sparse on all transects in

the upper *Balanus–Fucus* zone (Figure 31), a small terrestrial plant, *Cochlearia officinalis arctica* (Figure 3), appeared at the upper elevations, particularly on the tideflat transect.

## Littorina Zone

The *Littorina* zone extends from +10.0 ft to the uppermost limits of intertidal organisms. Flora here was limited to terrestrial plants, including *Cochlearia officinalis arctica*. This plant occurred in increasing numbers up to +11.0 ft, where it was replaced by another terrestrial plant, *Potentilla pacifica*. Both these species were frequently submerged in salt water. Of the intertidal animals, only *Littorina scutulata*, *Littorina sitkana*, and *Balanus balanoides* were found in this highest zone. Peak densities of *L. sitkana* occurred well up in this zone on beach transect 2 and somewhat lower on beach transect 1; most of these individuals were found in protective crevices or under rocks. An important factor in limiting the numbers of intertidal species and individuals at these high levels is the lack of wave splash, which restricts organisms to lower levels.

## OLSEN CREEK

The Olsen Creek sampling yielded 13 species of animals, 5 of which could be characterized as freshwater or dilute brackish-water organisms. The others were largely single occurrences of typically marine species, probably invaders from the adjacent tideflat or gravel beaches, who were tolerant of the prevailing conditions (Figure 33). The largely marine source of the Olsen Creek populations is reflected in the decrease in number of species found from lower to higher tide levels (Figure 34). The several species of microdrile oligochaetes,

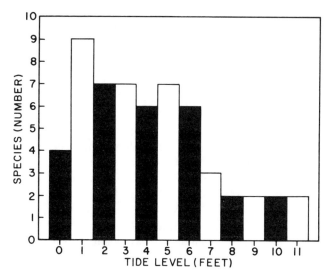

FIGURE 34   Numbers of species present per 1 ft of elevation, 0–11 ft, in intertidal Olsen Creek.

which were unidentified, constituted by far the greatest numbers of individuals in the stream collections. They approached densities of 100–150/ft$^2$ between +5.0 and +8.0 ft and were encountered at nearly every level sampled. Also abundant were three of the four species of amphipods, particularly *Anisogammarus confervicolus* (688 specimens in 35 quadrats). The fourth species of amphipod, *Micruropus alaskensis*, was represented by four individuals at the +5.0-ft level. The specimens of *M. alaskensis* collected at Olsen Bay were the basis for the descriptions of the species and are reported more fully by Bousfield and Hubbard (1968).

One nemertean, *Prostoma graecense*, was represented in small numbers at nearly all sampling levels. The three abundant amphipods, the nemerteans, and the oligochaetes all reached their lower limits at the +1.0-ft level in the stream; below this level, at 0.0, a few individuals of *Haploscoloplos elongata*, *Macoma inconspicua*, *Exosphaeroma oregonensis*, and young *Mya arenaria* were found. At +1.0 ft, single occurrences of *Eteone longa* and *Hemigrapsus oregonensis* were noted, and at +3.0 ft a single individual of *Upogebia pugettensis* was found; all these typically marine forms occurred near or below their lower limit of occurrence on the tideflat or beach habitat. *Exosphaeroma* appeared to be particularly tolerant of brackish conditions; its vertical range (mean lower low water to mean tide level) extended as high in the stream as on the tideflat. The upper limit of the amphipods varied from +6.0 ft for the two species of *Paramoera* to +7.0 ft for *Anisogammarus*. Nemerteans and oligochaetes were found up to the highest point sampled in the stream, the +11.0-ft level. Because sampling was carried out late in the summer, few insects in the larval or nymphal stages were encountered; those that were found occurred above the intertidal area.

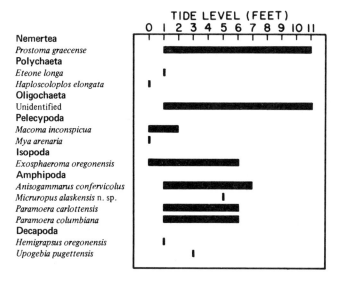

FIGURE 33   Vertical distribution of common invertebrates in Olsen Creek in 1965.

## SUMMARY OF SPECIES DISTRIBUTION

The three major habitats—beach, tideflat, and intertidal stream—displayed both similarities and differences in the distribution of species in the intertidal zone. These similarities and differences appear to be most closely related to the existence of particular combinations of substrate composition and tidal exposure; vegetational development and minor topographical variations appear to be of lesser importance.

The number of species on beach transect 1 exhibits a nearly normal distribution with the peak near mean tide level (Figure 32). Although several peaks of species distribution occurred below mean tide level on beach transect 2, vertical distribution of species was, in general, more uniform than on beach transect 1 or on the tideflat. In both beach transects the greatest number of species occurred below the mean tide line in conjunction with favorable substrates, greater algal cover, and shorter exposure time. Above the mean tide line the longer exposure time restricted the fauna to fewer species.

On the tideflat transect, the number of species from low to high levels also approximates a normal distribution with peak close to mean tide level (Figure 32). This point is also shown on Figure 35, where a sharp break between +6.0 ft and +6.5 ft marks the upper limit of many species. The substrate between the +4.0- and +6.0-ft levels that precedes the peak of this curve is firm mud and contains many species of organisms. The abrupt drop in number of species (mainly worms and bivalves) between +6.0 and +6.5 ft—the mean

tide level—is attributed to greater exposure to desiccation, shorter feeding time for filter feeders, and change from mud substrate to much coarser materials.

The number of species in intertidal Olsen Creek decreased steadily from lower to higher elevations (Figure 34). This difference is probably related primarily to changes in salinity and substrate composition.

## BIOLOGICAL EVIDENCES FOR EARTHQUAKE-RELATED UPLIFT

The uplift in the Olsen Bay area associated with the 1964 earthquake produced measurable changes in the distributions of certain intertidal organisms. It is possible to estimate the amount of the uplift by comparing the positions of these organisms before and after the earthquake. Although distributions of many other intertidal organisms do not provide direct evidence for the amount of uplift, they indicate that substantial environmental changes occurred in conjunction with the uplift.

The most obvious and reliable quantitative index of the uplift was the dead barnacle line, or upper limit of a band of barnacle tests, which was visible along nearly the entire shoreline from about +11.0 ft to a maximum of +14.0 ft. This band was composed of whitened entire tests and white calcareous bases, primarily of *Balanus glandula*. The living barnacles, on the other hand, were, for the most part, *Balanus balanoides*, a form with a membranous base, which

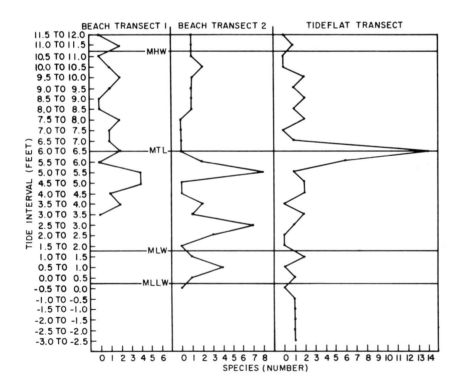

FIGURE 35   Numbers of species reaching their upper limits of distribution per ½ ft of elevation on tideflat and beach transects.

was observed to a maximum elevation of only +11.0 ft. Both species of barnacles occur within about the same vertical range. On the tideflat, evidence of preearthquake barnacle populations was found up to the +11.0-ft level, whereas living postearthquake barnacles were found only up to +8.0 ft. These figures indicate an uplift of about +3.0 ft.

An uplift of 3.0 to 3.5 ft is also indicated by the measurements of the upper limits of barnacles on the small rocky island at the mouth of Olsen Bay. The upper limit of barnacles before the earthquake, as indicated by the upper limit of the dead remains of mature *Balanus glandula*, was at +14.0 ft; after the earthquake, the upper limit of the living barnacles (composed of smaller preearthquake and postearthquake individuals) was at +10.5 ft. The lower limits of the barnacles were also determinable on this island: +7.0 ft for the mature preearthquake individuals (lower limit of larger individuals) and +4.0 ft for the postearthquake barnacles (lower limit of smaller individuals).

Before the earthquake, the most abundant barnacle was *Balanus glandula*, but in 1965 the dominant species was *B. balanoides*. This apparent reversal in dominance is discussed by Haven (1971, this volume), who postulates that it could have occurred if, at the time of the earthquake, *B. balanoides* had just released its larvae into the water, whereas many *B. glandula* were killed by the uplift before they had a chance to spawn, particularly those at higher elevations. Larvae of *B. balanoides* were then free to colonize the newly uplifted area and appropriate sites occupied by dead *B. glandula.*

Further evidence of recent uplift is indicated by the abnormal abundance of mollusk-shell remains, particularly of the larger bivalves, which indicates altered environmental conditions. In regions of maximum known uplift, such as on Montague Island (Figure 1), mollusk shells were piled in long windrows. At Olsen Bay, where the uplift was moderate, such evidence of high mortality was less marked. On beach transect 1, no large numbers of empty shells were encountered at any elevation, perhaps because the lack of suitable habitat precluded development of large populations before the uplift. On transect 2, empty shells of mature *Macoma nasuta* were common in conjunction with a few living individuals at postearthquake elevations of 0.0 to +1.6 ft. The scarcity of live *M. nasuta* suggests that existence is now marginal at these higher levels.

On beach transect 2, many empty shells of *Protothaca staminea* were found from +4.0 to +6.0 ft (remains of 75 individuals per 0.25 m$^2$ were present at +6.0 ft), and many living individuals were found at +3.0 to +5.0 ft (Figure 20). It appears, from the evidence of high mortality in the +5.0- to +6.0-ft zone (above the upper limit of living individuals), that those preearthquake individuals residing in the uppermost foot of the normal vertical range of the species were not able to survive the combination of

uplift and high population density. At lower elevations (+4.0 to +5.0 ft), however, there were conditions that allowed survival of a relatively large population. The fact that no small living individuals were observed with the large numbers of older individuals in the +3.0 to +5.0-ft area indicates a greater survival potential of the older individuals. The absence of small empty shells of several other clams also indicates poor reproduction in the years immediately preceding the earthquake.

On the tideflat, comparison of the preearthquake vertical range of *Protothaca* (+1.5 to +2.5 ft) with the postearthquake range of greatest abundance (+4.0 to +6.0 ft) indicates an uplift of 3.5 ft.

On beach transect 2, live *Saxidomus giganteus* were found from 0.0 to +3.5 ft and were most abundant between +2.0 and +3.5 ft (Figure 21). Most were large adults 20–70 mm long (about 4–10 years old). Large empty shells were found from 0.0 to +3.5 ft and were most abundant at +1.6 ft (35/0.25 m$^2$), +2.5 ft (45/0.25 m$^2$), +3.0 ft (72/0.25 m$^2$), and +3.5 ft (34/0.25 m$^2$). This high density of empty shells in the same vertical range as that of the living individuals probably indicates that they were sensitive to postearthquake conditions over the entire range. The close correlation between numbers and occurrence of living individuals and of empty shells seems to indicate a preearthquake range of about 3.5 ft and the uplift of the entire vertical range above the preearthquake upper limit. The absence of younger individuals in the present vertical range indicates little postearthquake reproductive success at these levels, emphasizing the probability that the entire range of this species was uplifted above the region formerly occupied. The absence of remains of small individuals probably indicates that reproduction was also extremely limited before the earthquake. The presence of mud, a substrate unfavorable for *Saxidomus*, at levels below +1.0 ft has prevented development of postearthquake populations at levels equal to those occupied by this species before the uplift.

Only a few live or dead *Saxidomus* were found on the tideflat, an indication that they were not abundant here before the earthquake. Helle and others (1964) give +1.5 ft as the upper limit of *Saxidomus* here; the postearthquake upper limit was +4.5 ft (Figure 21), a difference of 3.0 ft.

*Saxidomus giganteus* was not found on beach transect 1, probably because of the presence of mud up to the upper limit of the preearthquake vertical range (0.0-ft level).

The upper limits of several other tideflat organisms, before and after the earthquake, appear to substantiate the assumption of an uplift of 3.0–4.0 ft. *Abarenicola pacifica* had an upper limit of +2.5 to +3.0 ft before the earthquake (Helle and others, 1964) and now is found up to +6.0 ft, a difference of 3.0 to 3.5 ft. *Nereis* sp. (probably *vexillosa*) had a preearthquake upper limit of +2.5 ft and is now found up to +6.5 ft; its greatest density is at +5.5 ft. *Echiurus echiurus alaskensis*, formerly found from +1.5 to +3.0 ft, is now most common from +4.0 to +6.0 ft, an indication of an approximate 3.0-ft uplift.

Empty shells of *Macoma inconspicua*, *Macoma nasuta*, and *Mya arenaria* were also observed on the tideflat at the upper limit of living individuals of the same species. These species apparently were relatively unaffected by ecological changes accompanying the uplift, however, since the indication of die-off was slight and was observed only among individuals that had been living near the preearthquake upper limit of their vertical range. As on the beach transects, all empty shells on the mudflat were of larger, older individuals. Empty shells of younger individuals were not observed; this would not be unexpected if the premise holds true that younger individuals are generally found lower in the vertical range than are older individuals. Thus, if a species with a relatively broad vertical range is only moderately uplifted, the younger individuals at the lower levels will come to occupy the former upper limits of the range, and only the older individuals at the higher levels will be elevated sufficiently above the former upper limit to suffer high mortality.

In Olsen Creek, many of the numerous empty shells of mature *Saxidomus giganteus*, *Clinocardium nuttallii*, and *Macoma nasuta* in the streambed between +2.0 and +3.0 ft were probably postearthquake casualties from the adjacent tideflat or lower beach areas, through which the stream had cut its many channels. The occurrence of these shells in the streambed may have been the result of the stream cutting down into substrate containing an abundance of these species below the old streambed, or uplift may have altered the various stream channels in the lower end of the stream sufficiently to have caused erosion of these mature individuals from previously stable and unaffected areas. Only large shells were found; smaller weaker individuals exposed at the same time may have been washed away.

Most of the living bivalves found on the tideflat and beach transects in 1965 were more than 2 years old; that is, they were survivors of the earthquake. Younger individuals of some species were found, an indication of more specific differences in postearthquake spawning success. At the time of sampling, one full growing season and part of another had passed since the uplift, so that clams from postearthquake spawning should have had one annual ring.

Although *Macoma inconspicua* was extremely abundant on the Olsen Bay tideflat (Figure 15), only a few were taken in the length range of 0–5 mm. Individuals this small must have settled in the spring of 1965. Beanland (1940) gives approximate age–length relationships for this species in the Dover (England) estuary as follows: first season, 1–3 mm; and second season, 3–7 mm. After the second season, indistinct growth rings made such determinations unreliable. At Olsen Bay, most *M. inconspicua* fell within the range of 5–10 mm or 10–15 mm. The former were probably in their second season and were from postearthquake spawning, whereas the latter were from preearthquake spawning, and individuals larger than 15 mm were at least 3 years old. The scarcity of individuals smaller than 5 mm indicates a poor survival from the 1965 spawning, but it is possible that individuals that settled in 1965 grew so rapidly that most of them were larger than 5 mm when most samples were taken (during July and August). The wide tidal-elevation range of this species seems to eliminate the lack of favorable settlement areas as a cause of scarcity of young produced in 1965.

Reproduction by *Mya arenaria* and *Protothaca staminea* has not been very successful at Olsen Bay since the earthquake. The few *Protothaca* (less than 8 mm) found during this study had probably settled since the earthquake; the larger, mature specimens (15–45 mm, about 3–10 years) were survivors of the earthquake and were more common. The most common ages found were in the range of 5–8 years. Small *Mya* (6–10 mm) that had settled since the earthquake were not as plentiful as small *P. staminea* of the same age; but slightly larger *Mya* (10–30 mm, about 3–5 years) that had survived the earthquake were abundant. As was typical of most species of the bivalves at Olsen Bay after the earthquake, larger and older individuals of *Mya* (30–80 mm, about 5–10 years) were found at higher elevations, whereas smaller and younger individuals occurred mainly in the lower half of the vertical range.

The size and age distributions of *Macoma nasuta* and *Macoma inquinata* with elevation were similar to those of *Mya arenaria* and *Protothaca staminea*. Small to moderate numbers of small individuals occurred at lower elevations, and large numbers of intermediate-sized individuals (15–30 mm, about 3–8 years) at higher elevations. Large specimens of *M. inquinata* were scarce, whereas specimens of *M. nasuta* (30 to 65 mm long) were common.

Although reproduction by *Clinocardium nuttallii* has been at least moderately successful in some parts of Prince William Sound since the earthquake (Haven, 1971, this volume), this has not been true at Olsen Bay. The dominant length of individuals settled since the earthquake would have been less than 10–15 mm, but at Olsen Bay these sizes were scarce, and the 20–50-mm lengths predominated.

From these size and age comparisons, many of the bivalves do not appear to be experiencing much reproductive success, although sizable surviving preearthquake populations are evident.

Some of the intertidal mollusks have reproduced quite successfully since the earthquake. Littorines (*Littorina scutulata* and *L. sitkana*) appeared to have suffered little from the uplift; small individuals, obviously postearthquake settlers, were abundant. Small postearthquake individuals of *Mytilus edulis* were present and were especially abundant in the occasional dense beds on gravel beaches.

In conclusion, the distribution of old (preearthquake) and young (postearthquake) animals indicates an uplift of 3.0 to 3.5 ft in the Olsen Bay area. Differential susceptibility to the effects of uplift (increased exposure time and desiccation, greater temperature extremes), widths of vertical ranges, and adaptability to different substrates appear to account for most of the differences in survival of older organisms and success of young, within and between species. In view of the absence of either living or dead small individuals of some bivalves, the possibility of their existence elsewhere or of little reproductive success in the years immediately preceding the earthquake, should be considered in the interpretation of the data. Species with a wide vertical range generally fared better after the uplift than did those with a narrow range. Mortality varied widely between species, but within a species, mortality often appeared to be highest among the older individuals, not necessarily because of greater sensitivity to environmental changes, but because the higher tide levels often occupied by these older individuals were uplifted above the usual vertical range of the species. After the uplift, these were the individuals most likely to encounter marginal conditions for survival.

## ACKNOWLEDGMENTS

My special thanks go to Theodore R. Merrell, Jr., and Fredrik V. Thorsteinson, Bureau of Commercial Fisheries Biological Laboratory, Auke Bay, Alaska, for providing the opportunity to accomplish the fieldwork, and to the Auke Bay Laboratory staff for their support and assistance.

Jane Forsyth, Bowling Green State University, assisted in editing the manuscript, for which I am especially grateful. I gratefully acknowledge the efforts of the following people in assisting with the identification of the specimens: Cyril Berkeley, Pacific Biological Station, Fisheries Research Board of Canada (Polychaeta); E. L. Bousfield, National Museum of Canada (Amphipoda); Josephine F. L. Hart, Victoria, British Columbia (Decapoda); Myra Keen, Stanford University, and James McLean, Los Angeles County Museum (Mollusca); David Malcolm, Portland (Oregon) State College (Pseudoscorpionida); and Nathan Riser, Northeastern University (Nemertea).

I wish, also, to express my appreciation to Stoner Haven, Simon Fraser University, British Columbia, for his advice on special problems and to George Y. Harry, Jr., Bureau of Commercial Fisheries Biological Laboratory, Ann Arbor, Michigan, for his encouragement during the preparation of the manuscript.

## REFERENCES

Beanland, F. L., 1940. Sand and mud communities in the Dover estuary. *Journal of the Marine Biological Association of the United Kingdom,* 24, 589–617.

Bousfield, E. L., and J. D. Hubbard, 1968. New records of gammaridean amphipod crustaceans from the intertidal zone of Prince William Sound. Ottawa: National Museum of Canada, Natural History Paper 40. 11 p.

Haven, Stoner B., 1971. Effects of land-level changes on intertidal invertebrates, with discussion of postearthquake ecological succession *in* The Great Alaska Earthquake of 1964: Biology. NAS Pub. 1604. Washington: National Academy of Sciences.

Helle, John H., Richard S. Williamson, and Jack E. Bailey, 1964. Intertidal ecology and life history of pink salmon at Olsen Creek, Prince William Sound, Alaska. U.S. Fish and Wildlife Service Special Scientific Report–Fisheries 483. Washington: Government Printing Office. 26 p.

Plafker, George, 1969. Tectonics of the March 27, 1964, Alaska earthquake. U.S. Geological Survey Professional Paper 543-I. Washington: Government Printing Office. 74 p. Also *in* The Great Alaska Earthquake of 1964: Geology. NAS Pub. 1601. Washington: National Academy of Sciences, 1971.

Ricketts, Edward F., and Jack Calvin, 1962. Between Pacific tides. Third edition (revised by J. W. Hedgpeth). Stanford, California: Stanford University Press. 502 p.

U.S. Coast and Geodetic Survey, 1964. Tide tables, high and low water predictions, 1965, west coast North and South America, including the Hawaiian Islands. Washington: Government Printing Office. 224 p.

BONITA J. NEILAND
UNIVERSITY OF ALASKA

# Possible Effects of Land-Level Changes on Forest–Bog Tension Areas in South Coastal Alaska: A Preliminary Report

## INTRODUCTION

A study of the possible long-range effects of topographic changes on forest and bog (sometimes called "muskeg") in south coastal Alaska was begun in 1965. The project has two purposes: to ascertain the effects of changes in elevation and associated hydrological changes on relatively stable plant communities and on the tension areas between them; and to obtain information of potential value in interpretation of results of an earlier vegetational study south of the earthquake-affected region but in the same vegetational province. The "south coastal" area referred to here is that portion of coastal Alaska that extends from the southern border (with British Columbia) to northeastern Kodiak Island; it is a narrow border along the immediate coast and includes the islands of the Alexander Archipelago, those located in Prince William Sound, and those near northern Kodiak Island. The landward boundary of the region is the high ice-capped mountain ranges that parallel the coast; the area is largely coincident with the Pacific Coastal Forest (Cooper, 1957). Because this study is a long-term project, no results are yet available; the present report includes a description of the background of the project, the methods employed, the progress to date, and some preliminary observations.

## GENERAL VEGETATION OF THE REGION

### FOREST AND BOG

Two major forests are recognized by Cooper (1957) on the North Pacific coast of North America—the Pacific Coastal Forest and the Pacific Subalpine Forest. These two forests gradually merge toward their northern limits. My concern is with the vegetation near sea level, and further remarks will be restricted to the Pacific Coastal Forest or to the blend of the two forests. Although the entire area is desig-

ABSTRACT: A study was begun in 1965 to look for alterations in the relative positions of forest and bog vegetation types that may result from topographic and hydrologic changes due to differential land displacement during the 1964 earthquake. The study is an extension of work already in progress on forest–bog relationships in southeastern Alaska. Records were made of vegetation and substrate conditions along 91 transects established across forest–bog transitions in the Prince William Sound and Kodiak Island areas; similar data will be taken at intervals in the future. Observations indicate that rapid and temporary invasion by salt water during the tsunamis that followed the earthquake had only transient effects on bog vegetation.

FIGURE 1 General surface view of forest and bog vegetation on Perry Island, Alaska.

nated as one characterized by forest formations, bog and vegetation types intermediate to forest and bog occupy approximately as much land area in the Alaska portions of this Northwest American Province (Cooper's term) as does true upland forest.

The bogs occur in a wide variety of locations, surface characteristics, and stages of maturity. They include types that agree with the descriptions of Pearsall (1950), Sjors (1961), Tansley (1939), Gorham (1957), Jessen (1949), and Heusser (1960) for topogenous bogs, chiefly under the influence of topographically determined water accumulation; soligenous bogs, under the influence of moving surface water; and ombrogenous bogs, probably formed from both of the preceding types, but with their present surfaces under the influence of precipitation only with respect to mineral and water supplies. Such bogs are also referred to, in order, as flat or valley bogs, slope bogs, and raised and blanket bogs. Strictly topogenous bogs were not considered in this study.

Average precipitation in the region is high (Cordova, 18-year annual average, 89.9 in.; Whittier, 17-year annual average, 166.95 in.); there is no true dry season, and annual temperatures are cool (Cordova, 18-year July average, 53.1°F; Whittier, 14-year July average, 56.3°F. U.S. Weather Bureau, 1965). There seems to be a pronounced tendency toward bog formation by paludification, as bog mosses, which may become established in swampy areas, impede drainage, increase waterlogging of various sites, and spread over previously nonbog areas. (See Auer, 1930, and Heinselman, 1963, for discussion of this process.) The possible occurrence at present of such paludification is discussed later, but it apparently has gone on extensively in

the past. Only the steepest slopes or areas underlain by deep, permeable substrates have not been subjected to bog formation. Even on such sites, waterlogging and marsh or bog formation can be found along watercourses. The bogs are most common on slopes of 10 percent or less (Zach, 1950), but well-developed blanket bogs and slope-blanket mixtures occur on slopes of up to 20 percent (Neiland, 1971). Forest vegetation is best developed on moderate to steep slopes, and a decrease in its quality usually corresponds to a decrease in slope angle (Godman, 1952). The only exceptions occur on deep alluvial deposits or other well-drained sites, which are relatively uncommon. Figure 1 shows the two types of vegetation—forest and bog.

Vegetation types intermediate between the two extremes occupy fairly extensive areas and are increasingly common toward the southern part of the study region. Depending on various drainage features, such vegetation varies from narrow transitions between stands of forest and bog (see Figure 2) to fairly extensive and homogeneous stands many acres in size. Vegetation of the narrow transitions grades rapidly from open bog to "bog woodland," dominated by open stands of *Chamaecyparis nootkatensis* and tall erect *Pinus contorta;* to "bog forest" of more closed structure and dominated by mixtures of bog and forest species; and, finally, to closed upland forest. Any one of these may occur in fairly uniform stands wherever topographic gradients are not steep.

## PAST AND PRESENT RELATIONSHIPS BETWEEN FOREST AND BOG

Questions have been raised in the literature about the relationships between bog and forest under present and past

FIGURE 2   Closeup of transition between forest and bog vegetation, Perry Island, Alaska.

climatic conditions. Dachnowski-Stokes (1941) and Heusser (1960) describe peat profiles for many bogs of the southern coast and note that ligneous layers, which occur in nearly all of these, indicate former forest occupancy of the present bog sites.

More questions remain unanswered with respect to the contemporary status of bogs and forests of the area than with respect to their past relationships. Possible hypotheses are (a) change in either direction is so slow at present that the two types are, in effect, static; (b) forests are actively invading the majority of the bogs; and (c) bogs are continuing to develop and expand at the expense of the forest. Heusser (1952) states that "the forests that have reinvaded the muskegs are indicative of a certain amount of drying since 1750." Zach (1950), Lawrence (1958), and Cooper (1957), on the other hand, suggest that bogs, at least in some areas, either are spreading into the forest or are developing within the forests. Although the evidence is not conclusive, my own observations indicate that as long as present physiographic and climatic conditions remain fairly constant, many, if not most, of the present bog areas will remain stable.

## SOUTHEASTERN ALASKA PROJECT

To obtain more detailed and specific information on the contemporary forest–bog relationship than is possible from observation alone, studies of vegetation and substrate of the intermediate communities were begun in 1961, in conjunction with a more general investigation of the regional

vegetation of southeastern Alaska. Belt transects were run from open bog across the transitional areas and into closed forest on 36 sites. Information was obtained on relative species patterns, substrate conditions and stratification, and, through extensive collection of increment cores, rates and patterns of tree growth. At a few places, bog was clearly invading adjacent forest, and in a few others, forest was clearly invading adjacent bog, but for most of the stands, possible conclusions must await further analysis. Some of the transitions are permanently marked for long-range observation, but, unless there is a major rapid and widespread climatic shift, changes over a large area probably will be extremely slow. Any conclusions drawn from the study of the contemporary transitional areas will, of necessity, be based on circumstantial evidence.

## EARTHQUAKE AREA PROJECT

The 1964 earthquake provided an opportunity to study relationships between the forest and bog communities on a time scale much reduced from that previously possible. Although the coastal area affected by the earthquake is north and west of the southeastern Alaska area of the original study, the general vegetational types and most of the major species are continuous within the range of coastal coniferous forest. In the earthquake area, vertical displacements of large land areas range from about −6 ft to +33 ft (U.S. Coast and Geodetic Survey, 1966). Too little is known of the hydrology of the southern coast for accurate prediction of possible changes, and nothing is known of the hydrological relations of the Alaskan bogs. The assumption seems safe that local drainage patterns have been altered and that such alteration will be intensified as new patterns are established. As a much simplified working hypothesis, it is suggested that in areas of uplift, rates of loss of surface and immediately subsurface waters will be higher and that in areas of subsidence, rates of loss of these waters will be lower, compared with preearthquake conditions. Such topographical and hydrological changes occurring under a constant climate might be reflected by much the same vegetational changes as would result from certain climatic changes over a physiographically stable area.

If the positions of the present forest–bog tension areas (whether static or slowly successional) are related largely to the combined effects of climate and topography on the moisture regime, drastic changes in one major controlling factor might be reflected in relatively rapid changes in these positions. The changes, however, will undoubtedly be subtle and complex. Some of the communities, especially the ombrogenous bogs, may be too stable as communities for a relatively slight change in elevation to produce measurable vegetational responses. There seems to be a complete lack of either published or unpublished information on the effects of land-level changes on wholly terrestrial vegetation; for that reason alone, the problem seems worth investigating.

The entire bog surface or the entire forest undoubtedly will eventually reflect any alterations of soil-moisture supply, but the most rapid and conspicuous changes probably will occur in the forest–bog transitional areas. These tension areas, more open than the forests and more closed than the bogs, are the most readily accessible for invasion by seed or vegetative means by species of both types.

Ninety-one permanent transects were established across forest–bog transitions in areas of known vertical displacement, and various attributes of possible importance were recorded along these transects. The transects will be resampled at intervals in the future. In addition to the transect studies, floristic analyses were made and will continue to be made in forest and bog stands adjacent to the transects to determine their similarity to other stands in the coastal areas. All areas to be included in the study were established during the summer of 1965, except for those near Whittier, which were established a year later.

METHODS

Specific research sites were clustered in five major localities of differing land-level changes (Figure 3). Locality selection was based on considerations of spread along the total array of available vertical displacement, of time available for work, and of accessibility. The localities (designated by the nearest town or other named place) are Cordova (uplift about 6 ft);

southwestern Perry Island (uplift 1–2 ft); Shotgun Cove, near Whittier (subsidence about 6 ft); MacLeod Harbor, Montague Island (uplift about 30 ft); and northeastern Kodiak Island (subsidence 3–4 ft) (uplift and subsidence data from U.S. Coast and Geodetic Survey, 1966). The vegetation of Kodiak Island is not directly comparable with that of the other areas because of the very recent occupation of the area by *Picea sitchensis* (Griggs, 1934), the complete lack of forest vegetation in many nonbog sites, and the much greater mixture of tundra and boreal species. It was included because the subsidence area within the Pacific Coastal Forest was of much lesser extent than was the uplifted area and because the Kodiak Island area seemed more suitable than inland or western portions of the Kenai Peninsula.

Bog and forest stands selected for study in the five major localities showed no signs of human disturbance, and, as far as could be determined, no such disturbance is planned. Sites near the sea or near very large streams were selected, if other criteria were met, on the assumption that these sites might reflect changed drainage patterns sooner than would sites farther from such major drainages. Sites in a given major locality were placed as far apart as possible to minimize local effects. Tension areas studied were those between stands of well-developed blanket or slope bog and relatively well-drained forest. Because only terrestrial effects were to be studied, sites inundated by tsunamis, or seismic sea waves, were avoided as far as possible. All known sources of information on sea-wave occurrence were consulted, and sites were examined carefully for presence of water-deposited debris and possibly salt-killed vegetation. One Kodiak Island stand of known wave inundation, which showed extensive damage to vegetation but is not below the new high-tide mark, was included to provide some information on the effects of temporary saltwater invasion.

The basic transect unit was a line extending from open bog across the transitional area and into forest. This line was expanded into belts of various widths for sampling different attributes. Four or five transects were placed across the transition between each bog and forest "stand pair." The lines were located more or less evenly around a given bog, so that the transitions on the slope contour, those with the forest upslope from the bog, and those with the forest downslope from the bog were included. Narrow transitions in which the bog changed to forest in a short distance were selected if a choice was available. A steel tape, stretched tightly at a height of approximately 2 in. above the surface of the mosses, was used to locate the transect center line. If the topography was uneven, the line was held at the proper height with respect to the ground surface by steel ring pins; records were kept of the location of the pins. Some permanence in line location was achieved with wooden

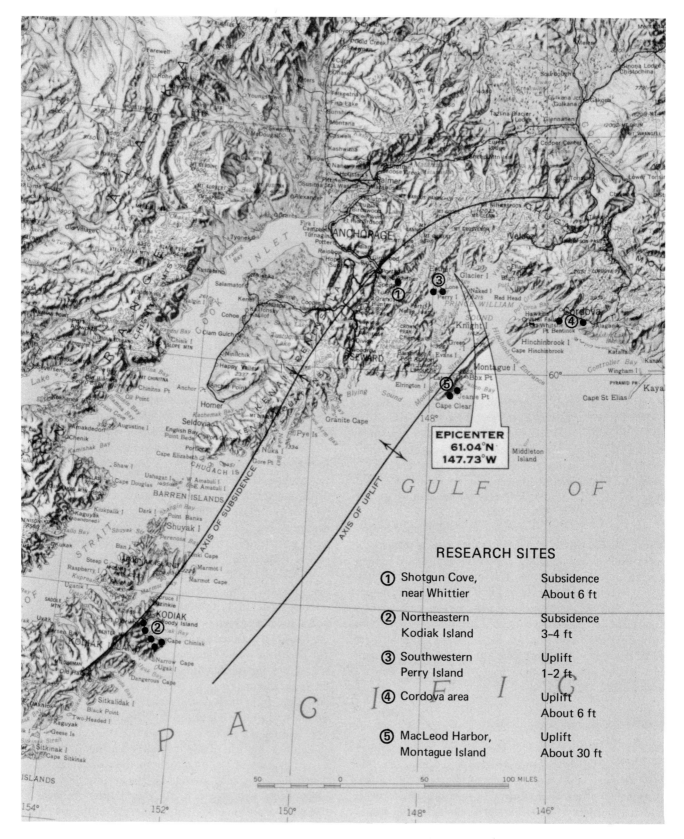

FIGURE 3　Specific research sites in five major localities with differing land-level changes (U.S. Geological Survey base map).

stakes, which were placed at the ends and in the center of the line. To ensure further that the lines could be relocated, even should some of the stakes be removed, a tree on either side of the line was blazed and the line ends were located by triangulation from these trees. Line lengths varied between 20 and 75 ft. In the few transitions that contained dense shrub growths, guide wires were fastened in place under the tape line to facilitate relocation of the line.

Qualitative observations were made along the lines to record the location of conspicuous vegetational changes, ponds, and other surface features. Quantitative records for the various life forms were made in belt transects of differing widths. Tree individuals more than 4 in. dbh (diameter breast height) that extended over the line were recorded by species and diameter. Standing dead trees within 5 ft of either side of the line were recorded by species, when possible, and by distance from and point of intercept with the line. Tree saplings (individuals between 1 ft in height and 4 in. dbh) were counted in contiguous 5-ft segments of a belt transect that was 2 ft wide and centered on the line. Shrubs were recorded by species and by the amount of line intercepted by each of the species. In the uncommon situation in which two or more shrub species were densely intermingled, the percentage that each contributed to the recorded shrub cover for that distance was estimated. Presence of dead shrub stems within 1 ft of the line was recorded. Tree seedlings (individuals between 1 in. and 1 ft in height) were counted in contiguous 2-ft segments of a belt transect that was 1 ft wide. Species of herbaceous plants, bryophytes, and lichens were recorded by presence in the 2-ft segments.

The surface topography of the transect was surveyed with hand-held equipment, and the general slope angles of the bog, forest, and transition area were recorded. Depth to sand, silt, clay, or gravel was determined along a line parallel with the transect line and approximately 4 ft away from it to provide a profile of the underlying sediment surface. A few peat and soil corings were made in each transition well away from any of the transects.

The transects were photographed in 1965, except for those on Kodiak Island and a few near Cordova. Continuous rain made photography impossible while I was in these areas in 1965; the Cordova photographs were completed in 1966. A fairly common type of transition is shown in Figure 1 and a view of the adjacent bog and forest in Figure 2.

The stand pairs of forest and bog were described in qualitative terms; species lists were compiled and were weighted by estimates of relative abundance. Data were entered on forms, which will allow rapid comparisons with material collected on subsequent samplings of these same transitions.

The following table summarizes the localities, sites, and numbers of stand pairs and transects dealt with during the two summers:

| Locality | Site | Stand Pairs | Transects |
|---|---|---|---|
| Cordova | Hartney Bay Road | 2 | 10 |
|  | Copper River Highway | 3 | 13 |
| Perry Island |  | 5 | 21 |
| Montague Island | MacLeod Harbor | 3 | 15 |
| Shotgun Cove |  | 4 | 16 |
| Kodiak Island | Cape Chiniak | 2 | 8 |
|  | Near Middle Bay | 2 | 8 |

## DISCUSSION

I did not begin the study of the earthquake-area communities until the summer of 1965, and I had been somewhat concerned that important modifications might be missed. Information from the southeastern Alaskan studies indicated, however, that the long-lived perennial plants that dominate these communities still would be easily detectable, at least in the uplifted areas, even if conditions had become unsuitable for them. It also had seemed probable that some stream cutting would be necessary before much surface-moisture change would occur. Even should the average amount of surface water increase immediately in the subsided areas, striking and immediate vegetational changes would not be expected. A certain amount of surface-moisture fluctuation normally must occur in response to annual fluctuations in precipitation and in rapidity of snowmelt, and the transitions must be tolerant of a fairly wide range of these conditions. Field observations supported these opinions; the transitions in the earthquake area in 1965 looked entirely "normal" when compared with those studied in southeastern Alaska.

The phytosociological analyses of bogs, forest, and transitions in the earthquake-affected area confirmed my original impressions (a) that the vegetation types, physical features, and community–environmental complexes are quite similar to those of southeastern Alaska and (b) that data from these two areas can be used to derive information about all of south coastal Alaska. The bogs of the Prince William Sound area differ in appearance from those of southeastern Alaska, but this difference is due chiefly to the absence of lodgepole pine; this pine is conspicuous in the southeastern bogs but apparently has little or no effect on the overall composition of these bogs. The only earthquake study locality departing strongly from these generalizations is Kodiak Island. Even there, the well-established spruce forests are similar in structure to Alaskan coast forests elsewhere. The bogs differ from those in southeastern and coastal south central Alaska in several important respects, some of which are probably related to the presence of thick ash layers from the 1912 eruption of Mount Katmai. The data from Kodiak Island will be useful chiefly (a) for a more detailed study of that specific area and of its response to subsidence and (b) for broad comparisons with stands and transitions in the other areas.

One conclusion that already seems warranted, with respect to the effects of rapid and temporary saltwater invasion of the bogs, is that any effects on the vegetation are probably transient. Areas obviously invaded by one or more tsunamis on Kodiak Island possessed conspicuous patches of blackened dead mosses and sedges, but in 1965 regrowth by the same species and apparently from some still living parts of the original plants was obvious. A line of water-deposited debris clearly marked a portion of a bog on Montague Island as having been invaded by seawater; careful checking of the invaded area and portions of the bog that could not have been invaded by seawater revealed no detectable differences between the two as far as the vegetation was concerned. This is not unexpected since oceanic bogs in other parts of the world are known to receive fairly large amounts of salt spray (Tolpa and Gorham, 1961; Sjors, 1961), and the vegetation would be assumed to be tolerant of higher salt levels than ordinarily occur on land. Because the waves retreated rapidly and the ground was frozen or snow-covered at the time of invasion, presumably little percolation occurred, and the amount of residual salt was small. The high precipitation during the summer of 1964 may have returned these areas to nearly normal salt concentrations.

The time of transect resampling cannot be estimated at present. After 1970, some of the transects will be inspected each year, and all will be resampled when there is reason to think that useful information might be obtained. Trees in many of the transitional areas eventually will be bored and the ring patterns analyzed for possible growth correlations with the occurrence of the earthquake.

## SUMMARY

An investigation of forest and bog relationships was conducted in southeastern Alaska between 1960 and 1964. Occurrence of the 1964 earthquake in areas containing the same general vegetation types led to the hypothesis that differential land-level changes might cause modifications in the tension areas between forest and bog that would be of interest in themselves and might be useful in interpretation of some of the data already collected from southeastern Alaska. A project begun in 1965 was designed to detect and measure any such modifications. Ninety-one permanent transects were established across forest–bog transitions in the Prince William Sound area and on Kodiak Island. The bog and forest stands adjacent to these transitions have been described qualitatively, and various attributes of the vegetation, the substrate, and the topography were recorded along the transects. The transects will be resampled at intervals to detect shifts in the relative position of the two major vegetation types, should such occur.

## ACKNOWLEDGMENTS

The project was supported chiefly by the National Science Foundation, Grant GB-3503; study for 1 month in 1966 was supported by McIntire-Stennis funds (U.S. Department of Agriculture, Cooperative State Research Service).

Appreciation for assistance during the project is expressed to the Comstock brothers of Perry Island, Alaska; to Mr. John Ireland of Whittier, Alaska; to Dr. William Meehan, Mr. Benjamin Ballenger, and Mr. Alfred Thomas of the Alaska Department of Fish and Game, Kodiak; and to Mr. K. A. Neiland, of the Alaska Department of Fish and Game, Fairbanks.

## REFERENCES

Auer, Vaino, 1930. Peat bogs of southeastern Canada. Geological Survey of Canada Memoir 162. Ottawa: Canadian Department of Mines. 32 p.

Cooper, W. S., 1957. Vegetation of the Northwest American Province. Proceedings of the Eighth Pacific Scientific Congress, Quezon City, November 16–28, 1953, v. 4, p. 133–138.

Dachnowski-Stokes, A. P., 1941. Peat resources in Alaska. U.S. Department of Agriculture Technical Bulletin No. 769. Washington: Government Printing Office. 84 p.

Godman, R. M., 1952. A classification of the climax forest of southeastern Alaska. *Journal of Forestry,* 50 (No. 6), 435–438.

Gorham, Eville, 1957. The development of peat lands. *Quarterly Review of Biology,* 32 (No. 2), 145–166.

Griggs, R. F., 1934. The edge of the forest in Alaska and the reasons for its position. *Ecology,* 15 (No. 4), 80–96.

Heinselman, M. L., 1963. Forest sites, bog processes and peatland types in the glacial Lake Agassiz region, Minnesota. *Ecological Monographs,* 33 (No. 4), 327–374.

Heusser, C. J., 1952. Pollen profiles from southeastern Alaska. *Ecological Monographs,* 22 (No. 4), 331–352.

Heusser, C. J., 1960. Late-Pleistocene environments of North Pacific North America. New York: American Geographical Society Special Publication 35. 308 p.

Jessen, Knud, 1949. Studies in the late Quaternary deposits and flora-history of Ireland. *Proceedings of the Royal Irish Academy,* 52, section B, 85–200.

Lawrence, Donald B., 1958. Glaciers and vegetation in southeastern Alaska. *American Scientist,* 46 (No. 2), 89–112.

Neiland, B. J., 1971. The forest-bog complex of southeast Alaska. *Vegetatio,* 22 (No. 1/3), 1–65.

Pearsall, W. H., 1950. Mountains and moorland. London: Collins. 312 p.

Sjors, Hugo, 1961. Surface patterns in boreal peatlands. *Endeavour,* 20 (No. 80), 217–224.

Tansley, A. G., 1939. The British Islands and their vegetation. Cambridge: Cambridge University Press. 980 p.

Tolpa, Stanislaw, and Eville Gorham, 1961. The ionic composition of waters from three Polish bogs. *Journal of Ecology,* 49 (No. 1), 127–134.

U.S. Coast and Geodetic Survey, 1966. The Prince William Sound, Alaska, earthquake of 1964 and aftershocks. Fergus J. Wood, editor. Volume I: Operational phases of the Coast and Geodetic Survey program in Alaska for the period March 27 to December 31, 1964. Washington: Government Printing Office. 263 p.

U.S. Weather Bureau, 1965. Climatic summary of the United States, 1951-1960, Supplement, Alaska. Climatography of the United States, No. 86-43. Washington: Government Printing Office. 67 p.

Zach, Lawrence W., 1950. A northern climax, forest or muskeg? *Ecology,* 31 (No. 2), 304–306.

# III
# EFFECTS ON FISH
# AND SHELLFISH

# Introduction

Alaska's most important industry depends on the fish and shellfish resources of the state. For the period 1962-1966 the average annual landings of fish and shellfish were worth $62 million to the fishermen of Alaska. Because of the importance of the fisheries to the state, the possible adverse effects of the earthquake on these resources and the damage to fishing vessels and processing plants caused great concern. The potential impact on the economy of Alaska was so significant that state and federal agencies immediately began to assess the damage to the resource and to the industry. The Alaska Department of Fish and Game conducted the state program, and the Bureau of Commercial Fisheries Biological Laboratory at Auke Bay carried out the federal program. Within a few days after the earthquake, a general assessment of damage had been made, and areas of possible critical damage to the resource had been indicated. This assessment, together with subsequent more extensive surveys by the Alaska Department of Fish and Game, resulted in the comprehensive report by Noerenberg, documenting the earthquake damage to the fisheries and fishing industry of Alaska.

The preliminary surveys yielded no evidence of damage to the marine fish and shellfish resources such as shrimp, king crab, or halibut. Consequently, no extensive biological studies of earthquake effects on these resources were undertaken.

The fishery of greatest value to the Alaska economy is that for salmon, and of the five species of Alaska salmon, the two of greatest importance are pink salmon (*Oncorhynchus gorbuscha*) and sockeye salmon (*Oncorhynchus nerka*). These two species contributed about 74 percent of the total value of all Alaska salmon for the period 1962-1966.

Sockeye salmon ascend river systems with lakes and spawn in the lake tributaries or just offshore from lake beaches, usually many miles from the sea. Seismic waves and changes in land elevation, therefore, probably had no appreciably harmful effect on this species. Aerial surveys of the major tributaries used by sockeye salmon in the Bristol Bay area, which is by far the most important sockeye spawning region of Alaska, yielded no evidence of landslides or snowslides that might have blocked salmon migration routes. All streams were running clear and at normal levels in the period immediately following the earthquake. Considerable ice scouring resulting from earthquake action was evident on lake beaches, and some beach spawning areas of sockeye salmon may have been disturbed; most lake spawning, however, occurs at depths not likely to be affected by ice action. Because there appeared to be little damage to the sockeye salmon resource, no extensive studies of earthquake effects were planned for this species.

Unlike sockeye salmon, pink and chum salmon (*O. keta*) usually spawn in short coastal streams, often in the intertidal reaches of these streams. The greatest potential damage to the salmon resource of Alaska was in the Prince William Sound area, where 50 to 75 percent of the pink and chum salmon spawn in intertidal zones of streams. Changes in elevation caused by the earthquake could have drastically affected the spawning environment of salmon in these zones. Research on the effects of the earthquake on salmon production was therefore concentrated in this region; two major papers resulted from these studies (see the papers by Thorsteinson and others and by Roys). The altered intertidal environment also affected clams of Prince William Sound, and Baxter's paper summarizes these effects.

Although there was no extensive damage to the salmon resource in the Kodiak Island area, tsunamis surging into some lowland lakes after the earthquake and high tides regularly washing into other depressed lowland lakes caused interesting changes in the environment of lakes and in the fish production from them. These changes are documented in the paper by Marriott and Spetz.

The adverse effect of the earthquake on the fish and shellfish resource of Prince William Sound will be felt for several years—at least until the intertidal zones and streams once again become stabilized. The recovery of this resource will be documented by the state and federal fishery agencies by means of research projects in the area.

GEORGE Y. HARRY, JR.
National Marine Fisheries Service
National Oceanic and Atmospheric Administration

WALLACE H. NOERENBERG
ALASKA DEPARTMENT OF FISH AND GAME

# Earthquake Damage to Alaskan Fisheries*

ABSTRACT: The Alaska earthquake of 1964 caused extensive physical damage and economic loss to the state's fisheries and related enterprises. Coastal streams and lakes were inundated by tsunamis that destroyed freshwater habitats by intruding salt water, destroying outlet spits, moving gravel in spawning streams, and silting lake and stream spawning areas. Land subsidence and uplift destroyed intertidal salmon-spawning areas and clam beds and created new spawning habitat in places where land subsidence drowned out preearthquake impassable falls and velocity barriers. The subsidence and uplift also temporarily dewatered streams and lakes because of fissures, landslides, and land tilting.

Tsunamis, together with land subsidence and uplift, destroyed or extensively damaged fishery facilities. In the Kodiak area, where 14 canneries were affected—one at Shearwater Bay was completely destroyed—losses to fish-processing facilities were estimated at $3,900,000, losses of products at $200,000, and losses of vessels at $2,400,000. In Cook Inlet and on the Kenai Peninsula, effects varied from minor damage at Snug Harbor to complete destruction at Seward. Travel on the Kenai Peninsula was restricted, and sport fishing there was halved; in the Seward area it was completely eliminated in the early season.

In the Prince William Sound area, both uplift and subsidence affected the salmon-spawning environment. Uplift caused silting and gravel shifts in such previously stabilized areas as Hinchinbrook and Montague islands and altered stream-flow velocities, which moved the salmon spawning areas downstream in the intertidal zone. Subsidence in some areas created new intertidal spawning riffles upstream in larger bed gravels. Uplift also produced high mortality in clam habitats in Prince William Sound and Copper-Bering River areas. In Prince William Sound, nearly half the clam habitat was lost and the number of accessible clams above 3-ft tide level was reduced about a third.

In the Copper River area, the habitats were changed by sloughing and sedimentation that covered shoreline salmon spawning areas with silt and debris, as well as by tide action that pushed sand and gravel into many stream mouths so as to partly or totally block fish movement. Access routes to commercial-fishing and waterfowl-hunting areas were lost when sloughs shallowed from loss of tidal action.

*Compiled from works of authors listed in the Acknowledgments at the end of this paper.

At Valdez the loss of two canneries and the dockside business area as a result of a tsunami and underwater landslide was estimated at more than half a million dollars. Nineteen small vessels and 15 purse seiners, valued at $338,000, as well as 76 small sport-fishing boats worth some $100,000, were known to have been lost. Although lakes did not appear to have been changed in the area, loss of bridges, housing and eating facilities along highways temporarily affected the sport fishery and related tourism.

## INTRODUCTION

The Alaska earthquake of 1964 seriously disrupted Alaska's fisheries in the Kodiak, Cook Inlet, and Prince William Sound areas. Land uplift and subsidence, in conjunction with tsunami action, dewatered lakes and streams and caused extensive silting. The changes in land level also altered the spawning and migrational habitats of salmon and destroyed eggs and fry; they destroyed intertidal clam beds and damaged or destroyed harbor and shore fishery facilities and related business, including vessels and gear, docks, canneries, and processing plants. Sport-fishing activities and related tourism in the affected areas were temporarily restricted. The immediate economic losses incurred by the state's fisheries from the disaster amounted to millions of dollars; the long-term ecological effects will not be fully evident for many years as the altered biological habitats become stabilized.

## KODIAK AND AFOGNAK ISLANDS

### SUMMARY OF OBSERVATIONS

In the Kodiak–Afognak area (Figure 1), the earthquake brought major changes to some of the spawning and rearing streams of pink (*Oncorhynchus gorbuscha*), chum (*O. keta*), sockeye (*O. nerka*), and coho (*O. kisutch*) salmon and also to many low-level lakes.

The shaking caused by the earthquake itself resulted in only minor changes; the major damage was done by land subsidence and tsunamis. The shaking motion compacted some gravels on lake beaches that were used for spawning by sockeye salmon, but it seems unlikely that this compaction appreciably harmed the spawning or rearing areas. No landslide damage to creeks or resultant stream dewatering was noted immediately after the earthquake.

*Alaska Department of Fish and Game*

FIGURE 1 Reference map to Kodiak and Afognak islands.

The tsunamis brought major destruction only to the eastern coast of Kodiak and Afognak islands. In Chiniak Bay, Kodiak Island, a series of five major waves was recorded between 6 p.m. and 12 midnight. These waves were 20–22 ft above the existing tide level. Because of land subsidence and the incoming tide level, however, the fifth wave reached a height corresponding to a preearthquake level of 37 ft above mean lower low water. The previous high-tide line in this area had been just under 11 ft above mean lower low water.

The tsunamis inundated coastal streams and lakes with considerable force in many areas. This action deposited salt water in numerous lakes or washed away the outlet spits, destroying or drastically altering these lakes as freshwater habitat. The action within the streams, which was similar to that of extreme flooding conditions, was particularly critical because it came when pink salmon fry were just emerging from the gravel or entering the creek-mouth estuaries.

Land subsidence of about 5 ft on Afognak Island and the north end of Kodiak Island caused the major changes in salmon spawning habitat. Lesser changes were noted on the west side of Kodiak Island, and the rest of the Kodiak Island group was unaffected. In the subsided areas, permanent damage to spawning and rearing habitat occurred mainly in the intertidal zone and to a lesser degree in former freshwater portions of streams used by pink and chum salmon; parts of streams used by sockeye and coho salmon were little affected. The new intertidal areas formed by subsidence of stream mouths have a steeper gradient and hence are much smaller than the former intertidal zone, which is now largely submerged. Intertidal zones in the Kodiak-Afognak area are not the most important areas for pink and chum salmon spawning, and the major pink and sockeye salmon areas in the southern half of Kodiak Island were not affected; overall damage to the Kodiak fishery therefore was minor.

Sport fishing around Kodiak was temporarily reduced because of damage to roads. Many lagoon-type lakes with significant potential for sport fishing were changed, but none of the principal lakes now used by sportsmen and kept stocked with fish was seriously damaged. The only important damage to stream fishing was the loss of former stream-mouth fishing sites in Chiniak Bay and the Afognak River. A more detailed description of the immediate and long-term effects of tsunamis and land subsidence on two lakes of Kodiak Island is given by Marriott and Spetz (1971, this volume).

## TECHNIQUES USED IN SURVEYING EARTHQUAKE EFFECTS

Extensive aerial and ground surveys of the Kodiak and Afognak islands area were performed using the following methods:

1. Observations, fish counts, and measurements.
    a. Extent of driftwood deposited upstream and around lake shores.
    b. Dead or dying shoreline and aquatic vegetation.
    c. Slides, fissures, gravel shifting, and silting.
    d. Measurement of length of old and new intertidal zones. For the purpose of this report, the intertidal areas suitable for salmon are between the +5-ft and +10-ft tide levels. Levels were determined from tides at the time of observation, and measurements were made from these points. Old tide lines were established from visual observations and previous knowledge, or from reference points previously established.
    e. Dead and live fish counts and estimates.
2. Egg counts.
    Live and dead egg counts in the new intertidal areas were compared with those from studies conducted in previous years. Random segments of the spawning gravels were excavated hydraulically as in the past.
3. Economic studies.
    Economic losses were determined by personal contact with owners and superintendents of vessels and canneries where fishing and processing had been suspended.

## SPECIFIC OBSERVATIONS

Streams in the Kodiak–Afognak islands area were intensively studied during the 1964 field season to determine the effects of the earthquake on salmon production (Table 1). Some streams, such as Malina Creek, Seal Bay Creek, Baumanns Creek, Little River, Spiridon River, and Sulua Creek, exhibited little or no change.

The Olds and American rivers were extensively damaged. The Olds River, observed from July to October, was the main spawning stream in Kalsin Bay and was the most changed of any river on Kodiak Island. The tsunami deposited driftwood more than 1 mi inland in the vicinity of the river and probably killed many pink salmon fry emerging from the gravel in the river estuary. The lower riverbed was covered by salt water at most tide stages, and heavy siltation had taken place. Approximately 4,500 ft of the river, including three major spawning riffles, were lost as spawning areas. In future years during extreme low-water levels, the entire run of Olds River pink salmon may be forced to spawn in about 600 ft of stream containing only one good area—an intertidal riffle about 130 ft long and 80 ft wide. Kalsin Bay before and after the earthquake is shown in Figures 2 and 3.

In the American River (Middle Bay area), observed from July to October, tsunamis carried driftwood 1½ mi inland, up to 1,000 yd above the old bridge, which was washed out; they probably caused high mortality over this distance among emerging pink salmon fry. High tides of 9 ft now

TABLE 1  Kodiak–Afognak Islands Streams Affected by the Earthquake

| Streams | Average Number of Salmon Spawners[a] | Loss of Stream Spawning Area[b] | | Remarks |
|---|---|---|---|---|
| | | Intertidal Zone | Freshwater Zone | |
| Paramanof Creek | 8,500 | Unknown | Unknown | Slight tsunami action |
| Danger Bay creeks | 7,900 | 1,700 ft | 865 ft | Little tsunami action |
| Perenosa creeks | 18,000 | Extensive | Extensive | Major tsunami action |
| Marka Creek | 13,000 | 1,800 ft | 2,600 ft | Minor tsunami effect |
| Back Bay creeks | Unknown | Unknown | 605 ft | Tsunami-deposited ash on tidal area |
| Afognak River | 20,500 | 3,000–4,000 ft | 825 ft | Considerable tsunami change |
| Elbow Creek | 12,050 | Unknown | Unknown | Light tsunami change |
| Kizhuyak River | 11,100 | Unknown | Unknown | Moderate tsunami change |
| Terror River | 41,000 | Considerable | Considerable | No tsunami effect noted |
| Uganik River | 67,000 | Considerable | Considerable | No tsunami effect noted |
| Zachar River | 61,750 | Considerable | Considerable | No tsunami effect noted |
| Kaguyak Creek | 25,250 | Considerable | Minor | Considerable tsunami change |
| Kaiugnak Creek | 13,000 | Considerable | Some | Heavy fry loss in tsunamis |
| Barling River | 30,000 | Considerable | Considerable | Heavy fry loss; tsunamis deposited driftwood for ½ mi |
| Kiliuda creeks | 16,350 | 3,000–5,000 ft | 1,900 ft | Little tsunami effect noted |
| Eagle Harbor Creek | 9,500 | 500 ft | 850 ft | Some fry loss, tsunami action |
| Saltery Cove Creek | 44,000 | 1,040 ft | 570 ft | Fry loss possibly severe |
| Monashka Creek | 4,550 | Unknown | Considerable | Heavy tsunami action; spawning area will be damaged by subsidence |
| Anton Larsen Creek | 2,850 | Unknown | Extensive | Important spawning area lost |
| Olds River | 32,800 | Considerable | 4,500 ft | Heaviest tsunami damage noted; heavy fry loss |
| American River | 16,900 | Considerable | Considerable | Heavy fry loss |

[a]Calculated from peak escapement estimates during the past 12 years.
[b]Linear measurements.

bring seawater to the bridge site, but the entire portion below the bridge was not an important spawning area. The good spawning habitat began at the first riffle above the bridge. Sampling of this riffle in the autumn of 1964 produced less than one fourth of the overall stream average, although total egg recoveries were much above normal because the number of spawning fish was unusually large. For about 400 ft above the riffle, much gravel had been removed from the bed and banks of the streams, and 97 percent of the eggs recovered in this part of the river were dead; fortunately this stretch of the stream is not a major spawning area.

ECONOMIC IMPACT

The economy of the area was dealt a severe blow by damage or loss of gear, fishing vessels, and fish-processing facilities. Tsunamis and the effects of subsidence were the major causes of destruction of gear and vessels. These waves damaged or destroyed 14 canneries in the area, one of which, Kadiak Fisheries at Shearwater Bay, was completely destroyed.

The tsunamis also completely destroyed Kodiak's Alaska Packers Association clam and king crab plant, Alaska King Crab's crab plant, Martin's King Crab plant, and Ouzinkie Packing Company's plant at Ouzinkie. In addition, considerable damage was sustained at Kodiak by King Crab, Inc. (crab, salmon, shrimp), and the Alaska Ice and Storage plant (cold storage: halibut, salmon, crab). (See Table 2.) Approximately $200,000 worth of processed products were lost because of the tsunamis. Subsidence caused the immediate or ultimate loss of canneries and their facilities, which have since been inundated by the higher tides (Table 3). Rebuilding of canneries has required considerable land refill, particularly in the channel area near the town of Kodiak. This requirement has placed an additional financial burden on plant owners. The economic loss of fishing vessels damaged or destroyed on Kodiak Island was nearly $2½ million. Because landmarks used by vessel operators in the area were lost, several vessels were damaged or sunk in collisions with submerged obstacles. The approximate values of fishing vessels destroyed are listed in Table 4. Total losses are shown in Table 5.

*G. C. Ameigh*

FIGURE 2  Kalsin Bay before the land subsided.

*Alaska Department of Fish and Game*

FIGURE 3  Kalsin Bay showing tidal infiltration after earthquake.

The effects of the earthquake brought the processing of shellfish to a standstill in the Kodiak area in 1964. The approximate loss in king crab was $275,000 to fishermen, and the loss to the packing industry was estimated at $687,000, on the basis of previous years' catches for the same period.

The capacity of the salmon industry was reduced by severe damage to the San Juan cannery at Uganik, which was unable to function in 1964, a bumper salmon year during which the facility could have operated at capacity. This two-line cannery could have processed 150,000 cases of 48 1-lb cans—about 2,700,000 fish. The approximate wholesale value of the production to the industry would have been $3,375,000, and the approximate value to the fishermen would have been $750,000.

TABLE 2 Approximate Value of Kodiak Area Cannery Losses and Damage

| Cannery | Location | Type | Value |
|---|---|---|---|
| *Canneries destroyed* | | | |
| Kadiak Fisheries | Shearwater Bay | Salmon | $ 500,000 |
| Alaska Packers Association | Kodiak | Clam, king crab | 750,000 |
| Alaska King Crab | Kodiak | King crab | 500,000 |
| Martin's King Crab | Kodiak | King crab | 60,000 |
| Ouzinkie Packing Co. | Ouzinkie | King crab | 300,000 |
| Subtotal | | | $2,110,000 |
| *Canneries damaged* | | | |
| King Crab, Inc. | Kodiak | Salmon, crab, and shrimp | $ 100,000 |
| Alaska Ice and Storage | Kodiak | Halibut, crab, and shrimp | 400,000 |
| Subtotal | | | $ 500,000 |
| Total | | | $2,610,000 |

TABLE 4 Approximate Value of Kodiak Area Fishing Vessel Losses

| Vessels Lost | Port | Loss Category | Value ($) |
|---|---|---|---|
| 13 | Kodiak | Total loss | 266,500 |
| 19 | Kodiak | Aground or swamped | 700,000 |
| Subtotal | | | 966,500 |
| Value of vessels lost or severely damaged on remainder of Kodiak Island | | | 1,000,000 |
| Value of miscellaneous minor damage to vessels on entire island | | | 500,000 |
| Subtotal | | | 1,500,000 |
| Total | | | 2,466,500 |

TABLE 5 Total of Kodiak Area Fishery Losses from All Causes

| | |
|---|---|
| Cannery losses | $2,610,000 |
| Losses due to land subsidence | $1,340,000 |
| Vessel losses | $2,466,500 |
| Total | $6,416,500 |

TABLE 3 Kodiak Area Facilities Lost Because of Land Subsidence

| Company and Location | Type | Loss | Value ($) |
|---|---|---|---|
| Washington Fish and Oyster, Port Williams | Halibut, crab, salmon | Complete | 500,000 |
| Wakefield Fisheries, Port Wakefield | King crab | Complete | 500,000 |
| West Point Cannery Co., Uganik Bay | Salmon | Complete | 80,000 |
| Kadiak Fisheries, Port Bailey | Salmon | Ways destroyed | 30,000 |
| San Juan Fishing and Packing Co., Uganik Bay | Salmon | Ways and dock level[a] | 75,000 |
| Parks Canning Co., Uyak Bay | Salmon | Ways and dock level[a] | 75,000 |
| Alaska Packers Association, Larsen Bay | Salmon | Dock level[a] | 80,000 |
| Total | | | 1,340,000 |

[a]Level unsatisfactorily low following subsidence.

The effects of subsidence and tsunamis on the salmon-spawning streams and sport-fishing lakes were studied from July to November, 1964. Records of economic losses from damage to the commercial-fishing fleet, local canneries, and cold-storage plants were compiled in April, and the losses were further documented during the commercial-fishing season.

## COOK INLET–KENAI PENINSULA

### SUMMARY OF OBSERVATIONS

An evaluation of the Cook Inlet–Kenai Peninsula fishery was begun in April 1964 and continued to October, when this report was begun. The area includes fishery habitat extending from Cape Resurrection in Blying Sound on the east, to Cape Douglas at the entry to Cook Inlet on the west, then north along Cook Inlet, including Knik and Turnagain arms (Figure 4).

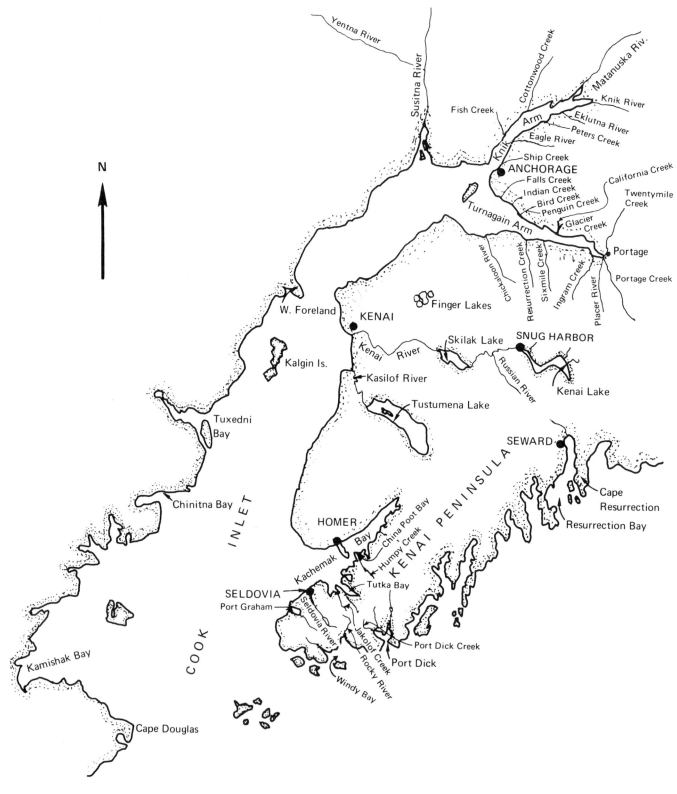

*Alaska Department of Fish and Game*

FIGURE 4   Upper Cook Inlet and the Kenai Peninsula.

In Cook Inlet and on the Kenai Peninsula the earthquake affected the fishery by causing land subsidence, tsunami action, and dewatering of freshwater habitat. Landmass subsidence occurred along most of the coastline and took two different forms: actual sinking of the entire landmass and compaction of soil material. Subsidence appears to have been greatest in the southern portion of the Kenai Peninsula. The overall effect of the sinking was a direct loss of intertidal salmon-spawning areas in streams from Kachemak Bay to Port Dick and in Turnagain Arm.

The tsunamis caused extensive damage in Port Dick and Resurrection Bay but very little along most of the shore of Cook Inlet. Two kinds of tsunami damage to fishery resources can be distinguished: movement of gravel in streams with resultant loss of fry and loss of freshwater habitat by saltwater intrusion.

Dewatering and the resultant loss of freshwater habitat were noted at three places in Cook Inlet: The Kasilof River slowed to a trickle for an undertermined time following the earthquake; Ship Creek at Anchorage stopped flowing for an estimated 18 hours; and two of the Finger Lakes on the Kenai Peninsula lost water at a rate of several inches per month.

The amount of damage to fishing-industry facilities varied; facilities at Snug Harbor were almost untouched, while those at Seward were completely destroyed. Homer and Seldovia facilities were jeopardized because land subsidence left them within reach of high tides. The fishing industry at Kenai and Ninilchik appears to have been unaffected.

Sport fishing decreased noticeably because of highway damage and disruption of other means of travel. The sport fishery on the Kenai Peninsula in 1964 decreased to about one-half its volume for the previous year, with an attendant loss to the peninsula's economy.

## TECHNIQUES USED IN SURVEYING EARTHQUAKE EFFECTS

Two biologists were employed specifically to investigate the effects of the earthquake. When possible, they observed each stream on foot to determine what physical changes had resulted from the earthquake. Streams that were inaccessible on foot were observed from aircraft. The Susitna River drainage was surveyed mainly by air, but some boat trips were made in the course of routine observations during the summer.

On the Kenai Peninsula, data on intertidal changes and tsunami effects were obtained by personal observation and through direct communication with biologists familiar with particular streams and areas. The amount of intertidal spawning area lost was either estimated from past high-tide marks or measured from known histories of the streams.

Information on lake-level lowering was obtained by using measuring stakes and by monthly observations. The dewatering of the Kasilof River was observed and reported by a biologist immediately after the earthquake.

Residents who were familiar with local conditions pertaining to land subsidence and clam beaches were interviewed.

A study of stream-gravel movement and substrata freezing that had been initiated in December 1963 made it possible to determine causes of salmon-egg and fry mortality resulting from the earthquake. Perforated ping-pong balls and sealed water-filled glass vials in vertical columns had been buried in the spawning gravel. The balls were painted six different colors to indicate burial depth. The vials were placed at the top and bottom of each ping-pong-ball column to determine depths of freezing. When these columns were examined immediately after the earthquake, broken vials were taken as indicators that freezing conditions had occurred, and missing balls indicated that the gravels had moved.

A study was also under way at the time of the earthquake to determine the abundance of preemergent pink and chum salmon fry in 10 streams. This study was expanded in an effort to determine what additional mortality the earthquake had caused. Sampling was done with a hydraulic pump that washed the fry out of the gravel and into a wire collecting screen.

Pertinent data and photographs to supplement the data on the fishery resources gathered by field investigations were obtained by a biologist who contacted people who had been in the area immediately after the earthquake. In Anchorage most of the information was obtained from personal interviews tailored to their fields of interest. For example, employees of the U.S. Geological Survey were asked for data on siltation and change in stream and lake water levels; the U.S. Coast and Geodetic Survey was asked for information on tidal changes; the U.S. fish and Wildlife Service was asked to provide published material and personal observations; the U.S. Army, Bureau of Land Management, U.S. Forest Service, and Air Photo Tech, Inc., were asked for aerial photographs of areas changed by the earthquake; and bush pilots were requested to give personal observations on earthquake-caused terrain changes. As available data were gathered, other sources of information were sought from each contact.

## SPECIFIC OBSERVATIONS

Biologists who conducted stream surveys in northern Cook Inlet reported that minor changes had occurred from Cape Douglas through the Susitna River drainage. Landslides were observed on the Susitna, Kashwitna, Chulitna, and Talachulitna rivers, Alexander Creek, and Beluga Lake (Figure 5). Landslides in Cook Inlet had occurred on bluffs near Three-mile Creek, Point Possession, and in the much-publicized

FIGURE 5   Typical landslide in the Cook Inlet area. This one is on the Susitna River about 5 mi above the mouth of Yentna River.

*Alaska Department of Fish and Game*

and spectacular Turnagain area. Numerous fissures were observed near the mouths of the Susitna and Knik rivers.

Streams between the Knik River and Bird Creek sustained little damage from subsidence other than some loss of intertidal spawning streams. One interesting observation was that the lower part of Ship Creek had been dry for 18 hours immediately after the earthquake.

As a result of land subsidence in the Portage area, high tides now extend 1–2 mi farther upstream, resulting in a considerable loss of freshwater habitat. Two small unnamed lakes, with a total of 12 acres near the mouth of Kern Creek, were completely destroyed by silting. These lakes had been popular for Dolly Varden (*Salvelinus malma*) fishing. About 1.5 mi of Twentymile Creek were lost to salmon, trout, and smelt (*Thaleichthys pacificus*) spawning. In addition, a parking area used by smelt fishermen, which had accommodated as many as 600 cars, was no longer usable. Table 6 summarizes the upper Cook Inlet streams that were surveyed and the changes, if any, that had occurred.

On the south side of Turnagain Arm, mud deposits encroached on mouths of streams. A great change in the character of these intertidal areas was observed in Ingram, Sixmile, and Resurrection creeks over a 2-month period. Ingram Creek lost an undetermined amount of freshwater habitat because of land subsidence accompanied by mud deposits up to the new high-tide elevation. An area of about 2,000 yd² of gravel previously used by pink salmon was lost under mud deposits at the mouth of Sixmile Creek. The mouth of Resurrection Creek had subsided about 3.5 ft, and an estimated 1,500 yd² of pink salmon spawning area were lost. In August 1964, pink and chum salmon were observed spawning in those three streams above the areas no

longer suitable for habitat. However, another series of observations in October revealed increased mud deposits in the areas used for spawning. An undetermined amount of pink salmon spawning area was affected in the Chickaloon River because of subsidence and resultant mud deposits.

The Finger Lakes, located near the Swanson River road on the Kenai Moose Range, are spring-fed, separated by glacial moraines, but with marshy connecting areas. Sloughing on the sides of these moraines had toppled many trees into the lakes. Field observations on October 26, 1964, indicated that water levels had gradually lowered about 5 ft. Measuring stakes had been placed in two lakes when they were initially surveyed in the fall of 1964 to record water-level fluctuation. By these means it was possible to record the dewatering that appeared to be taking place in these lakes, possibly through fissures in the lake bottom; the cause might also have been restriction of incoming spring water by the compaction of the stratum through which it flows.

These lakes range from 50 to 100 ft in depth and are spring fed; there was therefore no problem of oxygen depletion. However, spawning areas may have been lost to the large numbers of resident char. No streams enter or leave these lakes; the fish may therefore have spawned along the gravelly shores that are now exposed (Figure 6).

At Kenai Lake the earthquake had initiated a large wave that traveled the length of the lake and caused considerable ice shift. Figure 7 illustrates ice movement on the shores at the mouth of the Trail River in Kenai Lake and the barking of trees by lake ice to a height of 20 ft. Sockeye salmon spawn in unknown numbers in the shallow shore water of the lake. Thus, preemergent salmon fry along the shore may have been destroyed by the scouring effect of the shifting

TABLE 6  Streams Surveyed in Upper Cook Inlet

| Drainage | Stream or Tributary | Changes Observed |
|---|---|---|
| Turnagain Arm | | Overall subsidence ranging from 3.5 ft at Anchorage to 5 ft at Portage |
| | Falls Creek | None |
| | Indian Creek | Trees slid into stream, no barriers |
| | Bird Creek | Subsidence at mouth |
| | Penguin Creek | None |
| | Glacier Creek | Subsidence at mouth |
| | California Creek | None |
| | Twentymile Creek | Land subsidence. Vegetation dying because of salt water |
| | Portage Creek | Land subsidence |
| | Portage Lake | Parking lot damaged by fissures and unequal settling |
| | Placer River | Land subsidence |
| Knik Arm | | Overall subsidence ranging from about 2.5 ft at Eklutna flats to 3.5 ft in Anchorage |
| | Ship Creek | Subsidence at mouth |
| | Eagle River | Subsidence at mouth |
| | South Fork | None |
| | Peters Creek | Subsidence at mouth |
| | Eklutna River | Subsidence at mouth |
| | Bird Creek | None |
| | Eklutna Lake | Sinking by outlet to aqueduct; fissures at upper end of lake |
| | Knik River | Fissures throughout drainage |
| | Jim Creek | None |
| | Friday Creek | None |
| | Hunter Creek | Crevices and fissures prevalent |
| | Cottonwood Creek | Subsidence and crevices at mouth |
| | Fish Creek | Subsidence at mouth and small landslide |
| Susitna River | | Landslides but no blockage, main stem and tributaries |
| | Beluga Lake | Landslides but no blockage |

ice. Near the eastern end of Kenai Lake, 12 acres of wooded area had sloughed into the water.

An interesting phenomenon occurred at the Kasilof River immediately after the earthquake: its flow was halted to such an extent that a biologist was able to walk up its channel the following day wearing overshoes. A few dead Dolly Varden trout were observed. Although the exact cause of dewatering is unknown, it is believed to be the tilting of Tustumena Lake toward its eastern end and away from the outlet.

The most substantial changes and probably the most detrimental effects were encountered in the southern and eastern area of the Kenai Peninsula. The effects of the land subsidence and tsunamis on the pink and chum salmon spawning streams from Homer to Port Dick will take many years to determine accurately. Several streams were studied in this area. Humpy Creek, located in Kachemak Bay, is a major pink-salmon-producing stream; land subsidence caused some loss of intertidal spawning habitat there (Figure 8). Sampling of fry in the gravel after the earthquake indicated numbers close to the 1963 level, and fry mortality was not abnormal.

Tutka Bay Lagoon lost intertidal spawning area as a result of land subsidence, but the spawning stream was not visibly damaged by the tsunami. The gravel-shift and freezing-level indicators were virtually intact. In one minor spawning zone, 1–2 in. of gravel had been deposited. The fry counts were average for this system.

No gravel-shift or freezing-level indicators had been placed in the Seldovia River (at the head of Seldovia Bay) before the earthquake, but no obvious earthquake-caused changes were observed. The intertidal portion of the spawning area contained above-average numbers of salmon fry compared to those of previous years, but the area above the intertidal zone contained below-average numbers.

The Port Graham River lost some intertidal spawning area because of land subsidence, but tsunami action did not appear to have changed the spawning habitat appreciably.

The gravel-shift indicators located in Rocky Bay had not been disturbed by the earthquake or tsunami. No preemergent fry were found. Their absence cannot be directly attributed to the earthquake, however, because this stream had been subjected to extreme flooding during the fall of 1963.

FIGURE 6   Beach exposure caused by dewatering of Long Finger Lake, which is located in the Swanson River area of the Kenai Peninsula.

*Alaska Department of Fish and Game*

No gravel-shift or freezing-level indicators were located in Middle Creek (Port Dick), but observation indicated that some gravel movement had occurred, probably caused by the tsunami. The sampling indicated very low densities of pink and chum salmon fry in the stream's very fine, loose gravel.

Island Creek (Port Dick) flows through a grassy tide flat for approximately ½ mi. Tsunami action had removed ping-pong-ball setup markers along the stream bank, and the first 15 setups could not be located. There were no fry present in the gravel in this portion of the stream, although fish spawn in the area. Other setups were found upstream, away from the tide flats, with 2-3 in. of new gravel deposited over them. The attached plastic-string markers were all lying in an upstream position, indicating that an upstream current (tsunami) had deposited the gravel. Fry mortality in the upstream area was much lower than in the more exposed tidal flat.

At Port Dick Creek, an area of about 175,000 ft² of spawning gravel had been lost because of land subsidence (Figure 9). This creek lies at the head of a tapering bay, and there were indications that a surge of water had passed upstream through the creek. A log, 2 ft in diameter and about 15 ft long, was found lodged in a spruce tree approximately 15 ft above the extreme-high-tide mark. Ping-pong balls and freezing-vial setups in the lower portion of the main spawning area were covered by as much as 2 ft of gravel. In the upstream area, where the gravel is larger, missing ping-pong balls showed that scouring had occurred. There was heavy mortality among fry throughout the creek.

At Seward, damage resulted from tsunamis and from subsidence in a lagoon that served as a rearing area for sockeye and coho salmon. The salinity of this lagoon had been regulated by tide gates at its outlet to Resurrection Bay. The tsunami had swept over the Seward Highway and into the lagoon, destroying the tide gates and temporarily ruining this rearing area. The salinity of the lagoon was raised and much mud and debris had been deposited, causing a possible loss of two year classes of coho and one year class of sockeye salmon fry in the lower portion of Dairy Creek. This

FIGURE 7 Movement of ice near mouth of Trail River of Kenai Lake shortly after the earthquake. Note the barked trees. Scouring of gravel may have taken place.

*Art Kennedy, U.S. Forest Service*

creek is a tributary to the lagoon and supports a coho salmon run of about 600 fish.

The spawning areas used in 1964 and areas lost because of land subsidence are listed in Table 7. There is no evidence that subsidence of clam beaches has limited the availability of hard-shell clams to sport and commercial diggers.

Some possible detrimental effects of the earthquake could not be evaluated during the short time of study. The demonstrated land subsidences resulted in the loss of intertidal spawning area that may cause pink and chum salmon to spawn farther upstream. These upstream areas where spawning could take place may, however, be susceptible to adverse environmental conditions such as flooding, silting, and low water flows, with consequent freezing of exposed stream areas. Some streams appear to be carrying greater sediment loads as a result of stream-bank loosening and sloughing.

## ECONOMIC IMPACT

Damage to gear, vessels, and fish-processing facilities ranged from almost none at Snug Harbor to complete destruction at Seward. Canneries at Homer and Seldovia were within reach of high tides because of land subsidence. The Kenai and Ninilchik facilities appear to have been unaffected.

The recreational fishery and related enterprises declined markedly in value on the Kenai Peninsula in 1964. Land subsidence in the Portage area closed the Seward Highway, which leads from Anchorage to the Kenai Peninsula. The road was opened daily for short periods while repairs were taking place. Much of the sport-fishing effort on the peninsula is carried out by anglers from Anchorage, many of whom were unwilling to travel the almost-impassable highway. As a result, recreational fishing and all retail sales and service on the Kenai Peninsula were drastically reduced. It is difficult to determine the actual loss in sales, but the reduction of fishing effort can be seen in Table 8. The yearly differences are greater than indicated here because sport-fishing on the Kenai Peninsula had been increasing each year. Accordingly, there would probably have been more fishing in 1964 than in 1963 had not the earthquake occurred.

## PRINCE WILLIAM SOUND–COPPER RIVER BASIN

### SUMMARY OF OBSERVATIONS

The upper Copper River Basin was initially inspected less than 10 days after the earthquake for indications of the effects of the earthquake on the fishery habitat. The area comprises the lakes and streams in the Copper River drainage above the town of Chitina.

Two types of action caused by the earthquake were responsible for most of the changes in the upper Copper River Basin: the sloughing of the shoreline and the forcing of sand

FIGURE 8 Humpy Creek at Kachemak Bay. Top: area before earthquake. Bottom: same area at postearthquake high tide.

*Alaska Department of Fish and Game*

and gravel into stream mouths by large blocks of ice. Thirteen salmon-spawning streams were either partly or totally blocked to fish movement by the ice action that pushed up ridges of sand and gravel. Approximately 12 mi of shoreline spawning gravel were covered by silt and debris as a result of shoreline damage; any fish in the underlying gravel, or in that scoured by ice, were undoubtedly destroyed.

Of 14 lakes that were checked in the Cordova area, soundings and other observations indicated that only Hartney Lake had been altered significantly. Before the earthquake, salt water had entered through its outlet during high tides, and it supported a good population of Dolly Varden and cutthroat trout. Since the land around the lake rose in response to the earthquake, the lake has contained only fresh water. Tests made in the summer of 1964 revealed a low population of fish. Four lakes were checked that summer in the Valdez area, but none had been altered by the earthquake.

Extensive clam mortality occurred as a result of the earthquake-caused elevations of the beaches on the Copper-Bering rivers and on Prince William Sound. It will take several years to replace hard-shelled-clam habitat lost in the up-

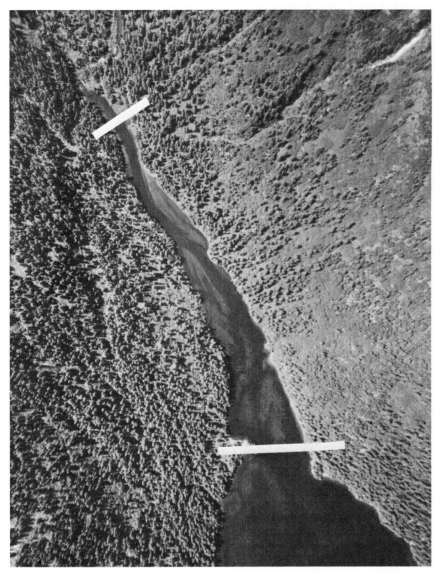

FIGURE 9 Port Dick Creek, located in Kenai Peninsula's southern district. The area between the lines has been lost to pink salmon spawning because of land subsidence.

*U.S. Army*

lifted areas where entire populations of some beaches were lost. Once suitable habitat is rebuilt and seeded with clams, 8–12 years are required for them to reach commercial size.

Some Dungeness crab were killed, but no significant change was noted in the catch per unit of effort in the commercial fishery.

Many schooling areas used by salmon before moving upstream to spawn can no longer be used for this purpose because of the 6½-ft land rise of the Copper River Delta.

In Prince William Sound the immediate or short-term effects of the earthquake were losses of pink and chum salmon eggs and fry in the gravel. The continued or long-term effects were alterations in the environment of spawning salmon. These changes were caused by the creation of new riffles in the intertidal zone and the uplift of intertidal rif-

fles that then became freshwater areas, by tsunami action depositing silt and debris in riffles or scouring riffles and by subsidence creating riffles in new intertidal zones through the encroachment of salt water and "drowning out" of normal riffles.

In 1964, 86 streams were examined during the pink salmon-spawning months of July, August, and September. New spawning-bed materials in uplifted zones varied considerably—from silt and small gravel to boulders and cobbles and some mussel beds. Erosion had occurred in some streams, and streams had occasionally gone underground. In uplifted areas, spawning salmon had shifted downstream; in subsided areas, they had moved upstream. The tsunami deposited sediments over spawning beds in four streams.

The effect of the earthquake on salmon production in

TABLE 7    Extent of Known Kenai Peninsula Spawning Areas Actually Used in 1964 and of Potential Spawning Areas Lost to Salmon as a Result of Subsidence in Kenai Peninsula Streams

| Stream | Spawning Area Used in 1964 (ft$^2$) | Lost Area (ft$^2$) |
|---|---|---|
| Port Dick Creek | 82,275 | 175,000 |
| Middle Creek | 16,000 | 8,750 |
| Island Creek | 38,500 | 27,500 |
| Rocky River | Not surveyed | – |
| Windy Bay (right) | 52,500 | Negligible |
| Windy Bay (left) | 48,800 | Negligible |
| Port Graham | Not surveyed | – |
| Seldovia River | 128,875 | 30,000 |
| Tutka Bay | 49,375 | 20,800 |
| Humpy Creek | 212,000 | 8,800 |
| China Poot Bay Creek | Unknown | 18,000 |
| Jakolof Creek | Unknown | 16,000 |
| Ingram Creek (Turnagain Arm) | Unknown | 4,500 |
| Sixmile Creek (Turnagain Arm) | Unknown | 36,000 |
| Resurrection Creek (Turnagain Arm) | Unknown | 27,000 |

TABLE 8    Comparative Numbers of Fishermen or Man-Days Fished in 1963 and 1964 in the Kenai Peninsula Sport Fisheries

| Sport Fisheries | Fishermen (Estimated) | | Man-Days Fished | |
|---|---|---|---|---|
| | 1963 | 1964 | 1963 | 1964 |
| Opening-day counts along the road from Seward to Soldotna | 200 | 25 | – | – |
| Resurrection Bay coho salmon fishery | – | – | 15,430 | 7,540 |
| Russian River sockeye salmon fishery | – | – | 7,880 | 4,940 |

Prince William Sound is described more fully elsewhere in this volume by Roys; by Thorsteinson and others; and by Baxter. Accordingly, only summary statements by Roys and Baxter have been included in this discussion.

## TECHNIQUES USED IN SURVEYING EARTHQUAKE EFFECTS

When possible, observers investigated lakes and streams on foot; their observations were supplemented by aerial surveys. Numbers and species of fish were checked visually and with gill nets. Bottom sampling was conducted with Eckman dredges. Changes in salmon-spawning areas were determined by comparisons with past data, established markers, old shorelines, and stream channels.

## SPECIFIC OBSERVATIONS

After the initial postearthquake survey of the area, a more intensive study was conducted from July to October by airplane, by boat, and on foot. The lakes and streams in the Copper River drainage above the town of Chitina (Figure 10) and 14 lakes in the Cordova–Valdez area were examined.

### Tazlina Lake and Associated Streams

Tazlina Lake lies in a glaciated valley approximately 24 air mi southwest of Glennallen. This large body of water, at an altitude of 1,700 ft, is 21 mi long, averages 2 mi in width, and has a relatively straight shoreline with few bays and no islands. The water is silt-laden from the flow of water from Tazlina Glacier and Nelchina River. Soundings revealed depths of over 200 ft. Almost all the shoreline is composed of washed gravel and is typical sockeye salmon spawning area. The length of Tazlina Lake extends north and south and is subjected to frequent strong winds blowing off the glacier.

The water level dropped at least 2 ft after or during the earthquake, probably because of drainage through fissures in the lake bottom. Considerable ice movement also occurred; huge ice masses, estimated to be 30 ft in diameter and 4 ft thick, were forced onto the shore and then returned to the lake, loaded with debris (Figure 11). Seven miles of shoreline had sloughed into the lake (Figures 12, 13). In the past, this shoreline had been considered a good spawning area for sockeye salmon. Bottom samples taken in the lake showed the area to be covered with silt and debris. This earthquake-caused deposition was found at depths of up to 30 ft along the shoreline. Any eggs or fry in the gravel at the time of the earthquake were undoubtedly lost. Bottom samples taken where the shoreline had not been disturbed showed clean gravel down to the 20–25-ft water depth.

Before the earthquake, all inlet streams of Tazlina Lake had been open to fish movement. Twenty-three inlet streams were surveyed on foot; 11 of them were either totally or partly blocked to fish movement (Figure 12) by barriers of rock and gravel that had been pushed up by the earthquake. During the earthquake the ice was broken up into large masses, which, when forced up on the shore, "bulldozed" rocks and gravel into the stream mouths (Figure 14), undoubtedly causing considerable destruction of sockeye salmon fry. Tokina Creek was partly blocked at the lake by fallen trees, but fish were still able to move upstream. Two of the larger unnamed streams cut new channels into the lake and were open to fish movement by October. Mendeltna and Kaina creeks, two of the better salmon streams in the Tazlina Lake drainage, were not affected.

### Klutina Lake and Associated Streams

Klutina Lake, at an altitude of 1,700 ft, is approximately 28 mi south of Glennallen. L-shaped, with its long leg bear-

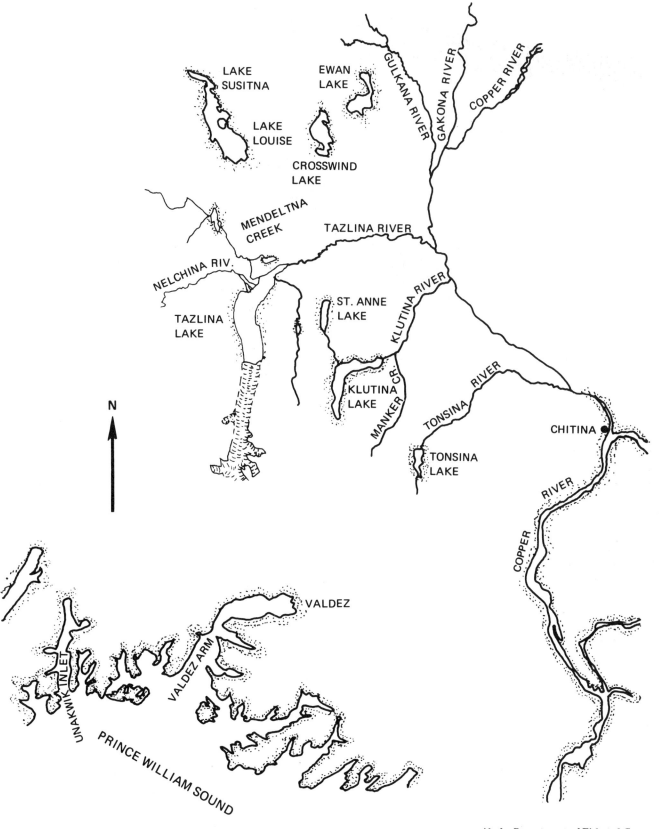

*Alaska Department of Fish and Game*

FIGURE 10    The upper Copper River area.

FIGURE 11   Debris on Tazlina Lake drawn back onto lake ice following the earthquake.

*Alaska Department of Fish and Game*

ing north and south, the lake is 16 mi long and averages 1½ mi in width. Soundings taken in the summer of 1964 showed depths of over 300 ft just off the southeast shoreline. The best sockeye salmon spawning areas are along the northwest shoreline where good gravel is found in most places. Approximately half the shoreline could be considered suitable salmon spawning area. About 3 mi of the shoreline had sloughed into Klutina Lake. Although this cracking and breaking off was not as extensive as that on Tazlina Lake, any salmon fry in the area would have been lost under the heavy cover of silt.

Klutina Lake showed less disturbance as a result of the earthquake than did Tazlina Lake. Most of the broken ice was located at the end of the lake near its outlet, where a peculiar formation was observed; debris and mud that had been thrown onto the ice formed a whirlpool pattern that covered an area of several acres. No cause for this phenomenon was established, but it can be surmised that a subsurface loss of water had occurred.

The Klutina River appeared to be flowing normally at the lake outlet, but about 9 mi downstream from Klutina Lake the river was completely blocked by an earthquake-caused landslide (Figure 15). Water was flowing below the barrier, however, indicating that the river was cutting under and through the ice and silt. There was only a slight indication of any backing up behind the slide; before the spring breakup, the river had begun to cut a new channel around it, and by midsummer the channel routing had been completed (Figure 16). The flow of the river downstream near the Richardson Highway was normal. The presence of salmon in Klutina Lake during the summer indicated that fish movement had not been restricted.

Ground surveys of Klutina Lake and its 14 inlet streams during the summer and in September of 1964 (Figure 17) failed to locate a complete barrier on any of the salmon streams. Although some sand and gravel had been pushed into the mouth of St. Anne Creek, this partial barrier did not prevent the movement of fish upstream.

*Tonsina Lake and Associated Streams*

Tonsina Lake is the smallest of the three lakes investigated in the upper Copper River drainage. It lies at an elevation of 1,900 ft, 44 mi southeast of Glennallen. The lake is 6 mi long from north to south, with an average width of ¾ mi.

Tonsina Lake showed evidence of more violent disturbance from the earthquake than did any of the other lakes in the upper Copper River area. Large blocks of ice were observed at least 100 ft lakeward of the normal shoreline where they had come to rest, apparently after skidding up onto the shore and then back into the lake (Figure 18). Trees and brush were picked up by this action and deposited several hundred yards out in the lake. Spruce trees along the shoreline gave evidence of having been barked as high as 30 ft above the ground by this ice action.

The best sockeye salmon areas of Tonsina Lake are found on both shorelines near the outlet and along most of the west shoreline. The east shoreline offers little opportunity for salmon to spawn because the drop-off is almost vertical to depths of over 200 ft about 50 yd offshore. Many small springs enter the lake along the west shore near the outlet, and these areas are heavily used by spawning sockeye salmon. This part of the shoreline had been subjected to violent ice action, but the bottom did not appear to be covered too heavily with silt and debris.

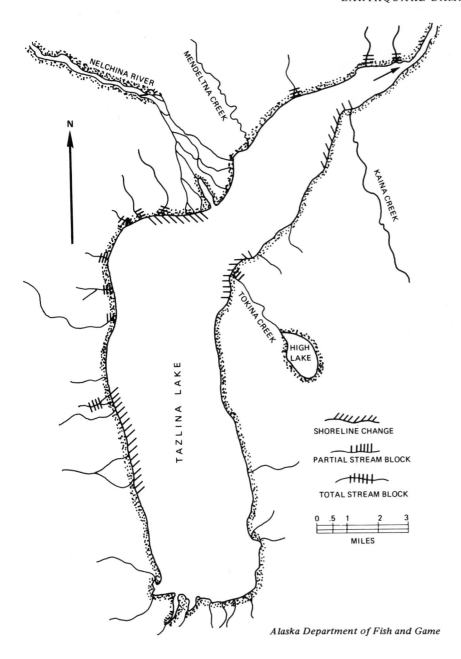

FIGURE 12  Tazlina Lake.

*Alaska Department of Fish and Game*

The Tonsina River had not been blocked by landslides and was flowing normally. Tonsina Creek had been partly blocked by ice action, which it had circumvented by cutting a new channel into the lake. The velocity of the stream increases considerably at the point where the stream now enters the lake, and when the streamflow is low, salmon will be unable to enter the creek. None of the other seven inlet streams flowing into Tonsina Lake appears to have been changed (Figure 19).

*Other Lakes and Streams*

The lower Copper River sustained some slides, but none had been large enough to block its flow completely. A few small slides went into the Chitina River, and some large fissures were evident in the river bottom. No permanent changes were observed.

The streams and lakes in the Gulkana River drainage did not appear to have been disturbed. Some ice had broken around the shoreline of Paxson, Summit, and Crosswind lakes, but very little ice had cracked in the center of the lakes. In several small lakes, mud and detritus from the bottom had been heaved up and deposited on the ice. In at least one site (Mae West Lake), the disturbance was probably responsible for a winter kill of arctic grayling.

Of the 14 lakes checked in the Cordova area, only Hartney Lake was affected to any great degree. Most of the

*Alaska Department of Fish and Game*

FIGURE 13   Shoreline change on Tazlina Lake. Note fissures in middle background.

*Alaska Department of Fish and Game*

FIGURE 14   Tazlina Lake inlet stream blocked by ridge of gravel.

damage to the sport fishery in the area was indirect. Beyond Mile 27 of the Copper River Highway, all the bridges had been destroyed or damaged to the extent that they were closed to vehicular travel. The amount of recreational fishing taking place in Cordova in 1964 was not sufficient to make this loss of access critical because many fishing locations were still easily accessible.

The 6½-ft uplift (Figure 20) caused many significant changes in the commercial fishing areas off the deltas of the Copper and Bering rivers. Both ends of the Copper River flats receive less fresh water because exposed bars divide the flats at most tide levels; there appeared to be little permanent loss of habitat for salmon spawning. The water in Bering Lake was lowered 2–3 ft, however, destroying some shoreline spawning areas.

FIGURE 15 Landslide blocking the Klutina River.

*Alaska Department of Fish and Game*

FIGURE 16 Klutina River. At the left is the landslide area and the old streambed. The river has cut a new channel.

*Alaska Department of Fish and Game*

ECONOMIC IMPACT IN THE PRINCE WILLIAM SOUND AREA

Two canneries were completely lost when the tsunami and an underwater landslide destroyed the Valdez dock and dockside business area. One of the canneries had custom-processed fish caught by sportsmen. The new Valdez cold-storage and crab processing plant, which had been scheduled to go into operation for the 1965 season, was lost when the Valdez dock was swept away. Also lost from the harbor was a small, family-operated, hand-pack cannery. The estimated value of the canneries alone exceeded $250,000, and the loss of the other facilities at dockside was far more costly. Shortly after the earthquake a list of known damages to docks, floats, and pilings showed an estimated loss of about $763,000. Nineteen small vessels and 15 purse seiners worth about $338,000 were lost at Valdez, in addition to about

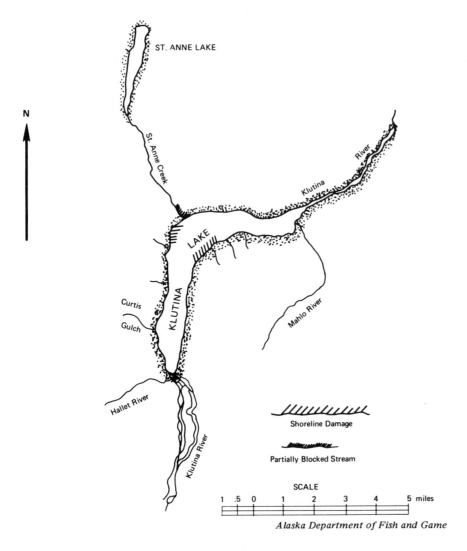

*Alaska Department of Fish and Game*

FIGURE 17   Klutina Lake.

*Alaska Department of Fish and Game*

FIGURE 18   Shoreline disruption on Tonsina Lake.

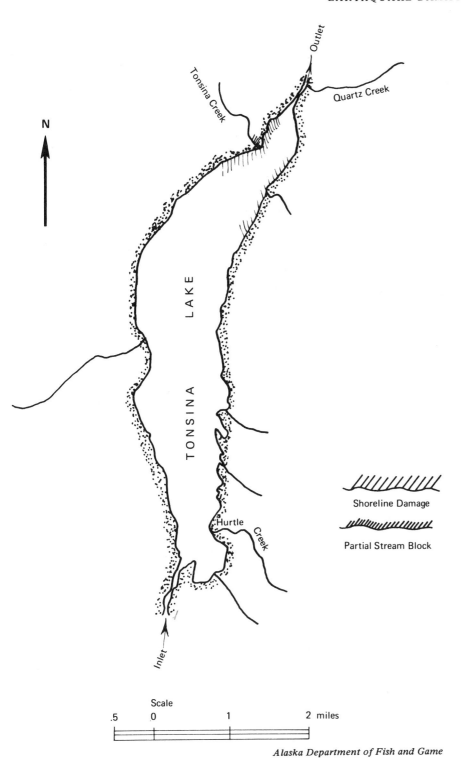

Shoreline Damage

Partial Stream Block

FIGURE 19  Tonsina Lake.

*Alaska Department of Fish and Game*

76 small sport-fishing boats valued at approximately $100,000.

The economic value to the community of the recreational fishing and other tourist attractions was temporarily eliminated. Many of the vessels and small boats that were

destroyed had been rented to or chartered by out-of-town saltwater anglers; their loss, together with the loss of other tourist and travel facilities, seriously impaired the economy of Valdez.

Loss of property was widespread throughout the

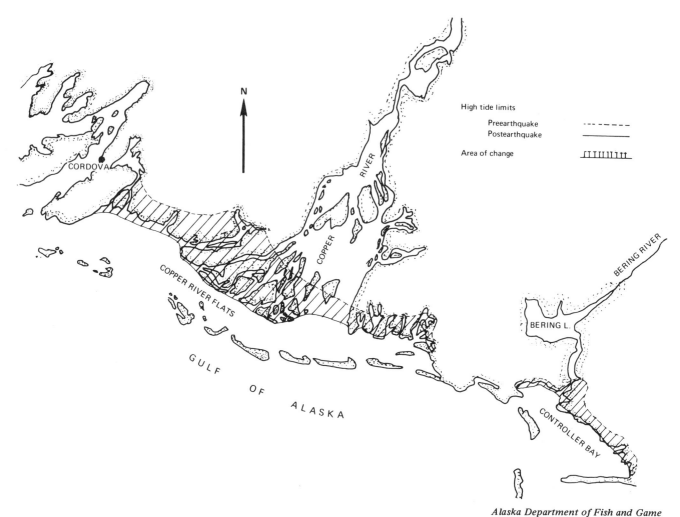

*Alaska Department of Fish and Game*

FIGURE 20   Mean high-tide limits before and after the earthquake in the Copper River and Bering River areas.

earthquake-affected area, and all communities in Prince William Sound suffered some loss. Hardest hit were the village of Chenega, which was literally wiped off the hillside by a tsunami, and the city of Valdez, where an underwater landslide and tsunami destroyed the waterfront docks, warehouses, and fish-processing plants and inundated the business district of the town.

Unknown amounts of fishing gear, vessels, and related equipment were lost throughout Prince William Sound. One fisherman submitted an itemized list for losses estimated at $3,759; another reported losses of $2,853.

Land uplift caused a number of transportation problems, particularly for the drift-gill-net fishery. The Crystal Falls Fish Company salmon cannery, located at Mountain Slough, became inaccessible to fishermen because of the uplift of land and was declared a complete loss by the owners. Lower tide levels prevented the use of moorages and anchorages, and restricted travel across the Copper and Bering rivers tidal flats, except at certain high-tide levels. Dredging of

waterways, harbors, and dockside areas in Orca Inlet, Sawmill Bay, and Valdez was necessary to carry on routine fishing activities. During the 1964 season in the Prince William Sound uplift areas, three purse seiners hit submerged rocks and were extensively damaged. The uplifted area made travel in the fishing waters of Prince William Sound extremely dangerous. On the Copper River Delta, several fishermen lost valuable fishing time when their vessels became stranded during lower tide levels.

## ACKNOWLEDGMENTS

This paper was adapted from "Postearthquake Fisheries Evaluation," an original report of the Alaska Department of Fish and Game, which was compiled from the joint efforts of the following staff members:

*Kodiak and Afognak Islands Section.*
    Dexter Lall, Richard A. Marriott, Robert J. Simon, and Carl E. Spetz.

*Cook Inlet–Kenai Peninsula Section.*

Allen S. Davis, Ben L. Hilliker, Sidney N. Logan, John C. McMullen, William Pilkington, James D. Reardon, Julius L. Reynolds, and Frank A. Stefanich.

*Prince William Sound–Copper River Basin Section.*

Rae E. Baxter, Darwin E. Jones, Ralph B. Pirtle, Robert S. Roys, and Fred T. Williams.

The original report was edited by Louis S. Bandirola and Caramel Walder.

## REFERENCES

Alaska Department of Fish and Game, 1965. Post-earthquake fisheries evaluation. An interim report on the March 1964 earthquake effects on Alaska's fishery resources. Juneau: Alaska Department of Fish and Game. 72 p.

Baxter, Rae E., 1971. Earthquake effects on clams of Prince William Sound *in* The Great Alaska Earthquake of 1964: Biology. NAS Pub. 1604. Washington: National Academy of Sciences.

Marriott, Richard A., and Carl E. Spetz, 1971. Effects of seawater intrusion into lakes of Kodiak and Afognak Islands *in* The Great Alaska Earthquake of 1964: Biology. NAS Pub. 1604. Washington: National Academy of Sciences.

Roys, Robert S., 1971. Effect of tectonic deformation on pink salmon runs in Prince William Sound *in* The Great Alaska Earthquake of 1964: Biology. NAS Pub. 1604. Washington: National Academy of Sciences.

Thorsteinson, Fredrik V., John H. Helle, and Donald G. Birkholz, 1971. Salmon survival in intertidal zones of Prince William Sound streams in uplifted and subsided areas *in* The Great Alaska Earthquake of 1964: Biology. NAS Pub. 1604. Washington: National Academy of Sciences.

FREDRIK V. THORSTEINSON
JOHN H. HELLE
DONALD G. BIRKHOLZ
U.S. BUREAU OF COMMERCIAL FISHERIES *

# Salmon Survival in Intertidal Zones of Prince William Sound Streams in Uplifted and Subsided Areas

ABSTRACT: Large numbers of pink salmon, *Oncorhynchus gorbuscha* (Walbaum), and chum salmon, *O. keta* (Walbaum), spawned each year in intertidal portions of streams in the Prince William Sound area where the Alaska earthquake of March 27, 1964, was centered. Changes in land elevation associated with the earthquake caused physical changes of great ecological significance in intertidal zones of streams. Many of these changes could affect the survival of pink and chum salmon in streams. Subsidence caused an upstream shift in the intertidal zone, which shortened the lengths of the streams and reduced the amount of available spawning space. Uplift extended the lengths of streams, and the downstream shift of the intertidal zone created potentially productive stream areas never before used by spawners. The new channel environments contained much silt, however, and were often very unstable. Detailed studies of the effects of changes in land level were made at Olsen Creek (uplifted about 4 ft), a stream for which a large amount of preearthquake data existed. General studies were made at three other streams—two in areas that were uplifted 10 ft and one in an area that subsided 6 ft. Despite relocation of intertidal spawning beds in relation to tidal levels, the areas occupied by the runs of returning pink and chum salmon were at approximately the same levels and in the same proportions as before the earthquake. The distribution of spawners and survival of eggs at different tide levels in the new intertidal spawning beds were similar to those observed before the earthquake. The first spawners occupied upper intertidal areas, and those that came later spawned at lower levels; very few fish spawned below the 6-ft tide level. Survival of eggs was high in upper areas and lower in downstream areas. Stream slope adjustments caused by changes in elevation created unstable streambed conditions. Scour, fill, and channel shifts that occurred because of regrading increased mortality of eggs and alevins (yolk-sac fry) buried in the streambed. The amount of streambed movement in Olsen Creek was measured by detailed topographic surveys before and after

spawning and just before the spring outmigration of fry. The relation between the amount of streambed movement and the numbers of eggs or alevins in the streambed was inverse—the larger the amount of scour or fill, the smaller the number of eggs or alevins remaining. We estimate that these secondary effects of the earthquake caused the disappearance of 7.27 million pink salmon eggs and 1.1 million chum salmon eggs from the Olsen Creek intertidal streambed during the summer and fall of 1965 and 0.54 million pink salmon alevins and 0.43 million chum salmon alevins during the 1965–1966 winter.

## INTRODUCTION

The annual harvest of Pacific salmon in Prince William Sound, where the Alaska earthquake of March 27, 1964, was centered (Figure 1), is worth millions of dollars. Pink salmon, *Oncorhynchus gorbuscha* (Walbaum), and chum salmon, *O. keta* (Walbaum), are the most abundant species of salmon in the Sound. From 1960 to 1965, pink salmon runs ranged from 3.2 to 8.7 million fish, and chum salmon runs from 0.4 to 1.4 million (Roys, 1966).

The life cycle of pink salmon is 2 years, and that of chum salmon is 3 to 5 years. In Prince William Sound the spawning season for both species occurs from late June to early September. Eggs buried in the streambed hatch from November to January, and fry emerge the following spring. Pink salmon fry leave the stream to enter the sea from April to June and return as adults about 15 months later; chum salmon leave the stream concurrently with the pink salmon but spend from 1 to 3 more years in the sea. About 75 percent of the chum salmon in Prince William Sound return as 4-year-olds, and the remainder return as 3- and 5-year-olds in about equal numbers (Thorsteinson and others, 1963).

After completing the marine phases of their lives, pink

---

*Now the National Marine Fisheries Service, National Oceanic and Atmospheric Administration.

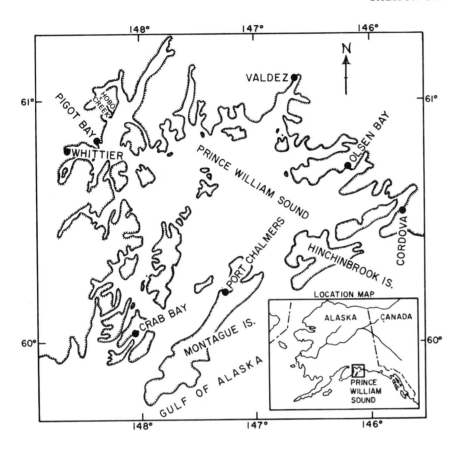

FIGURE 1    Prince William Sound, Alaska.

and chum salmon return to the coast and spawn in numerous streams that drain from the mountainous mainland and islands that rim the Sound. Most of the streams are short because the coastal mountains rise abruptly from the sea, and many have impassable falls a short distance from salt water. Because of the limited amount of accessible freshwater spawning space, the proportion of pink and chum salmon that spawn in intertidal stream channels is larger in Prince William Sound than elsewhere in Alaska. About 45 percent of the pink salmon spawn in the intertidal zone in odd-numbered years and about 75 percent in even-numbered years (Noerenberg, 1963); the proportion of chum salmon that spawn in intertidal zones has not been determined but is believed to be substantial.

The 1964 earthquake caused physical changes in streams of Prince William Sound that are of great ecological significance for pink and chum salmon. Uplift in some areas and subsidence in others changed the relation of the streambed surface to sea level and created new intertidal areas in most of the streams. New intertidal spawning beds in uplifted areas became unstable as streams began to regrade in response to changes in their base level. Lower portions of streams were drowned in areas of subsidence, and valuable spawning grounds were lost. These changes raised serious questions about the future of pink and chum salmon stocks that spawn in intertidal zones.

From observations of pink and chum salmon alevins (yolk-sac fry) that had been incubating in streambeds when the earthquake occurred, it appeared that the first effects of the earthquake on salmon abundance were slight. Noerenberg and Ossiander (1964) compared the numbers of dead pink salmon alevins found in beds of representative streams in April, 1–3 weeks after the earthquake, with those found in the same streams in April in previous years. They found many dead alevins whose deaths could be attributed to mechanical shock from shifting of streambed gravel and shaking during earth movements and to suffocation resulting from deposition of mud and sand on streambeds by seismic waves. Because of these additional mortalities, the authors forecast a reduction of 235,000 adult pink salmon in the return to Prince William Sound in 1965.

Changes in land elevation could affect the survival of future generations of pink and chum salmon by changing the amount of spawning grounds available and the quality of intertidal spawning ground. In this report we describe the general changes in the spawning grounds of Prince William Sound and the effects of altered intertidal environments on the survival of pink and chum salmon in four streams.

*J. M. Olson, U.S. Bureau of Commercial Fisheries*

FIGURE 2   Quadra Creek, Hanning Bay, Montague Island, November 1, 1964, at the 4.6-ft tide stage. This area was uplifted 25 ft. The new intertidal spawning area is between the waterline and snowline. The former high-tide line is near the tree line.

## SIGNIFICANCE OF UPLIFT AND SUBSIDENCE FOR FUTURE PRODUCTION OF PINK AND CHUM SALMON IN PRINCE WILLIAM SOUND

The amount of uplift and subsidence varied throughout Prince William Sound. Plafker (1969) determined changes in land level by measuring displacement of the common acorn barnacle, *Balanus balanoides* (Linnaeus) and *B. glandula*, whose upper distribution limit corresponds closely to the annual mean high-tide line. In areas without barnacles, Plafker used the displacement of the rockweeds, *Fucus furcatus* (Agardh) and *F. distichus*, whose upper limit of distribution is near that of the barnacle, and the encrusting lichen, *Verrucaria* sp., which occupies the splash zone above the barnacle line. He stated that the error of the barnacle-line method for displacement determination was probably less than 1 ft. Plafker found that the land area along the eastern shore and adjacent islands was uplifted from 1 to 8 ft. Along the southwestern shore and nearby islands, uplift was as great as 11 ft. The greatest uplift was in southern Prince William Sound, where it ranged from 6.4 ft on the northeast side to almost 38 ft on the southwest side of Montague Island. The greatest subsidence, 8 ft, was in the northwest portion of the Sound. Only a few streams in a small area of land across the north-central part of the Sound remained unchanged.

Streams of Prince William Sound were presumably stable or graded at the time of the earthquake, and a serious effect of uplift or subsidence on the stream ecology was disruption of this grade. The soft materials of the former sea floor, now in the intertidal zone of uplifted streams, were especially subject to readjustments of stream slope. The two physical changes that are biologically more important as a stream regains equilibrium are scouring and filling, which often result in braided and abandoned channels. These processes can destroy buried salmon eggs or alevins by dislodgment and mechanical shock or exposure to predators (scouring), suffocation (filling), and desiccation or freezing (abandoned channels). The physical consequences of uplift on a salmon stream—extension of stream length, relocation of the intertidal zone, and braiding and abandonment of channels resulting from adjustments of stream slope—are shown in a photograph of Quadra Creek, Montague Island (Figure 2).

In a few streams, particularly in the northeast portion of Montague Island, velocities and loads were not great enough to cut through uplifted beach surfaces; these streams disappeared into loose beach materials, thus denying access to salmon (Figure 3).

The physical consequences of subsidence on a salmon stream—reduction in available spawning space and dead or dying vegetation along stream channels—are shown in a photograph of Swanson Creek, Pigot Bay (Figure 4). The trees killed by saltwater intrusion in subsided areas are potential hazards. Dead trees are likely to be blown down, and if they

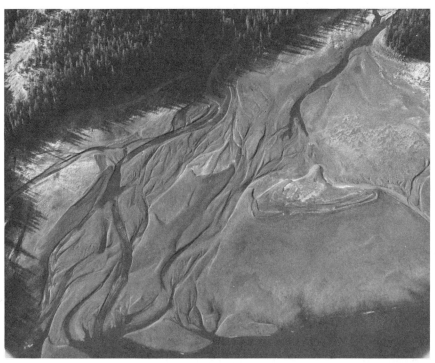

FIGURE 3   Streams at Zaikof Bay, Montague Island, September 28, 1965; uplifted 8.0 ft. Tide height was 2.2 ft. The stream in the upper right-hand quadrant disappears into loose beach materials.

*J. M. Olson, U.S. Bureau of Commercial Fisheries*

*J. M. Olson, U.S. Bureau of Commercial Fisheries*

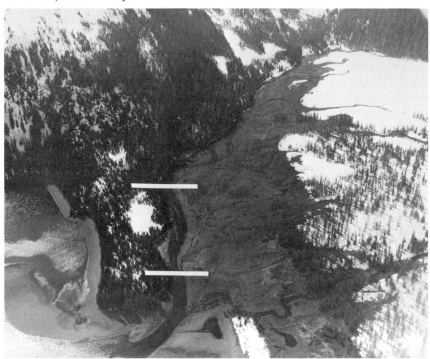

FIGURE 4   Swanson Creek, Pigot Bay, northwest mainland, September 28, 1965. This area subsided 6 ft. The former upper intertidal zone, which was productive, lies between the white lines in the left-central part of the picture. The upper limit of the new intertidal zone is indicated by the snowline. Tide height was 4.0 ft.

fall into a stream, they can form pools or barriers that further reduce spawning space. It is doubtful that the spawning space now available in Swanson Creek will support pink and chum salmon runs at their former population level.

Subsidence was not always detrimental to salmon, however. The drowning of a barrier near the mouth of Hobo Creek in the northwest arm of the Sound allowed access to an area suitable for spawning that had been unavailable during periods of high streamflow before the earthquake (Alaska Department of Fish and Game, 1965).

The physical and chemical quality of spawning beds in new intertidal zones can also affect survival of incubating pink and chum salmon eggs. Survival varies with the tidal elevation at which eggs are deposited (Hanavan and Skud, 1954; Kirkwood, 1962; Helle and others, 1964; Thorsteinson, 1965). Survival is highest at upper intertidal levels and, in general, becomes progressively less in lower levels. The amount of spawning below the 4-ft tide level is small, and survival is usually nil.

At depths where eggs are buried in the intertidal streambed, the temperatures and salinities of the intragravel water fluctuate with the tide and approximate those of the overlying salt water when the area is covered by the tide (Helle and others, 1964). Rockwell (1956) determined that mortality of pink and chum salmon alevins maintained in constant salinities (without freshwater relief) increased with length of exposure and that the tolerance to saline water increased with decreasing temperatures. Bailey (1966) reared pink salmon eggs in the laboratory in a simulated intertidal environment and exposed them to seawater with a salinity of 28 parts per thousand for amounts of time that were equal to saltwater exposure at different tide levels of Olsen Creek, Prince William Sound. He found that seawater had no adverse effects on eggs that were exposed for 4 hours twice a day (equivalent to tide cover at the 8-ft tide level), whereas 50 percent of those exposed for 6.67 hours (the 6-ft tide level) died. All eggs exposed for 9.33 hours twice daily (the 4-ft tide level) died.

The intragravel water surrounding the egg must contain an adequate amount of oxygen or the embryo will not survive, and, in general, the more permeable the gravel, the greater will be the flow of intragravel water and the rate of delivery of oxygen to the egg. Wickett (1958) showed a direct relation in three British Columbia streams between survival of pink and chum salmon embryos and permeability of the spawning bed. McNeil and Ahnell (1964) compared six streams in southeastern Alaska; they found that the more silt in the spawning beds, the smaller the populations of spawners. McNeil (1966a) noted that in the intertidal zones of two streams in southeastern Alaska the streambed with the smaller amount of fine material had the more favorable oxygen supply and an indication of lower egg mortality.

As the tide floods, flow velocities in the intertidal stream channel decrease the capacity of the stream to carry sediments, and the amount of fine materials deposited in the lower portions of the intertidal zone and stream delta increases.

Intertidal streambeds uplifted from former lower intertidal areas or stream deltas (depending on the amount of elevation change) thus contained a higher proportion of fine materials than is normal for these usually productive levels of the intertidal zone. Old intertidal spawning beds in subsided streams become totally unproductive because of prolonged exposure to seawater. Sediments accumulate in lower portions of new intertidal spawning beds as streams aggrade.

We categorized the streams of Prince William Sound according to number of spawners and changes in land elevation to determine the potential for damage to the stocks of pink and chum salmon. Estimates of the number of spawners in streams of Prince William Sound in 1962–1964 were compiled from reports issued by the Alaska Department of Fish and Game (Noerenberg and others, 1964; Roys and others, 1965; Roys, 1966), and the major streams (those with 5,000 or more pink or chum salmon) were grouped according to changes in land level. In 1962–1964, about 84 percent of the pink salmon and from 64 to 76 percent of the chum salmon spawned in about one fourth of the streams in Prince William Sound (Table 1). Most of these streams are in areas where land level changed, and resultant variations in intertidal spawning-bed stability and quality can seriously affect survival of pink and chum salmon using them. Roys (1966) estimated that in 1964, 0.5 million pink salmon, or about 28 percent of the 1.8 million that spawned in Prince William Sound streams that year, utilized new spawning beds in uplifted areas—areas that were below the lower limit of productive spawning before the earthquake.

Marked changes in land elevation have occurred in the Prince William Sound area in the comparatively recent past. DeLaguna (1956) cited observations made by Captain George Vancouver while he was anchored in Port Chalmers, Montague Island, during May and June 1794: " . . . stumps of trees, with their roots still fast in the ground, were also found in no very advanced state of decay nearly as low down as the water of spring tides." Evidence of this subsidence, or perhaps a more recent one, is shown by stumps still standing on the bare beach along Wild Creek in Port Chalmers (Figure 5). Grant and Higgins (1910) also found evidence of changes in land elevation at various points in Prince William Sound. Tarr and Martin (1912), who surveyed the Yakutat area in 1905 (where massive changes in land elevation occurred during the 1899 earthquake), found subsidence of as much as 7 ft, areas of little or no change, and uplift of more than 40 ft. They reported trenching of 20 ft or more in uplifted streams deltas and remarked that streams were then aggrading.

TABLE 1  Major Pink and Chum Salmon Streams Surveyed in Prince William Sound, Grouped According to Changes in Land Elevation and Percentage of Total Available Salmon Using Them, 1962–1964

| | Pink Salmon | | | | | | Chum Salmon | | | | | |
|---|---|---|---|---|---|---|---|---|---|---|---|---|
| | 1962 | | 1963 | | 1964 | | 1962 | | 1963 | | 1964 | |
| Change in Elevation of Land (ft) | Major Streams Surveyed | Percent of Total Escapement | Major Streams Surveyed | Percent of Total Escapement | Major Streams Surveyed | Percent of Total Escapement | Major Streams Surveyed | Percent of Total Escapement | Major Streams Surveyed | Percent of Total Escapement | Major Streams Surveyed | Percent of Total Escapement |
| −4 to −6 | 7 | 13.0 | 5 | 10.6 | 8 | 10.1 | 4 | 12.9 | 1 | 17.0 | 6 | 22.1 |
| −2 to −4 | 3 | 6.6 | 4 | 13.6 | 7 | 11.3 | 1 | 1.1 | 1 | 2.8 | 1 | 2.2 |
| 0 to −2 | 9 | 10.1 | 6 | 6.7 | 9 | 12.8 | 4 | 8.5 | 3 | 14.5 | 3 | 9.7 |
| 0 to 2 | 9 | 7.9 | 4 | 2.1 | 9 | 7.2 | 4 | 10.0 | 1 | 2.8 | 4 | 12.8 |
| 2 to 4 | 14 | 14.5 | 11 | 10.3 | 12 | 12.9 | 7 | 19.7 | 5 | 13.2 | 4 | 13.9 |
| 4 to 6 | 21 | 15.9 | 23 | 35.1 | 22 | 22.1 | 6 | 17.9 | 3 | 10.3 | 4 | 10.7 |
| 6 to 10 | 8 | 4.0 | 4 | 2.8 | 6 | 3.6 | 0 | 0 | 0 | 0 | 0 | 0 |
| 10 to 20 | 11 | 6.6 | 4 | 2.1 | 6 | 2.6 | 2 | 6.3 | 2 | 3.0 | 1 | 5.0 |
| >20 | 3 | 5.7 | 0 | 0 | 2 | 1.8 | 0 | 0 | 0 | 0 | 0 | 0 |
| Total | 85 | 84.3 | 61 | 83.3 | 81 | 84.4 | 28 | 76.4 | 16 | 63.6 | 23 | 76.4 |
| Streams surveyed | 339 | | 353 | | 383 | | 132 | | 194 | | 134 | |
| Total escapement | 2,001,200 | | 1,344,700 | | 1,844,700 | | 486,850 | | 371,100 | | 442,550 | |

199

FIGURE 5  Wild Creek, Port Chalmers, September 22, 1964. This area was uplifted 10 ft by the 1964 earthquake. Photograph was taken at preearthquake 10-ft tide level, looking downstream. Stumps along left bank are evidence of a previous land subsidence. An abandoned channel is apparent near center of photograph.

*J. M. Olson, U.S. Bureau of Commercial Fisheries*

The changes in tributaries of Prince William Sound brought about by the 1964 earthquake clearly have impaired the reproductive potential of the salmon runs. Evidence indicates that salmon runs have recovered from earlier changes in land level. They will probably recover again, but the length of time required for recovery is unknown.

## CHANGES IN THE INTERTIDAL ENVIRONMENT AND SURVIVAL OF PINK AND CHUM SALMON EGGS AND ALEVINS IN THE SPAWNING BED

We studied the effects of changes in elevation of intertidal spawning beds on survival of pink and chum salmon by determining the location, abundance, and fate of eggs deposited in altered environments and by monitoring streambed shifting. The major effort was concentrated at Olsen Creek, where ecological studies had been carried out before the earthquake. General studies were made in three other streams that were selected as representative of changes throughout the Sound: Wild Creek (uplifted), O'Brien Creek (uplifted), and Swanson Creek (subsided).

### STUDIES AT WILD, O'BRIEN, AND SWANSON CREEKS

Our observations at Wild, O'Brien, and Swanson creeks were intended to show the effects on the survival of pink and chum salmon of major alterations in the intertidal environ-

ment resulting from uplift or subsidence. The general methods and techniques used followed those developed in earlier studies at Olsen Creek. Maps of the intertidal stream sections were drawn by measuring at right angles along a base line the distance between wetted edges of the low-flow channel at 10-ft intervals. Bench marks and base lines were established by reference to the stage of the tide [calculated from tide tables of the U.S. Coast and Geodetic Survey (1964) and corrected to the nearest reference station]. Stream elevations in this report are referred to zero tide level. Randomly chosen 0.1-m² plots were sampled with a hydraulic sampler (McNeil, 1964) to determine the number of eggs in the streambed after spawning and the number of alevins the next spring shortly before they emerged as fry from the gravel.

### Wild Creek

Wild Creek enters Port Chalmers on the northwest side of Montague Island in an area uplifted 10 ft. Before the earthquake, escapements of pink salmon to Wild Creek ranged from 3,000 to 8,000 fish, and most spawning took place in the intertidal zone and the freshwater area immediately above it. Roys (1966) estimated that the 1964 escapement was 3,830 pink salmon.

We sampled the spawning beds between the present 19.5- and 21-ft levels (former 9.5- to 11-ft tide levels) and between the 9.5- and 11-ft levels (former −0.5- to +1-ft tide levels). The upper area, formerly in the intertidal zone, is now en-

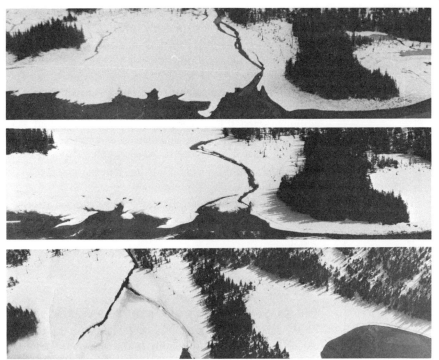

FIGURE 6  Aerial photographs of the channel of Wild Creek on October 31, 1964 (top), April 9, 1965 (center), and April 13, 1966 (bottom).

*J. M. Olson, U.S. Bureau of Commercial Fisheries*

tirely in fresh water. The lower area was previously below the level used by spawners. In September 1964, the abundance of eggs was low in both areas, compared with the abundance at similar tide levels in other streams; scouring had probably dislodged many eggs before the samples were collected. Most of the eggs were alive, indicating that both the old and the new intertidal environments were satisfactory. Much channel shifting and streambed scouring took place between September 1964 and April 1965 (Figures 6 and 7); we found no eggs or alevins in April 1965. During the winter the stream had left its old bed at the 21-ft elevation and rejoined it again at the 11-ft level; this change left the old channel dry between these two points. Deep scouring occurred below the 11-ft level.

*O'Brien Creek*

O'Brien Creek is a small stream entering Crab Bay, Evans Island, on the western side of Prince William Sound in an area uplifted 10 ft. Escapements of pink salmon have ranged from 5,000 to 15,000; 10 to 20 percent of the fish spawned in the former intertidal zone. Roys (1966) estimated that the escapement in 1964 was 8,200 pink salmon. The stream delta, an extensive mudflat now exposed by low tides, is unsuitable for survival of salmon embryos. It is easily dissected by freshets (Figure 8). The former lower intertidal area, the 9.5- to 11-ft tide levels (former −0.5- to +1.0-ft levels) was not used by spawners before the earthquake because of the long period of tide cover. Although we

found an average of 1,665 eggs per m$^2$ in this area in late September 1964 (after spawning), only 42 percent of the eggs were alive. We attribute the low survival to the low intragravel waterflow and low oxygen concentrations resulting from the high silt content of the streambed.

Between September 1964 and April 1965, a new channel was formed at the 10-ft tide level, and the old channel was abandoned (Figure 7). Eggs and alevins in the abandoned channel presumably were killed by freezing or desiccation. Only 0.13 percent of the live eggs in the streambed between the 10- and 11-ft tide levels in September survived the winter. This low survival resulted from a combination of dislodgment of eggs and alevins by scouring and a generally unfavorable streambed environment. It is doubtful that the intertidal zone will ever contribute significantly to the production in O'Brien Creek. In 1964, pink salmon spawned heavily (1,711 eggs per m$^2$) in the old upper intertidal zone (between the new 19.5- and 21-ft elevations), now a freshwater area. We were unable to sample this section completely in April 1965 because of snow and ice along the stream edges, but we found excellent survival in the samples taken.

*Swanson Creek*

Swanson Creek is a relatively large stream that enters Pigot Bay in northwestern Prince William Sound in an area that subsided 6 ft. Annual escapements in this stream in recent years have ranged from 40,000 to 80,000 pink salmon. Before the earthquake, more than 75 percent of the fish

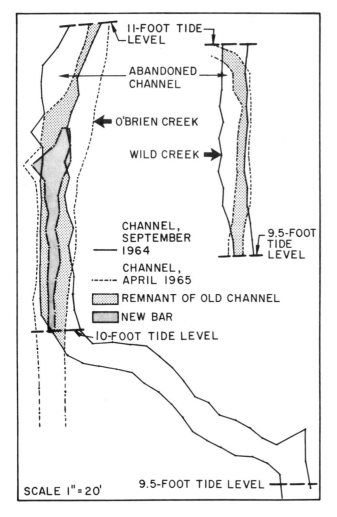

FIGURE 7 Overwinter channel changes between the 9.5- and 11-ft tide levels of Wild and O'Brien creeks, 1964–1965.

riffle. Female pink salmon spawned throughout the upper area in September 1964. In April 1965, we found that the survival of eggs was nil in the low-gradient portion and high in the high-gradient portion.

Our observations at Wild, O'Brien, and Swanson creeks (Table 2) demonstrated that pink salmon consistently selected spawning areas on the basis of present tide levels, although some of the areas had never before been used. Mortalities of salmon eggs and alevins were attributable to the secondary effects of uplift and subsidence—chiefly streambed scouring, channel shifting, and the presence of unfavorable streambed environments in what otherwise would be productive intertidal levels. High survival after spawning in some portions of new intertidal zones indicates that pink salmon that spawn in intertidal areas could maintain themselves if streambeds were stable.

## STUDIES AT OLSEN CREEK

Early in the studies of the effects of changes in land level on the survival of salmon in Prince William Sound, we decided to make an intensive study of the immediate physical changes in a stream, the gradual return to normal, and the accompanying response of salmon. Olsen Creek was selected because of the large amount of preearthquake information available on the physical nature of the stream and the biology of the salmon that use it.

We conducted postearthquake studies at Olsen Creek to learn the distribution and abundance of spawners on the old and new intertidal spawning beds, to determine the number and survival of eggs deposited in these beds, to measure experimentally the rate of egg dislodgment from spawning beds, and to measure streambed movements in relation to the disappearance of eggs and alevins.

During previous studies at Olsen Bay, we have developed the hypothesis that the populations of pink and chum salmon that spawn in the intertidal area are discrete from those that spawn in the freshwater portion of the stream. An obligatory use of the intertidal zone by a certain segment of a run would make that segment especially vulnerable to the secondary effects of an earthquake. The hypothesis of discreteness of freshwater and intertidal spawning populations is supported by the following points: (a) The environments of the intertidal and freshwater areas are drastically different. (b) Late-run pink salmon of the even-year line spawn almost entirely within the intertidal zone (Figure 9); pink salmon of both the odd- and even-year lines are bimodal in time of appearance in Olsen Creek, and the early spawners of both lines and the late spawners of the odd-year line spawn in both the freshwater and intertidal environments. (c) More than 90 percent of the chum salmon in Olsen Creek spawned in the intertidal zone even though spawning areas farther upstream were accessible and uncrowded.

spawned in the intertidal zone. As a result of subsidence, the productive former upper intertidal area is now located between the 3.5- and 5-ft levels and is covered with tidewater about 75 percent of the time. This area is now rarely used by spawners. We found an average of only four pink salmon eggs per m² in September 1964, after the spawning season, whereas in this same area the average number of live alevins per m² was 60 in the spring of 1958 and 120 in the spring of 1959, after overwinter mortalities (data on file, Bureau of Commercial Fisheries Biological Laboratory, Auke Bay, Alaska).

The upper area of Swanson Creek, between the present 8- and 9-ft tide levels, is now covered by tidewater about 25 percent of the time; before the earthquake, only the highest tides reached this area. The upper two thirds of the study area has a low gradient and slow current and is generally a poor spawning area, whereas the lower third has a greater gradient and velocity and is an excellent spawning

FIGURE 8  New intertidal area of O'Brien Creek, September 25, 1964. Photograph is from present 8-ft level, looking downstream. Ten-foot uplift exposed extensive mudflat over which the stream now flows.

*J. M. Olson, U.S. Bureau of Commercial Fisheries*

*Methods*

In April 1964, we determined the amount of uplift at Olsen Creek to be about 4.5 ft by measuring changed tidal elevations from bench marks established before the earthquake. J. Hubbard (1971) observed differences of 3.0 to 3.5 ft between the preearthquake and postearthquake barnacle lines in Olsen Bay during the summer of 1965. In comparisons of preearthquake and postearthquake intertidal zones at Olsen Creek, we have assumed that the uplift was 4 ft but acknowledge a probable error of ±1 ft.

In earlier studies at Olsen Creek, the 12-ft tide level (about mean high tide) was arbitrarily used as the boundary between intertidal and freshwater spawning populations (Helle and others, 1964; Helle, 1970). To facilitate observations of distribution of spawners and of survival of eggs and alevins in various tide zones, the intertidal zone was divided into sections according to elevation (Table 3). Tide predictions for Cordova (with Snug Corner Cove correction; U.S. Coast and Geodetic Survey, 1960) were used to establish boundaries for the sections. Each section was surveyed, and a permanent base line was established parallel to the long axis of the stream to permit accurate orientation within the study area.

The 4-ft uplift caused by the earthquake changed three of the intertidal study sections to freshwater environments and raised some of the unproductive lower intertidal areas to more productive tide levels. For example, the section of the stream formerly between the 3- and 6-ft levels is now be-

tween the 5.9- and 9.4-ft levels. Before the earthquake, this section produced practically no salmon fry, but now (1965) the environmental conditions there approximate those in the old 6- to 9.5-ft section, where survival from live eggs to live fry was moderate to good—5.8 percent for the 1962 brood year and 14.1 percent for 1963. Since the earthquake, we have used the present 12.9-ft tide level as the upper limit of intertidal spawning instead of the 12-ft level used earlier, so that the upper limit would coincide with the boundary between sections 3 and 4. In our discussions of the intertidal sections, sections 1 to 3 make up that portion of the preearthquake intertidal zone that is now above mean high tide, and sections 4 to 6 make up the postearthquake intertidal zone (Figure 10 and Table 3). Section 2 is omitted from further figures and from the discussion that follows because it is a deep pool in which very little spawning takes place.

The total numbers of pink and chum salmon that spawned in the study sections of Olsen Creek were estimated from counts of the spawning grounds made on foot. The method was described by McNeil (1966b) and evaluated at Olsen Creek before the earthquake (Helle, 1970). The total population is the sum of the daily counts (total fish-days) divided by the average redd life (average number of days a fish spends on the spawning grounds). Redd life was determined by daily observations of individual fish marked with large numbered Petersen disk tags. The number of eggs in the streambed after spawning and the number of fry the

TABLE 2 Description of Intertidal Spawning Areas before and after Earthquake and Pink Salmon Egg and Alevin Survival in September 1964 and April 1965, in Wild, O'Brien, and Swanson Creeks[a]

| Creek and Intertidal Area | Description of Area | | | | | | Egg Deposition and Overwinter Survival | | | | | | | | | | | |
|---|---|---|---|---|---|---|---|---|---|---|---|---|---|---|---|---|---|---|
| | Preearthquake | | Postearthquake | | | | September 1964 | | | | | | | April 1965 | | | | |
| | Tidal Elevation of Section Studied (ft) | Time Covered by Tide Water (%) | Primary Composition of Streambed Materials | Tidal Elevation of Area Studied (ft) | Time Covered by Tide Water (%) | Stability of Streambed | Points Sampled | Area Sampled (m²) | Live Eggs per m² Mean | 90% Confidence Interval | Dead Eggs per m² Mean | 90% Confidence Interval | % of Eggs Alive | Points Sampled | Area Sampled (m²) | Live Alevins per m² Mean | 90% Confidence Interval | Overwinter Survival (%) |
| **Wild** | | | | | | | | | | | | | | | | | | |
| Lower | −0.5–1 | >95 | Sand, fine gravel | 9.5–11 | ≃5 | Unstable | 100 | 186 | 1,140 | ±280 | 184 | ±57 | 86 | 30 | 69[b] | 0 | – | 0 |
| Upper | 9.5–11 | ≃5 | Coarse gravel | 19.5–21 | 0 | Unstable | 100 | 112 | 407 | ±155 | 62 | ±31 | 87 | c | – | 0 | – | 0 |
| **O'Brien** | | | | | | | | | | | | | | | | | | |
| Lower | −0.5–1 | >95 | Mud, silt, fine gravel | 9.5–11 | ≃5 | Unstable | 100 | 595 | 681 | ±162 | 984 | ±253 | 42 | 39 | 133[b] | 4 | ±4 | 0.13 |
| Upper | 9.5–11 | ≃5 | Coarse gravel | 19.5–21 | 0 | Stable | 100 | 1,449 | 1,500 | ±361 | 211 | ±85 | 88 | 55 | 906[d] | 922 | ±151 | 61.5[d] |
| **Swanson** | | | | | | | | | | | | | | | | | | |
| Lower | 9.5–11 | ≃5 | Sand, fine gravel | 3.5–5 | ≃75 | Stable | 100 | 5,610 | 2 | ±1.9 | 2 | ±1.9 | 50 | e | – | – | – | – |
| Upper | 14.0–15 | 0 | Sand, fine gravel | 8.0–9 | ≃25 | Stable | 100 | 1,840 | 1,509 | ±317 | 272 | ±90 | 85 | 50 | 1,840 | 173 | ±93 | 11.5 |

[a] Before the earthquake, all areas except the −0.5- to 1-ft sections of Wild and O'Brien creeks were heavily used by spawners.
[b] Remnant of fall channel; area reduced by scouring and channel shifting.
[c] Channel abandoned; therefore no survival was assumed.
[d] Open water only; ice and snowbanks covered edges of stream.
[e] Not sampled.

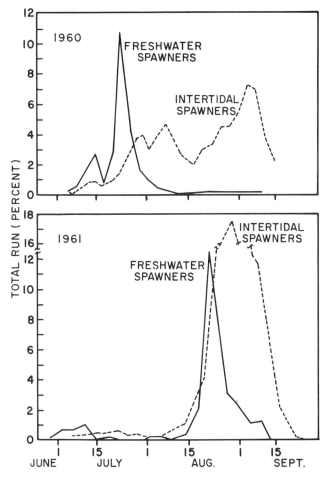

FIGURE 9   Time of appearance of pink salmon on the freshwater and intertidal spawning grounds, Olsen Creek, 1960 and 1961 (from Helle and others, 1964).

next spring, shortly before they emerged from the gravel, were estimated by use of a hydraulic sampler (McNeil, 1964).

Changes in streambed relief were measured by comparing periodic topographic surveys. Streamflow was determined by stream-level recorders on the East Fork and West Fork of the Olsen Creek system during 1964 and 1965. Olsen Creek is typical of the short coastal streams of Prince William Sound. It is subject to rapid fluctuations in the volume of flow because it depends largely on surface runoff, which varies with rainfall. Helle and others (1964) reported that floods at Olsen Creek were frequent and at times caused minor changes in the riffle area of the lower intertidal area by shifting the gravel.

*Distribution and Abundance of Spawning Salmon in Olsen Creek, 1964–1965*

In Olsen Creek, the relative abundance and time of appearance on the spawning ground of intertidal and freshwater spawners differ between odd- and even-year lines of pink

salmon, but these features are nearly constant for chum salmon. We studied the abundance of spawners and the time and place of spawning for pink and chum salmon in 1964 and 1965 to determine the response of the fish to the altered environments of the old and new intertidal spawning beds.

Before the earthquake the late run of the even-year line of pink salmon spawned only in the intertidal zone of Olsen Creek. The late run also used the intertidal zone in 1964, though the upper limit of spawning was not at the new boundary between fresh water and intertidal water but at the upper limit of the old intertidal zone—as if the uplift had not occurred.

In 1964, pink salmon first began to spawn in Olsen Creek in the upstream portions of the East and West forks in mid-July. By the end of July, spawning fish were present throughout both forks and below their confluence down through section 4. No pink salmon spawned in section 6 until early September.

By September 8, pink salmon were spawning in all the study sections, but most were in the three lower sections (4 to 6, Figure 11), and by mid-September more than 90 percent of the fish were spawning in sections 5 and 6. Thus the use of the lower intertidal areas gradually increased with the progress of the season, an indication of a preference for the lower intertidal areas by the later fish.

The proportion of pink salmon of the even-year line that spawned below the old 12-ft level before and after the earthquake was similar (74 percent in 1960 and 70 percent in 1962, as compared with 77 percent in 1964), but the distribution within this zone was markedly different. In 1964, more than 36 percent of the total population spawned in the former lower intertidal and sea-floor sections (5 and 6), as compared with less than 5 percent before the earthquake; 25 percent spawned in section 4 (Table 4). Thus, 61 percent of the fish spawned in the new intertidal zone and only 15 percent in the portion of the old intertidal zone (sections 1 to 3 and East and West fork sections, now fresh water) that was used by about 60 percent of the intertidal spawners in 1962.

Before the earthquake, the early and late runs of pink salmon of the odd-year line spawned in both the intertidal and freshwater environments. Late-run spawners were more abundant in the intertidal zone than in fresh water, however, and spawning tended to persist longer in the intertidal zone.

The earlier pattern of occurrence of odd-year spawners persisted in 1965, when about 61 percent of the total escapement of pink salmon spawned below the preearthquake 12-ft tide level and about 45 percent spawned in the new intertidal zone (sections 4 to 6). A smaller proportion of the early-run spawners occupied sections 1 to 3 in 1965 than in 1964. As the season progressed, however, most of the late-run fish spawned in sections 4 and 5 (Figure 12).

**TABLE 3**   Descriptions of Study Sections of Olsen Creek Intertidal Zone Showing Elevation and Grade before and after the Earthquake

| Preearthquake Name for Study Section | Postearthquake Number for Study Section | Length (ft) | Base-Line Reference (ft) | General Description (Postearthquake) | Preearthquake (July 1963) | | Postearthquake (July 1965) | |
|---|---|---|---|---|---|---|---|---|
| | | | | | Tidal Elevation (ft) | Grade (%) | Tidal Elevation (ft) | Grade (%) |
| Upper intertidal | 1 | 309 | 1,382 to 1,700 | Good riffle area, stable streambed, heavy use by spawners | 9.7–11.0 | 0.42 | 14.0–15.0 | 0.32 |
| Holding pool | 2 | 133 | 1,250 to 1,382 | Deepwater resting area | 9.6–9.7 | 0.08 | 13.6–14.0 | 0.30 |
| Low gradient | 3 | 228 | 1,022 to 1,250 | Poor-grade, silt-bottom overlap of pool | 9.5–9.6 | 0.04 | 12.9–13.6 | 0.30 |
| Middle intertidal | 4 | 776 | 250 to 1,022 | Good riffle area, steep grade causing some streambed shifting, heavy spawning | 6.0–9.5 | 0.45 | 9.4–12.9 | 0.46 |
| Lower intertidal | 5 | 696 | −442 to 250 | Start of silt-settling area, part of section unstable | 3.0–6.0 | 0.43 | 5.9–9.4 | 0.50 |
| Former bay floor | 6 | 158 | −442 to −1,016 | Unstable, silt-laden bed, covered by tide more than 50 percent of time | <3.0 | – | <5.9 | 0.56 |

Only 2.3 percent of the run spawned in section 6 in 1965, whereas 14.1 percent spawned there in 1964 (Table 4). When the sizes of the even- and odd-year lines are about the same, the odd-year line might be expected to have fewer fish in the lower areas because both the early and late runs on the odd year have freshwater and intertidal components, whereas the late run of the even-year line has only intertidal spawners.

Before the earthquake, about 95 percent of the chum salmon in Olsen Creek spawned in the intertidal zone; the earlier spawners used the upper intertidal area, and gradually over the season the later fish used the lower area down to the 6-ft tide level (lower limit of section 5).

In the summer after the earthquake, the early chum salmon spawners occupied Olsen Creek as though the area had not been uplifted—that is, they spawned in section 1, a former intertidal section that is now always above tidewater. As the season progressed, however, spawning increased in the lower intertidal sections, and by early August about one third of the chum salmon in Olsen Creek were spawning in streambed areas that were rarely or never used before be-

cause of the low tidal elevation (sections 5 and 6) but that are now within the preferred tide range (Figure 13).

The number of chum salmon that spawned in the unchanged freshwater areas and in the preearthquake (old) and postearthquake (new) intertidal zones are given in Table 5 by stream sections. In 1964, as before the earthquake, about 95 percent of the chum salmon spawned below the former 12-ft tide levels but, because sections 1 and 3 are now fresh water, the percentage of fish spawning in the intertidal zone was lower after the earthquake. Fifty-five percent of the chum salmon spawned in the new intertidal zone in 1964, and the rest spawned upstream. Distribution of chum salmon spawners in the new intertidal zone in 1964 was similar to that in the old intertidal zone before the earthquake. Fish began spawning in the upper reaches of the zone (section 4) and gradually progressed downstream over the season (into sections 5 and 6). An insignificant number of chum salmon spawned below section 6.

The chum salmon run into Olsen Creek was slightly smaller in 1965 than in 1964. About 99 percent of the fish spawned below the preearthquake 12-ft tide level, and 64

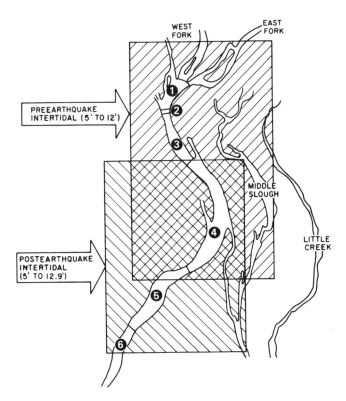

FIGURE 10   Location and numbers of Olsen Creek study sections and their position in relation to preearthquake and postearthquake intertidal zones.

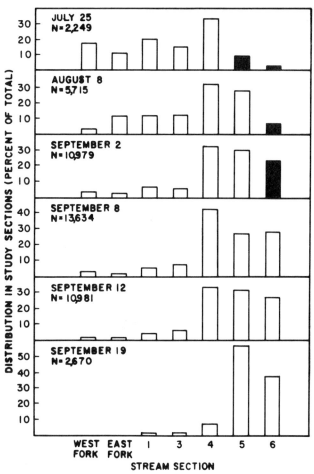

FIGURE 11   Intraseasonal occupation of old and new intertidal stream sections by pink salmon, in percentage of total fish present at time of each survey, Olsen Creek, 1964. Solid bars represent prespawning fish moving to the spawning grounds.

percent spawned in the new intertidal zone (Table 5). Early spawners concentrated in freshwater sections 1 to 3 (old upper intertidal zone) and moved into intertidal sections (4 and 5) as the season progressed (Figure 14). Only 14 chum salmon spawned in section 6 (below the 6-ft tide level).

*Egg Deposition and Overwinter Survival of Pink and Chum Salmon, 1964–1965 and 1965–1966*

The number of eggs deposited and the number that survived over the winter were estimated by use of the hydraulic sampler in October after spawning and again in April just before the fry emerged from the gravel.

The abundance of pink salmon eggs and alevins in the various sections of Olsen Creek in October 1964 and April 1965 and in October 1965 and April 1966 and estimates of overwinter survival are summarized in Tables 6 and 7. The mean density of pink salmon eggs (alive and dead) in the Olsen Creek streambed in October 1964 ranged from 1,055 per m² in section 6 to 3,836 per m² in section 4, and the percentage of live eggs ranged from 72 percent in section 6 to 83 percent in section 4 (Table 6).

The relation between overwinter survival before and after the changes in land level varied markedly among the stream sections. Survival of pink salmon eggs to alevins over

the winter of 1964–1965 in section 1 (10.6 percent, Table 6) was the lowest recorded for this area since research began at Olsen Creek in 1960. Overwinter survival in section 1 was 54 percent in 1960–1961 (Helle and others, 1964), about 32 percent in 1962–1963, and 15 percent in 1963–1964 (Thorsteinson, 1965). Dislodgment of eggs and alevins by gravel movement that accompanied regrading of the streambed was suspected to be responsible for the low survival in 1964–1965. Survival of pink salmon eggs and fry in section 6 was expected to be negligible because this area never produced live fry before the earthquake (Helle and others, 1964; Thorsteinson, 1965). Our estimate of survival of pink salmon over the winter of 1964–1965 (10.9 percent, Table 6), however, was as high as that for the other sections, although the large confidence interval reduces the significance of this difference (only 14 of the 100 points sampled in section 6 contained fry, and only three points contained more than 100 fry).

TABLE 4   Distribution of Spawning Pink Salmon in Olsen Creek, 1964–1965

| Stream Section | Section Number | Tidal Elevation (ft) | | Pink Salmon | | | |
| | | New | Old | 1964 | | 1965 | |
| | | | | No. | Percent of Total | No. | Percent of Total |
|---|---|---|---|---|---|---|---|
| Unchanged fresh water, East and West forks | – | >16.0 | >12.0 | 16,835 | 23.0 | 28,371 | 38.6 |
| Old intertidal | | | | | | | |
| West Fork | – | 15.0–16.0 | 11.0–12.0 | 1,754 | 2.4 | 1,223 | 1.7 |
| East Fork | – | 15.0–16.0 | 11.0–12.0 | 2,163 | 3.0 | 1,510 | 2.1 |
| Upper intertidal | 1 | 14.0–15.0 | 9.7–11 | 3,447 | 4.7 | 3,397 | 4.6 |
| Low gradient | 3 | 12.9–13.6 | 9.5–9.6 | 3,972 | 5.4 | 5,531 | 7.5 |
| New intertidal | | | | | | | |
| Middle intertidal | 4 | 6.0–9.5 | 9.4–12.9 | 18,403 | 25.1 | 20,409 | 27.8 |
| Lower intertidal | 5 | 5.9–9.4 | 3.0–6.0 | 16,268 | 22.2 | 11,313 | 15.4 |
| Former bay floor | 6 | < 3.0 | 5.0–5.9 | 10,346 | 14.1 | 1,685 | 2.3 |
| Total | – | – | – | 73,188 | 99.9 | 73,439 | 100.0 |

The relative survival of pink salmon eggs and fry among the intertidal study sections in 1965–1966 (Table 7) was apparently similar to that in years before the earthquake. Because of ice and snow, only sections 5 and 6 could be sampled completely in the spring of 1966. On the basis of survival at equivalent tide levels in 1960, 1962, and 1963, the survival of 18 percent in section 5 (Table 7) over the winter of 1965–1966 was close to the expected maximum. In contrast to the high survival in 1964–1965, no live pink salmon fry were found in section 6 in April 1966.

The number of chum salmon eggs and preemergent fry in the various sections of Olsen Creek in October 1964 and April 1965 is summarized in Table 8. In October the mean density of chum salmon eggs, live and dead, varied only slightly among study sections 1–5, despite sizable variations in the density of spawners. For example, although more than twice as many chum salmon spawned in section 4 as in any other section (Table 5), the mean number of eggs per m² (live plus dead) was only slightly larger than in the other sections. This lack of correlation between the density of spawners and density of eggs in the streambed was probably due to the loss of eggs as the streambed gravel shifted and to increased dislodgment of eggs by late-spawning females in areas where spawning fish were abundant. Spawning of only 82 chum salmon in section 6 resulted in a mean density of 0.06 dead egg per m² (Table 8). No live chum salmon eggs were found in this area in 1964.

Survival of chum salmon over the winter of 1964–1965 was 36 percent in section 1, 13 percent in section 4, and only 0.1 percent in section 5 (Table 8). Before the earthquake, no chum salmon eggs survived the winter in section 5. Because of its present elevation between the 5.9- and 9.4-ft tide levels, we expected survival over the winter in sec-

tion 5 to be 10 to 20 percent. The difference between the expected and the actual survival was attributed to movement of the streambed gravel.

Fewer adult chum salmon returned to Olsen Creek in 1965 than in 1964, and the abundance of eggs after spawning was correspondingly lower (Table 9). The density of eggs in the streambed in October was highest in section 1 (301 per m²) and lowest in section 6 (0.6 per m²). A greater proportion of the eggs were alive in four of the five sections at the end of spawning in 1965 than in 1964. In the spring of 1966 the survival was unexpectedly high (57 percent) in section 5 (see Table 9), but no live chum salmon fry were found in section 6; sections 1, 3, and part of 4 were not sampled.

Most of the pink and chum salmon that spawned in Olsen Creek below the old 12-ft tide line in 1964 and 1965 used the new intertidal zone. This behavior supports the hypothesis that intertidal spawners are a discrete population and that they select their spawning ground in relation to tidal elevation. The new intertidal area had the same general decreasing rate of egg deposition and increasing mortalities from upper to lower tide levels that were observed in the old intertidal area before the earthquake.

The disappearance of large numbers of eggs from the new intertidal area was apparently a direct result of the instability of the streambed. Efforts to determine the extent and cause of this disappearance are described below.

*Experimental Measurement of Egg Dislodgment from the Spawning Bed*

We expected that the movement of streambed gravel caused by floods would increase after the earthquake because of the increased grade caused by the land uplift. We expected fur-

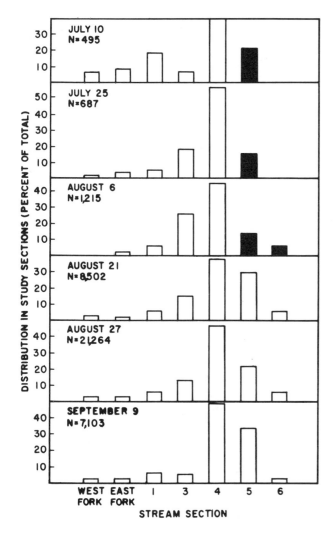

FIGURE 12 Intraseasonal occupation of old and new intertidal stream sections by pink salmon, in percentage of total fish present at time of each survey, Olsen Creek, 1965. Solid bars represent prespawning fish moving to the spawning grounds.

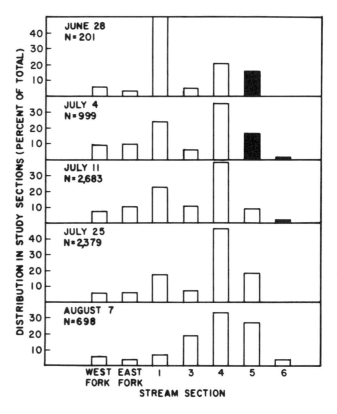

FIGURE 13 Intraseasonal occupation of old and new intertidal stream sections by chum salmon, in percentage of total fish present at time of each survey, Olsen Creek, 1964. Solid bars represent prespawning fish moving to the spawning grounds.

ther that this movement would dislodge buried eggs, but the extent of the dislodgment could not be predicted.

In 1964, we conducted an experiment in a spawning bed in the West Fork of Olsen Creek to measure egg dislodgment. We buried 6,136 preserved pink salmon eggs in pockets, each pocket containing about 35 eggs. These eggs had been dyed dark red to differentiate them from natural pink salmon eggs. The pockets were spaced 3 ft apart in rows across the stream, and the rows were 4 ft apart (Figure 15). All the eggs in each row were at the same depth—eggs in row 1 were buried 6 in. deep; row 2, 9 in. deep; and row 3, 12 in. deep. This sequence was repeated in successive series of rows in the plot. An array of nets was placed at the lower end of the plot to catch dislodged eggs, both natural and dyed, as they drifted downstream. Thirty-eight female chum salmon had spawned in the experimental area before the dyed eggs were

buried, and an additional 63 female chum salmon and 434 female pink salmon spawned in the area by August 29. The dyed eggs were buried July 17-18 and were recovered August 25-29 by digging them from each pocket with the hydraulic sampler.

Daily records were kept of stream discharge, number of salmon spawning in the experimental plot, and catch of drift eggs (natural and dyed) in the net array below the experimental plot (Figure 16).

Stream discharge was moderate, about 50 cfs (cubic feet per second) in late July, and gradually decreased through August 19. On August 20, the discharge increased sharply to about 300 cfs, and between August 20 and 26, it reached a peak of 375 cfs—almost 10 times the base discharge. After this flood, flows diminished until September 23-24, when a smaller flood with a peak discharge of 205 cfs occurred.

The number of eggs dislodged seemed to depend on a combination of spawning activity and stream discharge (Table 10). Between July 20 and August 19, when the number of spawners was increasing, the average catch of drift eggs per day was 111 natural eggs and 3 dyed eggs. The flood of August 20-26 occurred at the peak of spawning. For the 3 days we were able to hold the nets in the stream

TABLE 5    Distribution of Spawning Chum Salmon in Olsen Creek, 1964–1965

| Stream Section | Section Number | Tidal Elevation (ft) | | Chum Salmon | | | |
| | | New | Old | 1964 | | 1965 | |
| | | | | No. | Percent of Total | No. | Percent of Total |
|---|---|---|---|---|---|---|---|
| Unchanged fresh water, East and West forks | – | >16.0 | >12.0 | 278 | 4.5 | 40 | 0.7 |
| Old intertidal | | | | | | | |
| West Fork | – | 15.0–16.0 | 11.0–12.0 | 400 | 6.5 | 129 | 2.3 |
| East Fork | – | 15.0–16.0 | 11.0–12.0 | 412 | 6.7 | 54 | 0.9 |
| Upper intertidal | 1 | 14.0–15.0 | 9.7–11 | 1,092 | 17.7 | 718 | 12.6 |
| Low gradient | 3 | 12.9–13.6 | 9.5–9.6 | 580 | 9.4 | 1,113 | 19.5 |
| New intertidal | | | | | | | |
| Middle intertidal | 4 | 6.0–9.5 | 9.4–12.9 | 2,375 | 38.6 | 1,957 | 34.3 |
| Lower intertidal | 5 | 5.9–9.4 | 3.0–6.0 | 934 | 15.2 | 1,683 | 29.5 |
| Former bay floor | 6 | < 3.0 | 5.0–5.9 | 82 | 1.3 | 14 | 0.2 |
| Total | – | – | – | 6,153 | 99.9 | 5,708 | 100.0 |

(August 20, 25, and 26), the average catch of drift eggs was 1,028 natural and 2 dyed eggs per day. After the peak of spawning, the average catches of drift eggs were 165 natural and less than one dyed egg per day. During 9 days after the last spawning fish had disappeared, the average daily catch was nine natural and no dyed eggs.

The catches of dyed eggs cannot be compared with the catch of natural drift eggs from the experimental area because natural eggs could have originated anywhere in the stream above the nets. The catch of natural eggs indicates that the number of drift eggs per day increased as the number of spawners, the density of eggs in the spawning bed, and stream discharge increased.

In a regrading stream, successfully buried salmon eggs are dislodged from the spawning beds by the combined action of scouring of the streambed and digging by late-spawning salmon. The rate of dislodgment increases as the water velocity and the number of late-spawning salmon increase. The dyed eggs buried the deepest were dislodged at the lowest rate—66 percent disappeared from 12-in. depths, 71 percent from 9-in. depths, and 86 percent from 6-in. depths. The (weighted) average loss of dyed eggs at all depths was 71 percent.

*Streambed Movement and Disappearance of Salmon Eggs and Alevins in New and Old Intertidal Areas of Olsen Creek, 1965–1966*

Our 1964 observations of the effects of changes in land level in the intertidal area indicated that salmon eggs and alevins were removed from the streambed by scouring and were smothered or stranded by filling and channel shifting that occurred with slope adjustments. In 1965 we began a series of detailed topographic surveys of the Olsen Creek streambed in the intertidal area to describe changes in the streambed. Surveys were made in July and October 1965 and in April 1966, before and after spawning and just before the out-migration of fry. The changes were considered in relation to changes in the abundance of eggs and alevins. Similar surveys are to be made each year until major slope adjustments are completed and the stream has returned to normal.

For the study of changes in the topography of the Olsen Creek streambed, we surveyed the area between the present 5- and 15-ft tide levels. The 5-ft level is the lower limit of potential production in the new intertidal study area. Bench marks and a permanent base line (2,300 ft long) were established adjacent and parallel to the long axis of the stream. Stream cross-section stations were located every 20 ft along the base line. Elevations were recorded at 10-ft intervals along each cross section (or at any marked deviation in bottom elevation), at the edges of the wetted channel, and for a short distance beyond the wetted edge at each station. Standard surveying procedures were used to measure elevation to the nearest 0.1 ft, and precision was estimated to be ±0.1 ft.

The net movement of streambed material between surveys was determined by comparing the relief of the bed recorded on succeeding surveys. The contour of successive surveys of each cross section was plotted on the same graph to determine where net changes in elevation occurred and the amount and direction, i.e., increase or decrease. The points of changed elevation of 0.2, 0.6, 1.0, and >1 ft were plotted on the cross section drawn on an outline map of the stream-

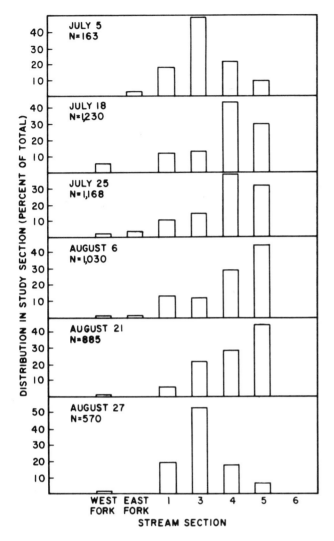

FIGURE 14   Intraseasonal occupation of old and new intertidal stream sections by chum salmon in percentage of total fish present at time of each survey, Olsen Creek, 1965.

bed; points of equal change were connected to construct a map of changes in relief. This process is illustrated for three cross sections in Figures 17 and 18 for three surveys. We did not consider streambed changes of less than 0.2 ft because most pink and chum salmon eggs are buried deeper than this. The surface area of streambed in each category of change was determined by measuring the surface within each contour on the map with a polar planimeter.

The points sampled with the hydraulic sampler to determine abundance of eggs or preemergent fry were plotted on the streambed relief maps, and the data obtained from hydraulic sampling were grouped according to increments of change in streambed elevation.

Changes in stream slope were accelerated during floods. Obvious changes in the streambed occurred during three floods when the discharge exceeded 400 cfs in the West Fork of Olsen Creek (Figure 19), which is about half the discharge of the main stream in the intertidal zone. Some movement of streambed occurred in all study sections between July 5, 1965, and October 3, 1965. Between July and October 1965, the elevation of about 56 percent of the streambed area between the present 5- and 15-ft levels was changed more than 0.2 ft; 35 percent of the area was scoured, and 21 percent was filled. The greatest amount of streambed movement occurred in the central portion of the present intertidal zone (centered near the boundary of sections 4 and 5, Figure 20).

In October 1965, after spawning, the highest density of buried eggs per m² was in the areas of no change in elevation. There was an inverse relation between the amount of apparent change in elevation and the number of eggs remaining in the streambed: the greater the change, the fewer the eggs (Table 11).

In calculating the loss of eggs due to scouring or filling in the intertidal study areas, we assumed that the abundance of eggs in the unchanged streambed was representative of what the abundance in the entire study area would have been without scouring or filling. Egg losses in the 1965 spawning season due to scouring or filling in the former and present intertidal areas were estimated to be 7.27 million pink salmon eggs and 1.1 million chum salmon eggs (Table 11). Salmon are seldom 100 percent efficient in depositing their eggs, however; differences between actual and potential egg deposition are frequently great. Bailey (1964) estimated that the actual deposition in the Olsen Creek intertidal zone in 1962 was 40 percent of the potential deposition for pink salmon and 32 percent for chum salmon. The average fecundity of female pink salmon in Olsen Creek in 1965 was 1,961 eggs; the estimated egg loss was therefore equivalent to the eggs of 3,705 females or, if spawning efficiency in 1965 was similar to that in 1962, the loss from the effects of the earthquake would represent the actual deposition of about 9,260 female pink salmon. The average fecundity of female chum salmon in Olsen Creek in 1965 was 2,936 eggs, and the loss of chum salmon eggs from the streambed was equivalent to the full potential of 373 females (or the actual deposition of 1,165 females at 32 percent efficiency).

We estimated that 42,335 pink salmon and 5,485 chum salmon spawned between the former 11-ft tide level and the present 5-ft level in 1965. Assuming a 1:1 sex ratio, these totals represented 21,167 female pink salmon and 2,742 female chum salmon. The true losses caused by scouring and filling in the intertidal area, expressed in terms of loss of female spawners, probably lie between the estimates based on potential and actual deposition (3,705 and 9,260 pink salmon, and 373 and 1,165 chum salmon) and represent a significant proportion of the females that spawned in this section of stream.

TABLE 6 Abundance of Pink Salmon Eggs and Alevins in October 1964 and April 1965 in Olsen Creek and Estimates of Survival

| | | October 2–5, 1964 | | | | | | April 15–19, 1965 | | | |
| | | Live Eggs per m² | | | Live and Dead Eggs per m² | | | Live Alevins per m² | | | |
| Stream Section | Section Number | Samples | Mean | 90% Confidence Interval | Mean | 90% Confidence Interval | Percent of Eggs Alive | Samples | Mean | 90% Confidence Interval | Percent Survival |
|---|---|---|---|---|---|---|---|---|---|---|---|
| Upper intertidal | 1 | 100 | 1,832 | ±284 | 2,251 | ±316 | 81 | 97 | 194 | ±73 | 10.6 |
| Low gradient | 3 | 99 | 2,396 | ±336 | 3,033 | ±375 | 79 | 37 | 6 | ±5 | 0.3 |
| Middle intertidal | 4 | 140 | 3,200 | ±498 | 3,836 | ±351 | 83 | 84 | 321 | ±117 | 10.0 |
| Lower intertidal | 5 | 158 | 2,159 | ±29 | 2,729 | ±35 | 79 | 101 | 50 | ±28 | 2.3 |
| Former bay floor | 6 | 158 | 763 | ±176 | 1,055 | ±204 | 72 | 100 | 83 | ±71 | 10.9 |

TABLE 7 Abundance of Pink Salmon Eggs and Alevins in October 1965 and April 1966 in Olsen Creek and Estimates of Survival

| | | October 2–5, 1965 | | | | | | April 11–13, 1966 | | | |
| | | Live Eggs per m² | | | Live and Dead Eggs per m² | | | Live Alevins per m² | | | |
| Stream Section | Section Number | Samples | Mean | 90% Confidence Interval | Mean | 90% Confidence Interval | Percent of Eggs Alive | Samples | Mean | 90% Confidence Interval | Percent Survival |
|---|---|---|---|---|---|---|---|---|---|---|---|
| Upper intertidal | 1 | 102 | 1,938 | ±326 | 2,169 | ·±346 | 89 | a | – | – | – |
| Low gradient | 3 | 99 | 1,311 | ±346 | 1,523 | ±397 | 86 | a | – | – | – |
| Middle gradient | 4 | 148 | 1,394 | ±236 | 1,622 | ±260 | 86 | 43b | 39 | ±23 | – |
| Lower intertidal | 5 | 137 | 418 | ±157 | 471 | ±160 | 89 | 155 | 75 | ±21 | 18 |
| Former bay floor | 6 | 72 | 25 | ±32 | 32 | ±33 | 78 | 42c | 0 | – | 0 |

a Not sampled; stream frozen above 11-ft tide level.
b Area only partially sampled because of ice cover.
c Stream channel had shifted at midpoint of this section.

212

TABLE 8 Abundance of Chum Salmon Eggs and Alevins in October 1964 and April 1965 in Olsen Creek and Estimates of Survival

| | | October 2–5, 1964 | | | | | | April 15–19, 1965 | | | |
| | | Live Eggs per m² | | | Live and Dead Eggs per m² | | | Live Alevins per m² | | | |
| Stream Section | Section Number | Samples | Mean | 90% Confidence Interval | Mean | 90% Confidence Interval | Percent of Eggs Alive | Samples | Mean | 90% Confidence Interval | Percent Survival |
|---|---|---|---|---|---|---|---|---|---|---|---|
| Upper intertidal | 1 | 100 | 516 | ±187 | 593 | ±204 | 87 | 97 | 187 | ±112 | 36 |
| Low gradient | 3 | 99 | 562 | ±263 | 651 | ±278 | 86 | 37 | 11 | ±1 | 2 |
| Middle intertidal | 4 | 140 | 590 | ±180 | 655 | ±194 | 90 | 84 | 77 | ±48 | 13 |
| Lower intertidal | 5 | 158 | 446 | ±152 | 515 | ±160 | 87 | 101 | 0.6 | ±0.04 | 0.1 |
| Former bay floor | 6 | 158 | 0 | — | 0.06 | — | 0 | 42 | 0 | — | — |

TABLE 9 Abundance of Chum Salmon Eggs and Alevins in October 1965 and April 1966 in Olsen Creek and Estimates of Survival

| | | October 2–5, 1965 | | | | | | April 11–13, 1966 | | | |
| | | Live Eggs per m² | | | Live and Dead Eggs per m² | | | Live Alevins per m² | | | |
| Steam Section | Section Number | Samples | Mean | 90% Confidence Interval | Mean | 90% Confidence Interval | Percent of Eggs Alive | Samples | Mean | 90% Confidence Interval | Percent Survival |
|---|---|---|---|---|---|---|---|---|---|---|---|
| Upper intertidal | 1 | 102 | 295 | ±128 | 301 | ±133 | 98 | a | — | — | — |
| Low gradient | 3 | 99 | 48 | ±6 | 55 | ±61 | 87 | a | — | — | b |
| Middle intertidal | 4 | 148 | 179 | ±119 | 186 | ±119 | 96 | 43[b] | 18 | ±19 | b |
| Lower intertidal | 5 | 137 | 79 | ±49 | 92 | ±53 | 86 | 155 | 45 | ±52 | 57 |
| Former bay floor | 6 | 72 | 0.6 | ±0.4 | 0.6 | ±0.4 | 100 | 42[c] | 0 | — | 0 |

[a] Not sampled; stream frozen above 11-ft tide level.
[b] Area only partially sampled because of ice cover.
[c] Stream channel had shifted at midpoint of this section.

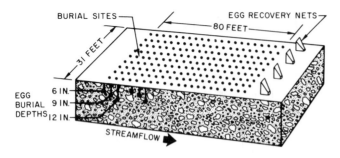

FIGURE 15  Diagram of stream section, showing layout for egg-dislodgment experiment, July 17 to August 29, 1964.

The April 1966 topographic surveys and hydraulic sampling of preemergent fry were done only between the 5- and 11-ft levels because upstream areas were covered by ice. We found less change in streambed elevation between October 1965 and April 1966 than between July 1965 and October 1965—37 and 66 percent, respectively. The area filled over the winter was about the same as in the summer (24 percent), but only 13 percent was scoured, as compared with 35 percent in the summer. The density of alevins was greatest in the unchanged streambed area, and, as we had previously observed with eggs, the trend was toward a decrease in the density of alevins with an increase in the depth of scouring (Table 12). Mortalities due to movement of streambed materials from October 1965 to April 1966 were estimated to be 0.54 million pink salmon and 0.43 million chum salmon eggs and alevins between the 5- and 11-ft tide levels (Table 13).

The losses of eggs and alevins due to movement of streambed materials after the March 1964 earthquake were reflected in 1966 in the small number of adult pink salmon in the intertidal zone of Olsen Creek and the general scarcity in Prince William Sound. When it became evident that the return of pink salmon to the Sound in 1966 was less than the anticipated 6.3 million (Roys, 1967), the Alaska Department

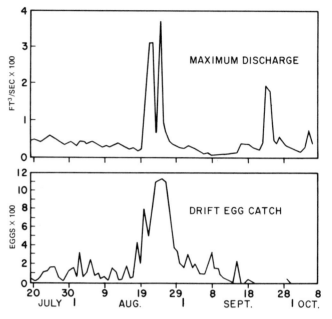

FIGURE 16  Daily maximum stream discharge and daily catch of drift eggs (natural and dyed) in East Fork of Olsen Creek, July 1 to October 8, 1964.

of Fish and Game curtailed commercial fishing in time to protect the important late intertidal runs. Despite this protection, Olsen Creek had only about half as many pink salmon spawning in the intertidal zone in 1966 as in the parent year 1964. Although pink salmon in both the even- and odd-year runs have continued to spawn in the new intertidal portion of Olsen Creek, the runs have not increased. The proportion of each run that spawned in the new areas has been about the same as it was during the first two seasons after the earthquake—1964 and 1965. The return of pink salmon to Olsen Creek in 1967 was less than half that of the parent year, 1965, and odd- and even-year runs have both remained at this low level in Olsen Creek through 1970.

TABLE 10  Daily Maximum Stream Discharge, Type of Spawning Activity, and Average Daily Catch of Drift Eggs (Natural and Dyed), West Fork of Olsen Creek, July 20 to October 6, 1964

| Period | Water Level | Daily Maximum Discharge (range, in cfs) | Type of Spawning Activity | Average Daily Catch | |
|---|---|---|---|---|---|
| | | | | Natural Eggs | Dyed Eggs |
| July 20 to August 19 | Normal | 22–49 | Active spawning | 111 | 3 |
| August 20, 25, 26 | Flood | 61–375 | Active spawning | 1,028[a] | 2 |
| August 27 to September 21 | Normal to low | 11–41 | Active spawning | 165 | <1 |
| September 22–27 | Flood | 186–205 | End of spawning | [b] | [b] |
| September 28 to October 6 | Normal to high | 26–82 | No spawning | 9 | 0 |

[a]Nets fished only 3 full days because of flood.
[b]Nets not fished because of flood.

Since the earthquake, most of the chum salmon in Olsen Creek spawned in the preearthquake intertidal portion of the stream, and the runs have increased slightly. Returns of 4-year-old chum salmon to Olsen Creek were slightly greater in 1968, 1969, and 1970 than in their respective postearthquake brood years—1964, 1965, and 1966.

Major changes in the streambed, caused by flooding and stream regrading that occurred in 1964 and 1965, continued through the fall of 1967. Only minor changes occurred in the streambed in 1968-1970.

Returns of pink and chum salmon in Prince William Sound are expected to remain relatively small until major stream regrading is complete and spawning beds approach their former stability.

## ACKNOWLEDGMENTS

Many individuals on the staff of the Bureau of Commercial Fisheries assisted with field observations. Merritt Mitchell gave advice and assistance with the topographic surveys at Olsen Creek.

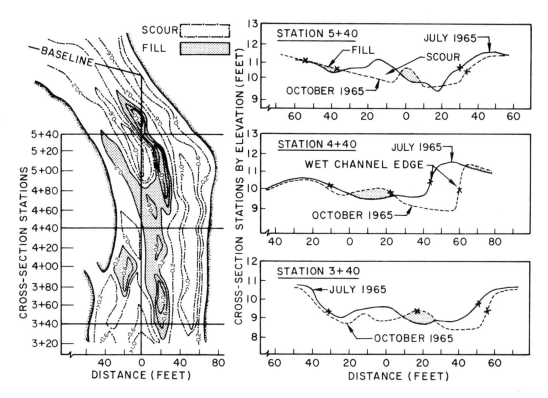

FIGURE 17  Streambed relief map and cross-section profiles, showing changes in streambed elevation between July and October 1965, in a section of Olsen Creek. In the cross sections, the edge of the wetted channel is indicated by X.

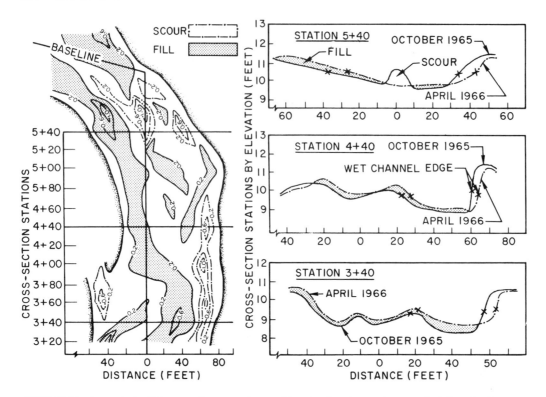

FIGURE 18   Streambed relief map and cross-section profiles, showing changes in streambed elevation between October 1965 and April 1966 in a section of Olsen Creek. In the cross sections, the edge of the wetted channel is indicated by X.

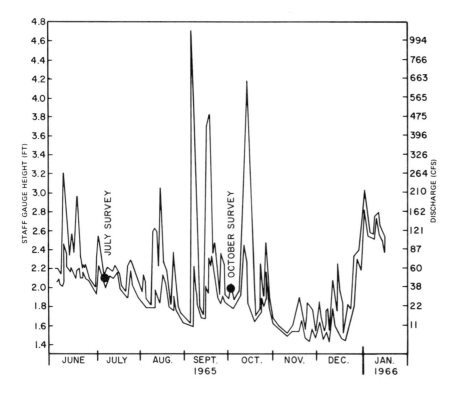

FIGURE 19   Daily maximum and minimum discharges for West Fork of Olsen Creek from June 1965 to January 1966.

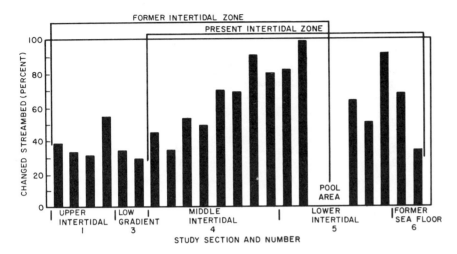

FIGURE 20  Histogram showing portions of former and present intertidal streambed at Olsen Creek that changed between July 5 and October 3, 1965. Data are shown for each 100-ft unit of the study section. No observations were made in the pool area.

TABLE 11  Average Density of Pink and Chum Salmon Eggs at End of Spawning and Estimated Loss of Eggs in Olsen Creek during the 1965 Spawning Season

| Type of Change in Streambed and Amount of Movement (ft) | Area of Streambed (m²) | Pink Salmon Eggs | | | Chum Salmon Eggs | | |
|---|---|---|---|---|---|---|---|
| | | Average Density per m² | Deviation from Average Density in Unchanged Area | Estimated Loss | Average Density per m² | Deviation from Average Density in Unchanged Area | Estimated Loss |
| Unchanged | | | | | | | |
| <±0.2 | 5,931 | 1,904 | — | — | 241 | — | — |
| Scour | | | | | | | |
| 0.2–0.6 | 3,500 | 1,228 | −676 | 2,366,000 | 51 | −190 | 665,000 |
| 0.6–1.0 | 1,011 | 29 | −1,875 | 1,895,625 | 76 | −165 | 166,815 |
| >1.0 | 284 | 15 | −1,889 | 536,476 | 0 | −241 | 68,444 |
| Fill | | | | | | | |
| 0.2–0.6 | 2,230 | 1,380 | −524 | 1,170,750 | 225 | −16 | 35,680 |
| 0.6–1.0 | 535 | 30 | −1,874 | 1,000,590 | 14 | −227 | 121,445 |
| >1.0 | 155 | 0 | −1,904 | 295,120 | 0 | −241 | 37,355 |
| Total | — | — | — | 7,266,561 | — | — | 1,094,739 |

TABLE 12   Average Density of Pink and Chum Salmon Alevins between the 5- and 11-ft Tide Levels of Olsen Creek in April 1966

| Type of Change in Streambed and Amount of Movement (ft) | Area of Streambed (m$^2$) | Percent of Streambed | Points Sampled | Average Density of Live Alevins per m$^2$ | |
|---|---|---|---|---|---|
| | | | | Pink Salmon | Chum Salmon |
| Unchanged | | | | | |
| <±0.2 | 3,455 | 62.8 | 27 | 315 | 226 |
| Scour | | | | | |
| 0.2–0.6 | 499 | 9.1 | 94 | 34 | 13 |
| 0.6–1.0 | 157 | 2.8 | 35 | 31 | 54 |
| >1.0 | 39 | 0.7 | 17 | 1 | 1 |
| Fill | | | | | |
| 0.2–0.6 | 1,186 | 21.6 | 42 | 67 | 9 |
| 0.6–1.0 | 137 | 2.5 | 22 | 36 | 42 |
| >1.0 | 24 | 0.4 | 9 | 66 | 7 |

TABLE 13   Average Density of Pink and Chum Salmon Alevins and Estimated Loss between the 5- and 11-ft Tide Levels of Olsen Creek from October 1965 to April 1966

| Type of Change in Streambed and Amount of Movement (ft) | Area of Streambed (m$^2$) | Pink Salmon Alevins | | | Chum Salmon Alevins | | |
|---|---|---|---|---|---|---|---|
| | | Average Density per m$^2$ | Deviation from Average Density in Unchanged Area | Estimated Loss | Average Density per m$^2$ | Deviation from Average Density in Unchanged Area | Estimated Loss |
| Unchanged | | | | | | | |
| <±0.2 | 3,455 | 315 | – | – | 226 | – | – |
| Scour | | | | | | | |
| 0.2–0.6 | 499 | 34 | −281 | 140,219 | 13 | −213 | 106,287 |
| 0.6–1.0 | 157 | 31 | −284 | 44,588 | 54 | −172 | 27,004 |
| >1.0 | 39 | 1 | −314 | 12,246 | 1 | −225 | 8,775 |
| Fill | | | | | | | |
| 0.2–0.6 | 1,186 | 67 | −248 | 294,128 | 9 | −217 | 257,362 |
| 0.6–1.0 | 137 | 36 | −279 | 38,223 | 42 | −184 | 25,208 |
| >1.0 | 24 | 66 | −249 | 5,976 | 7 | −219 | 5,256 |
| Total | – | – | – | 535,380 | – | – | 429,892 |

# REFERENCES

Alaska Department of Fish and Game, 1965. Post-earthquake fisheries evaluation. An interim report on the March 1964 earthquake effects on Alaska's fishery resources. Juneau: Alaska Department of Fish and Game. 72 p.

Bailey, Jack E., 1964. Intertidal spawning of pink and chum salmon at Olsen Bay, Prince William Sound, Alaska (unpublished manuscript). Auke Bay, Alaska: Bureau of Commercial Fisheries Biological Laboratory.

Bailey, Jack E., 1966. Effects of salinity on intertidal pink salmon survival *in* Proceedings of the 1966 Northeast Pacific Pink Salmon Workshop. William L. Sheridan, editor. Alaska Department of Fish and Game Informational Leaflet 87. Juneau: Alaska Department of Fish and Game. p. 12–15.

DeLaguna, Frederica, 1956. Chugach prehistory: the archaeology of Prince William Sound, Alaska. University of Washington Publications in Anthropology, v. 13. Seattle: University of Washington. 289 p.

Grant, U. S., and D. F. Higgins, 1910. Reconnaissance of the geology and mineral resources of Prince William Sound, Alaska. U.S. Geological Survey Bulletin 443. Washington: Government Printing Office. 89 p.

Hanavan, Mitchell G., and Bernard Einar Skud, 1954. Intertidal spawning of pink salmon. U.S. Fish and Wildlife Service Fishery Bulletin 56. Washington: Government Printing Office. p. 167–185.

Helle, John H., 1970. Biological characteristics of intertidal and fresh-water spawning pink salmon at Olsen Creek, Prince William Sound, Alaska, 1962-63. U.S. Fish and Wildlife Service Special Scientific Report–Fisheries 602. Washington: Government Printing Office. 19 p.

Helle, John H., Richard S. Williamson, and Jack E. Bailey, 1964. Intertidal ecology and life history of pink salmon at Olsen Creek, Prince William Sound, Alaska. U.S. Fish and Wildlife Service Special Scientific Report–Fisheries 483. Washington: Government Printing Office. 26 p.

Hubbard, Joel D., 1971. Distribution and abundance of intertidal invertebrates at Olsen Bay in Prince William Sound, one year after the earthquake *in* The Great Alaska Earthquake of 1964: Biology. NAS Pub. 1604. Washington: National Academy of Sciences.

Kirkwood, James B., 1962. Inshore-marine and freshwater life history phases of the pink salmon, *Oncorhynchus gorbuscha* (Walbaum), and the chum salmon, *O. keta* (Walbaum), in Prince William Sound, Alaska (Ph.D. thesis). Louisville: University of Kentucky. 300 p.

McNeil, William J., 1964. A method of measuring mortality of pink salmon eggs and larvae. U.S. Fish and Wildlife Service Fishery Bulletin 63. Washington: Government Printing Office. p. 575–588.

McNeil, William J., 1966a. Effects of the spawning bed environment on reproduction of pink and chum salmon. U.S. Fish and Wildlife Service Fishery Bulletin 65 (No. 2). Washington: Government Printing Office. p. 495–523.

McNeil, William J., 1966b. Distribution of spawning pink salmon in Sashin Creek, southeastern Alaska, and survival of their progeny. U.S. Fish and Wildlife Service Special Scientific Report–Fisheries 538. Washington: Government Printing Office. 12 p.

McNeil, William J., and Warren H. Ahnell, 1964. Success of pink salmon spawning relative to size of spawning bed materials. U.S. Fish and Wildlife Service Special Scientific Report–Fisheries 469. Washington: Government Printing Office. 15 p.

Noerenberg, Wallace H., 1963. Salmon forecast studies on 1963 runs in Prince William Sound. Alaska Department of Fish and Game Informational Leaflet 21. Juneau: Alaska Department of Fish and Game. 54 p.

Noerenberg, Wallace H., and Frank J. Ossiander, 1964. Effect of the March 27, 1964, earthquake on pink salmon alevin survival in Prince William Sound spawning streams. Alaska Department of Fish and Game Informational Leaflet 43. Juneau: Alaska Department of Fish and Game. 26 p.

Noerenberg, Wallace H., Robert S. Roys, Theodore C. Hoffman, Asa T. Wright, and Allen S. Davis, 1964. Forecast research on 1964 Alaskan pink salmon fisheries. Alaska Department of Fish and Game Informational Leaflet 36. Juneau: Alaska Department of Fish and Game. 52 p.

Plafker, George, 1969. Tectonics of the March 27, 1964, Alaska earthquake. U.S. Geological Survey Professional Paper 543-I. Washington: Government Printing Office. 74 p. Also *in* The Great Alaska Earthquake of 1964: Geology. NAS Pub. 1601. Washington: National Academy of Sciences, 1971.

Rockwell, Julius, Jr., 1956. Some effects of sea water and temperature on the embryos of the Pacific salmon, *Oncorhynchus gorbuscha* (Walbaum) and *Oncorhynchus keta* (Walbaum) (Ph.D. thesis). Seattle: University of Washington. 417 p.

Roys, Robert S., 1966. Forecast of 1966 pink and chum salmon runs in Prince William Sound. Alaska Department of Fish and Game Informational Leaflet 80. Juneau: Alaska Department of Fish and Game. 48 p.

Roys, Robert S., 1967. Forecast of 1967 pink and chum salmon runs in Prince William Sound. Alaska Department of Fish and Game Informational Leaflet 104. Juneau: Alaska Department of Fish and Game. 49 p.

Roys, Robert S., Allen S. Davis, and Wallace H. Noerenberg, 1965. Forecast research on 1965 central Alaska pink salmon fisheries. Alaska Department of Fish and Game Informational Leaflet 65. Juneau: Alaska Department of Fish and Game. 54 p.

Tarr, Ralph S., and Lawrence Martin, 1912. The earthquakes at Yakutat Bay, Alaska, in September, 1899. U.S. Geological Survey Professional Paper 69. Washington: Government Printing Office. 135 p.

Thorsteinson, Fredrik V., 1965. Effects of the Alaska earthquake on pink and chum salmon runs in Prince William Sound *in* Science in Alaska, 1964: Proceedings Fifteenth Alaskan Science Conference, College, Alaska, August 31 to September 4, 1964. George Dahlgren, editor. College: Alaska Division American Association for the Advancement of Science. p. 267–280.

Thorsteinson, Fredrik V., Wallace H. Noerenberg, and Howard D. Smith, 1963. The length, age, and sex ratio of chum salmon in the Alaska Peninsula, Kodiak Island, and Prince William Sound areas of Alaska. U.S. Fish and Wildlife Service, Special Scientific Report–Fisheries 430. Washington: Government Printing Office. 84 p.

U.S. Coast and Geodetic Survey, 1960. Tide tables, high and low water predictions, 1961, west coast North and South America, including the Hawaiian Islands. Washington: Government Printing Office. 223 p.

U.S. Coast and Geodetic Survey, 1964. Tide tables, high and low water predictions, 1965, west coast North and South America, including the Hawaiian Islands. Washington: Government Printing Office. 224 p.

Wickett, W. Percy, 1958. Review of certain environmental factors affecting the production of pink and chum salmon. *Journal of the Fisheries Research Board of Canada*, 15. Ottawa: Queen's Printer and Controller of Stationery. p. 1103–1126.

ROBERT S. ROYS
ALASKA DEPARTMENT OF FISH AND GAME

# Effect of Tectonic Deformation on Pink Salmon Runs in Prince William Sound

## INTRODUCTION

Four days after the great Alaska earthquake, an Alaska Department of Fish and Game research team began the annual sampling of pink salmon (*Oncorhynchus gorbuscha*) spawning beds in Prince William Sound streams. This program, a continuing effort in existence since 1960, gives an index of abundance of pink salmon alevins before their emergence from the spawning beds and migration to the sea. The index is used as a basis for predicting the return of adult pink salmon some 15 months before their arrival (Noerenberg, 1961, 1963, 1964; Roys and others, 1965; Roys, 1966, 1967, 1968).

During this sampling program, which so closely followed the major shock and resultant tsunamis, awesome changes in tide levels and severe stream damage were observed (Noerenberg and Ossiander, 1964). Tide-level changes reflected the amount of uplift or subsidence that had occurred. Streams could be expected to adjust to uplift by eroding the channel and to subsidence by depositing sediments. The areas most likely to be affected would be the newly created intertidal zones in those streams where uplift or subsidence had occurred. These areas were the most productive spawning areas in Prince William Sound before the earthquake.

The Alaska Department of Fish and Game, which is responsible for the management of the pink salmon resource of the state, realized that production of this species would be affected and considered that a broad approach to the problem would be necessary. Detailed studies on four or five streams might not have produced sufficient data for analysis to establish a method of managing the resource. Our approach was, therefore, to determine how many streams were affected and to what degree. We could then recommend steps to protect or rehabilitate those runs that were in jeopardy and still allow a harvest of the runs that were not.

Our method was (a) to categorize the streams by amount of uplift or subsidence, (b) to determine annually the abundance and distribution of spawners in as many affected and

ABSTRACT: Tectonic deformation associated with the Alaska earthquake of March 27, 1964, caused base-level changes in nearly all pink salmon (*Oncorhynchus gorbuscha*) streams in Prince William Sound. Of 223 primary producers, 138 were uplifted 3–31.5 ft, 43 subsided 2–6 ft, and 42 remained at essentially the same level (−1 to +2 ft). Streams reacted to a lowering of the base level (uplift) by cutting channels downward, and to the raising of the base level (subsidence) by depositing sediments.

Before deformation, between 70 and 77 percent of the even-year pink salmon escapement and 35–57 percent of the odd-year escapement spawned in intertidal reaches.

After deformation, pink salmon spawners reacted to uplift by displacing downstream into newly created unstable reaches of streams and responded to subsidence by displacing upstream.

Analysis of escapement and alevin data showed that as deformation increased, escapements, subsequent alevin densities, and, by inference, adult runs declined.

A crude estimate of the economic loss to the salmon fishery of Prince William Sound for the 3 years 1966–1968 was $3,355,000 to the fishermen, $9,601,000 to the canneries, and $13,888,000 to the retailers.

unaffected streams as possible, (c) to compare overwinter survival of eggs in predetermined sections of newly created spawning beds with survival in preearthquake spawning beds, and (d) to monitor pink salmon alevin production in as many streams as budgetary considerations would allow.

Our purpose here is to present the results of these studies, conducted from 1964 to 1968, without repeating specific details on sampling procedures and population enumerations that have been described by Noerenberg (1961) and Roys (1967).

## BACKGROUND INFORMATION ON PINK SALMON RUNS IN PRINCE WILLIAM SOUND

Adult pink salmon return to spawn in the coastal streams of Prince William Sound between June and September, when they bury their eggs in the intertidal and freshwater riffles of these streams. Spawner distribution varies between even-numbered years and odd-numbered years. W. H. Noerenberg's investigations for the Fisheries Research Institute (1953-1959) and the Alaska Department of Fish and Game (1960-1963) showed that for the years 1953-1963, 70-77 percent of the even-year spawners selected intertidal riffles for egg deposition, but only 35-57 percent of the odd-year spawners used these areas. The 6-12-ft tide level is the productive intertidal zone. Below the 6-ft level, few alevins are produced, although this area is sometimes used for spawning. Noerenberg also observed that even-year spawners rarely migrated very far above the 12-ft tide level but that odd-year fish spawned in the headwaters of many systems (personal communication). These differences are particularly noticeable in less glaciated areas, such as Hawkins and Hinchinbrook islands. In many streams, spawning migrations of both odd- and even-year cycles are limited to the intertidal areas or to short distances upstream by the presence of cascades or falls. These situations are most common in the more rugged areas of the Sound (Figure 1).

Eggs deposited in the spawning gravels develop and usually hatch between November and February. The alevins remain covered by gravel until spring, emerge from the gravel during the period between April and June, and migrate to sea as fry. The number of pink salmon fry emerging from the spawning beds each spring is controlled by a variety of factors.

Factors limiting fry production in southeastern Alaska have been investigated by McNeil (1966). His evidence indicated that mortalities of pink salmon eggs and alevins in spawning beds are often attributable to the following reasons: (a) removal of eggs and alevins by scouring of the streambed during high stream discharge, (b) lethal dissolved-oxygen levels associated with extremely low stream discharge, (c) freez-

ing of eggs and alevins associated with low stream discharge and continuous subfreezing temperatures, and (d) superimposition of late redds over those of earlier spawners.

After emerging from the spawning gravels and out-migrating from their natal streams, pink salmon fry begin to feed in the estuaries and bays and eventually work their way to the high seas. Approximately 15 months after this out-migration they return as adult spawners, usually to the streams where they themselves were spawned.

Plafker's report (1965) described the extent of tectonic deformation in Prince William Sound. With his report and a detailed map that he provided, it was simple to determine which streams had been uplifted or had subsided and to what extent. Of 223 salmon producers, 138 were uplifted 3-31.5 ft, 43 subsided 2-6 ft, and 42 remained at essentially the same level (-1 to +2 ft).

Where subsidence or uplift was relatively small (-1 to +2 ft), streams were considered "normal," and for the purpose of this report are used as controls. Figure 1 shows the tectonically uplifted and subsided categories in the Prince William Sound area.

## CONDITION OF POSTEARTHQUAKE SPAWNING BEDS

Concern for postearthquake pink salmon spawners in uplifted streams is based on the knowledge that streams are reacting to base-level changes by degrading and will continue to do so until equilibrium is again reached. If pink salmon eggs are deposited in this degrading environment, unusual mortalities will result (Figure 2). Where uplift was highest (Montague Island, 8-31.5 ft of uplift), we expected to witness very rapid lateral and vertical movement of streambeds, and where uplift was lowest (Port Fidalgo, 1-3 ft of uplift), we expected to observe little movement. During surveys of spawner assessment, egg deposition, and alevin abundance in the summer and fall of 1964 and 1965 and in the spring of 1965 and 1966, we observed astounding channel changes, particularly on Montague Island. In September 1964, for example, we staked certain newly created spawning sections of MacLeod Creek (uplift 31.5 ft) for egg-depositional studies (Figure 3). When we returned the following October to determine the egg deposition of these sections, we could not locate the stakes, and the stream channel did not even look familiar. The stream appeared to be flowing 100 m northwest of the streambed location in September. We sampled the new channel but did not recover any eggs.

Wild Creek (Figure 4) is an excellent example of vertical displacement of a streambed. In general, very rapid displacement of stream channels was observed in 1964 and 1965 in the newly created reaches of all uplifted streams, but by spring 1966, signs of unusual streambed movements were de-

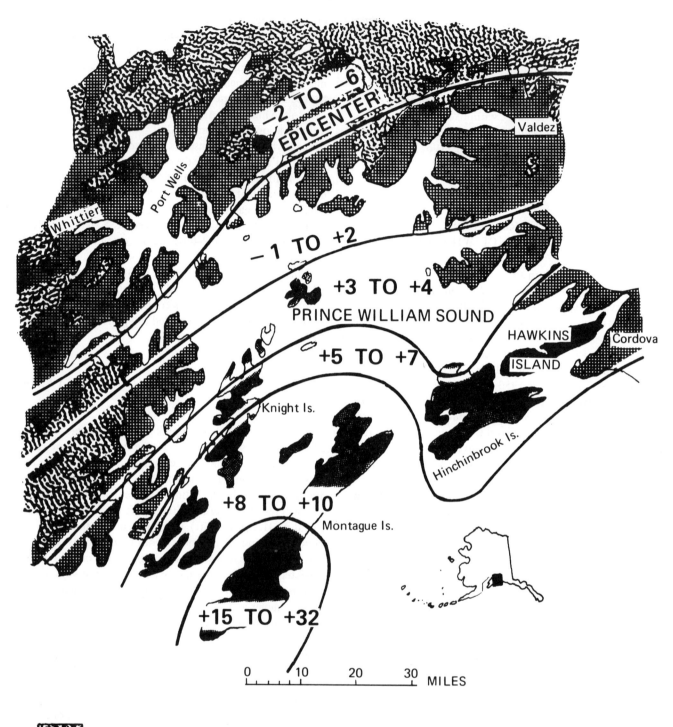

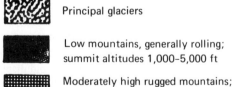

Principal glaciers

Low mountains, generally rolling;
summit altitudes 1,000–5,000 ft

Moderately high rugged mountains;
summit altitudes 5,000–10,000 ft

FIGURE 1  Tectonic deformation in Prince William Sound and approximate physiographic divisions. The most extensive freshwater spawning areas are found on Hawkins and Hinchinbrook islands. Little intertidal or freshwater spawning area is available on Knight Island, where the drainage forms a radial pattern.

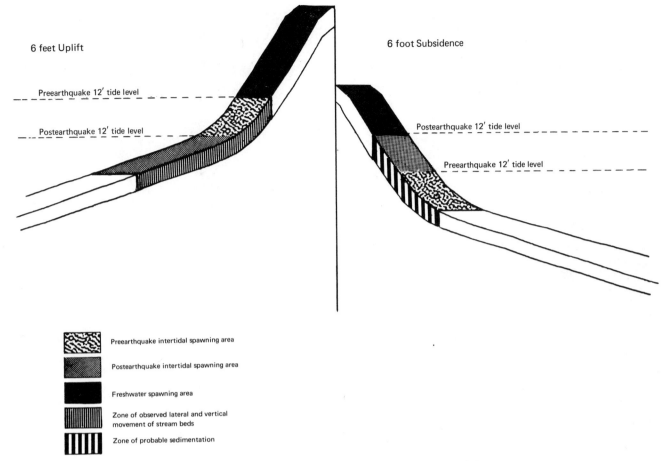

6 feet Uplift

Preearthquake 12' tide level

Postearthquake 12' tide level

6 foot Subsidence

Postearthquake 12' tide level

Preearthquake 12' tide level

Preearthquake intertidal spawning area

Postearthquake intertidal spawning area

Freshwater spawning area

Zone of observed lateral and vertical
movement of stream beds

Zone of probable sedimentation

FIGURE 2  Schematic diagram of reaction of streams to base-level changes.

tected and were quite obvious in the preearthquake intertidal reaches.

Lateral or vertical movement of streambeds was not the
only problem observed that could cause losses of salmon
eggs and alevins in the uplifted streams; disappearance of
streamflows underground during low streamflows made it impossible for salmon to ascend further. We observed this type
of problem in 16 relatively small streams on Montague Island.
Disappearance of streams underground not only prevented
passage of spawners upstream but in some instances caused
mortality of adult spawners. Spawners would begin to deposit eggs in newly created intertidal riffles and become
stranded when the tide receded and the streams disappeared
underground. Spawners trapped in this manner usually died
before the return of the tide (Figure 5) and before they were
able to discharge eggs and milt.

Lowered streamflows or disappearance of streams underground after successful spawning also caused mortality
through desiccation or freezing of eggs or alevins. On at least
three different occasions, we have observed successful spawning in newly created reaches of streams, only to find on our
return the following fall or spring that these reaches were
dry or frozen solid.

Maximum subsidence amounted to only 6 ft, as opposed
to the 31.5-ft maximum uplift, but it affected spawning beds
almost as much as did uplift (Figure 2). Productive intertidal
areas of subsided streams now lie deeper below salt water
by the amount of their subsidence. In subsided streams
where falls or cascades prohibit upstream movement by
spawners, the once-productive intertidal areas are lost
through subsidence for the period required by natural forces
to rebuild them.

Harrison Lagoon Creek, an area of 6-ft subsidence, is an
example of lost intertidal spawning ground. Before the earthquake, a 30-ft falls located at the 13-ft tide level permitted
productive spawning in a 500-yd reach below the falls; subsidence reduced the length of this area to 100 yd (Figure 6).

Even where new upstream areas are available for spawning, subsided streams present problems in a region such as
Prince William Sound where intertidal spawning is so important. Preearthquake intertidal spawning zones were of excellent quality, as is shown by past production, particularly in
even-numbered years, but the quality of the postearthquake
intertidal spawning area is questionable. Many new intertidal
areas no longer consist of the relatively smooth, constant-
gradient gravel riffles previously extant. New intertidal zones

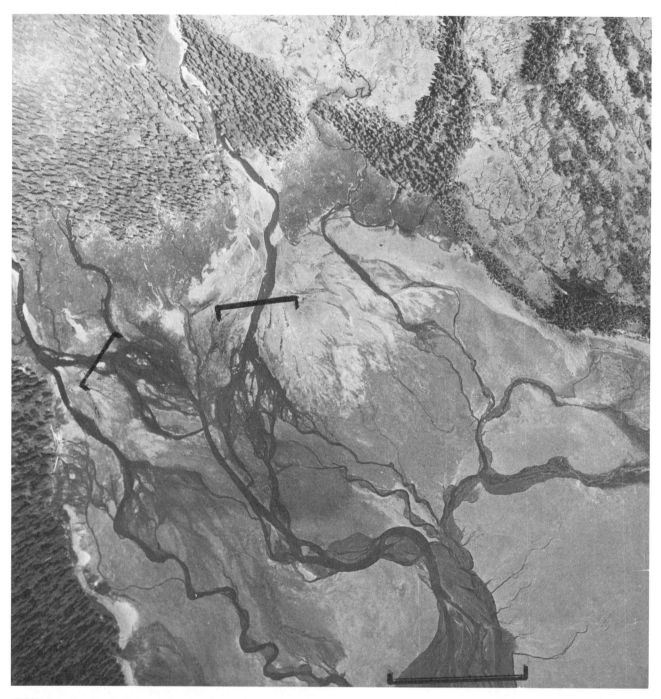

FIGURE 3  Brackets indicate newly created spawning area of MacLeod Creek (1964) that was former sea floor. The pink salmon run to this system has been virtually destroyed. Note braided stream channels.

FIGURE 4   Preearthquake 4-ft tide level of Wild Creek, Montague Island. By 1966, stream flows had cut the channel downward approximately 8 ft. Land was raised 10 ft in this area.

FIGURE 5   Mortality of intertidal salmon spawners (encircled) in 1964, when tide receded and streams disappeared underground. Udall Creek, Montague Island.

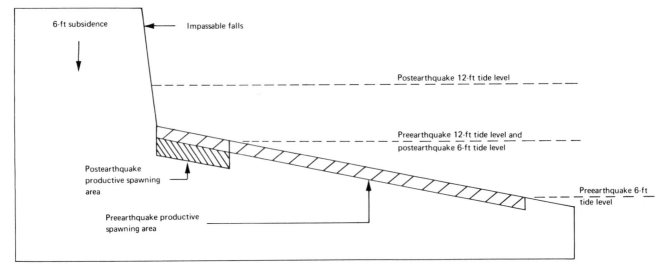

FIGURE 6   Diagram illustrating the significant reduction in length of the spawning area at Harrison Lagoon Creek because of subsidence. The saline content of the water below the 6-ft tide level effectively eliminates productive spawning.

now consist in many places of pools, formed by fallen trees, which were the preearthquake upstream sections. The intrusion of salt water to higher levels resulting from land subsidence is killing more stream-bank trees and will compound this problem.

## COMPARISON OF PRE- AND POSTEARTHQUAKE SPAWNING POPULATIONS

### ZONAL DISTRIBUTION OF SPAWNERS: SURVEY METHODS

One hundred and two streams containing pink salmon were observed by walking the course of the streams during the key spawning months of July, August, and September each year from 1964 to 1968. These investigations were supplemented by aerial surveys, particularly on Hawkins and Hinchinbrook islands, where odd-year spawners migrate considerable distances upstream from the 12-ft tide level. Procedures were (a) to locate the approximate boundaries of the preearthquake 4–12-ft tide zone in each stream from maps drawn before the earthquake (Figure 7); (b) to plot the postearthquake 4–12-ft tide level on these maps by observing actual tide levels; and (c) to estimate the number of spawners utilizing the preearthquake intertidal (4–12-ft tide level) and freshwater zones and the newly created spawning areas. Newly created spawning areas could be intertidal or freshwater areas, depending on the amount of uplift.

By conducting surveys in this manner, and by comparing the data assembled with preearthquake survey data, it was possible to approximate for each of the six tectonic categories (Figure 1) the behavior of spawners relative to uplift or

subsidence and to ascertain whether spawning populations were increasing or decreasing.

The amount of downstream displacement of spawners into entirely new spawning areas created by uplift from 1964 to 1968 was determined from an index of 14 streams: four in the 3–4-ft category, five in the 5–7-ft category, four in the 8–10-ft category, and one in the 15–32-ft category. Very few spawners returned to the 15–32-ft category in 1966, 1967, and 1968; displacement in that category therefore had to be calculated from observations on one stream. These indices show that as uplift increased, the displacement of spawners downstream also increased (Table 1), and even-

TABLE 1   Mean Percentage of Spawners Observed in Newly Created Spawning Areas, by Uplift Category

| Uplift Category (ft) | 1964 | 1965 | 1966 | 1967 | 1968 |
|---|---|---|---|---|---|
| 3–4 | 24.4 | 18.9 | 24.8 | 20.4 | 28.0 |
| 5–7 | 63.2 | 26.3 | 53.9 | 19.7 | 55.7 |
| 8–10 | 66.5 | 25.5 | 74.8 | 39.8 | 64.6 |
| 15–32 | 92.3 | 79.9 | 88.9 | 78.9 | 86.3 |

year spawners were more influenced by uplift than were odd-year spawners. Because more even- than odd-year pink salmon spawned in intertidal zones before the earthquake, even-year spawners could be expected to show a greater tendency to downstream displacement than odd-year spawners.

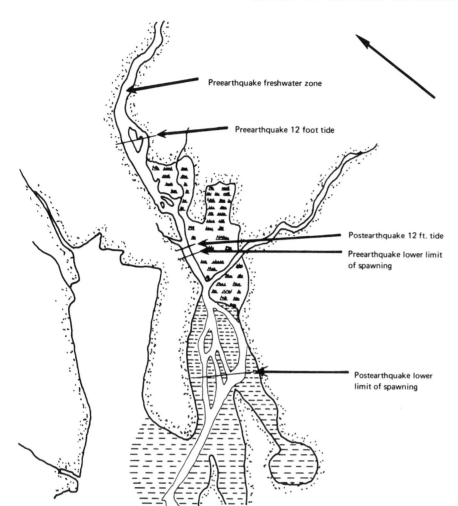

Preearthquake freshwater zone

Preearthquake 12 foot tide

Postearthquake 12 ft. tide

Preearthquake lower limit of spawning

Postearthquake lower limit of spawning

FIGURE 7   Stream map of Constantine Creek, Hinchinbrook Island, showing downstream shift of spawning area because of uplift.

## INFLUENCE OF THE TIDE

If the cause of initial displacement in 1964 and 1965 was strictly a genotypical response of spawners to the relocation of intertidal zones downstream, then the percentage utilization of intertidal zones after the earthquake should be similar to intertidal percentages observed before the earthquake. The author recognizes that it is difficult to prove or disprove this postulate with the type of data on hand. Nevertheless, the data presented in Table 2 suggest that factors other than a genotypical response were involved in causing initial downstream displacement. The calculations in Table 2 were derived from ground estimates made to a point approximately 300 m upstream from the preearthquake 12-ft tide level and during similar time periods. Unfortunately, comparable ground counts were not obtained in 1962 and 1963 or in the 8–10-ft category in 1966. Spawners had a choice in 1964 and 1965 of spawning intertidally or upstream. Evidence in Table 2 suggests that after the earthquake, percentage utilization of intertidal zones by spawners in control and subsided

streams did not differ a great deal from utilization observed before the earthquake. Percentage utilization of the relocated uplifted intertidal zones, however, was not the same as before the earthquake: as uplift increased, the percentage utilization of the relocated intertidal zones decreased. The most striking example of nongenotypic response was observed in MacLeod Creek (Figure 3), where less than 5 percent of the spawners in 1964 and 1965 were observed in the newly created intertidal zone. Furthermore, spawners did not occupy the old spawning areas but instead chose rapidly eroding newly created freshwater riffles above the new 12-ft tide level but below the preearthquake 4-ft tide level.

The evidence in Table 2 substantiates the hypothesis that the intertidal homing instinct is stronger for even-year pinks than for odd-year pinks, but this instinct may be subjugated by other factors, such as the quality of the new intertidal riffles. New intertidal riffles that were not used to a great extent by spawners in 1964 and 1965 were quite odoriferous and were composed of rapidly eroding mud, mussel beds, or fine sand.

TABLE 2  Mean Percentage of Spawners Observed in Intertidal Areas, by Vertical Change Category

| Vertical Change Category (ft) | Odd-Numbered Years | | | Even-Numbered Years | | | |
|---|---|---|---|---|---|---|---|
| | 1961 | 1965 | 1967 | 1960 | 1964 | 1966 | 1968 |
| Uplift | | | | | | | |
| 3–4 | 39.3 | 35.2 | 29.9 | 89.6 | 67.3 | 68.4 | 56.5 |
| 5–7 | 42.2 | 30.3 | 17.7 | 82.3 | 64.1 | 55.3 | 52.2 |
| 8–10 | 50.9 | 24.5 | 6.3 | 88.2 | 43.3 | – | 33.6 |
| 15–32 | 62.1 | <5 | <5 | 88.7 | <5 | <5 | <5 |
| Normal-controls | | | | | | | |
| −1 to +2 | 55.1 | 69.0 | 56.9 | 75.1 | 76.2 | 82.1 | 80.7 |
| Subsidence | | | | | | | |
| −2 to −6 | 63.4 | 72.8 | 62.2 | 82.4 | 80.8 | 76.5 | 78.0 |

We have dealt mainly with the behavior of pink spawners relative to uplift and have mentioned only briefly that the percentage utilization of intertidal zones after the earthquake did not change significantly in the control or subsided streams. The intertidal zones of subsided streams were relocated upstream during deformation. During postearthquake surveys (1964–1967), we noted that many intertidal reaches of streams that had been used extensively for spawning before deformation were practically devoid of spawners. It was not until 1968, when more manpower was available, that we conducted surveys specifically to determine the extent of upstream relocation of salmon spawners in three streams that had subsided about 6 ft. These three streams (in Port Wells) were selected because spawners were able to displace upstream in response to tidal relocation; we could not obtain a representative example of displacement if the passage upstream were blocked by falls. In addition, good records had been kept of the numbers of spawners observed in various reaches in 1960. Mean percentages of spawners that utilized three reaches of these streams are given for 1960 and 1968 in Table 3. Spawners in 1968 were obviously not distributing themselves as they had in 1960. Populations, at least in 1968,

had displaced upstream with the new tide level.

In streams where cascades or falls blocked displacement upstream, considerable crowding was observed. In 1964, during the first postearthquake spawning, approximately 11,000 pink salmon spawned in Harrison Lagoon Creek, and a significant number spawned at the new 2–4-ft tide level (preearthquake 8–10-ft tide level), where few eggs can survive because of lethal salinities. Apparently, overcrowding at the base of impassable falls forced the use of this lethal downstream intertidal reach (Figure 6). There are six subsided streams where spawners are unable to displace upstream.

## ESCAPEMENTS, BY TECTONIC CATEGORY

The term "escapement" denotes the number of adult salmon that escape marine predation and the commercial fishery and successfully enter the stream areas to spawn. Escapement in a given brood year provides only a rough idea of the magnitude of the subsequent adult return 2 years later, because freshwater survival of spawn varies considerably. However, if very few spawners are observed in one stream or a group of streams in a given year, we seldom observe large returns 2 years later. Conversely, when escapement levels are good or spawners are abundant, fair to good returns are generally observed.

Spawners reacted to deformation by displacing either upstream, in the case of subsidence, or downstream, in the case of uplift. Where deformation consisted of uplift of less than 2 ft or subsidence of 1 ft, displacement was not detected. Spawners in the subsided and control categories are still using the reaches used for spawning before the earthquake, but in uplifted streams, significant percentages of spawners are no longer using the preearthquake spawning areas.

TABLE 3  Mean Percentage of Spawners Observed in Pre- and Postearthquake Intertidal Zones of Three Streams That

| Year | Preearthquake 6–12-ft Tide Zone (Postearthquake 0–6-ft Tide Zone) | Preearthquake 12–18-ft Tide Zone (Postearthquake 6–12-ft Tide Zone) | Preearthquake 18–21-ft Tide Zone (Postearthquake 12–15-ft Tide Zone) |
|---|---|---|---|
| 1960 | 76.9 | 15.4 | 7.7 |
| 1968 | 20.8 | 58.3 | 21.5 |

What are the changes in the magnitude of the escapement in the preearthquake spawning areas following deformation? If escapements have declined in the preearthquake spawning areas, adult production would probably also decline in these areas. If we assume that the percentages of displacement by tectonic uplift category and year derived in Table 2 are representative of the behavior of spawners in each uplift category, then we can approximate the magnitude of the escapement that has been observed either in the preearthquake spawning areas or in the newly created spawning areas. We can then also compare preearthquake spawning-area escapements with those observed after deformation in the same area and can detect whether these escapements have increased or decreased.

## ESCAPEMENTS IN THE PREEARTHQUAKE SPAWNING AREAS

Escapements before and after deformation in the preearthquake spawning areas of 102 streams (17 normal, used as controls; 14 subsided; and 71 uplifted) are summarized and averaged by mean amount of tectonic change in Table 4.

Examination of these data indicates that although annual escapements in control streams have fluctuated considerably, average escapements were quite similar before and after deformation (250,975 versus 280,050). Subsided-category escapements also fluctuated annually, but the average escapement declined slightly, from 340,125 before deformation to 312,400 after deformation.

The most striking changes in escapement levels have been observed in the preearthquake spawning areas of 71 streams that were later uplifted. The uplifted streams were divided

into four uplift categories averaging +3.68 ft, +5.98 ft, +9.96 ft, and +18.65 ft. The distribution of the 71 streams into these categories was 15, 22, 10, and 24, respectively. Average escapements of pink salmon by category before and after deformation are shown in Table 4 to range from a preearthquake high of 373,000 in the +5.98-ft category to 1,975 in the +18.65-ft category. Even more revealing is the percentage change column, which shows drastic postearthquake reductions in all uplift categories from 41.5 percent at the +3.68-ft category to nearly 98 percent at the +18.65-ft category on Montague Island. These data indicate that as uplift increased, average escapements to preearthquake spawning areas declined. More detailed data suggest that odd-year spawners have, in general, been more abundant than even-year spawners in the preearthquake spawning area of uplifted streams, but both have been much less abundant than before deformation.

## ESCAPEMENTS IN THE NEWLY CREATED SPAWNING AREAS

Estimates (calculated from Table 1) of pink salmon escapements observed in newly created spawning areas of 71 uplifted streams are summarized in Table 5. Examination of these data indicates that in 1964 and 1966, 55.6 and 44.8 percent, respectively, of the escapement observed in 71 uplifted streams was in newly created reaches that have been subjected to rapid vertical and lateral movement of streambeds. In 1964 and 1966, therefore, 25.3 and 15.7 percent, respectively, of the total escapement in 102 streams was observed in poor-quality spawning environment. The situation was not quite as serious for odd-year runs. In 1965 and 1967,

TABLE 4   Comparison of Average Estimated Escapements of Pink Salmon and Percentage Change in Preearthquake Spawning Areas before and after Displacement, by Categories of Mean Tectonic Change

| Mean Tectonic Change Category (ft) | Streams Surveyed | Escapements | | | | | | |
| | | Before Displacement (1960–1963) | | | After Displacement (1964–1967) | | | |
| | | Annual Range | | | Annual Range | | | |
| | | Lower | Upper | Average | Lower | Upper | Average | Percent Change |
| Control | | | | | | | | |
| +0.88 | 17 | 158,300 | 399,400 | 250,975 | 88,300 | 384,900 | 280,050 | +11.6 |
| Subsidence | | | | | | | | |
| −4.04 | 14 | 173,700 | 429,600 | 340,125 | 197,900 | 456,100 | 312,400 | −8.2 |
| Uplift | | | | | | | | |
| +3.68 | 15 | 178,100 | 250,200 | 194,375 | 95,200 | 133,400 | 113,700 | −41.5 |
| +5.98 | 22 | 179,400 | 585,000 | 373,000 | 89,100 | 203,000 | 156,025 | −58.2 |
| +9.96 | 10 | 36,600 | 82,700 | 63,650 | 5,500 | 20,400 | 13,150 | −79.3 |
| +18.65 | 24 | 14,000 | 157,000 | 94,300 | 300 | 5,000 | 1,975 | −97.9 |

TABLE 5    Estimated Pink Salmon Escapements Observed in the Newly Created Spawning Areas of Uplifted Streams

| Mean Uplift (ft) | Streams Surveyed | Estimated Escapements | | | |
|---|---|---|---|---|---|
| | | 1964 | 1965 | 1966 | 1967 |
| 3.68 | 15 | 43,100 | 28,400 | 31,400 | 26,900 |
| 5.98 | 22 | 220,700 | 72,400 | 104,200 | 49,800 |
| 9.96 | 10 | 28,700 | 7,000 | 16,500 | 8,100 |
| 18.65 | 24 | 60,200 | 9,700 | 2,000 | 1,300 |
| Total | 71 | 352,700 | 117,500 | 154,100 | 86,100 |
| Percentage of total escapement in 71 uplifted streams | – | 55.6 | 25.2 | 44.8 | 21.2 |
| Percentage of total escapement of 102 streams (all categories) | – | 25.3 | 15.2 | 15.7 | 8.1 |

15.2 and 8.1 percent, respectively, of the escapement in 102 streams was observed in newly created areas.

For all practical purposes, from 1964 to 1967, 710,400 pink salmon out of a total indexed spawning population of 4,219,000 were observed in poor-quality environment that was and still is reacting to base-level changes.

## OVERWINTER SURVIVAL OF EGGS

Since deformation, a significant portion of the total pink salmon escapement deposited eggs in newly created, obviously unstable reaches of uplifted streams. Eggs deposited in such an environment initially had little chance of survival. As time passes, however, and streams again become relatively stable, these newly created reaches should begin to produce harvestable levels of adult pink salmon, if there are any adult pinks left to deposit eggs.

We began to monitor egg deposition in October 1964 and subsequent survival to the alevin stage in March and April of that brood year in selected sections of the preearthquake spawning area and the newly created spawning area. Figure 8 illustrates the equipment used for sampling. Excavated eggs were counted by species for each sample in the fall, and alevins were counted by species for each sample in the spring.

We observed some mortality of eggs during handling procedures in fall 1964 that we did not observe in later years, although some may have occurred. Our finances did not allow for a separation of live and dead eggs by chemical methods; mean survival of eggs to alevins (Table 6) was therefore calculated from the total number of eggs present. Survival of eggs to the alevin stage in the newly created spawning areas of sampled uplifted streams since 1964 has been poor (between 4 and 8 percent) compared with survival in the preearthquake spawning areas of either uplifted (16–25 per-

cent) or control streams (17–41 percent). Survival may have been even poorer in the newly created areas than the data indicated. Very few pink salmon spawners were observed in any of the sampling sections after September 15, which indicated that very few eggs were deposited after that date. Fall sampling did not begin until October 7, 1964; a period of at least 3 weeks between cessation of deposition and the beginning of sampling was therefore left, during which time eggs could have been dislodged and carried out to sea. If eggs were lost at a higher rate in the newly created areas than in the preearthquake areas, estimates of survival in the newly created areas are probably too high. I suspect that this was the case, particularly in 1964 and 1965, when newly created stream reaches were degrading rapidly. Survival in the newly created areas was about twice as great for brood year 1967 (8.97 percent) as it was for brood year 1964 (4.50 percent), but egg deposition in 1967 (324 per $m^2$) was about one half what it was in 1964 (654 per $m^2$).

## PINK SALMON ALEVIN DENSITIES IN PREEARTHQUAKE SPAWNING AREAS

The abundance of pink salmon alevins in the spawning gravels just before emergence and migration to sea each spring is a reflection of the number of viable eggs deposited the previous summer and the postspawning or overwinter survival of these eggs.

Since brood year 1960, the abundance of pink salmon alevins has been determined each spring during late March and early April after most of the mortality has occurred in the streams. Randomly selected points have been hydraulically excavated each year (Figure 8) from intertidal and immediate upstream zones of at least 22 similar streams distributed widely in Prince William Sound. Thus far there has been a direct relation between abundance of pink salmon

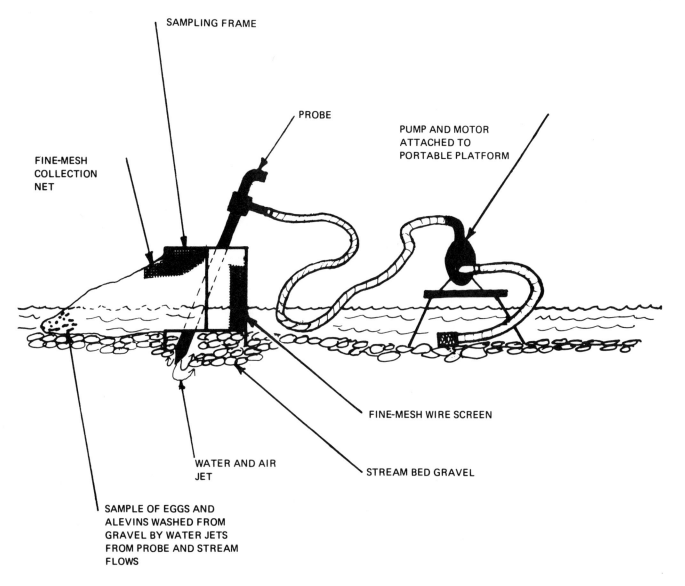

SAMPLING FRAME

PROBE

PUMP AND MOTOR
ATTACHED TO
PORTABLE PLATFORM

FINE-MESH
COLLECTION
NET

FINE-MESH WIRE SCREEN

WATER AND AIR
JET

STREAM BED GRAVEL

SAMPLE OF EGGS AND
ALEVINS WASHED FROM
GRAVEL BY WATER JETS
FROM PROBE AND STREAM
FLOWS

FIGURE 8   Sampling equipment used in the field. The frame is located over a sampling point, and the probe removes eggs and alevins from the gravel.

alevins, expressed in terms of mean number of alevins per $m^2$, and the returning adult runs (Roys, 1967).

When weighted mean alevin densities have been high, good runs of adults have returned. Conversely, when alevin densities are low, poor runs of adults have returned (Table 7). Intertidal and freshwater-zone alevin densities were weighted to compensate for the differences in the amount of spawning area utilized by odd- and even-year spawners.

Alevin densities may vary annually because of abundance and fecundity of spawners or because of poor postspawning survival conditions. Our best chance of detecting any decline in the earthquake-triggered alevin density in preearthquake spawning areas is therefore to average densities for the 4

brood years after deformation changes (1964–1967). Averages will smooth out the effects of annual fluctuations in numbers of spawners and of postspawning survival conditions.

Mean weighted alevin density for the 4-year period before spawner displacement (brood years 1960–1963) was approximately 280 alevins per $m^2$. After spawner displacement (1964–1967), however, the 4-year average alevin density in the same area declined to 189 alevins per $m^2$; the ratio of these two densities (189/280) is 0.675. Before displacement the adult pink salmon runs (progeny of brood years 1960–1963) averaged about 6 million. After displacement the 4-year (1964–1967) average will be about 4.3 million (1969 mean

TABLE 6   Comparison of Pink Salmon Egg-to-Alevin Survival in the Preearthquake and Newly Created Spawning Areas

| Brood Year | Streams | Sections | Samples | Mean Deposition of Eggs per $m^2$ | Mean Percentage Survival |
|---|---|---|---|---|---|
| | | | Preearthquake Spawning Area | | |
| No elevation change | | | | | |
| 1964 | 2 | 5 | 50 | 2,313 | 17.22 |
| 1965 | 2 | 5 | 38 | 975 | 23.04 |
| 1966 | 2 | 5 | 50 | 931 | 17.78 |
| 1967 | 2 | 5 | 44 | 1,091 | 41.74 |
| Uplifted | | | | | |
| 1964 | 7 | 12 | 95 | 1,996 | 16.02 |
| 1965 | 7 | 15 | 80 | 1,058 | 20.67 |
| 1966 | 7 | 15 | 103 | 1,251 | 16.07 |
| 1967 | 7 | 17 | 111 | 1,099 | 25.80 |
| | | | New Spawning Area (Uplifted) | | |
| 1964 | 6 | 8 | 85 | 654 | 4.50 |
| 1965 | 7 | 10 | 54 | 611 | 5.32 |
| 1966 | 7 | 12 | 99 | 354 | 8.35 |
| 1967 | 9 | 12 | 85 | 324 | 8.97 |

TABLE 7   Mean Weighted Pink Salmon Alevin Densities and Adult Returns (All Tectonic Categories Combined)[a]

| Brood Year | Alevin Density per $m^2$ | Adult Return (Millions) |
|---|---|---|
| 1960 | 358 | 8.7 |
| 1961 | 314 | 6.6 |
| 1962 | 300 | 6.0 |
| 1963 | 149 | 3.4 |
| 1964 | 209 | 4.0 |
| 1965 | 138 | 3.8 |
| 1966 | 144 | 3.5 |
| 1967 | 266 | 5.9 |

[a]Newly created spawning-area data not included; the coefficient of determination, $r^2 = 0.9143$.

forecast is included in the calculations). The ratio of these two averages is 0.717, fairly close to the alevin density ratios.

Alevin densities in the preearthquake spawning areas for the 4-year period after displacement averaged below predisplacement levels, and the returning runs have also averaged lower. These data, however, do not indicate whether the decrease was a function of deformation or of displacement. Evidence has been presented to indicate that as uplift increased, displacement of spawners downstream into newly created areas increased, and escapements in the preearthquake spawning areas declined. These declines contrasted with observations in the control category, where escapements increased slightly. Average alevin densities observed in the pre-

earthquake spawning areas after displacement could also be expected to decline according to the amount of uplift, and average alevin densities in the control area should reflect a slight increase. Subsided streams should also show a decrease in alevin density because many reaches were no longer used by spawners, and samples were collected from those little-used areas.

Examination of pink salmon alevin data for the two 4-year periods presented in Table 8 indicates that after displacement

TABLE 8   Ratio of 4-Year Mean Pink Salmon Alevin Densities after Spawner Displacement (1964-1967) to Densities before Displacement (1960-1963)

| Mean Tectonic Change Category (ft) | Mean Alevin Density per $m^2$ | | Ratio |
|---|---|---|---|
| | 1960-1963 | 1964-1967 | |
| Controls | | | |
| +0.88 | 273 | 282 | 1.033 |
| Subsided | | | |
| -4.04 | 219 | 166 | 0.758 |
| Uplifted | | | |
| +3.68 | 267 | 259 | 0.970 |
| +5.98 | 226 | 184 | 0.814 |
| +9.96 | 262 | 96 | 0.366 |
| +18.65 | 244 | 0 | 0.0 |

the average alevin density increased slightly (ratio 1.033) in control streams and declined in those with greater uplift or subsidence. I have plotted the ratios of predisplacement to postdisplacement mean alevin densities by tectonic category in Figure 9, and the relation between amount of deformation and decline of alevin abundance is obvious.

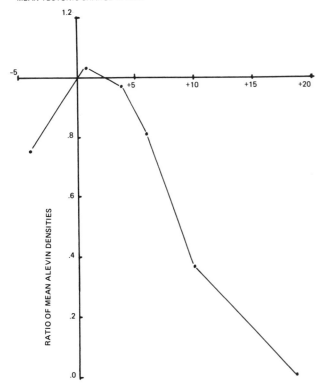

FIGURE 9  Ratio of pink salmon alevin densities after displacement to those before displacement in the preearthquake spawning areas, by mean amount of tectonic change.

In streams uplifted more than 3 ft, even-year declines in densities of pink salmon alevins are much more severe than odd-year declines. This is what we would expect, because even-year spawners, with the exception of those on Montague Island, have exhibited a stronger tendency than odd-year spawners to displace to newly formed spawning areas.

## ALEVIN DENSITIES IN NEWLY CREATED SPAWNING AREAS

Alevin densities of pink salmon observed since 1964 in the newly created areas of sampled uplifted streams are listed in Table 9. These data are based on samples collected from 15 streams and corroborate the evidence presented in the survival section (Table 6). There was no correlation between

TABLE 9  Mean Pink Salmon Alevin Densities in Newly Created Spawning Areas of 15 Streams Uplifted More Than 3 ft

| Brood Year | Density per m$^2$ |
| --- | --- |
| 1964 | 55 |
| 1965 | 31 |
| 1966 | 41 |
| 1967 | 49 |

amount of uplift and abundance of alevins; scarcity of alevins was observed in areas uplifted 3.68 ft as well as in streams uplifted 10 ft or more.

The newly created spawning areas are for the most part still unstable, and it is too early to determine how much spawning area will eventually be gained. It is impossible to calculate the portion of the total adult run that may have originated in the newly created areas, but the alevin densities are so low that this is probably a very small portion of the adult run.

Since 1964, because of tectonic uplift, at least 710,000 pink salmon have spawned in areas that are not yet capable of good production.

## RELATION BETWEEN DECLINE IN ESCAPEMENTS AND SUBSEQUENT ALEVIN INDICES

Because there is a relation between the decline of average escapements in preearthquake spawning areas and the amount of tectonic deformation, and a relation between average alevin density declines and amount of deformation, there should be a relation between average escapement declines and subsequent average alevin density declines relative to the amount of deformation. For ease of interpretation, instead of plotting ratios as in Figure 9, I have expressed the relationship (Figure 10) in terms of percentage increases or decreases. Figure 10 demonstrates that the decline in 4-year mean alevin densities is related to reduced escapement levels, and reduced escapement levels were a function of displacement and amount of deformation.

There is little evidence to support the postulate that escapement declines in the preearthquake spawning areas of deformed streams were caused by a selective commercial fishery that harvested pink salmon runs at a rate directly related to the amount of uplift. On the contrary, commercial fishing operations in many areas of Prince William Sound, particularly in those areas uplifted more than 3 ft, have been severely restricted. Montague Island, an area of substantial uplift, has been closed to commercial fishing since the first week of August 1966. These closures (Figure 11) effectively re-

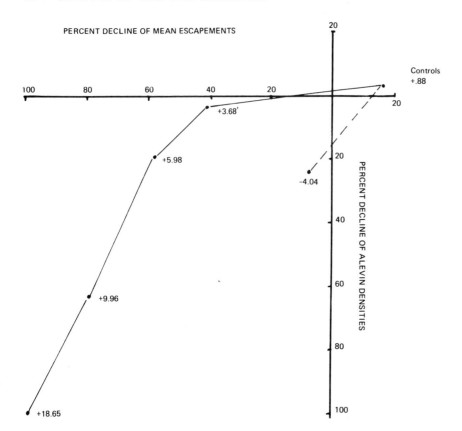

PERCENT DECLINE OF MEAN ESCAPEMENTS

FIGURE 10   Relation of mean escapement declines and sequential mean alevin densities, by tectonic category.

duce harvest rates, making the percentage of tectonically affected runs removed by the commercial fishery less than the percentage removed in control areas.

There is a relation between mean alevin densities and the total returning adult run in spawning streams sampled. From this and from the declines in alevin densities caused by the deformation, we may infer that deformation has reduced the adult runs in proportion to the amount of uplift, despite contributions from the new spawning areas.

## ECONOMIC LOSS

To determine economic losses caused by the declines in pink salmon production, we shall have to estimate the magnitude of the runs if the earthquake had not occurred. The difference between the actual runs and the estimated size of the runs if the earthquake had not occurred represents the economic loss.

Problems in determining either the size of the actual run or the size of the projected run to a particular tectonic category cause inaccurate estimates. It is not possible to determine accurately the percentage contribution of each tectonic category to the total run before or after deformation because a very significant portion of the commercial catch is composed of pink salmon whose destination is unknown. Pinks

caught in subsided bays and passages may or may not be destined for the normal zone, and the numbers destined for each category cannot be separated. In addition, commercial fishing regulations vary annually. When fish are abundant, regulations are relaxed; when fish are not abundant, restrictive measures are employed. If we assume that fishing mortality is constant for stocks of all categories in a given year, then any restrictive measure employed in one area and not in another will lead to an overestimate of the magnitude of the total run to the restricted area. After the earthquake, unusually severe restrictions were imposed in those areas that were uplifted more than 3 ft, in particular on Montague Island.

Despite these problems, it is necessary at least to approximate what the losses have been; estimated losses of pink salmon for the 3-year period affected are listed in Table 10, and gross dollar value lost is listed in Table 11.

These computations are based on assumptions that, before the earthquake, fluctuations in the magnitude of pink salmon runs in the control category were proportional to fluctuations of runs in the other tectonic categories. It is also assumed that the magnitude of the escapement to the spawning grounds reflected the magnitude of the runs in each tectonic category before and after deformation.

I have undoubtedly underestimated losses where restrictions on commercial fishing operations were in effect and overestimated losses where fishing was intense, but these er-

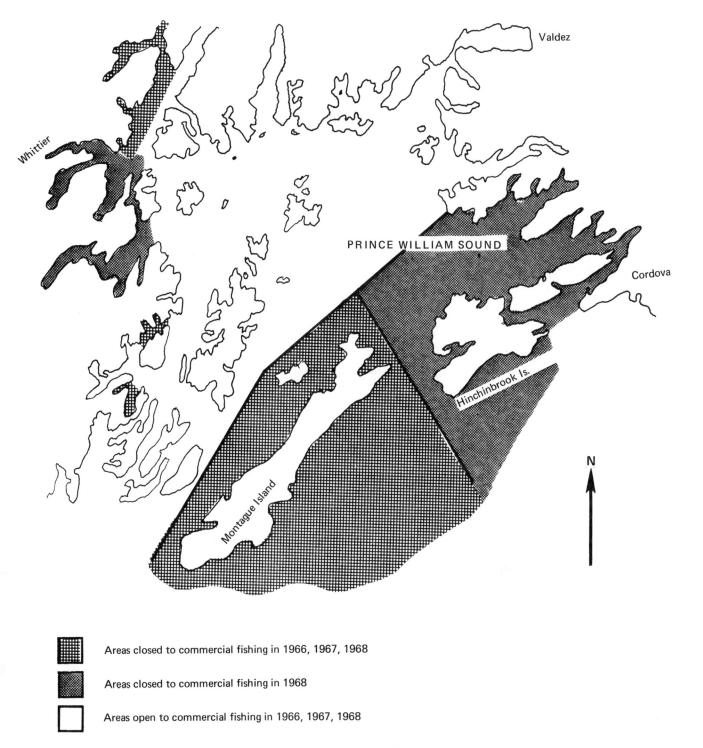

FIGURE 11   Areas closed to commercial fishing because of poor runs.

TABLE 10  Estimated Losses of Pink Salmon (by Tectonic Change Category)

| | Mean Change (ft) | | | | | | |
| | | Uplift | | | | | |
| Year | Controls, +0.88 | +3.68 | +5.98 | +9.96 | +18.65 | Subsidence, −4.04 | Total, All Categories |
|---|---|---|---|---|---|---|---|
| 1966 | 0 | 315,700 | 807,100 | 112,900 | 304,000 | 935,700 | 2,475,400 |
| 1967 | 0 | 96,000 | 1,450,900 | 186,500 | 123,400 | 203,800 | 2,060,600 |
| 1968 | 0 | 276,300 | 706,300 | 98,800 | 274,300 | 818,800 | 2,174,500 |
| Total | 0 | 688,000 | 2,964,300 | 398,200 | 701,700 | 1,958,300 | 6,710,500 |

TABLE 11  Gross Dollar Value of Pink Salmon Lost for 3-Year Period (1966-1968) by Tectonic Change Category and Segment of the Industry

| | Mean Change (ft) | | | | | | |
| | | Uplift | | | | | |
| Group | Controls, +0.88 | +3.68 | +5.98 | +9.96 | +18.65 | Subsidence, −4.04 | Totals |
|---|---|---|---|---|---|---|---|
| Fishermen[a] | 0 | $   344,000 | $1,482,000 | $199,000 | $   351,000 | $   979,000 | $   3,355,000 |
| Canneries[b] | 0 | 984,000 | 4,241,000 | 570,000 | 1,004,000 | 2,802,000 | 9,601,000 |
| Retailers[c] | 0 | 1,424,000 | 6,135,000 | 824,000 | 1,452,000 | 4,053,000 | 13,888,000 |

[a]$0.50 per fish.
[b]$28.00 per 48-lb case (19.57 pink salmon per case).
[c]$40.50 per 48-lb case.

rors probably balance each other out. It this is true, between 1966 and 1968 the fishermen of Prince William Sound lost approximately $3,355,000 in income because of the earthquake. This is roughly $6,000 per fisherman for the 3-year period 1966-1968. Approximate gross value lost to the canning industry during the same period was $9,601,000, and the retail value lost was $13,888,000.

## SUMMARY

Before the tectonic deformation caused by the earthquake, 70-77 percent of the even-year pink salmon escapement and 35-57 percent of the odd-year escapement spawned in intertidal reaches.

The tectonic deformation caused base-level changes in nearly all the pink-salmon-producing streams in Prince William Sound. Of 223 principal producers, 138 were uplifted 3-31.5 ft, 43 subsided 2-6 ft, and 42 remained at essentially the same level (−1 to +2 ft).

The uplift caused the intertidal zone to relocate downstream, and new stream reaches that increased the spawning area were created. Subsidence caused the intertidal zone to relocate upstream and to submerge lower reaches of the stream, thus reducing the amount of spawning area.

Newly created reaches of uplifted streams are degrading, and lateral and vertical displacement of newly created streambeds was observed, particularly where streams were uplifted 5 ft or more. These newly created reaches were still relatively unstable in 1968.

Streams were grouped in six categories, based on amount and type of deformation. One category with little uplift or subsidence was used as a control. Spawning areas were divided into two categories, preearthquake and newly created. The preearthquake spawning areas were reaches of streams used by spawners before deformation; the newly created spawning areas were reaches of uplifted streams downstream from the preearthquake areas that had not been used for spawning before deformation.

Extensive spawner-assessment surveys, conducted from 1964 to 1968 on uplifted streams, revealed that spawners moved downstream into newly created unstable areas and that displacement was related to the amount of uplift but not necessarily to the relocation of the intertidal zone. In subsided streams, spawners moved upstream, if possible, but distributed themselves normally in the control streams.

Continued displacement and smaller adult runs in uplifted streams have reduced average escapements in the preearthquake spawning areas. Average escapements also declined in subsided streams, particularly on the even-year cycle, but not as seriously as in most uplifted streams. In the control streams during this same period (1964–1968), average escapements increased slightly.

Overwinter egg-survival studies indicated that in brood year 1967 the newly created spawning areas were not capable of sustaining good production.

Alevin densities, which reflect the magnitude of the adult return, were found to average lower than preearthquake levels in preearthquake spawning areas of uplifted and subsided streams, and declines reflected the amount of uplift. Alevin densities in the control streams increased slightly between 1964 and 1968; in the newly created areas, alevin densities were poor and had increased little by brood year 1967.

A very crude estimate of loss for the 3-year period 1966–1968 was $3,355,000 to the fishermen, $9,601,000 to the canneries, and $13,888,000 to the retailers.

## CONCLUSION

Any change in the base level of streams can be expected to affect deleteriously populations of organisms that depend on streambed stability during some phase of their life cycle. If the organism is as economically important as the pink salmon, the people who depend on it for their livelihood are bound to suffer. Special restrictions must be placed on the commercial harvesting of pink salmon if our runs are to regain or exceed former levels of abundance, especially in those areas uplifted more than 5 ft and during even-year runs. These restrictions will be necessary until the newly created spawning areas become reasonably stable.

Restrictions alone will not bring back completely destroyed runs such as the majority of those located on Montague Island. In that area, streams must be stabilized by modern engineering techniques and restocked, using sound biological techniques.

The Alaska Department of Fish and Game, with the help of the U.S. Forest Service, is engaged in a stream-rehabilitation program in cooperation with the U.S. Bureau of Commercial Fisheries, under provisions of the Anadromous Fish Act.

## ACKNOWLEDGMENTS

Several people provided invaluable field assistance in determining displacement of spawners. Wallace H. Noerenberg, Alaska Department of Fish and Game, in correspondence, in conversations, and on numerous field trips, pointed out many aspects of displacement that would otherwise have gone unnoticed. Richard B. Nickerson assisted in the surveys of 1967 and 1968.

I particularly wish to express my appreciation to Captain Harry P. Curran of the M.V. *Shad*, whose knowledge of the waters of Prince William Sound and whose dedication to the salmon resource are unsurpassed.

My thanks are also extended to Steven Pennoyer and Melvin C. Seibel for editorial comments and to George C. Cunningham for engineering assistance.

The evaluation and rehabilitation work in Prince William Sound since February 1967 has been jointly funded by the U.S. Bureau of Commercial Fisheries under the Anadromous Fish Act, Public Law 89-304, as Project Number AFC-3, and by the State of Alaska.

## REFERENCES

McNeil, William J., 1966. Effects of the spawning bed environment on reproduction of pink and chum salmon. U. S. Fish and Wildlife Service Fishery Bulletin 65 (No. 2). Washington: Government Printing Office. p. 495–523.

Noerenberg, Wallace H., 1961. Observations on spawning and subsequent survival of fry of the 1960 salmon runs in Prince William Sound, Alaska. Alaska Department of Fish and Game Memorandum 5. Cordova: Alaska Department of Fish and Game. 22 p.

Noerenberg, Wallace H., 1963. Salmon forecast studies on 1963 runs in Prince William Sound. Alaska Department of Fish and Game Informational Leaflet 21. Juneau: Alaska Department of Fish and Game. 54 p.

Noerenberg, Wallace H., 1964. Forecast research on 1964 Alaska pink salmon fisheries. Alaska Department of Fish and Game Informational Leaflet 36. Juneau: Alaska Department of Fish and Game. 51 p.

Noerenberg, Wallace H., and Frank J. Ossiander, 1964. Effect of the March 27, 1964, earthquake on pink salmon alevin survival in Prince William Sound spawning streams. Alaska Department of Fish and Game Informational Leaflet 43. Juneau: Alaska Department of Fish and Game. 26 p.

Plafker, George, 1965. Tectonic deformation associated with the 1964 Alaska earthquake. *Science*, 148 (June 25), 1675–1687.

Roys, Robert S., 1966. Forecast of 1966 pink and chum salmon runs in Prince William Sound. Alaska Department of Fish and Game Informational Leaflet 80. Juneau: Alaska Department of Fish and Game. 48 p.

Roys, Robert S., 1967. Forecast of 1967 pink and chum salmon runs in Prince William Sound. Alaska Department of Fish and Game Informational Leaflet 104. Juneau: Alaska Department of Fish and Game. 49 p.

Roys, Robert S., 1968. Forecast of 1968 pink and chum salmon runs in Prince William Sound. Alaska Department of Fish and Game Informational Leaflet 116. Juneau: Alaska Department of Fish and Game. 50 p.

Roys, Robert S., Allen S. Davis, and Wallace H. Noerenberg, 1965. Forecast research on 1965 central Alaska pink salmon fisheries. Alaska Department of Fish and Game Informational Leaflet 65. Juneau: Alaska Department of Fish and Game. 54 p.

RAE E. BAXTER
ALASKA DEPARTMENT OF FISH AND GAME

# Earthquake Effects on Clams of Prince William Sound

## INTRODUCTION

Changes in land elevation associated with the Alaska earthquake of 1964 considerably altered the intertidal zone of Prince William Sound. The earthquake tilted a huge local area of the earth's crust, causing relocation of the supratidal, intertidal, and subtidal life zones. Within Prince William Sound the movement was mainly upward, resulting in more uplifted than subsided habitat.

The Alaska Department of Fish and Game undertook a short-term study to evaluate the effects of changes in elevation on the potential commercial clam resource and to determine methods of handling problems associated with the management of this resource in Prince William Sound. The study consisted of three surveys in the spring of 1965.

The objective of the first survey, which was conducted in March 1965 on the outer islands, Hinchinbrook and Montague, was to develop methods of determining the clam mortality caused by the earthquake and of measuring elevation change. The objective of the second survey was to measure specific changes in the clam habitat and population structure caused by the uplift. This second survey concentrated on the area of maximum uplift in the southeastern part of the Sound from April 26 to May 14. The third survey was conducted in July throughout the Sound; its purpose was to examine and compare a number of areas with those examined in the second survey.

The principal economically important clams of Prince William Sound are called hard-shell clams. The name "hard-shell clam," as commonly used in Alaska, includes all species of pelecypods utilized for human consumption, with the exception of razor clams (*Siliqua*), mussels (*Mytilus*), and scallops (*Pecten, Chlamys,* and *Hinnites*). By far the most commercially valuable hard-shell clam is *Saxidomus giganteus.* All species of pelecypods collected during fieldwork connected with the present study and with other studies in the Sound are listed in Baxter (1967).

ABSTRACT: The changes in land elevations associated with the Alaska earthquake of 1964 affected the intertidal populations of hard-shell clams in Prince William Sound. Mortality was estimated at 36 percent. Studies established that 29 percent of the surviving hard-shell clams were in the optimum habitat zone between mean low water and lowest low water; before the earthquake, 82 percent of the hard-shell clams were in the optimum zone. No species of hard-shell clam is in danger of disappearing from the fauna of Prince William Sound. Ninety-nine species of pelecypods were tentatively identified during studies in the Sound.

## METHODS

### METHOD OF DETERMINING UPLIFT

On the first survey a method suggested by Dr. G Dallas Hanna was developed for estimating the amount of uplift caused by the earthquake. Changes from the preearthquake levels of land elevation were determined from the upper limit of growth of the common acorn barnacles *Balanus balanoides* and *Balanus glandula* (Plafker and Mayo, 1965), an upper limit that is generally sharply defined near the mean high tide level. The differences between the upper limit of living postearthquake-spawned barnacles and the upper limit of the dead *in situ* shells of the preearthquake population were assumed to represent the change in elevation. This method of determining elevation change is probably accurate to 6 in. or less. Semiprotected areas not exposed to the open Sound were chosen to obtain the most accurate results with this method. The effects of waves and surge wash in areas exposed to the open Sound cause the uneven upper limit of the barnacles. In general, the upper limit of barnacles appeared to be at a constant elevation throughout the semiprotected areas of Prince William Sound.

### METHOD OF OBTAINING SUBTIDAL SAMPLES

Subtidal samples were taken with a dredge that consisted of a 3-ft length of 16-in.-diameter pipe ¼ in. thick; it weighed 85 lb and held approximately 3 ft³ of material. The lower end was covered with a fine-mesh screen that allowed water to pass through but retained most of the bottom materials. The towing bridle was fastened off-center, so that the dredge would immediately dig into the bottom. The dredge gouged a groove roughly 1 ft deep and from 4 to 10 ft long, depending on the type of bottom. This dredge captured razor clams, which move very rapidly vertically in the sand. It was therefore assumed that it adequately sampled other slower-moving species of clams in deep water. The dredge was towed at 4–10 knots, according to the depth of the water; when it hit bottom, there was one hard jerk and the dredge was full. When the dredge took either *Saxidomus giganteus* or their siphons, they were known to be present. When a series of samples contains no signs of a species, the species is presumed not to be present in significant numbers. The dredge was effective in 70 fathoms, the deepest water sampled. Dredging was conducted on known clam beds at random depths and locations. The bottom samples were washed through a series of graduated screens so that all mollusks over 1 mm could be examined.

### METHOD OF DETERMINING DENSITY OF CLAM POPULATION

During the second survey, single transects were established at 11 locations known to contain hard-shell clams (Table 1 and Figure 1). The transects were established perpendicular to the shoreline, extending from the upper limit of the preearthquake clam population to the lowest tide level that could be sampled on the date of the survey. Each transect was divided, using a level and rod, into segments representing a 6-in. change of elevation. A sampling trench 8 in. wide and 1 ft deep was dug with a shovel at each transect. The length of sampling trench in each 6-in. elevation segment was dependent on the length of the segment and the type of ground. More than half of each segment, or at least 20 lineal feet, was dug unless large rocks or bedrock interfered. The number of clams per square foot of surface area was calculated on the basis of the samples.

TABLE 1  Second Survey Transects Used To Sample Hard-Shell Clams in Prince William Sound in 1965

| Area | Location | | Date of Sample | Estimated Uplift (ft) |
| --- | --- | --- | --- | --- |
| | West Longitude | North Latitude | | |
| 1. Knight Island (lower passage) | 147°35′ | 60°28′ | May 13 | 3.3 |
| 2. Sheep Bay | 146°00′ | 60°41′ | May 14 | 4.4 |
| 3. Hartney Bay[a] | 145°43′ | 60°30′ | May 2, 3 | 5.1 |
| 4. Hawkins Island, Canoe Passage | 146°10′ | 60°31′ | April 26 | 5.2 |
| 5. Crocker Island | 146°21′ | 60°29′ | April 29 | 5.2 |
| 6. Knight Island, Dryer Bay | 147°50′ | 60°18′ | May 12 | 5.6 |
| 7. Simpson Bay | 145°55′ | 60°38′ | April 30 | 5.7 |
| 8. Hinchinbrook Island, Port Etches | 146°39′ | 60°21′ | April 28 | 6.0 |
| 9. Evans Island, Port Ashton | 148°04′ | 60°03′ | May 12 | 7.9 |
| 10. Green Island, Gibbon Anchorage | 147°24.8′ | 60°17.8′ | May 10 | 8.2 |
| 11. Montague Island, Wilby Island | 147°13′ | 60°15′ | May 9 | 9.7 |

[a]Two transects were established at Hartney Bay.

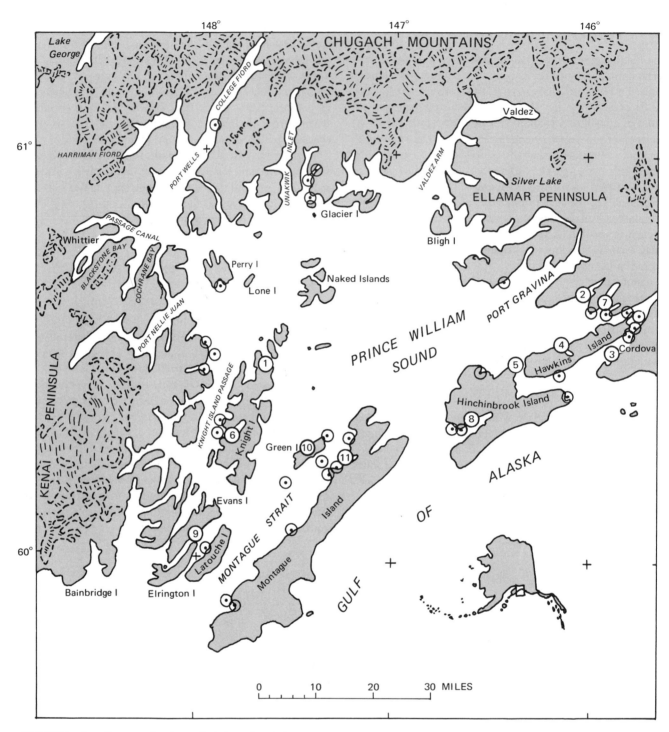

FIGURE 1    Sampling areas for clams. Circled numbers indicate sampling locations (see Table 1 for data). Circled dots indicate stations surveyed on foot.

## METHOD OF DETERMINING CLAM MORTALITY

In the third survey, 19 additional intertidal clam beds were sampled to determine mortality of clams. Incidental surveys conducted during the summer examined 13 more intertidal sites (Figure 1) for elevation-change effects. Sampling included areas of uplift, areas in the pivot zone where elevation was unchanged, and areas in the subsided northern part of the Sound. During the third survey, 28 dredge samples were taken, in addition to about 60 that had been taken at other times in the subtidal area, to ascertain the total tidal range inhabited by the species of hard-shell clams being studied. Clams from each transect sample were identified and examined to determine whether they were alive or dead of presumed earthquake causes, and the tidal elevation was recorded where the sample was collected. Other information taken at each sampling location included substrate composition and average age and size of the commercially important species of clams. Samples of substrate from intertidal areas were screened to determine numbers of young clams that might have been missed during the normal gross sampling with the shovel.

Mortality caused by the earthquake was defined as any clam death that occurred in the spring and summer of 1964 and in the winter of 1964–1965. Criteria for establishing time of death were (a) the decomposed clam body inside the shell; (b) no mud or other external debris filling the inside of the paired connected valves; (c) the clam shell *in situ* at normal depth and orientation; and (d) the resilium complete and not decomposed or sloughed away.

One inherent error is that natural mortality between the winter before the earthquake and the date of sampling was included in earthquake-caused mortality. This natural mortality is presumed to be low because the incidence of dead clams in the postearthquake optimum tidal zone for the clams was very low, although most clams were mature and near maximum size.

## FINDINGS

The 12 transect samples were assumed to be representative of the earthquake-elevated areas of Prince William Sound where clams were present, and it was also assumed that in areas of subsidence no immediate mortality resulted. The third survey, conducted throughout the Sound to evaluate the findings derived from the transect data obtained during the second survey, substantiated the assumption that no immediate mortality resulted in the subsided areas within a year after the subsidence.

Information on the relative density of hard-shell clams before and after the earthquake is shown in Table 2 and Figure 2. This information is not representative of the entire Sound because the transects were established only in areas of known populations, but it does give a measure of relative change in the abundance of hard-shell clams for Prince William Sound.

The term "optimum habitat" is defined as that area where the density of commercially utilized hard-shell clams exceeds 2 clams per ft$^2$. Harvesting by hand digging with a

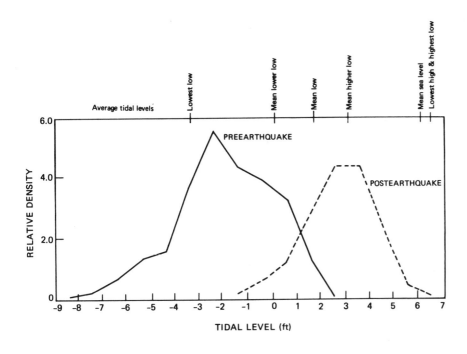

FIGURE 2  Distribution, by tidal level, of mature hard-shell clams in uplifted areas of Prince William Sound before and after the earthquake. The average numbers of clams per square foot for each foot of change in tidal elevation in each transect are totaled. The relative density is the average for the 12 transects.

TABLE 2  Relative Density of Clams per Square Foot by Species in Each 6-in. Tidal Level before and after (1965) the Earthquake in Prince William Sound

| Tidal Level (ft) | Preearthquake[a] | | | | | | | Postearthquake | | | | | | |
|---|---|---|---|---|---|---|---|---|---|---|---|---|---|---|
| | Saxidomus | Protothaca | Macoma | Humilaria, Mya, Tresus | Clinocardium | Total | Percentage | Saxidomus | Protothaca | Macoma | Humilaria, Mya, Tresus | Clinocardium | Total | Percentage |
| 7.0 to 6.5 | | | | | | | | | | | | | | |
| 6.5 to 6.0 | | | | | | | | 0.08 | 0.08 | | | | 0.16 | 1.0 |
| 6.0 to 5.5 | | | | | | | | 0.08 | 0.08 | | | 0.03 | 0.19 | 1.1 |
| 5.5 to 5.0 | | | | | | | | 0.10 | 0.09 | | | 0.05 | 0.24 | 1.5 |
| 5.0 to 4.5 | | | | | | | | 0.10 | 0.09 | | | 0.05 | 0.24 | 1.5 |
| 4.5 to 4.0 | | | | | | | | 0.89 | 0.48 | 0.54 | 0.01 | 0.05 | 1.97 | 11.9 |
| 4.0 to 3.5 | | | | | | | | 0.95 | 0.48 | 0.54 | 0.01 | 0.04 | 2.02 | 12.2 |
| 3.5 to 3.0 | | | | | | | | 0.80 | 0.79 | 0.59 | 0.13 | 0.05 | 2.36 | 14.3 |
| 3.0 to 2.5 | | | | | | | | 0.77 | 0.79 | 0.59 | 0.14 | 0.08 | 2.37 | 14.3 |
| 2.5 to 2.0 | 0.10 | | | | | 0.10 | 0.4 | 0.33 | 0.43 | 0.92 | 0.25 | 0.10 | 2.03 | 12.3 |
| 2.0 to 1.5 | 0.10 | | | | | 0.10 | 0.4 | 0.32 | 0.43 | 0.92 | 0.24 | 0.08 | 1.99 | 12.0 |
| 1.5 to 1.0 | 0.16 | 0.59 | 0.42 | | | 1.17 | 4.5 | 0.16 | 0.47 | 0.22 | 0.02 | 0.03 | 0.90 | 5.4 |
| 1.0 to 0.5 | 0.16 | 0.59 | 0.42 | | | 1.17 | 4.5 | 0.12 | 0.47 | 0.22 | 0.02 | 0.03 | 0.86 | 5.2 |
| 0.5 to 0.0 | 0.49 | 0.52 | 1.03 | | 0.02 | 2.06 | 8.0 | 0.10 | 0.13 | 0.14 | | 0.03 | 0.40 | 2.4 |
| 0.0 to −0.5 | 0.49 | 0.52 | 1.03 | | 0.02 | 2.06 | 8.0 | 0.12 | 0.13 | 0.13 | | 0.04 | 0.42 | 2.5 |
| −0.5 to −1.0 | 0.35 | 0.36 | 0.99 | 0.07 | 0.07 | 1.84 | 7.2 | 0.02 | | 0.11 | | 0.07 | 0.20 | 1.2 |
| −1.0 to −1.5 | 0.41 | 0.36 | 0.84 | 0.08 | 0.08 | 1.77 | 6.9 | 0.02 | | 0.10 | | 0.07 | 0.19 | 1.1 |
| −1.5 to −2.0 | 0.92 | 0.72 | 0.61 | 0.10 | 0.03 | 2.38 | 9.3 | | | | | | | |
| −2.0 to −2.5 | 0.99 | 0.64 | 0.63 | 0.10 | 0.08 | 2.44 | 9.5 | | | | | | | |
| −2.5 to −3.0 | 0.78 | 1.00 | 0.92 | 0.27 | 0.13 | 3.10 | 12.1 | | | | | | | |
| −3.0 to −3.5 | 0.78 | 1.02 | 0.90 | 0.27 | 0.11 | 3.08 | 12.0 | | | | | | | |
| −3.5 to −4.0 | 0.27 | 0.16 | 0.18 | 0.04 | 0.06 | 0.71 | 2.8 | | | | | | | |
| −4.0 to −4.5 | 0.35 | 0.17 | 0.20 | 0.04 | 0.05 | 0.81 | 3.1 | | | | | | | |
| −4.5 to −5.0 | 0.26 | 0.28 | 0.13 | 0.02 | 0.07 | 0.76 | 3.0 | | | | | | | |
| −5.0 to −5.5 | 0.16 | 0.28 | 0.20 | 0.03 | 0.07 | 0.74 | 2.9 | | | | | | | |
| −5.5 to −6.0 | 0.15 | 0.13 | 0.16 | 0.08 | 0.04 | 0.56 | 2.2 | | | | | | | |
| −6.0 to −6.5 | 0.16 | 0.12 | 0.01 | 0.08 | 0.02 | 0.39 | 1.5 | | | | | | | |
| −6.5 to −7.0 | 0.11 | 0.10 | | | 0.01 | 0.22 | 0.9 | | | | | | | |
| −7.0 to −7.5 | 0.10 | 0.10 | | | | 0.20 | 0.8 | | | | | | | |
| −7.5 to −8.0 | 0.01 | | | | 0.02 | 0.03 | 0.1 | | | | | | | |
| −8.0 to −8.5 | 0.01 | | | | 0.02 | 0.03 | 0.1 | | | | | | | |
| Totals | 7.31 | 7.66 | 8.67 | 1.18 | 0.90 | 25.72 | | 4.96 | 4.94 | 5.02 | 0.82 | 0.80 | 16.54 | |

[a]Preearthquake population is the sum of the postearthquake surviving population and the clams killed by the earthquake adjusted for elevation change.

242

shovel is considered uneconomical if the density of clams is fewer than 2 per ft². Hard-shell clams were considered to be of commercial size when more than 1½ in. in diameter.

## CLAM HABITATS

Tidal habitats of preearthquake populations of hard-shell clams of potential commercial importance ranged from +2.5 ft to –8.5 ft. Tides in Prince William Sound vary from the highest high tide of about 14.8 ft to the lowest low tide of about –3.6 ft. The optimum habitat tidal range for *Saxidomus giganteus* was from +1.5 ft to –3.5 ft, or from mean low water to lowest low water. The optimum habitat for the other species of hard-shell clams was approximately the same.

Under preearthquake conditions, 82 percent of the commercially important species of hard-shell clams were in the zone of optimum habitat, 17 percent were below this zone, and 1 percent were above it. In uplifted areas, adult hard-shell clams are now surviving to about the postearthquake 6-ft tide level, or to mean sea level.

Below the lowest low water tidal zone, in those areas that are seldom exposed to waves or strong surges, the subtidal habitat just offshore from the hard-shell clam population is composed of soft decaying organic silty mud. Beneath the surface of this silt layer, free oxygen may be deficient, but no oxygen determinations were actually made. I found that this subsurface was characterized by a strong hydrogen sulfide smell, black color, and the absence of all larger organisms other than a few worms and fewer adult pelecypods. In protected bays, this silty layer covers the bottom; in the other areas of the Sound, from lowest low water down to about 8 fathoms, it fills the interspaces between the rocks, gravel, and sand. Below this zone, much less organic material appears to be in the mud, except in the bottoms of the deeper basins. In areas without this highly organic silt, such as the outer shores facing the Gulf of Alaska and in lower Cook Inlet, dredging operations took *S. giganteus* to about the –10-ft tide level.

In Prince William Sound, either the cause or the effect of this stagnant silt zone is the lower limiting factor of the habitat of *S. giganteus*.

## SURVIVAL AND MORTALITY

The factor limiting the establishment of a stable clam population at upper tide levels is the unsuitability of the habitat for young clams. Adult clams can survive at higher elevations, as demonstrated by their presence in areas of uplift at elevations at which no adult clams were living before the earthquake. Three and a half years after the uplift, the clams of this displaced population were still living, and mortality appeared to approximate that of mature populations of hard-shell clams of the area that were living in the optimum zone. This information was obtained by comparison digs in the two zones in 1967.

In the area of subsidence, the change in the population structure differed from that in the uplifted areas. Much of the subsided area was immediately suitable for the deposition and survival of larval clams because it was composed of sand, gravel, and broken shells and contained a minimum of highly organic silt. Clams of the 1964 year class were found in the newly subsided habitat in the spring of 1965. This area was above mean low water before the earthquake.

In subsided areas the zone below the present lowest low tide now contains clams but probably will not be suitable for young clams after silting occurs. As the present populations of clams mature and die, the subtidal zone will probably cease to support most of the species of clams now living there.

In the areas of uplift, the present clam populations will gradually disappear above mean low water because the adults will not be replaced by young. Whether natural mortality of the uplifted population will increase is not known, but sampling in 1966 and 1967 indicated that the mortality was very low and did not appear to differ from populations in the lower tide zones.

The condition of the gonads of surviving clams at all tidal levels indicated that they apparently were all capable of spawning.

Much of the new habitat in the uplifted intertidal zone of Prince William Sound is unsuitable for clams because it consists of the preearthquake subtidal silty bottom material. Rain and wave action are washing out the silt, and eventually it will be suitable for the survival of young clams. No young clams of the 1964 year class spawn were found in this type of habitat in 1965, which suggests that the silt itself may be the limiting factor in survival of the young clams. Clam populations in the present optimum habitat zone of subsided areas will revert to preearthquake conditions before clams in the same habitat zone of uplifted areas. The new habitat in subsided areas was suitable for the survival of the larval clams the first season after the change in elevation, whereas in the uplifted areas it still was not suitable for their survival more than a year later.

### *Saxidomus giganteus*

My past work indicates that the habitat of *Saxidomus giganteus* is sharply bounded by tidal levels. Although the habitat extends sometimes to a depth of 10 ft, it is found primarily in the zone between mean low water and lowest low water. This range of habitat exists also in Humboldt Bay, California (tidal range about 10.2 ft); Prince William Sound (tidal range 18.4 ft); and Kasitsna Bay, near Seldovia in lower Cook Inlet, Alaska (tidal range 29.2 ft).

The narrow habitat range of *S. giganteus* is also the range of less economically important species of hard-shell clams. The change in elevation of the landmass has therefore had a profound effect on many other species of clams. Because adult hard-shell clams were capable of adjusting to an estimated average uplift of 4.7 ft, the estimated mortality of the clam population of the Sound was only 36 percent. Of the survivors, however, only 29 percent are in the optimum habitat tidal zone, compared with 82 percent in this zone before the earthquake (Table 3).

### Clinocardium nuttallii

Mortality resulting from the earthquake was 31 to 42 percent for the major species of hard-shell clams, except for the cockle *Clinocardium nuttallii*, for which mortality was estimated at 11.1 percent (Table 4). *C. nuttallii* is the only species of hard-shell clam in Prince William Sound living at or near the surface of the beds and capable of changing position in the adult stage. In one uplifted population that could be closely observed, movement was evidenced by tracks left by the clams on the surface of the mud flat. The tracks were generally circular and 5 to 10 ft in diameter, although some clams traveled in approximately straight lines, some made smaller circles, and some made other types of tracks. Although the tracks appeared to be in a random direction in level areas, they tended to move downward in sloping areas, probably because of gravity and the

round shape of the shell. The mortality figure of 11.1 percent for *C. nuttallii* in Table 4 is of questionable accuracy because of the probable disappearance of some shells. Stranded and exposed clams of all species, especially those at the surface as this species is, become quick prey for birds and mammals and thus cannot be retrieved.

In an area that had been uplifted 6.3 ft, *C. nuttallii* densities of about 4 clams per ft$^2$ were examined. These clams were all dead on the surface of the ground from 4 to 6 weeks after the earthquake. Their movements on the nearly level surface before they died appeared to be nondirectional and often covered more than 20 ft.

No horizontal movement of any other adult species of hard-shell clams was noted. Young hard-shell clams of most species, in age classes 0 to II, are capable of some horizontal movement, but it is unlikely that they would be able to move far enough to survive an uplifting if they were left in an unsuitable habitat. Adult hard-shell clams are capable of reburrowing if displaced.

### Tresus capax

Large numbers of hard-shell clams were washed out and deposited in windrows at the face of sandbars in Orca Inlet by the earthquake tsunamis. These clams, primarily *Tresus capax*, were starting to rebury themselves 3 days after the earthquake. Within a month the shells of the survivors were below the surface, and by midsummer they were deep enough to retract their siphons below the surface, which required a vertical movement of about 4 in. the first month

TABLE 3 Mortality and Changes in Accessibility and Habitat of Hard-Shell Clams in Prince William Sound Caused by the Great Alaska Earthquake

| Elevation Change (ft) | Area (mi$^2$)$^a$ | Percent Mortality | Percent of Population Accessible for Harvest$^b$ | Percent of Population Living in Optimum Habitat$^c$ |
|---|---|---|---|---|
| +20 to +30 | 396 | 100.0 | — | — |
| +10 to +19.9 | 370 | 100.0 | — | — |
| +8 to +9.9 | 368 | 82.3 | 100.0 | 0.3 |
| +6 to +7.9 | 961 | 54.7 | 100.0 | 6.2 |
| +4 to +5.9 | 1,608 | 16.0 | 98.0 | 31.8 |
| +2 to +3.9 | 1,094 | 0 | 97.2 | 62.7 |
| 0 to +1.9 | 514 | 0 | 88.6 | 80.6 |
| 0 to −1.9 | 410 | 0 | 54.7 | 54.9 |
| −2 to −3.9 | 305 | 0 | 21.0 | 21.0 |
| −4 to −5.9 | 530 | 0 | 0.6 | 0.6 |
| −6 to −7.9 | 288 | 0 | 0 | 0 |
| Averages$^d$ | — | 35.7 | 68.9 | 28.7 |

$^a$No figures are available for the area of clam habitat, either pre- or postearthquake, for Prince William Sound. The area of the entire Sound is used as a reference point against which to compare population changes caused by elevation changes.
$^b$The percentage of the population living above lowest low tide and capable of being harvested by current methods.
$^c$Optimum habitat zone is between mean low tide and lowest low tide.
$^d$Based on the average uplift of the Sound of 4.7 ft.

TABLE 4 Estimated Percentage Mortality of Commercially Important Hard-Shell Clams in Prince William Sound for a Habitat Change of +4.7 ft$^a$

| Scientific Name | Common Name | Percent Mortality |
|---|---|---|
| *Saxidomus giganteus* | Hard-shell clam | 32 |
| *Protothaca staminea* | Littleneck clam | 36 |
| *Macoma incongrua* *Macoma inquinata* *Macoma nasuta* | Mud clam | 42 |
| *Tresus capax* *Mya* cf. *priapus* *Mya* cf. *japonica* *Mya truncata* *Humilaria kennerleyi* | Gaper clam Soft-shell clam Soft-shell clam Northern soft-shell clam Ribbed hard-shell clam | 31 |
| *Clinocardium nuttallii* | Basket cockle | 11.1 |

$^a$Estimated average uplift of Prince William Sound caused by the earthquake was 4.7 ft.

and 1 in. a month thereafter until the clams had disappeared from view.

## Mytilus edulis

*Mytilus edulis*, the blue mussel, which was probably the most plentiful mollusk of Prince William Sound, was severely affected by the uplift. The normal tidal habitat of *M. edulis* is roughly limited to an area between mean sea level and mean lower high tide. Much of the habitat for *M. edulis* was uplifted sufficiently to destroy this mussel. Estimated mortality was about 90 percent. The year's young were found in all suitable areas examined in 1965, and the *M. edulis* population should shortly return to preearthquake levels. One reason for this potential stabilization of numbers is that the molluskan predators were also greatly reduced in number, and these predators are much slower in returning to preearthquake population levels. Mollusk predators on the mussels, which were greatly reduced in numbers by the uplift, include *Boreotrophon multicostatus* (Eschsholtz), *Thais lamellosa* (Gmelin), and *Thais lima* (Martyn).

## Siliqua patula

The mortality of *Siliqua patula*, the razor clam, caused by the uplift was extensive. No living clams were found in the four known beds located on the west side of Montague Island, an area that was uplifted 10–31 ft. The major *S. patula* beds of Orca Inlet experienced moderate mortality from an uplift of 6.5 ft. Any suitable habitat shortly will be replenished from the existing spawners on the Copper River Flats, because of the proximity of the Orca Inlet clam beds to favorable currents.

## ACKNOWLEDGMENTS

On the third survey in the summer of 1965, Mr. Robert Talmadge, a malacologist from Eureka, California, assisted in evaluating the effects of the habitat-elevation change on mollusks.

## REFERENCES

Baxter, Rae E., 1967. List of the bivalves of Prince William Sound collected 1962–1965 (unpublished manuscript). Bethel: Alaska Department of Fish and Game. 4 p. (Copy on file, Library, National Academy of Sciences–National Academy of Engineering, Washington, D.C.)

Plafker, George, and L. R. Mayo, 1965. Tectonic deformation, subaqueous slides and destructive waves associated with the Alaskan March 27, 1964, earthquake: an interim geologic evaluation. U.S. Geological Survey Open-File Report. Menlo Park, California: U.S. Geological Survey. 34 p.

RICHARD A. MARRIOTT
CARL E. SPETZ *
ALASKA DEPARTMENT OF FISH AND GAME

# Effects of Seawater Intrusion into Lakes of Kodiak and Afognak Islands

## INTRODUCTION

The freshwater lakes of Kodiak and Afognak islands were little damaged by the land tremors of the earthquake. Compaction of lakeshore sediments around inlet stream mouths of several lakes caused local shoreline settling of as much as 5 ft but produced no major change in lake habitats.

Lagoon-type lakes, on the other hand, were markedly affected by the land subsidence of 5-6 ft in the northeastern part of Kodiak Island and the eastern part of Afognak Island. Because the outlet spits were rapidly eroded, extreme high tides now enter most of these lakes, and at least two receive influxes of seawater at the peak of most higher tidal cycles.

Many coastal lakes were also severely damaged by the tsunamis generated by the earthquake. In Chiniak Bay (Figure 1), a series of at least four major waves was recorded at the Kodiak Naval Station during the 6 hours following the earthquake. These waves varied from 20 to 22 ft above the existing sea level. However, because of land subsidence and incoming-tide levels, the fourth wave reached a height of approximately 26 ft above the preearthquake high-tide level of 10.9 ft. Spits of several major lagoon-type lakes were washed out and converted into shallow bays by these tsunamis (Figure 2), and large amounts of seawater entered three lakes where the spits remained.

The major affected lakes in the Kodiak–Afognak area and the type of damage sustained are listed below (names are those used by the Alaska Department of Fish and Game; daggers indicate lagoon-type lakes with narrow seaward spits).

### Lakes Affected by Land Subsidence

Periodic seawater intrusion:

Lake Rose Tead (Kodiak Island)
Pauls Lake (Afognak Island)

ABSTRACT: The earthquake caused significant alteration of 13 major lakes on Kodiak and Afognak islands, as a result of land subsidence and of scouring and entry by tsunamis. Detailed studies of changes in fishery habitat were made in two of these lakes during the period 1964–1967. One of the lakes, which was subjected to a single massive intrusion of seawater, showed inverted temperature profiles, oxygen depletion, and sterile plankton conditions. In the other lake, which has experienced frequent recurring intrusion of seawater, alternate stratification and mixing has occurred; the transport of marine organisms into this lake is apparently responsible for accelerated growth and survival of a native population of coho salmon.

* Now at the Khutaghat Fish Farm, Bilaspur, India.

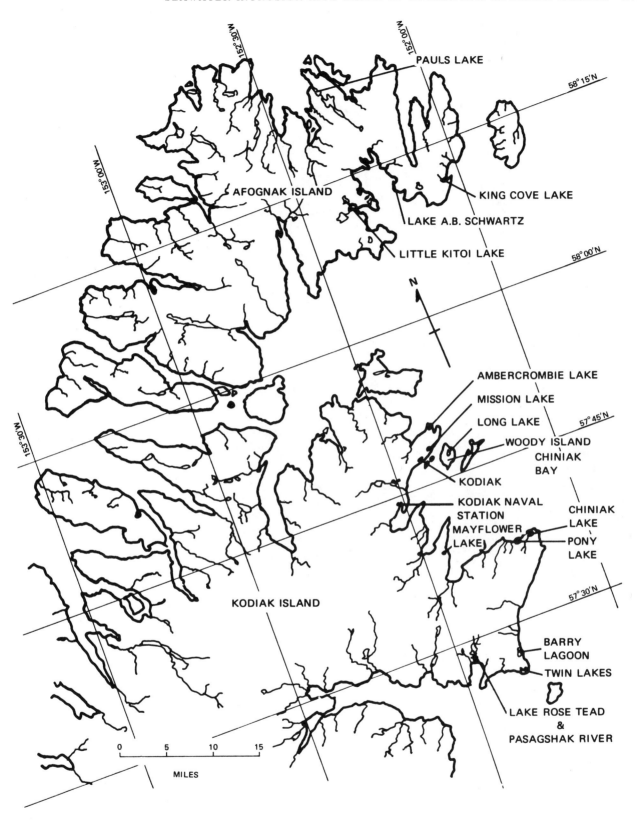

FIGURE 1   Afognak Island and northern Kodiak Island.

*Alaska Department of Fish and Game*

FIGURE 2   Outlet spit damage to King Cove Lake (foreground).

Occasional seawater intrusion:

† Chiniak Lake (Kodiak Island)
† Ambercrombie Lake (Kodiak Island)
† Barry Lagoon (Kodiak Island)

*Lakes Affected by Tsunami Scouring*

Permanent loss of seaward spit:

† King Cove Lake (Afognak Island)
† Lake A.B. Schwartz (Afognak Island)
† Twin Lakes (Kodiak Island)

Temporary spit loss, now repaired:

† Mission Lake (Kodiak Island)
† Pony Lake (Kodiak Island)

*Lakes Affected Only by Tsunami Entry*

Permanent stratification:

Mayflower Lake (Kodiak Island)

Temporary stratification:

Little Kitoi Lake (Afognak Island)
Long Lake (Woody Island)

A more detailed description of the general Kodiak–Afognak island area lake surveys made in 1964, including less important or undamaged lakes and measurements of streambed damage, may be found in "Post-earthquake fisheries evaluation," an interim report published by the Alaska Department of Fish and Game (1965).

Preearthquake biological studies of Karluk Lake on Kodiak Island were made by Croasdale (1958) and Hilliard (1959); Karluk Lake, however, was apparently not affected by the earthquake.

The methods of lake studies undertaken by the authors from June 1964 to November 1967 included aerial and ground observations of shoreline damage, salinity checks (1964) using a Kemmerer bottle and silver nitrate titration of samples, temperature readings using an electric thermometer, salinity-with-temperature readings (1965 and 1966) using a conductivity salinometer, oxygen samples using a Hach modified-Winkler titration procedure, vertical plankton hauls using a ½-m-diameter net of #20 nylon mesh, random bottom samples using a 9- by 9-in. Ekman dredge with sifting screens, and fish sampling using a 125- by 6-ft sinking gill net with variable mesh panels of ¾- to 2-in.-size webbing.

## MAJOR STUDIES

The more extensive follow-up studies were confined mainly to two lakes on the Kodiak road system: Mayflower Lake, a lake with initial but nonrecurring seawater intrusion; and Lake Rose Tead, a lake that has experienced periodic seawater intrusion since the earthquake. The principal purpose of these continuing studies is to detect gross alterations of the fish-rearing habitats.

### MAYFLOWER LAKE

Mayflower Lake is a low-lying lake ¼ mi inland from the Chiniak Road at Broad Point (mile 20½). In 1956 the Lake was mapped by alidade and plane table and the surface area calculated at 12.42 acres. The maximum depth was 28.6 ft and the volume 181 acre-ft. Although it lies at an elevation of only 16 to 17 ft (preearthquake level), the lake curves behind steep alder-covered hills and is protected from most winds. It is shaded by these hills during most of the winter. The lake bottom consists of compacted mud and silt, and there are several water-lily beds along the shallow shore areas. Two small inlets enter along the west shore, and the outlet stream (of approximately 3 cfs) flows through an extensive shallow weedy area and then directly to the ocean through two road culverts.

The lake was stocked as follows:

| | | |
|---|---|---|
| 1953 | 30,000 | ⎫ |
| 1954 | 20,000 | ⎪ |
| 1957 | 2,700 | ⎬ Rainbow trout (*Salmo gairdneri*) |
| 1958 | 6,500 | ⎪ |
| 1959 | 7,100 | ⎭ |
| 1963 | 2,750 | Coho salmon (*Oncorhynchus kisutch*) |

Mayflower Lake also contains native populations of three-spined sticklebacks (*Gasterosteus aculeatus*), Dolly Varden (*Salvelinus malma*), and coho salmon. The lake was rated as moderately poor for sport fishing before 1964, apparently mainly because of the low success of stocking in the face of natural predation and competition. Although a rehabilitation project had been proposed for this lake and an outlet weir designed, no actual work had begun on this project prior to the 1964 earthquake.

Initial observations of earthquake damage in June 1964 revealed marine driftwood deposited around the lakeshore 3–4 ft above the existing lake level. The lake outlet had been moderately scoured, and there was a heavy concentration of driftwood there. At least one tsunami had entered the lake, but subsequent high tides did not. A new road fill across the lower portion of the outlet stream, completed in September 1964, now gives further protection against future contamination. The lake surface in June 1964 was estimated at 12 ft above the new mean low water line.

Temperature profiles taken from July 1964 through July 1966 are shown in Figure 3, and the relationship of temperature with salinity is shown in Figure 4. Saline water, as much as 20 ppt (parts per thousand), has remained in the lake below 7½ ft, and an unusual inverted temperature profile has been created. The lake now contains a calculated 78.3 acre-ft of fresh water and 103.7 acre-ft of saline water. The saline water below the 10-ft depth has retained a temperature above 50°F while the freshwater stratum has fluctuated through seasonal changes ranging from 32°F (with a 22-in. ice cover) to 67°F. The freshwater layer is always colder than the upper portion of the saltwater layer; apparently the saline water initially absorbed heat from solar radiation and retained most of it each winter because of limited mixing with the freshwater layer.

The following oxygen concentrations were found in samples from Mayflower Lake:

| Date | Depth (ft) | Oxygen (ppm) |
|---|---|---|
| September 10, 1964 | Surface | 8.1 |
| | 10 | 10.0 |
| January 29, 1966 | 3.5 | 12.0 |
| | 25 | 0.0 |
| July 19, 1966 | 5 | 11.5 |
| | 25 | 1.6 |
| July 7, 1967 | 10 | 19.0 |
| | 20 | 0.6 |

The low oxygen levels in the lower hypolimnion are typical of stratified lake conditions. The extreme supersaturation observed on July 7, 1967, in the upper saltwater layer indicates that during early spring, mixing with oxygenated freshwater may occur down to the 10-ft level; however, water at this depth remains stratified during the summer and becomes

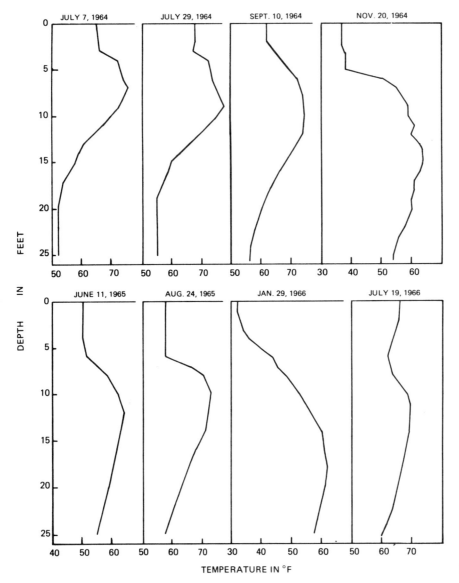

FIGURE 3   Mayflower Lake: temperatures.

supersaturated with oxygen. The mechanism producing the supersaturation is not known.

Vertical plankton hauls were made on July 7, September 10, and October 20, 1964, and on June 11, 1965. The 1964 hauls produced filamentous algae and a few unclassified marine-type adult copepods. Except for a small quantity of filamentous algae, the 1965 sample was virtually sterile.

Fish population observations were made on July 7, 1964. A 125-ft sampling gill net was set at approximately 4–16 ft. One 8.3-in. coho salmon and one 15.3-in. Dolly Varden were taken. They had been feeding on winged insects. On the same date, a shoreline count was made around the lake, and 250 coho fry, 160 three-spined sticklebacks (many of these dead), and two coho salmon fingerlings were observed in the shore areas. A similar 2-hour gill net set on October 20, 1964, produced one 14.2-in. coho salmon. Gonad and scale analy-

ses showed that it was a sexually ripe, nonmigratory male. Fisherman reports for 1966 and 1967 indicate that some "land-locked" coho salmon are continuing to be taken, but the lake has lost its reputation as a sport-fishing area.

*Conclusions*

The following conclusions may be drawn from the post-earthquake observations on Mayflower Lake:

1. The lake, which had previously been entirely fresh, received a large quantity of saline water during the March 1964 tsunamis.

2. This saline water, at concentrations of 9–20 ppt, has remained in the lake below a 10-ft depth and shows only a very slight dissipation.

3. The mean temperature of this saline water has consis-

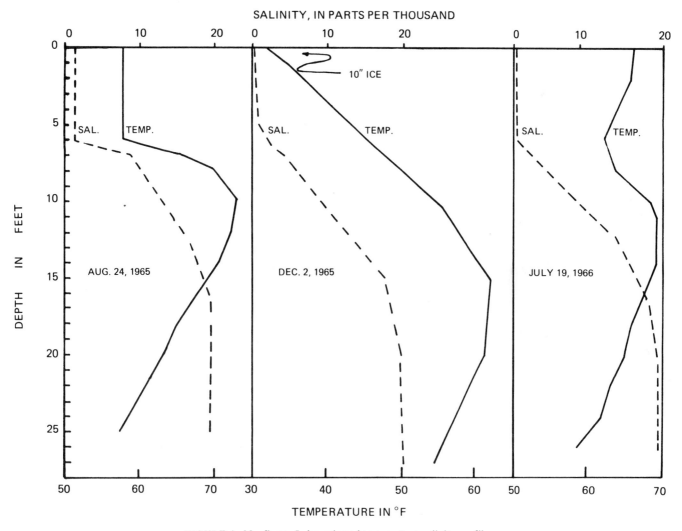

FIGURE 4   Mayflower Lake: selected temperature–salinity profiles.

tently remained higher than the overlying fresh water and has produced extreme temperature inversion profiles.

4. The lake became virtually sterile of freshwater plankton within the first year following seawater intrusion.

5. By the end of the first winter after seawater intrusion, the saline-water layer had developed a severe oxygen depletion and, to the present (1967), has remained below levels suitable for fish or zooplankton.

6. Except for small populations of coho salmon, Dolly Varden, and three-spined sticklebacks remaining in the freshwater layer, the lake has become unsuitable as a fish habitat and is likely to remain unsuitable for many years.

LAKE ROSE TEAD

Lake Rose Tead (Figure 5) is a large shallow lake along the Kodiak Island road system 36 mi south of the city of

Kodiak. Plane-table mapping of the main lake in February 1966 gave a calculated surface area of 234 acres; the maximum depth located in 1964 was 17 ft. The lake lies in a mountain valley and is fed by mountain drainage and several small spring-fed inlets on the northeast end. Lake outlet drainage into Ugak Bay is through 1½ mi of shallow lagoons and the Pasagshak River. Outlet measurements taken at the Pasagshak River during low flows (and at the extreme low-tide stage) established a minimum indigenous outflow of 60 cfs. Prior to the 1964 land subsidence, the lake surface was at an altitude of approximately 10.5 ft, and even extreme high tides did not enter the lake.

All the major 1964 tsunamis probably surged seawater into the lake; marine driftwood and the remains of the Pasagshak River bridge were deposited around the shores of the lake to a height of approximately 7 ft above the normal lake level. Lakeshore compaction of several feet occurred

Alaska Department of Fish and Game

FIGURE 5   Lake Rose Tead, showing shore-line subsidence and outlet lagoons in background.

along most of the east and northeast shores. Land subsidence and compaction totaling approximately 5 ft in the area of the Lake Rose Tead outlet left the lake surface at an altitude of 5.5 ft. Tide stages above this level now create a reverse current into the main lake.

Salinity observations were made during the crest of the 7.3-ft tidal cycle of Lake Rose Tead on October 2, 1964, and the following readings were obtained:

| Area | Salinity (ppt) |
| --- | --- |
| River separating upper and lower lagoons | 4.8 |
| Upper lagoon | 3.0 |
| Main lake outlet | 1.5 |
| Midlake surface | 1.0 |
| Midlake bottom (15 ft) | 1.7 |

On October 22, 1964, during the crest of a 10.0-ft tidal cycle, the following readings were obtained:

| Area | Salinity (ppt) |
| --- | --- |
| Main lake outlet | 13.2 |
| Southwest lake shore at 7 ft | 2.0 |
| Midlake surface | 2.0 |
| Midlake at 7 ft | 1.7 |
| Midlake bottom (15 ft) | 11.3 |

These observations indicate that although a tide above 5.5 ft will now create a reverse current into the lake, fresh water accumulating in the outlet lagoons prevents saline wa-

ter from entering the main lake until a tide stage of approximately 9 ft has been reached. This saline water periodically accumulates in the bottom of the main lake but is frequently mixed by wind action and dissipated between high tidal sequences.

Temperature readings from June 1964 through September 1966 (Figure 6) and the temperature–salinity relationship observed on June 4, 1965 (Figure 7), delineate the situation. Although the temperature profiles are all of the atypical inverted type similar to those found in Mayflower Lake, they give only a very general indication of salinity differences; for example, the extreme temperature inversion occurring October 2, 1964, developed from a salinity gradient of only 0.7 ppt.

The high level of salinity in the lake on June 16, 1964, was probably mainly from residual seawater deposited by the tsunamis; it appears to represent a maximum volume of seawater in the lake. However, inasmuch as bottom salinities since that time have fluctuated between 1.7 and 23.7 ppt, it is evident that dilution and wind action periodically mix the water mass and allow dissipation of the saline hypolimnion. This mixing was particularly noticeable in observations made on September 20, 1966, which followed a period of low tides, high winds, and heavy precipitation.

In the face of these recurring variations, a greatly modified fishery habitat can be anticipated in Lake Rose Tead. Before 1964, the lake contained a spawning population of 200–500 sockeye salmon (*Oncorhynchus nerka*), most of which spawned along the beaches in the southwest shore area. A population of 150–600 coho salmon spawned in the

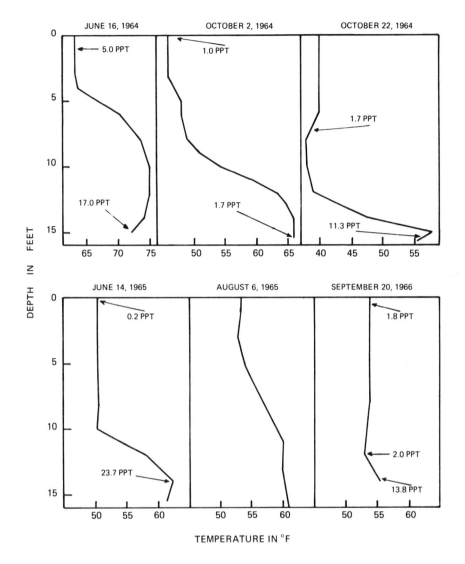

FIGURE 6   Lake Rose Tead: temperature profiles with salinity reference points.

northeast tributaries. Typically, the juveniles of these species were reared in the lake for 1 or 2 years. Small numbers of pink salmon (*Oncorhynchus gorbuscha*) also spawned in the northeast tributaries, and Dolly Varden were present in the lake and tributaries.

After the initial postearthquake observations, it was predicted that the lake would probably become less suitable for sockeye salmon rearing and more suitable for the rearing of more saline-tolerant coho salmon fingerlings; however, no direct fisheries observations were made in 1964. In June 1965, several hundred unusually large coho salmon smolts, some as long as 14 in., were taken at Pasagshak River by sport fishermen. A sampling gill net set for 1 hour in the lower outlet lagoon on June 23, 1965, produced 15 Dolly Varden and 2 coho salmon 9–10 in. long. All these fish were feeding on large numbers of marine amphipods (unclassified gammerids). A 9- by 9-in. Ekman dredge was used to locate the distribution of this feed, and the following samples were obtained:

| Area | Type of Organism | Number of Organisms (3-sample mean) |
|---|---|---|
| Lake Rose Tead | Caddis larvae | 3 |
| | Freshwater snails | 5 |
| Upper lagoon | Marine amphipods | 2 |
| Lower lagoon | Marine amphipods | 6 |
| Pasagshak River | Marine amphipods | 48 |

On July 12, 1965, a sampling gill net was set for 1 hour at a 6- to 12-ft depth in Lake Rose Tead; two Dolly Varden and one marine cottid (*Leptocottus armatus*) were caught. These fish were feeding heavily on marine euphausids (unclassified). The euphausids could not be collected in repeated vertical plankton hauls in the lake on this date; a virtually sterile plankton condition prevailed throughout the main lake. A previous plankton haul taken on October

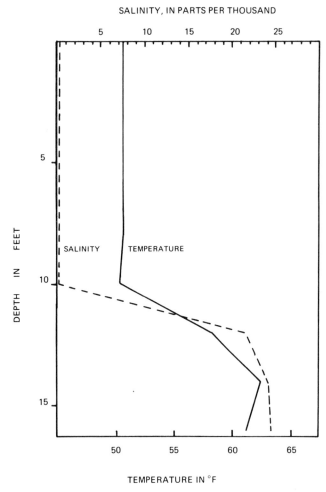

SALINITY, IN PARTS PER THOUSAND

TEMPERATURE IN °F

FIGURE 7 Lake Rose Tead: salinity–temperature profile on June 4, 1965.

2, 1964, produced a small number of unclassified but apparently marine copepods.

The incompatibility of this situation of heavily feeding fish in a plankton-poor environment may be attributed to physical or behavioral grouping of the larger marine plankters as they enter the lacustrine environment. The lagoon areas and narrow outlet of the main lake probably afford optimum grazing opportunities before the marine organisms disperse into the main lake. Coho salmon fingerlings and Dolly Varden characteristically depend on selection of larger bottom and surface organisms, rather than on the grazing of microscopic planktonic organisms. Inasmuch as seawater enters the main lake for at least 1 hour approximately 13 times per month and the lagoon areas receive seawater on nearly every high tide, it appears likely that this supplemental source of food would be enough to stimulate significantly the growth of coho salmon and Dolly Varden in this system and to contribute to increased survival for these species.

The 1966 and 1967 spawning-ground surveys at Lake Rose Tead have shown the following rapid increases in adult coho salmon returns:

| Year | Escapement Estimate | Female Age Composition, by Brood Year |
| --- | --- | --- |
| 1966 | 1,600+ | Nearly all from 1964 fry |
| 1967 | 2,600+ | 24 percent from 1964 fry; 76 percent from 1965 fry |

The 1966 and 1967 sockeye salmon escapement estimates ranged between 150 and 300 fish.

*Conclusions*

The following conclusions can be drawn from the postearthquake observations at Lake Rose Tead:

1. The lake was initially made almost completely saline by the 1964 tsunamis.
2. The main lake continues to receive additional influxes of saline water on tides above 9 ft.
3. Alternate periods of seawater intrusion and dilution and mixing with fresh water produce a fluctuating saline and thermal situation in the lake.
4. The intrusion of seawater apparently brings marine euphausids into the lake, but the subsequent mixing effect produces an environment unsuitable for either marine or freshwater plankton.
5. Marine amphipods have become established in the Pasagshak River and the outlet lagoons, but not in the main lake.
6. One species of marine cottid is now found in the lake.
7. The altered lacustrine environment apparently has improved coho salmon fingerling growth and survival and has produced an initial dramatic increase in the magnitude of the returning spawning populations in 1966 and 1967.

REFERENCES

Alaska Department of Fish and Game, 1965. Post-earthquake fisheries evaluation. An interim report on the March 1964 earthquake effects on Alaska's fishery resources. Juneau: Alaska Department of Fish and Game. 72 p.

Croasdale, Hannah T., 1958. Freshwater algae of Alaska (2). Some new forms from the plankton of Karluk Lake. *Transactions of the American Microscopical Society*, 77 (No. 1), 31–35.

Hilliard, D. K., 1959. Notes on the phytoplankton of Karluk Lake, Kodiak Island, Alaska. *Canadian Field-Naturalist*, 73 (No. 3), 135–143.

JAMES W. NYBAKKEN *
CALIFORNIA STATE COLLEGE OF HAYWARD

# Appendix:
# Preearthquake Intertidal Zonation of Three Saints Bay, Kodiak Island

## INTRODUCTION

The work reported here is part of a much larger quantitative ecological analysis of the intertidal zone of Three Saints Bay, Kodiak Island (Nybakken, 1969), which was done in the summer of 1963. This paper reports on the intertidal zonation as determined on several shores of a semiprotected bay about 9 months before the 1964 earthquake. To the author's knowledge, this is the only intertidal study from the earthquake zone before the earthquake; it thus is a basis for comparison and evaluation of changes since the earthquake that are reported in other papers in this volume. A considerable body of literature documents the zonation of intertidal areas in various places throughout the world, but scarcely any studies have been made on biotic zonation along the Alaska coast. The publications of Scagel (1959, 1961a, 1961b, 1962a, 1962b, and 1964) on the north Pacific coast flora are pertinent, however, and may serve as a basis for comparison with the following observations and as a basis for subsequent studies.

The works of Bousfield and McAllister (1962) and of Bousfield (1963) in this area consist only of lists of collecting stations in the area. Stephenson and Stephenson (1961a, 1961b) have discussed in detail the zonation of the shores around the southern end of Vancouver Island, but all other intertidal work on the Pacific coast of North America has been done south of Canada. Considerable work was done by Hewatt (1937) and by Gislén (1943, 1944) on Monterey Bay, California, by Shelford and others (1935) on Puget Sound, and by Rigg and Miller (1949) at Neah Bay in Washington. In addition to these regional studies, the work of Ricketts and Calvin (1962) is a comprehensive coverage of intertidal ecology, including zonation.

## DESCRIPTION OF THE AREA

Kodiak Island is about 100 mi long by 60 mi wide at its extremes and has an area of 3,588 mi$^2$ (Capps, 1937). The

ABSTRACT: A pattern of zonation existed on four intertidal areas of a semiprotected bay on Kodiak Island before the earthquake of 1964. Three zones could be distinguished on all shores that had a stable substrate. The lowest zone was dominated by eelgrass if the substrate was soft and by laminarian kelps if it was rocky. The middle zone on all shores was dominated by the alga *Fucus*, and the highest zone by one or more barnacle species. These zones varied in height and extent among the four sample areas, reflecting the different environmental conditions prevailing on each.

* Now at Moss Landing Marine Laboratories, Moss Landing, California.

island lies just southwest of Kenai Peninsula, of which it is geologically an extension, and about 40 mi off the Alaska Peninsula.

Three Saints Bay, an inverted L-shaped inlet (Figure 1) on the southern half of the island about 60 mi from the city of Kodiak, is ringed with steep-sided mountains that rise abruptly from the bay to heights of 3,000 ft on the south side and 2,000 ft on the north side.

Because of the abruptly rising mountains, there are few low-lying areas about the bay. Two such areas occur where streams enter, and two more extensive ones occur as small peninsulas (Figure 1). The remainder of the shoreline of the bay consists of solid rock faces and interspersed talus slopes or cobble beaches; many of the faces are nearly vertical.

Three Saints Bay is influenced by mixed tides and has a maximum tidal range of slightly more than 13 ft (13.2 ft in 1963, U.S. Coast and Geodetic Survey, 1962b). The mean tidal range is 8.3 ft. In the summer the lowest tides occur in early morning, usually between 4:00 and 8:00 a.m.

Water temperatures in the summer usually range from 48 to 54° F (9–12° C) at the surface (U.S. Coast and Geodetic Survey, 1962a). During the fieldwork in 1963, surface temperature measurements taken by the field party at various times during the summer averaged 51.8° F (11.0° C).

## SAMPLE AREAS

Four areas within Three Saints Bay were studied intensively enough to allow the establishment of zonation patterns (Figure 1, sample areas 1, 2, 3–4, and 6). The four were selected to include a representative of each of the various shoreline areas that existed in the bay at the time of this study:

1. The West Reef (sample area 1, Figure 1) was the northernmost outlier of a more extensive reef system that bordered the shore of the bay all the way to Cape Kasiak. The reef extended outward from the base of a steeply sloping gravel beach, which itself was almost devoid of marine life. It was composed of boulders 12–15 in. in diameter separated by areas of smaller cobbles. The reef was very low-lying and was exposed only at the lowest tides. On the seaward side it had no definite edge within the tidal range. The area was subject to extensive wave action.

2. The beach transect area (sample area 2, Figure 1) was a cobble beach that nearly enclosed a lagoon. It consisted of partly consolidated pieces of rock 5–7 in. in diameter that formed a pavement overlying finer material beneath. The cobbles continued from above high water downward to about the level of mean lower low water (MLLW) where the shore became mud or sandy mud. At its seaward edge this mud flat dropped off abruptly into the deeper waters of the

lagoon. The peninsula cut off the area from the bay proper and thus protected it from wave action. A freshwater stream entered the lagoon near the southern end of the sample area.

3. The vertical transect area (sample areas 3–4, Figure 1) consisted of nearly vertical flat slabs of dioritic rock that dropped abruptly into the water on the upper reaches of the west side of the bay. In this area, there were no beaches, and water depths adjacent to shore were 60 ft or more. Here the zonation of organisms was best displayed, and there was considerable wave action on south-facing cliffs.

4. The East Reef (sample area 6, Figure 1) was another boulder reef composed of rocks 10–12 in. in diameter separated by areas of cobbles and smaller rock fragments. This substrate sloped off toward the bay and terminated with a modified substrate of sand–silt. At its shoreward edge, the reef originated at the base of a gently sloping depauperate sand beach that did not extend throughout the entire tidal range, although it extended through a greater vertical range than the West Reef (5.00 ft as opposed to 1.65 ft). This reef also had a more pronounced slope than the West Reef (6.3 ft in 150 ft, as opposed to 1.97 ft in 150 ft). The East Reef had no definite edge within the tidal zone and continued subtidally as an extensive eelgrass bed (*Zostera*). The area was subject to moderate wave action because it faced the mouth of the bay and hence the incoming swell.

## METHODS

The methods used to study the zonation patterns varied with the type of area and were also governed by the fact that the primary effort was directed to quantitative ecological studies. The study was restricted to sedentary and semisedentary species of macroinvertebrates and algae.

Two methods of study were used. In the beach transect area and in the vertical transect area, a series of belt transects were run. Each belt transect consisted of a series of adjacent contiguous 0.25 m$^2$ quadrats in a line providing the transect. Each transect extended from the level of the lowest tide available at the time of sampling to well above the level of mean higher high water (MHHW). Five of these belt transects were run in the beach transect area and seven in the vertical transect area.

The second method, used on the West Reef and the East Reef areas, involved the establishment of random sampling stations on a surveyed grid system that covered the reef. At each station so established, a 0.25-m$^2$ quadrat was analyzed. The zonation pattern was then later built out of the analysis of quadrats taken in each physiognomically different zone, and the qualitative descriptions were recorded in field notebooks; this pattern is more subjective than that derived by the first method.

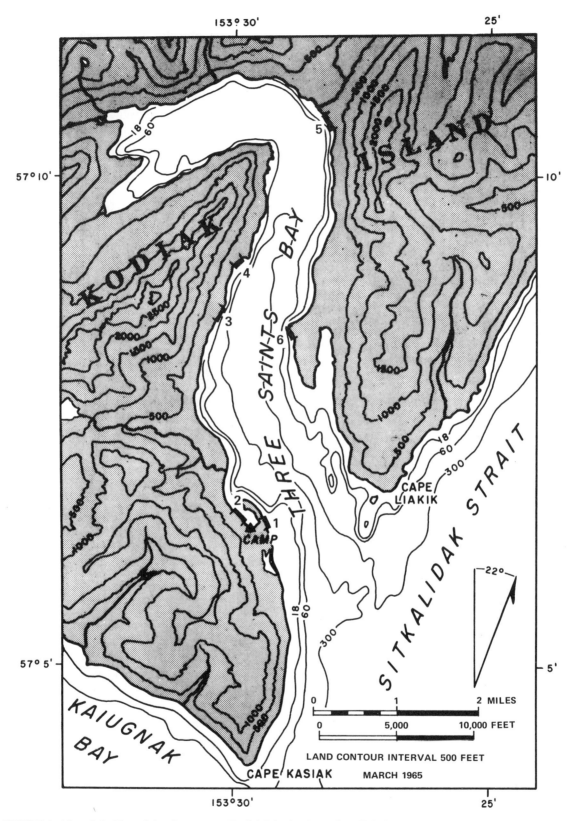

FIGURE 1   Map of the Three Saints Bay area on Kodiak Island redrawn from U.S. Geological Survey topographic map of the area. The numbers indicate the sampling sites described in the text: *1*, the West Reef; *2*, the beach transects; *3* and *4*, the vertical transects; *5*, a tidal pool described in Nybakken (1969); and *6*, the East Reef.

The establishment of zonation pattern by either method included the study of many photographs taken of the sample areas.

Tide levels on all sampling areas except the vertical transect area were similarly established. A surveying transit and level rod were used to measure the height of each quadrat. At the beginning and end of each day, a similar reading was taken of the height of the tide, and the time of the measurement was noted. It was then possible at a later time to convert these rod measurements to actual tidal levels by using standard conversion tables (U.S. Coast and Geodetic Survey, 1962b).

In the vertical transect area, the near-vertical faces made the transit unnecessary; the leveling rod was merely placed against the vertical face, and the water level and the times were noted for later conversion to tidal levels. The tidal datum was always MLLW (0.0 of the tide tables).

## ZONATION

The zonation patterns were somewhat different at each sampling area. The low-lying West Reef, which was exposed only at the lowest tides, did not support communities that ordinarily were found at higher tide levels. Both the ecological sampling and general observation demonstrated that this reef consisted of but a single zone, which was conspicuously dominated by a laminarian kelp, *Alaria pylaii*, and which may be classified as an isolated laminarian zone (Figure 2).

Although the reef was dominated by the *Alaria*, these algae were not continuous over the entire reef. Beneath the *Alaria* mat and also extending out over the cobble areas between the larger boulders was a conspicuous green encrusting sponge that covered rather extensive areas.

The large boulders that characterized the reef often stood out as islands above the *Alaria*. The tops of these rocks, whether or not surrounded by *Alaria*, had a growth of rockweed (*Fucus distichus*), and other algae, including especially sea lettuce, *Ulva* sp., *Halosaccion glandiforme*, and *Spongomorpha* sp. (Figure 2).

The large rocks also supported great numbers of the barnacle *Balanus cariosus*. The individuals of this species on this reef were the largest seen anywhere in the bay. Other invertebrate species conspicuously present on the reef included *Katharina tunicata*, *Acmaea scutum*, *Mopalia ciliata*, *Thais lamellosa*, *Leptasterias* sp., *Cucumaria curata*, and *Strongylocentrotus drobachiensis*. This reef supported the greatest number of species of any of the four sample areas.

The beach transect area consisted of three principal horizontal zones arranged in a regular series vertically. These bands were very obvious from a distance and remained so under closer observation in the transects.

The lowest zone was covered by a carpet of green eelgrass (*Zostera marina*). The substrate here was soft muddy sand and differed from the cobble substrate of the upper zones. It reached its upper limit near the 0.5-ft tide level (Figure 3). No large surface-dwelling invertebrates were found in the zone.

The second zone, dark yellow-brown in color, was covered primarily by *Fucus distichus*, but *Ectocarpus* sp. formed a mat over the *Fucus* at the lower levels. Large numbers of *Littorina sitkana* were visible on the fronds of the *Fucus*. Beneath the mat of *Fucus*, many *Mytilus edulis* mussels, usually in clumps, were attached to the larger rock cobbles or were partially buried in the cobble substrate. Small *Balanus cariosus* barnacles were also numerous under the *Fucus* mat, and *Acmaea pelta* limpets were common on the cobble *Fucus* fronds and on *Mytilus* shells.

The *Fucus* zone ended abruptly between 4.0 and 5.0 ft—slightly above mean tide level (MTL) (4.4 ft); from a distance, its upper boundary was the most marked line on the beach. The lower limit of this zone, which generally occurred between 0.5 and 1.0 ft, was less precise because of a transition area present at many places between the eelgrass and *Fucus* zone. This transition area was well marked in the two transects (4 and 5, Figure 3) where a reef of exposed *Mytilus edulis* occurred. In the other transects this transition area in most places was bare. At no point did the *Zostera* and *Fucus* zones meet in a sharp line.

Above the *Fucus*, the last zone, designated the barnacle zone, extended to the level reached by the highest tides. This zone was almost black because of the visible cobble substrate. Except for occasional small white patches of *Balanus cariosus*, nothing else was visible superficially in this zone. The only other species of the zone were *Mytilus edulis* and *Littorina sitkana*, both extending into this zone in lesser number from their areas of abundance in the *Fucus* zone below.

The vertical transect area showed the greatest vertical extent of development of the tidal zone found in the bay region. The very sharp distinct banding found at all levels on the beach transect area was not immediately apparent in this area, but further observation and the analysis of the transect revealed the presence again of three major zones.

The lowest of these vertical zones was continuous subtidally and of a dark brown color. It was dominated by the algae *Alaria pylaii*, *Odonthalia floccosa*, and *Laminaria platymeris* and has been termed the *Odonthalia–Laminaria* zone (Figure 4). Underneath the thick outer layer of this zone, the rock faces were extensively covered by bryozoans and tunicates. Few other large invertebrates were found here, and none were common. *Tonicella lineata* chitons, *Evasterias troschellii*, *Leptasterias* sp., and *Henricia leviuscula*, the latter three starfish, were found occasionally.

A second dark zone, dominated by *Fucus distichus*, ex-

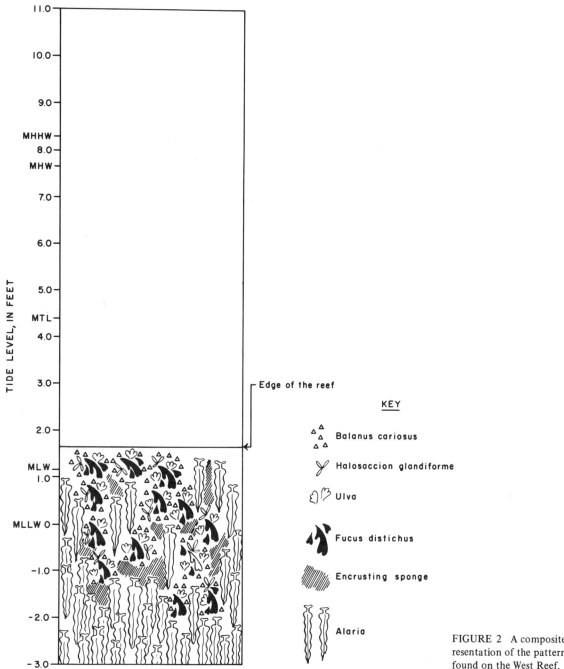

KEY

△△ △  Balanus cariosus
△△

У  Halosaccion glandiforme

Ulva

Fucus distichus

Encrusting sponge

Alaria

FIGURE 2   A composite diagrammatic representation of the pattern of zonation found on the West Reef.

tended up from about 1.0 to 2.0 ft, but there was no definite break between it and the *Odonthalia–Laminaria* zone below because of very large amounts of the alga *Odonthalia floccosa* that extended from a subtidal position through the lowest *Odonthalia–Laminaria* zone and well into the *Fucus* zone (Figure 4).

The covering of *Fucus* was attached to a layer of large *Balanus cariosus* barnacles, so dense in many places that no open rock substrate was to be found. Associated with the barnacles were several other species of invertebrates, of which *Mytilus edulis, Katharina tunicata*, and *Acmaea scutum* were the most common.

*Fucus distichus* extended almost to the 7.5-ft tide level, or very near mean high water (MHW). *Balanus cariosus* also reached its upper level in this region, and this line was the most visible one on the faces. The *Fucus* was dark, and the

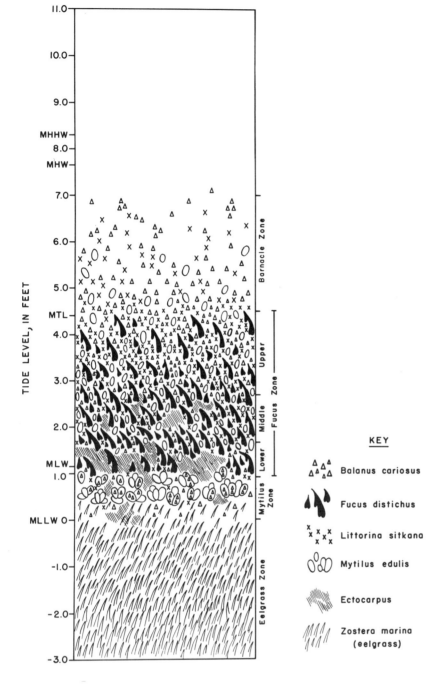

TIDE LEVEL, IN FEET

KEY

△ △ △
△ △ △   Balanus cariosus

Fucus distichus

x x x
x x x   Littorina sitkana

Mytilus edulis

Ectocarpus

Zostera marina
(eelgrass)

FIGURE 3   A composite diagrammatic representation of the pattern of zonation of the beach transect area taken at the level of transects 4 and 5.

line was accentuated by the presence of large numbers of light-colored barnacles immediately above and by a narrow band of the bright green alga *Enteromorpha intestinalis.*

The last and highest zone, the barnacle zone, above the *Fucus* zone, graded off above within a distinct, prominent band formed by the black *Verrucaria* lichens. This black-lichen band was itself delimited above by the lighter color of the rocks. The lichen band was not always continuous, and it varied in width and height above tidal datum. Where

the band occurred, its upper edge marked the upper limit of marine organisms.

This highest zone was characterized by an absence of large algae. The most prominent and numerous organisms in it were the barnacles *Balanus glandula* and *Chthamalus dalli* and the limpet *Acmaea digitalis* (Figure 4). In many places in this zone, these were the only organisms observed, and no others were common. The zone extended from about 7.5 ft to between 10.0 and 11.0 ft (Figure 4).

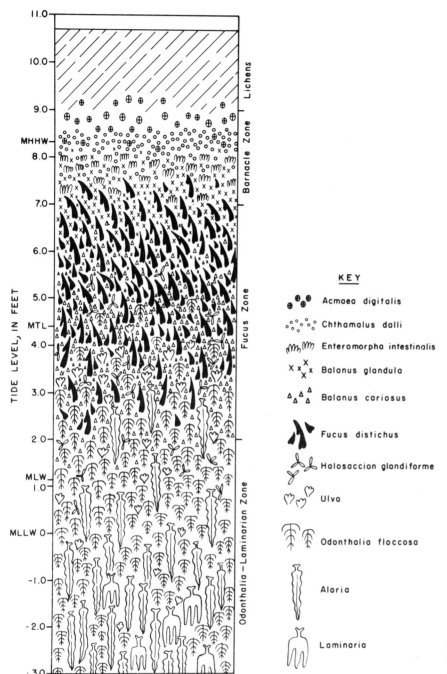

KEY

⊕ Acmaea digitalis

○ Chthamalus dalli

ᶭᶭ Enteromorpha intestinalis

x Balanus glandula

△ Balanus cariosus

🖌 Fucus distichus

⚜ Halosaccion glandiforme

♡ Ulva

🌿 Odonthalia floccosa

Alaria

Laminaria

FIGURE 4  A composite diagrammatic representation of the pattern of zonation of the vertical transect area.

On the East Reef, three distinct zones, much like those seen at the beach transect area, were distinguishable (Figure 5).

The lowest zone was dominated by a heavy cover of dark green eelgrass (*Zostera marina*). Interspersed in this blanket of green were patches of the brown alga *Rhodomela larix*, which surrounded the occasional rocks (Figure 5). This zone was continuous subtidally; it extended upward to between the −0.5- and 0.0-ft tide levels. Aside from the oc-

casional rocks, the substrate here was soft muddy sand. The only large invertebrates associated with this zone were starfish, *Pycnopodia helianthoides*, which was quite common, and *Dermasterias imbricata*, which was rare.

Extending shoreward above the eelgrass zone was a narrow dark brown zone dominated by the alga *Fucus distichus* associated with the filamentous brown alga *Ectocarpus* sp.; it was termed the *Fucus* zone (Figure 5). Other less common algae of this zone were *Cryptosiphonia*

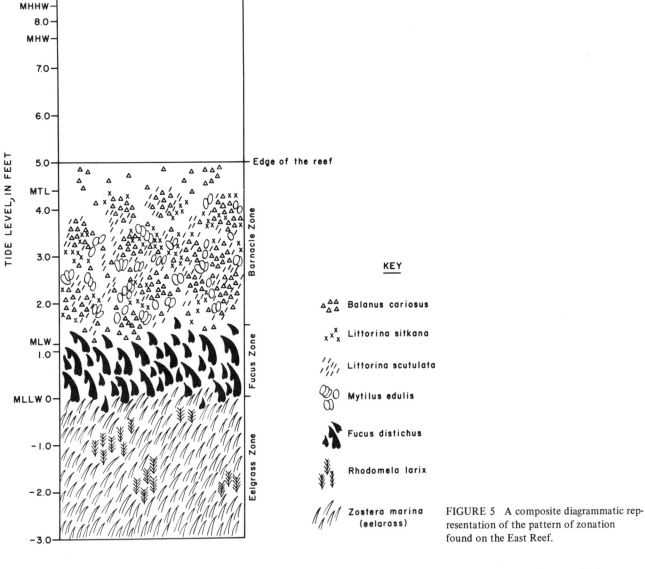

KEY

△△△ Balanus cariosus

ₓ ₓˣₓ Littorina sitkana

⫻ Littorina scutulata

◯◯ Mytilus edulis

Fucus distichus

Rhodomela larix

Zostera marina
(eelgrass)

FIGURE 5 A composite diagrammatic representation of the pattern of zonation found on the East Reef.

woodii, Enteromorpha sp., Rhodomela larix, and Spongomorpha sp.

This zone differed from the physiognomically similar zone in the beach transect area in that it was markedly lacking in populations of any of the larger invertebrates. It was especially notable for the almost total absence of Balanus cariosus and Mytilus edulis. Only hermit crabs (Pagurus hirsutiusculus) were common. Most of the other invertebrates found in this zone were stragglers from populations that reached their greatest densities in the next higher zone.

This narrow Fucus zone reached its upper limit between 1.0 and 1.8 ft. Near the lower edge of this zone, the substrate changed from the muddy sand of the eelgrass zone to the rock and boulder substrate, which in turn extended from the lower edge of the Fucus zone to the uppermost levels reached by the reef.

Above 1.8 ft, bare dark gray substrate was the characterizing feature of the uppermost zone. The otherwise uniform gray-black color was interrupted by numerous patches of contrasting white barnacles. These barnacles were the dominant surface invertebrates here, and hence the zone was named for them. The barnacles were of two species, *Balanus cariosus* and *Balanus glandula*. No large algae species occurred in this zone.

This upper zone was by far the richest of the three zones on the reef in terms of species of invertebrates and numbers of individuals. The most prominent and numerous species associated with the barnacles were *Mytilus edulis, Acmaea pelta, Littorina sitkana*, and *Littorina scutulata*.

The barnacle zone ended abruptly at a tidal level of about 5.0 ft at an interface between the reef and the sandy beach that extended through the remainder of the tidal zone. This substrate was unstable and nearly devoid of large invertebrates.

## DISCUSSION

The number of zones that were observed and established on the four sample areas coincided wherever there was enough vertical extent of stable substrates. There were typically three zones on the shore that differed among themselves physiognomically and often in species composition. The West Reef did not show three zones because it did not have enough vertical extent in the tidal zone.

The number of zones on any one shore was three or less, but the total number of types of zones from all areas was four. These four zones were named the barnacle zone, *Fucus* zone, eelgrass zone, and laminarian zone. All shores investigated with enough vertical extent in the tidal zone showed a similar upper zone dominated by barnacles and a similar middle zone dominated by the alga *Fucus distichus*. Differences between the sample areas appeared in the lowest zone, which was an eelgrass zone if the substrate was sand or muddy sand and a laminarian zone if the substrate was rock.

Despite the similarity of the zones among the different sample areas as to the dominating organisms, they showed considerable differences from area to area in height above tidal datum and in presence and abundance of component organisms.

The beach transect and East Reef sample areas had essentially the same zones. Both were gently sloping beaches. There was, however, a great contrast between the two areas in the animal species associated with each zone. The eelgrass zone of the East Reef had a small but persistent population of asteroids, whereas none were found in the beach transect eelgrass zone.

The *Fucus* zone of the two areas also showed marked differences. In the beach transect area, this zone was the richest in numbers and species of associated invertebrates.

*Mytilus edulis, Littorina sitkana, Acmaea scutum,* and *Balanus cariosus* were common. The East Reef *Fucus* zone, by contrast, was bare, and no other invertebrates of large size were common.

The barnacle zones of the two areas showed the greatest differences in terms of species and numbers. In the beach transect area, only *Balanus cariosus, Littorina sitkana*, and *Mytilus edulis* were found, and these were in small numbers compared to their abundance in the *Fucus* zone below. Indeed, the zone was composed of stragglers from the zone below. The East Reef, by contrast, had the greatest number of species and individuals concentrated in this zone, and none were stragglers from other zones. Also, except for *Balanus cariosus* and *Littorina sitkana*, the species in it were not found in the beach transects.

The population and species differences may be partly attributable to the differences in substrate, most notably the large boulders on the East Reef, but apparently the differences in exposure of the two areas and the presence near the beach transect area of freshwater outflow were the principal governing factors in the population and species differences.

Differences in zonal components between the vertical transect area and the other areas are most likely due to the steep slope of the substrate and the lack of crevices in the rock. Certain species, such as *Littorina*, that are not adapted to clinging could not have been expected on these faces. The very much higher extent of the zones on these faces as opposed to those on the other three areas probably results from their greater exposure to wave action and splash. The waves break against these surfaces much more readily than on sloping beaches.

In summary, an intertidal zonation pattern that consisted typically of three zones was determined for Three Saints Bay. The uppermost zone was typically dominated by barnacles, and the middle zone was dominated by the alga *Fucus distichus*. The lowest zone was an eelgrass zone if the substrate was sand or muddy sand and was a zone dominated by one or more large laminarian kelps if the substrate was hard rock. Species and population differences between similar zones in different areas can be attributed to differences in exposure and substrate.

## ACKNOWLEDGMENTS

The fieldwork for this research was supported by National Science Foundation Grant GS-136 to the University of Wisconsin.

## REFERENCES

Bousfield, E. L., 1963. Investigations on seashore invertebrates of the Pacific coast of Canada, 1957 and 1959: I, Station list. Ottawa: National Museum of Canada Bulletin 185. p. 72–90.

Bousfield, E. L., and D. E. McAllister, 1962. Station list of the National Museum marine biological expedition to southeastern Alaska and Prince William Sound. Ottawa: National Museum of Canada Bulletin 183. p. 76–103.

Capps, Stephen Reid, 1937. Kodiak and adjacent islands, Alaska. U.S. Geological Survey Bulletin 880-C. Washington: Government Printing Office. p. 111–184.

Gislén, Torsten, 1943. Physiographical and ecological investigations concerning the littoral of the northern Pacific, I. Lund: Lunds Universitet Årksskrift, Ny Foljd, avd. 2, bd. 39, No. 5. 63 p.

Gislén, Torsten, 1944. Physiographical and ecological investigations concerning the littoral of the northern Pacific, II-IV. Lund: Lunds Universitet Årsskrift, Ny Foljd, avd. 2, bd. 40, No. 8. 91 p.

Hewatt, Willis G., 1937. Ecological studies on selected marine intertidal communities of Monterey Bay, California. *American Midland Naturalist*, 18 (No. 2), 161–206.

Nybakken, James Willard, 1969. Pre-earthquake intertidal ecology of Three Saints Bay, Kodiak Island, Alaska. Biological Papers of the University of Alaska, Number 9, August. College: University of Alaska. 115 p.

Ricketts, Edward F., and Jack Calvin, 1962. Between Pacific tides. Stanford, California: Stanford University Press. 516 p.

Rigg, George B., and Robert C. Miller, 1949. Intertidal plant and animal zonation in the vicinity of Neah Bay, Washington. *Proceedings, California Academy of Sciences*, 26, Series 4 (No. 10), 323–351.

Scagel, Robert F., 1959. The role of plants in relation to animals in the marine environment *in* Marine Biology. Proceedings, 20th Annual Biology Colloquium. Corvallis: Oregon State College. p. 9–29.

Scagel, Robert F., 1961a. Ecology of marine algae. A synthetic approach to some problems in marine algal ecology. *Recent Advances in Botany*, University of Toronto Press, Vol. 1, p. 175–180.

Scagel, Robert F., 1961b. The distribution of certain benthonic algae in Queen Charlotte Strait, British Columbia, in relation to some environmental factors. *Pacific Science*, 15 (No. 4), 494–539.

Scagel, Robert F., 1962a. Benthic algal productivity in the north Pacific with particular reference to the coast of British Columbia. Proceedings of the Ninth Pacific Science Conference, v. 4, Bangkok, Thailand, 1962. p. 181–187.

Scagel, Robert F., 1962b. Coastal studies of marine algae in British Columbia and the North Pacific. D. S. Gorsline, editor. The First National Coastal and Shallow Water Research Conference, October 1961. p. 748–750.

Scagel, Robert F., 1964. Some problems in algal distribution in the north Pacific. Proceedings of the Fourth International Seaweed Symposium, Biarritz, France, September 18–25, 1961. New York: MacMillan Company. p. 259–264.

Shelford, V. E., A. O. Weese, Lucile Rice, D. I. Rasmussen, Archie MacLean, and H. C. Markus, 1935. Some marine biotic communities of the Pacific coast of North America. *Ecological Monographs*, 5 (No. 3), 249–354.

Stephenson, T. A., and Anne Stephenson, 1961a. Life between the tide marks in North America. IV-A: Vancouver Island, I. *Journal of Ecology*, 49 (No. 1), 1–29.

Stephenson, T. A., and Anne Stephenson, 1961b. Life between the tide marks in North America. IV-B: Vancouver Island, II. *Journal of Ecology*, 49 (No. 2), 227–243.

U.S. Coast and Geodetic Survey, 1962a. Surface water temperature and salinity, Pacific coast, North and South America and Pacific Ocean islands. Washington: Government Printing Office. 71 p.

U.S. Coast and Geodetic Survey, 1962b. Tide tables, high and low water predictions, 1963, west coast North and South America, including the Hawaiian Islands. Washington: Government Printing Office. 224 p.

# Annotated Bibliography

Alaska Department of Fish and Game. Post-earthquake fisheries evaluation. An interim report on the March 1964 earthquake effects on Alaska's fishery resources. Juneau: Alaska Department of Fish and Game, 1965. 72 p.
Finds that the tsunamis had caused extensive damage to fisheries and canneries throughout south central Alaska. The spawning environment in the Prince William Sound area had been altered by the land uplift, tsunami action, and subsidence.

Alaska Monthly Review of Business and Economic Conditions. Alaska's fisheries industry. College: University of Alaska, Institute of Business, Economic and Government Research. *Alaska Monthly Review of Business and Economic Conditions*, 2 (January 1965), 1–8.
Describes fisheries production in 1963, the management of Pacific salmon production, methods of fishing, the significance of earthquake damage to Alaska's fishing industry, and other economic aspects.

Alaska Review of Business and Economic Conditions. The Alaskan king crab industry. College: University of Alaska, Institute of Business, Economic and Government Research. *Alaska Review of Business and Economic Conditions*, 1 (November 1965), 1–8.
Describes the growth of the king crab industry, despite the loss of several crab-processing facilities in the Kodiak area; these were destroyed by the seismic waves that were generated by the earthquake. Also outlines regulations, methods of quality control, the function of the Convention of the Continental Shelf, by-products, and the future of the industry.

Alaska Review of Business and Economic Conditions. Alaska's economy in 1965. College: University of Alaska, Institute of Business, Economic and Government Research. *Alaska Review of Business and Economic Conditions*, 3 (January 1966), 1–8.
Indicates that, despite earthquake losses, the value of Alaska's fisheries production in 1965 was 14 percent above the value in 1964.

Alaska Review of Business and Economic Conditions. The Kodiak economic community. College: University of Alaska, Institute of Social, Economic and Government Research. *Alaska Review of Business and Economic Conditions*, 4 (April 1967), 1–8.
The 1964 earthquake destroyed 75 percent of downtown Kodiak but has ultimately resulted in an improved, reconstructed city and the promise of a more stable economic base. Kodiak's continued economic growth will depend on expansion and diversification of its booming fishing industry.

Baxter, Rae E. List of the bivalves of Prince William Sound collected 1962–1965 (unpublished manuscript). Bethel: Alaska Department of Fish and Game [1967]. 4 p. (Copy on file, Library, National Academy of Sciences–National Academy of Engineering, Washington, D.C.)
This tentative listing gives the scientific names and habitat preferences of 99 pelecypods collected by the author in Prince William Sound before and after the earthquake.

Baxter, Rae E. Earthquake effects on clams of Prince William Sound *in* The Great Alaska Earthquake of 1964: Biology. NAS Pub. 1604. Washington: National Academy of Sciences, 1971.
Estimates that the earthquake caused a 36 percent mortality in the clam population, and that only 29 percent of surviving hard-shell clams were in the optimum habitat zone after the earthquake. No species of hard-shell clam, however, was in danger of disappearing from the area.

Committee on the Alaska Earthquake. Toward reduction of losses from earthquakes: Conclusions from the great Alaska earthquake of 1964. Washington: National Academy of Sciences, 1969. 34 p.
Summarizes comprehensive study of the 1964 earthquake, gives recommendations of separate panels of the Committee, and advocates loss-reduction programs designed not only for earthquakes but also for other environmental hazards.

Crow, John H. Earthquake-initiated changes in the nesting habitat of the dusky Canada goose *in* The Great Alaska Earthquake of 1964: Biology. NAS Pub. 1604. Washington: National Academy of Sciences, 1971.
Finds that the nesting area of the dusky Canada goose has been severely diminished by uplift of the Copper River Delta. Studies the invasion of shrubs in the nesting area and the desalinization of the soil.

Davis, Allen S. Cook Inlet District gravel shift and freezing level studies, pink and chum salmon streams. Alaska Department of Fish and Game Report (unpublished manuscript). Homer: Alaska Department of Fish and Game, Division of Commercial Fisheries [1964]. 6 p. (Copy on file, Library, National Academy of Sciences–National Academy of Engineering, Washington, D.C.)
Describes results of studies to measure freshwater mortality of salmon eggs and preemergent fry caused by gravel shift and freezing.

Department of the Interior, Bureau of Land Management. Sport

Fisheries and Wildlife loses Kodiak patrol boat. *Our Public Lands*, 14 (July 1964), 17.
The Bureau of Sport Fisheries and Wildlife, despite its own losses, was able to assist the state in damage surveys. The Division of Wildlife studied waterfowl-habitat damages caused by the earthquake.

Eyerdam, Walter J. Alaska Earthquake Investigation—1965. Annual Reports for 1966 of the American Malacological Union. Marinette [Wisconsin]: American Malacological Union, 1966. p. 66-67.
Summarizes findings of investigations in Prince William Sound made in 1965 by a team led by Dr. Hanna. Tsunamis had severely damaged the shores, and earthquakes had caused many avalanches and landslides. Clam beds had been destroyed, but most crab species had survived. Very few shell-forming invertebrates were found alive in the tidal zone. Over 100 species of plants were collected. Sea otters were found to be making a notable comeback.

Eyerdam, Walter J. Flowering plants found growing between pre- and postearthquake high-tide lines during the summer of 1965 in Prince William Sound *in* The Great Alaska Earthquake of 1964: Biology. NAS Pub. 1604. Washington: National Academy of Sciences, 1971.
Reports on 75 species of flowering plants collected in the new land area between the former and present high-tide lines.

Hanna, G Dallas. Biological effects of an earthquake. *Pacific Discovery*, 17 (November–December 1964), 24–26. Also *in* The Great Alaska Earthquake of 1964: Biology. NAS Pub. 1604. Washington: National Academy of Sciences, 1971.
Reports losses of animals and plants that inhabited areas that had been elevated or had subsided as a result of the earthquake. In areas of extensive uplift, desiccation totally destroyed the flora and fauna, leaving masses of bleached shells. In subsided areas, forests and other vegetation were killed by seawater penetration.

Hanna, G Dallas. The great Alaska earthquake of 1964. *Pacific Discovery*, 20 (May-June 1967), 25-30.
Recounts how earthquake-caused uplift and subsidence were measured and describes subsequent findings on the mortality of the flora and fauna of the affected areas.

Hanna, G Dallas. Introduction: Biological effects of the earthquake as observed in 1965 *in* The Great Alaska Earthquake of 1964: Biology. NAS Pub. 1604. Washington: National Academy of Sciences, 1971.
Reports the organization and discoveries of a 1965 expedition to Prince William Sound made by a group of biologists to study the earthquake effects on the flora and fauna. Presents the records and locations of the 33 stations established.

Harry, George Y., Jr. Effects of the Good Friday earthquake on Alaska fisheries (unpublished paper). Auke Bay [Alaska]: U.S. Bureau of Commercial Fisheries Biological Laboratory, 1964. 13 p. (Copy on file, Library, National Academy of Sciences–National Academy of Engineering, Washington, D.C.)
Fears that uplifting of spawning areas by as much as 36 ft and downwarping to 6 ft may drastically affect spawning adult salmon. Tsunamis and elevation changes killed fish, clams, and possibly crabs.

Harry, George Y., Jr. General introduction, summary and conclusions *in* The Great Alaska Earthquake of 1964: Biology. NAS Pub. 1604. Washington: National Academy of Sciences, 1971.
Describes the research opportunities and problems in the areas of greatest damage. The usual difficulties limited the accomplishments, but research was nevertheless extensive and valuable because it related to commercial fishing, Alaska's main industry, which suffered losses amounting to about $14 million.

Harry, George Y., Jr. Introduction: Effects on fish and shellfish *in* The Great Alaska Earthquake of 1964: Biology. NAS Pub. 1604. Washington: National Academy of Sciences, 1971.
Briefly outlines the importance of the earthquake's effects on fish and shellfish and on the fishing industry. Tells of the studies and surveys that were carried out to assess these effects.

Haven, Stoner B. Effects of land-level changes on intertidal invertebrates, with discussion of postearthquake ecological succession *in* The Great Alaska Earthquake of 1964: Biology. NAS Pub. 1604. Washington: National Academy of Sciences, 1971.
Studies the ecological problems that arose in connection with the great physical upheaval, including both the fate of the displaced preearthquake populations and the development of new communities of organisms in the postearthquake tidal zone.

Hubbard, Joel D. Distribution and abundance of intertidal invertebrates at Olsen Bay in Prince William Sound, one year after the earthquake *in* The Great Alaska Earthquake of 1964: Biology. NAS Pub. 1604. Washington: National Academy of Sciences, 1971.
Seeks to determine the species composition of macroinvertebrate fauna on three major intertidal habitats; to determine their patterns of distribution, vertical zonation, and relative densities; and to evaluate any changes in community structure or distribution resulting from environmental changes caused by the earthquake.

Johansen, H. William. Effects of elevation changes on benthic algae in Prince William Sound *in* The Great Alaska Earthquake of 1964: Biology. NAS Pub. 1604. Washington: National Academy of Sciences, 1971.
Describes the environment and the extensive effects on the attached marine algae caused by the raising or lowering of shorelines resulting from the Alaska earthquake. Includes a list of the macroalgae collected during the summer of 1965.

Kirkwood, James B., and Robert M. Yancey. Effects of the March 27 earthquake on the shellfish resources of Alaska (unpublished manuscript). Auke Bay [Alaska]: Bureau of Commercial Fisheries Biological Laboratory, 1964. 13 p. (Copy on file, Library, National Academy of Sciences–National Academy of Engineering, Washington, D.C.) Abstract *in* Science in Alaska, 1964: Proceedings, Fifteenth Alaskan Science Conference, College, Alaska, August 31–September 4, 1964. College: Alaska Division, American Association for the Advancement of Science, 1965. p. 162.
Survey shows that habitats of some mollusks were affected by the earthquake, and razor clams, butter clams, and cockles were found dead on uplifted beaches. No direct evidence was found of mortality or habitat changes of the commercially important crustacean species of king crabs, shrimps, and Dungeness crab.

McRoy, C. Peter. A pre- and postearthquake survey of eelgrass on the Alaska Peninsula (unpublished manuscript). College: University of Alaska, Institute of Marine Science [1967]. 10 p. (Copy on file, Library, National Academy of Sciences–National Academy of Engineering, Washington, D.C.)
Survey shows that eelgrass was destroyed wherever it was lifted

above mean lower low water. Standing stocks of eelgrass in the Izembek Lagoon showed no significant change after an uplift of 20–60 cm by the earthquake.

Marriott, Richard A., and Carl E. Spetz. Effects of seawater intrusion into lakes of Kodiak and Afognak islands *in* The Great Alaska Earthquake of 1964: Biology. NAS Pub. 1604. Washington: National Academy of Sciences, 1971.
Gives results of studies to detect gross alterations of the fish-rearing habitats in lakes experiencing seawater intrusion.

Neiland, Bonita J. Possible effects of land-level changes on forest-bog tension areas in south coastal Alaska: A preliminary report *in* The Great Alaska Earthquake of 1964: Biology. NAS Pub. 1604. Washington: National Academy of Sciences, 1971.
Looks for alterations in the relative positions of forest and bog vegetation types that may result from topographic and hydrologic changes caused by the earthquake. Some 91 transects were established across forest-bog transitions, and later readings will be taken along these.

Nickerson, Richard B., George Cunningham, and Robert S. Roys. Synopsis of Prince William Sound stream rehabilitation project (unpublished preliminary report). Cordova: Alaska Department of Fish and Game, February 29, 1968. 33 p. (Copy on file, Library, National Academy of Sciences-National Academy of Engineering, Washington, D.C.)
Intertidal zones of many important salmon streams in Prince William Sound were found uplifted as high as 31.5 ft or subsided to a maximum of 6 ft. The pink salmon run was seriously reduced as a result of tectonic deformation; hence, a program of stream rehabilitation was put into effect.

Noerenberg, Wallace H. Earthquake damage to Alaskan fisheries *in* The Great Alaska Earthquake of 1964: Biology. NAS Pub. 1604. Washington: National Academy of Sciences, 1971.
Surveys and analyzes the effects of the earthquake on the state's fisheries and related businesses and studies their economic impact.

Noerenberg, Wallace H., and Frank J. Ossiander. Effects of the March 27, 1964 earthquake on pink salmon alevin survival in Prince William Sound spawning streams. Alaska Department of Fish and Game Informational Leaflet 43. Juneau: Alaska Department of Fish and Game, 1964. 26 p.
Lists and analyzes the available survey data and examines the environmental causes of alevin mortality in relation to the earthquake. Considers the future consequences of increased alevin mortality.

Nybakken, James Willard. Pre-earthquake intertidal ecology of Three Saints Bay, Kodiak Island, Alaska. Biological Papers of the University of Alaska, Number 9, August 1969. College: University of Alaska. 115 p.
Includes enumeration of major species of semisedentary and sedentary invertebrates present, delimitation of tidal ranges of these invertebrates, and description of horizontal belts or zones on various shores in 1963.

Nybakken, James Willard. Preearthquake intertidal zonation of Three Saints Bay, Kodiak Island *in* The Great Alaska Earthquake of 1964: Biology. NAS Pub. 1604. Washington: National Academy of Sciences, 1971.
Reports on the intertidal zonation determined on several shores of a semiprotected bay about 9 months before the earthquake. The

study will be a basis for comparison and evaluation of changes since the earthquake.

Oliver, William B. A shock to Alaska agriculture: earthquake damage spurs landowners to form conservation subdistrict. *Soil Conservation*, 30 (September 1964), 30–31.
Stresses the loss of animals, feed grain, and land used for hay production on Kodiak Island as a result of the 1964 earthquake; mentions the formation of a soil-conservation subdistrict and the emergency feed-grain programs needed because of transportation breakdown.

Olson, S. T. Reconnaissance of Copper River Delta following the March 27, 1964, earthquake. Alaska Department of Fish and Game Reconnaissance Report. Juneau: Alaska Department of Fish and Game, June 1964. 7 p.
Finds that the most significant earthquake-caused change was the drop in water levels caused by the rise of the land. New nesting areas might become available for a time, but a substantial loss of nesting habitat for geese and ducks could eventually result if the grass and sedge communities yielded to dense stands of willow and alder.

Olson, S. T. Re-examination of salmon habitat improvement projects in Prince William Sound to evaluate earthquake damage. Alaska Department of Fish and Game Reconnaissance Report. Juneau: Alaska Department of Fish and Game, June 1964. 3 p.
Finds that uplifted areas such as Olsen Creek became more suitable for a floodplain artificial spawning channel because of the uplift. Areas of subsidence previously suitable for salmon production might be submerged and lost.

Plafker, George. Tectonics of the March 27, 1964, Alaska earthquake. U.S. Geological Survey Professional Paper 543-I. Washington: Government Printing Office, 1969. 74 p. Also *in* The Great Alaska Earthquake of 1964: Geology. NAS Pub. 1601. Washington: National Academy of Sciences, 1971.
Reports method by which the displacement of sessile marine organisms, relative to sea level, and the zonation of plants and animals between tide levels resulting from the 1964 earthquake is used to determine the extent of uplift.

Plafker, George, and Reuben Kachadoorian. Geologic effects of the March 1964 earthquake and associated seismic sea waves on Kodiak and nearby islands, Alaska. U.S. Geological Survey Professional Paper 543-D. Washington: Government Printing Office, 1966. 46 p. Also *in* The Great Alaska Earthquake of 1964: Geology. NAS Pub. 1601. Washington: National Academy of Sciences, 1971.
Mentions that tides at Kodiak after the earthquake rendered many salmon-spawning areas nearly useless, requiring modification of fishing techniques and possibly affecting the migration pattern of the salmon.

Prescott, G. W. Introduction: Selected ecological effects *in* The Great Alaska Earthquake of 1964: Biology. NAS Pub. 1604. Washington: National Academy of Sciences, 1971.
Hopes that the research on the earthquake's effects on some species of organisms will encourage future studies of the numerous ecological problems resulting from the earthquake.

Roys, Robert S. Effect of tectonic deformation on pink salmon runs in Prince William Sound *in* The Great Alaska Earthquake of 1964: Biology. NAS Pub. 1604. Washington: National Academy of Sciences, 1971.

Notes adjustments in pink salmon spawning distributions and unusual mortalities among eggs, alevins, and fry caused by land-level changes. Estimates large economic losses to salmon fishermen, canneries, and retailers during 3 years 1966–1968 after the earthquake. Suggests restrictions limiting commercial harvest of pink salmon to enable runs to regain former levels, especially in areas of greatest uplift.

Shepherd, Peter E. K. A preliminary evaluation of earthquake damage to waterfowl habitat in south central Alaska. Paper presented at 45th Annual Conference of the Western Association of State Game and Fish Commissioners, July 7–9, 1965, Anchorage, Alaska. 9 p. (Copy on file, Library, National Academy of Sciences–National Academy of Engineering, Washington, D.C.)
Estimates a loss of 25 mi$^2$ of marshland (available for hunting) because of land subsidence in Cook Inlet, and alteration by land uplift of 300 mi$^2$ of waterfowl nesting habitat on the Copper River Delta.

Shepherd, Peter E. K. Current status of the Copper River Delta waterfowl habitat and the dusky Canada goose nesting population. Paper presented to Northwest Section Meeting of the Wildlife Society, March 25, 1966, LaGrande, Oregon. 7 p. (Copy on file, Library, National Academy of Sciences–National Academy of Engineering, Washington, D.C.)
Preliminary studies of vegetation on the Copper River Delta indicate that coniferous forests may eventually spread, bringing an increase in the number of mammalian predators on wild geese and ducks. The newly exposed mud flats do not appear extensive enough to support the present population of dusky geese. The survival of the waterfowl on the delta may depend on their adaptability to a changing environment.

Shepherd, Peter E. K., Ben L. Hilliker, and John H. Crow. Waterfowl report: Work plan segment report, federal aid in wildlife restoration (unpublished report). Alaska Department of Fish and Game Project W-13-R-2 and 3, Work Plan C, March 1968. Juneau: Alaska Department of Fish and Game. 39 p. (Copy on file, Library, National Academy of Sciences–National Academy of Engineering, Washington, D.C.)
Reports that desalinization and draining of formerly flooded areas, as a result of land uplift from the 1964 earthquake, have affected the Copper River Delta habitats of the dusky Canada goose.

Sheridan, William L. Salmon habitat improvement reconnaissance, Prince William Sound, Cordova, and Anchorage districts, September 1965. Branch of Wildlife Report, Division of Resource Management, U.S. Forest Service, Region 10. Juneau: U.S. Forest Service, 1965. 7 p.
Recommends various methods of improving salmon habitats, particularly in those streams that were greatly damaged by the earthquake.

Stanley, Kirk W. Effects of the Alaska earthquake of March 27, 1964, on shore processes and beach morphology. U.S. Geological Survey Professional Paper 543-J. Washington: Government Printing Office, 1968. 21 p. Also in The Great Alaska Earthquake of 1964: Geology. NAS Pub. 1601. Washington: National Academy of Sciences, 1971.
States that the emergence of large areas that were once below water and the permanent submergence of once-useful land areas as a result of the Alaska earthquake have led to problems of land use in addition to the destruction or relocation of wildfowl, shellfish, and salmon habitats.

Thorsteinson, Fredrik V. Effects of the Alaska earthquake on pink and chum salmon runs in Prince William Sound in Science in Alaska, 1964: Proceedings, Fifteenth Alaskan Science Conference, College, Alaska, August 31–September 4, 1964. College: Alaska Division American Association for the Advancement of Science, 1965. p. 267–280.
Finds that the earthquake produced drastic environmental changes in the spawning habitat of pink and chum salmon runs homing to streams in the Prince William Sound area. Discusses the results of preearthquake ecological studies on a Prince William Sound stream and their implications regarding future abundance of pink salmon in view of the earthquake-produced changes in spawning habitat.

Thorsteinson, Fredrik V. Aftermaths of the Alaska earthquake in Prince William Sound. Pacific Fisherman, 63 (May 1965), 10–11.
Finds disturbing initial effects of the earthquake on spawning streams in the Sound. Smaller than usual runs returning from the 1964 and perhaps the 1965 brood years were expected; runs should return to preearthquake levels when the streams stabilize.

Thorsteinson, Fredrik V., John H. Helle, and Donald G. Birkholz. Salmon survival in intertidal zones of Prince William Sound streams in uplifted and subsided areas in The Great Alaska Earthquake of 1964: Biology. NAS Pub. 1604. Washington: National Academy of Sciences, 1971.
Examines the effects of changes in land level on the survival of pink and chum salmon in various streams. Detailed studies were made at Olsen Creek, which was uplifted about 4 ft, and general studies were made at three other streams—two in areas that were uplifted 10 ft and one in an area that subsided 6 ft.

Tuthill, Samuel J. Survival and recolonization of vegetation on an earthquake-induced mudvent deposit (unpublished manuscript). New Concord [Ohio]: Muskingum College, 1968. 10 p. (Copy on file, Library, National Academy of Sciences–National Academy of Engineering, Washington, D.C.)
Provides an insight into plant succession in the region and deals with one aspect of biotic response to the earthquake.

# Contributors to This Volume

RAE E. BAXTER, Alaska Department of Fish and Game, Bethel, Alaska 99559

DONALD G. BIRKHOLZ, Biological Laboratory, National Marine Fisheries Service, National Oceanic and Atmospheric Administration, Auke Bay, Alaska 99821

JOHN H. CROW, Department of Botany, Rutgers—The State University, Newark, New Jersey 07102

WALTER J. EYERDAM, 7531 19th Street, N.E., Seattle, Washington 98115

G DALLAS HANNA, Department of Geology, California Academy of Sciences, San Francisco, California 94118 [deceased]

GEORGE Y. HARRY, JR., Marine Mammals Biological Laboratory, Naval Support Activity, Building 192, National Marine Fisheries Service, National Oceanic and Atmospheric Administration, Seattle, Washington 98115

STONER B. HAVEN, Department of Biological Sciences, Simon Fraser University, Burnaby 2, British Columbia, Canada

JOHN H. HELLE, Biological Laboratory, National Marine Fisheries Service, National Oceanic and Atmospheric Administration, Auke Bay, Alaska 99821

JOEL D. HUBBARD, Department of Biology, University of Colorado, Boulder, Colorado 80302

H. WILLIAM JOHANSEN, Department of Biology, Clark University, Worcester, Massachusetts 01610

RICHARD A. MARRIOTT, Alaska Department of Fish and Game, Juneau, Alaska 99801

BONITA J. NEILAND, College of Biological Sciences and Renewable Resources, University of Alaska, College, Alaska 99701

WALLACE H. NOERENBERG, Alaska Department of Fish and Game, Juneau, Alaska 99801

JAMES W. NYBAKKEN, Moss Landing Marine Laboratory, Moss Landing, California 95039

GERALD W. PRESCOTT, Biological Station on Flathead Lake, University of Montana, Big Fork, Montana 59911

ROBERT S. ROYS, Alaska Department of Fish and Game, Juneau, Alaska 99801

CARL E. SPETZ, Khutaghat Fish Farm, Post Rataupur, Bilaspur, Madhya Pradesh, India

FREDRIK V. THORSTEINSON, Biological Laboratory, National Marine Fisheries Service, National Oceanic and Atmospheric Administration, Auke Bay, Alaska 99821

# ENGLISH–METRIC CONVERSION TABLE

### LENGTH

| | | | |
|---|---|---|---|
| 1 inch (in.) | = | 2.54 | centimeters (cm) |
| 1 foot (ft) [12 in.] | = | 30.48 | cm |
| 1 yard (yd) [3 ft] | = | 91.44 | cm |
| | = | 0.914 | meter (m) |
| 1 mile (mi) [5280 ft] | = | 1.610 | kilometer (km) |

### AREA

| | | | |
|---|---|---|---|
| 1 square inch (in.$^2$) | = | 6.45 | square centimeters (cm$^2$) |
| 1 square foot (ft$^2$) | = | 929.0 | cm$^2$ |
| | = | 0.0929 | square meter (m$^2$) |
| 1 square yard (yd$^2$) | = | 0.836 | m$^2$ |
| 1 acre (a) [43560 ft$^2$] | = | 0.4047 | hectare (ha) |
| 1 square mile (mi$^2$) | = | 2.59 | square kilometers (km$^2$) |

### VOLUME

| | | | |
|---|---|---|---|
| 1 cubic inch (in.$^3$) | = | 16.4 | cubic centimeters (cm$^3$) |
| 1 cubic foot (ft$^3$) | = | 28.3 | $\times 10^3$ cm$^3$ |
| | = | 0.0283 | m$^3$ |
| 1 cubic yard (yd$^3$) | = | 0.7646 | cubic meter (m$^3$) |
| 1 cubic mile (mi$^3$) | = | 4.17 | cubic kilometers (km$^3$) |
| 1 quart (qt) [0.25 U.S. gallon (gal)] | = | 0.95 | liter |
| 1 gal [4 qt] | = | 3.79 | liter |
| 1 bushel (bu) [U.S. dry] | = | 35.24 | liter |

### MASS

| | | | |
|---|---|---|---|
| 1 pound (lb) [16 ounces (oz)] | = | 453.6 | grams (g) |
| | = | 0.4536 | kilogram (kg) |
| 1 U.S. ton (tn) [2000 lb] | = | 907.2 | kg |
| | = | 0.9072 | metric ton (MT) |
| 1 long ton (LT) [2240 lb] | = | 1.016 | MT |

### PRESSURE

| | | | |
|---|---|---|---|
| 1 pound per square inch (lb/in.$^2$ or psi) | = | 0.0704 | kilogram per square centimeter (kg/cm$^2$) |
| 1 pound per square foot (lb/ft$^2$) | = | 4.8824 | kilograms per square meter (kg/m$^2$) |
| 1 bar [1000 millibars (mb)] | = | 1.020 | kg/cm$^2$ |

### VELOCITY

| | | | |
|---|---|---|---|
| 1 foot per second (ft/s) | = | 0.3048 | meter per second (m/s) |
| | = | 1.097 | kilometer per hour (km/h) |
| | = | 0.5925 | international knot (kn) |
| 1 mile per hour (mi/h) | = | 1.609 | km/h |
| | = | 0.869 | kn |

# METRIC–ENGLISH CONVERSION TABLE

### LENGTH

| | | | |
|---|---|---|---|
| 1 millimeter (mm) [0.1 centimeter (cm)] | = | 0.0394 | inch (in.) |
| 1 cm [10 mm] | = | 0.3937 | in. |
| 1 meter (m) [100 cm] | = | 39.37 | in. |
| | = | 3.28 | feet (ft) |
| 1 kilometer (km) [1000 m] | = | 0.621 | mile (mi) |
| 1 international nautical mile [1852 m] | = | 6076.1 | ft |

### AREA

| | | | |
|---|---|---|---|
| 1 square centimeter (cm$^2$) | = | 0.155 | square inch (in.$^2$) |
| 1 square meter (m$^2$) | = | 10.76 | square feet (ft$^2$) |
| | = | 1.196 | square yards (yd$^2$) |
| 1 hectare (ha) | = | 2.4710 | acres (a) |
| 1 square kilometer (km$^2$) | = | 0.386 | square mile (mi$^2$) |

### VOLUME

| | | | |
|---|---|---|---|
| 1 cubic centimeter (cm$^3$) | = | 0.0610 | cubic inch (in.$^3$) |
| 1 cubic meter (m$^3$) | = | 35.314 | cubic feet (ft$^3$) |
| | = | 1.31 | cubic yards (yd$^3$) |
| 1 cubic kilometer (km$^3$) | = | 0.240 | cubic mile (mi$^3$) |
| 1 liter | = | 1.06 | quarts (qt) |
| | = | 0.264 | gallon (gal) |

### MASS

| | | | |
|---|---|---|---|
| 1 kilogram (kg) [1000 grams (g)] | = | 2.20 | pounds (lb) |
| | = | 0.0011 | ton |
| 1 metric ton (MT) [1000 kg] | = | 1.10 | ton |
| | = | 0.9842 | long ton (LT) |

### PRESSURE

| | | | |
|---|---|---|---|
| 1 kilogram per square centimeter (kg/cm$^2$) | = | 14.20 | pounds per square inch (lb/in.$^2$) |
| | = | 2048 | pounds per square foot (lb/ft$^2$) |

### VELOCITY

| | | | |
|---|---|---|---|
| 1 meter per second (m/s) | = | 3.281 | feet per second (ft/s) |
| 1 kilometer per hour (km/h) | = | 0.9113 | ft/s |
| | = | 0.621 | mile per hour (mi/h) |
| 1 knot (kn) [1852 m/h] | = | 1.6878 | ft/s |
| | = | 1.151 | mi/h |

# Index

*Figures in italics indicate major discussion of topic*

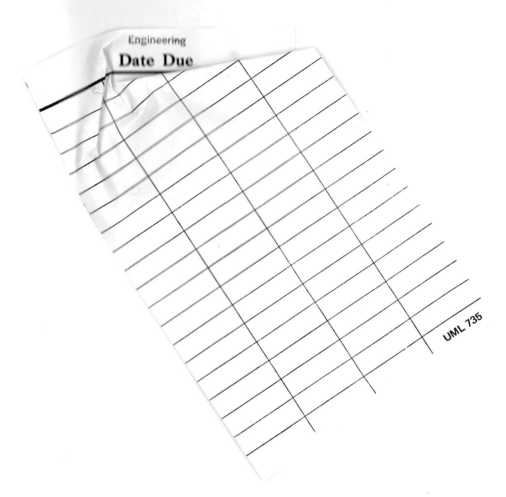